ISSUES IN
EDUCATING STUDENTS
WITH DISABILITIES

The LEA Series on Special Education and Disability
John Wills Lloyd, Series Editor

Lloyd, Kameenui, and Chard
Issues in Educating Students with Disabilities

ISSUES IN EDUCATING STUDENTS WITH DISABILITIES

Edited by

John Wills Lloyd
University of Virginia

Edward J. Kameenui
University of Oregon

David Chard
Boston University

LEA LAWRENCE ERLBAUM ASSOCIATES, PUBLISHERS
1997   Mahwah, New Jersey   London

Lawrence Erlbaum Associates, Inc., Publishers
10 Industrial Avenue
Mahwah, New Jersey 07430

Library of Congress Cataloging-in-Publication Data

Issues in educating students with disabilities / edited by John Wills
Lloyd, Edward J. Kameenui, David Chard.
    p.   cm.
    A festschrift in honor of Barbara D. Bateman.
    Includes bibliographical references and indexes.
    ISBN 0-8058-2201-1 (alk. paper). — ISBN 0-8058-2202-X (pbk. :
alk. paper).
    1. Handicapped children—Education—United States. 2. Learning
disabilities—United States. 3. Handicapped children—Education—
Law and legislation—United States. 4. Bateman, Barbara D.
I. Lloyd, John, Ph. D. II. Kameenui, Edward J. III. Chard, David.
LC4031.I84 1997
371.91—dc21   97-1095
                                                    CIP

Printed in the United States of America
10 9 8 7 6 5 4 3 2 1

CONTENTS

PART V: LEGISLATION AND POLICY

PART VI: INTEGRATION

PROLOGUE

Norris Haring
Professor Emeritus
University of Washington

This volume honors Barbara Bateman, whose brilliant career in two disciplines—special education and the law—has contributed significantly to the education of students with disabilities and to our understanding of the legal and ethical aspects of our practices. I am among the few special educators who has been a Bateman observer and acquaintance since she was in her final years of preparing for the Ph.D. at the University of Illinois, and I feel honored to introduce this book.

A good place to begin is to provide a brief review of Barbara's early contributions to the procedures for identifying, defining, and educating students with learning disabilities. During her studies at Illinois, she developed, along with her advisor, Sam Kirk, the first published definition of learning disability. She realized that to this point, circa 1962, almost all definitions and descriptions of students showing behavior characteristics of individuals with brain damage included labels involving dysfunctioning of the brain. Bateman's definition focused more on the behavioral aspects of learning. In keeping with that, the Kirk–Bateman (1962) definition stated:

> A learning disability refers to a retardation disorder or delayed development in one or more of the processes of speech, language, reading, writing, arithmetic, or other school subjects resulting from a psychological handicap caused by a possible cerebral dysfunction and/or emotional or behavioral disturbance. It is not the result of mental retardation, sensory deprivation, or cultural or instructional factors. (p. 8)

The process of defining learning disabilities began as early as the early 1940s when Strauss and Lehtinen differentiated learning problems into two categories—exogenous and endogenous. The exogenous category included learning disorders due to neurological dysfunctioning or brain damage. The endogenous category referred to disorders of learning similar to those in the exogenous category but without a history of brain damage (Strauss & Lehtinen, 1947). William Cruickshank, a psychologist working with Strauss at that time, compared a group of children with known brain damage, specifically children with cerebral palsy, to a matched group without brain damage to determine if there were significant differences with respect to their learning characteristics (Dolphin & Cruickshank, 1951). Cruickshank then conducted a major applied study in Montgomery County, Maryland, with a large number of subjects who had learning characteristics similar to those of children with brain damage but without the physical signs (Cruickshank, Bentzen, Ratzburg, & Tannhauser, 1961).

Throughout that early period, investigators from the medical disciplines in general, and the neurological sciences in particular, used such terms as brain damage and minimal cerebral dysfunction. On the other hand, Bateman (1965) began to follow a more educationally functional approach and offered a refinement of her earlier definition, which follows:

> Children who have learning disorders are those who manifest an educationally significant discrepancy between their estimated intellectual potential and actual level of performance related to basic disorders in the learning process, which may or may not be accompanied by demonstrable central nervous system dysfunction, and which are not secondary to generalized mental retardation, educational or cultural deprivation, severe emotional disturbance, or sensory loss. (p. 220)

Two aspects of Bateman's refined definition are very attractive because of their functional value. First, it identifies the conditions that are included and those that are not; second, it is concerned with a flawed learning process whether or not there is demonstrable brain injury. In addition, as far as I can find in my review, this definition is the first to introduce the discrepancy concept. A far better and more detailed discussion of this topic can be found in this volume in the chapter on defining learning disabilities by Kavale and Forness.

Another major contribution to the field of learning disabilities was Bateman's excellent research related to development of the Illinois Test of Psycholinguistic Abilities (ITPA; Kirk & McCarthy, 1961). This test was conceptualized to allow a trained clinician to pinpoint more precisely the nature of the learning disability, that is, whether there were visual or auditory reception or expression problems or whether the concerns were more related to central, cognitive processing problems. After several years of attempting to establish reliability and validity of the test and applying specific instructional strategies based on specific areas of deficit, Bateman abandoned research and development activities on the ITPA. In addition to her concerns about the test, several other researchers were critical of the fact that its diagnostic, predictive, and programming values were highly questionable; and that because validity and reliability were not conclusively established, clinicians and teachers were warned to be cautious in using the instrument (Haring & Bateman, 1977, p. 104). Some of the assumptions held by the authors of the ITPA have resurfaced among certain neuropsychologists in their efforts to advance the practice of identifying specific areas of brain damage through an analysis of performance deficits and behavioral characteristics (Reitan & Boll, 1973).

In any case, following Bateman's disenchantment with the instructional value of ITPA results, she turned her attention to a broader based approach to the educational identification, assessment, and evaluation of students with learning disabilities (Bateman & Schiefelbusch, 1969). After a thorough review of various assessment procedures, Bateman concluded that at some point in the application of diagnostic procedures, diminishing returns are reached and instructional strategies should be initiated. Further, she concluded that the most valuable information about the child's learning characteristics and patterns can be achieved by a systematic analysis of correct responses and errors in responding, by the child's rate of acquiring skills, and by his or her ability to use and generalize new skills.

Bateman provided a thorough review of the most common approaches to remediation in her textbook (Haring & Bateman, 1977). She identified three strategies applied to reading remediation for children with learning disabilities: the etiological, diagnostic–remedial, and task-analytic approaches.

The etiological approach assumes that remediation should begin with identifying the cause of the learning problem. Once the basic cause is found, remediation is based on treating it. For example, if the child has poorly established hemispheric dominance, exercises and activities designed to establish dominance would be in order. Bateman opposed the etiological approach on the grounds that it does not respond specifically and directly to the learning problem.

As noted by Bateman, the predominant strategy in the field of learning disabilities has been the diagnostic–remedial approach. This conceptualization is characterized by the medical model, prescriptive teaching, abilities and process training, psychometric phrenology, and psychoeducation. According to Bateman, this approach assumes that the child's cognitive, perceptual, sensorimotor, and other processes—as assessed by a variety of psychoeducational instruments—provide information about where the strong and weak functioning are occurring in the child's performance. After identifying these strong and weak functions, one tries to determine which among the deficits is primary. Remediation, then, is planned to overcome or circumvent the deficit. Bateman has criticized the diagnostic–remedial approach for these reasons: Research has not supported the assumption that deficiencies in psychological processes can be reliably and validly assessed; and remediation based on those procedures may not result in improved academic performance.

We come now to the task-analytic approach. Bateman's position was advanced because she believed that students with learning disabilities could be taught effectively by improved instruction through which any child with reading problems would learn to grade level. She began to focus on the task-analytic approach which was introduced and employed by behavioral technologists. In support of Bateman, DISTAR, a task-analytic based reading program, was validated by Project Follow-Through (Abt Associates, 1976). The national evaluation based on evidence from several approaches to teaching reading in Follow Through programs throughout the country confirmed that programs using DISTAR were so successful that poor, high-risk, bilingual, and other very low-achieving populations read at middle class grade-level norms by the end of the third grade. As Bateman points out, the task- analytic approach starts with an analysis of the child's beginning skills, specifies the objectives of the reading task, and builds the instructional sequence step-by-step that most directly aims toward the reading objective. This approach, also known as direct instruction, begins with identifying the prereading skills. The subskills are defined by a logical analysis of the reading task and by their demonstrated effect on the following reading achievement (Haring & Bateman, 1977, p. 140).

In this approach, sight-word recognition skills are based in three pre-reading skills: visual discrimination of letter strings (letter sequences), which requires letter recognition, attention to order of letters, and attention to the entire word; association and retention of labels for the letter sequence; and retrieval and articulation of labels when one is shown the sequences. The analysis of decoding identifies five subskills: letter differentiation; association of sound and letter; blending sounds; identification of a sound within a word and sound matching within a word; and sound matching within words.

Reading programs based on task-analytic procedures assume that children with learning disabilities proceed as well as children who have reading problems but not specific learning disabilities. Task-analysis provides a systematic way of teaching reading directly. The reading task is analyzed and taught with specific steps in the reader's sequence so precisely defined that additional practice on specific errors is provided until the full sequence is performed correctly (Haring & Bateman, 1977, p. 144).

Bateman's contribution to applying reading instruction approaches with students who have learning disabilities, based on her thorough and systematic review of research on reading remediation, can be summarized most succinctly by her statement: ". . . it is nevertheless clear that intensive, systematic decoding programs result in better reading achievement than do other kinds of beginning reading programs. It is just possible that intensive decoding instruction is even more vital for potential low achievers than for their easy-to-teach counterparts . . ." (Haring & Bateman, 1977, p. 144).

She states, further, that "the task-analytic approach teaches basic skills directly without prior remediation of possibly correlated problem areas. The what of teaching thus has been the specific skills and subskills directly necessary to achieve the academic objective and the how of teaching is to focus attention on relevant features to be learned and to provide adequate practice and appropriate reinforcement" (Haring & Bateman, 1977, p. 156).

Fast forward to Bateman's career in law, which began in 1974, when she became a staff member of the Oregon Law Review, and two years later was awarded a Doctorate in Jurisprudence. From then until now she has taught in the law school as well as the Department of Special Education.

Since 1975, Bateman's publications have reflected her significant competencies in law. Her first major publication, which proved to be most valuable for both administrators of special education and child advocates, was entitled "So You're Going to Hearing: Preparing for a P.L. 94-142 Hearing." In another book entitled "Better IEPs," Bateman made an important point concerning the specificity of IEP requirements with respect to the objectives of the IEP and the instructional techniques required to meet the specified outcomes. Bateman (1996) refers to others as "empty IEPs," IEPs that contain goals and objectives without specifying techniques and services to be delivered to meet them. The chapter on programming by Howell and Davidson in this volume thoroughly discusses this issue.

Bateman's brilliant, scholarly career in special education and the law has influenced policies and practices for more than three decades and her contributions will continue to be applied for years to come. It is a mark of great achievement to reach such stellar performance in two significant disciplines.

A Brief Statement Concerning This Volume

Issues in Educating Students With Disabilities brings to the field of special education the reassertion, prompted by recent criticisms of the field's value, that there is a substantial body of knowledge available to teachers, psychologists, and instructional support personnel that significantly strengthens their instructional effectiveness. Further, there is a trend, as a result of the full inclusion movement, to lessen the emphasis on the systematic application of specialized instruction. This book was conceptualized by the editors to reestablish the emphasis on special instruction, to sift through the current research and practices which show productive and successful outcomes, and to select authors known for their scholarly contributions to this field. Although this is a multiauthored volume, the planning and structure that the editors provided for the authors have enhanced the continuity of the content so successfully that readers will have a sense of reading a single-authored textbook.

REFERENCES

Abt Associates. (1976). *Education as experimentation: A planned variation model* (Vol. 171). Boston: Author.

Bateman, B. (1965). An educational view of a diagnostic approach to learning disorders. In J. Hellmuth (Ed.), *Learning disorders* (Vol. 1, pp. 219–239). Seattle: Special Child Publications.

Bateman, B. (1996). *Better IEPs*. Longmont, CO: Sopris West.

Bateman, B., & Schiefelbusch, R. (1969). Educational identification, assessment, and evaluation procedures. In N. Haring (Ed.), *Minimal brain dysfunction in children phase II (NINDS Monograph No. 2, U.S. Public Health Service Publication No. 2015)*. Washington, DC: Department of Health Education Welfare.

Cruickshank, W., Bentzen, F., Ratzburg, F., & Tannhauser, M. (1961). *A teaching method for brain-injured and hyperactive children*. Syracuse, NY: Syracuse University Press.

Dolphin, J., & Cruickshank, W. (1951). The figure-background relationship in children with cerebral palsy. *Journal of Clinical Psychology, 7*, 228–251.

Haring, N., & Bateman, B. (1977). *Teaching the learning disabled child*. Englewood Cliffs, N.J.: Prentice-Hall.

Kirk, S., & Bateman, B. (1962). Diagnosis and remediation of learning disabilities. *Exceptional Children, 28*(2), 73–78.

Kirk, S., & McCarthy, J. (1961). An approach to differential diagnosis. *American Journal of Mental Deficiency, 66*, 399–412.

Reitan, R., & Boll, T. (1973). Neuropsychological correlates of minimal brain dysfunction. Annals of the *New York Academy of Sciences, 205*, 65–88.

Strauss, A., & Lehtinen, L. (1947). *Psychopathology and education of the brain-injured child*. New York: Grune & Stratton.

INTRODUCTION

We are enormously privileged to serve as editors of this book, and one must look no further than the list of authors who have contributed to this effort to appreciate our unwitting good fortune. The contributors to this volume represent the prominent researchers and thinkers on issues in educating students with and without disabilities. We need not labor in our descriptions of their expertise, because their words speak sufficiently, mellifluously, and exactingly about their contributions to the education of all students, in particular those with disabilities.

This book is a *Festschrift*, a volume of essays contributed by many authors in honor of a colleague. It pays tribute to the work of Barbara D. Bateman, Ph.D., J.D., Professor Emeritus at the University of Oregon. As editors of this text and as former students, we owe much to her teaching, mentoring, and clear thinking, as well as her unambiguous personal and professional presence in special education, and most certainly in our lives.

The prologue and 19 chapters of this book are expressions of gratitude to someone with uncommon insight into common problems of teaching and learning . In most cases, Barb gave uncommon scrutiny to common practice, especially when that practice is widely or vigorously embraced. Friends and colleagues alike know well, for example, of Barb's disdain for the computer and other electronic gadgets that rush the fingers to advocate what the mind has yet to apprehend. At a time when most of us are thoroughly marinated in the cybersauce of communications networking, Barb's fierce independence in such matters is refreshing and is best captured by Henry David Thoreau's observations in 1854 about a similar technological gadget, the telegraph:

We are in great haste to construct a magnetic telegraph from Maine to Texas, but Maine and Texas, it may be, have nothing important to communicate. . . . We are eager to tunnel under the Atlantic and bring the Old World some weeks nearer to the New, but perchance the first news that will leak through into the broad, flapping American ear will be that Princess Adelaide has the whooping cough. (pp. 57–58)

As history would have it, John Thoreau founded the first quality pencil manufacturer in America and his son, Henry David, wrote this statement with a pencil he had made himself. (Interestingly, authors Steve Forness and Ken Kavale also share Barb's fervent commitment to the quill and have managed to evade the electronic glare of computers.) Like Thoreau, Bateman is determined above all else not to be impressed with the medium, be it the telegraph, the computer, the Internet, or the latest electronic thingamajig designed to make communication more efficient and timely.

For Barbara Bateman, the message is always supreme, and the medium is a fashionable formalism that invites monstrous trivialities. As editors of this text, we think we have duplicated as faithfully as possible Bateman's commitment to the message. It would be contemptibly silly for us to do anything less in honor of her contributions to the field of special education and to the clarity and incisiveness of thought that are her signature as a teacher, researcher, lawyer, advisor, and mentor. For Barb, the words are always important, worth the grappling and imbued for reflection. She wields a language that is notably parsimonious, intensely surgical, and immoderately effectual. She is equally comfortable discussing the intricacies of an instructional strategy in beginning reading, briefing a Supreme Court case involving the 14th Amendment Equal Protection Clause of the U.S. Constitution, and perfecting a student's IEP at the invitation of a school district.

In the prologue, Norris Haring points out that Samuel Kirk and Barbara Bateman first offered a definition of the term *learning disabilities* in 1962. However, it is rarely remembered that they did so as part of a percipient call for developing "a scientific pedagogy in the area of learning disabilities" (Kirk & Bateman, 1962, p. 74). The field remembered the term *learning disabilities* but forgot the message: "Of course, the field immediately took flight with the term and gave only ceremonial verse to its meaning. At the same time, the field unwittingly ignored Kirk and Bateman's real message about the need for the development of a pedagogy of learning disabilities based on scientific principles" (Kameenui, 1992, p. 249).

The message in this text is perhaps best captured by Naomi Zigmond's insightful, passionate, and eloquent summary (see chap. 19), in which she incites readers to reconsider "the meaning and practice of *special education*, now and in the future" (p. 378). For Zigmond, and we suspect the same is true for Bateman, special education taught students "things they hadn't learned before . . . and what they couldn't learn anywhere else" (p. 379). The special education teacher was a "detective and diagnostician . . . clever and creative . . . knew a lot about children and about instruction . . . But above all else, she was relentless. She did not give up until she and her students had been successful" (p. 379). At the end of her chapter, Zigmond states, "Special education was once worth receiving. It could be again" and she challenges readers to define "the nature of special education and the competencies of the teachers who will deliver it" (p. 389). Zigmond speaks passionately for all of us and reveals the "felt difficulty" (Dewey, cited in Larrabee, 1964, p. 98) that is only gained through the experience of being a special education teacher.

This Festschrift consists of six uneven parts. Of these parts, most peculiar in size and impassioned in voice is Part VI, which stands alone as the final part of the book and includes a single chapter by Naomi Zigmond. Our intent as editors was to allow her to comment freely on the previous 18 chapters, and as such, her chapter serves to summarize and inspire, without encumbrance and encouragement from the editors. We think Zigmond's chapter will provoke much thought and discussion.

Part I consists of four chapters, three of which serve to define learning disabilities, attention deficit disorders, and emotional or behavioral disorders. Fortunately, Kavale, Lerner, and Forness do not merely define; they explicate, muse, and reflect on matters that are notoriously complex and elusive. For example, Kavale and Forness (see chap. 1) dare to define definitions and invoke the likes of Aristotle and Kant in lamenting that the "definitional problem of LD is genuine" (p. 16). Their efforts are insightful, provocative, and informative. Likewise, Lerner (see chap. 2) grapples courageously and judiciously with the newest of diagnostic labels for children, attention deficit disorders (ADD), and aptly places it in proper ontological, historical, political, and pedagogical perspective. Forness and Kavale (see chap. 3) offer readers a thorough and instructive examination of the definitions of serious emotional disturbance or behavioral disorders that a range of agencies (e.g., Head Start, NIMH, Social Security, American Psychiatric Association) use to determine eligibility for special education or related services. Their call for a "collaborative network of care" between agencies as a precursor to the development of a comprehensive individual plan and a shared definition of emotional or behavioral disabilities is enormously sensible and long overdue. Finally, Speece and Harry (see chap. 4) boldly address how the classification of children is constructed from both social and scientific perspectives. In citing Annie Mae's response to Shirley Brice Heath (1983), "Whatcha *call* it ain't so important as whatcha *do* with it," Speece and Harry sharpen their own words on classification, while echoing Bateman's sentiments: "As it now stands, instruction is more of an afterthought that follows designation as handicapped rather than a driving force that explicates learning difficulties. We suggest that eligibility discussions take instruction as the primary issue, relegating measurement of a host of individual differences and the naming of the condition to secondary status" (p. 70).

Part II, on Assessment of Disabilities, is comprised of four chapters on progress monitoring, programming, social competence, and comorbidity of emotional and behavioral disorders. What we gain from these chapters is an unrequited respect for assessment that is of the character alluded to by Speece and Harry in their call for shifting the burden of classification and diagnosis from the child to teacher–child interactions around instruction. For example, Deno (see chap. 5) fully and masterfully delineates the psychometric, pedagogical, historical, conceptual, and political considerations of two approaches to progress monitoring, mastery monitoring, and general outcome measurement. Deno makes a persuasive case for the inescapable smartness of using progress monitoring as a basis for educational decision-making. However, one can hear the wistfulness in his voice as he pens the last sentence, "We can hope that the adoption of such beneficial practices will occur more rapidly than was true of the British Navy when it waited more than two hundred years after discovering that fresh fruit prevented scurvy to require that its ships carry such food" (p. 97).

In keeping with the theme of ocean-going vessels and assessment, Howell and Davidson (see chap. 6) call for evaluation decisions that "directly influence the actions of teachers and the learning of students" (p. 106), but their clever metaphorical call is from the bow of a boat off Orcas Island in the Pacific Northwest. Howell and Davidson's specification of the "actions to take" and the "things to think about" in programming for task-related and task-specific knowledge is meticulous and refreshing, which is naturally expected of researchers anchored in the Northwest.

In chapter 7, Haager and Vaughn tackle two decades of research on the assessment of social competence of individuals with learning disabilities, a most unenviable task. As expected, these researchers clearly deliver, and what we learn is that a model and the tools for gaining a comprehensive assessment of social competence continue to emerge empirically and conceptually. However, unusual diligence and care are required to disentangle a host of factors (e.g., learner characteristics, instrumentation, content, context, peers, raters) that determine whether social competence as a construct represents a slip knot or a Gordian knot for researchers and practitioners eager to launch intervention programs.

Comorbidity is a big word that is generally found seeking shelter in the damp basements of hospitals or medical labs. After all, "morbidity" is defined as the "condition of being diseased or morbid" (*Dorland's Pocket Medical Dictionary*, 22nd Edition, p. 422). Grim stuff for a Festschrift; however, Tankersley and Landrum (chap. 8) handle the intrigue surrounding the "co-occurrence" of emotional and behavioral disorders with aplomb. Their summary table of studies on the prevalence of comorbidity among specific emotional and behavioral disorders is indeed intriguing and itself worth a peek. In addition, the Tankersley and Landrum call for "a more thorough approach to assessment . . . at all stages of the assessment process" (p. 170) is important to testing the "purity" (i.e., the true morbidity) of specific, individual disorders.

Part III, on Instruction, consists of four chapters and serves to center the text, because it is rightfully at the heart of this Festschrift and the person it honors. This section opens with Engelmann's chapter on the theory of mastery and acceleration, and it is classic Engelmann—"The programs used to teach skills and academic content should be engineered so they are capable of inducing learning" (p. 179); "The material should be designed so it provides teaching demonstrations that are consistent with one and only one interpretation" (p. 180); "The teaching materials should provide for the mastery of all the skills that the child will need later in the sequence" (p. 181). Thankfully, Engelmann's restless and relentless call for our attention to the details of instruction is clear, unapologetic, and absolute. Rosenshine provides readers with a distillation of the "procedures and scaffolds" that comprise cognitive strategy instruction in reading. This offering, too, is classic Rosenshine, reducing a mass of information to the core features that render a body of work instructive and singular.

Individual differences when examined in the context of school learning (à la Carroll, 1963) are known as student heterogeneity, but when pressed into the language of the educational reform literature are writ large as "diversity" and accompany the popularized call to "educate all students" (e.g., curriculum standards for The National Council of Teachers of Mathematics, The National Center for History in the Schools, The National Science Education Standards, The Standards Project for English and Language Arts). Educating *all* students in heterogeneous classrooms, as Stevens and Salisbury point out, is enormously complex but preferable and more beneficial than educating all students in "relatively homogeneous classes for the entire day" (p. 225). Student heterogeneity, however, always requires important and strategic instructional and organizational supports, and the account of cooperative learning that Stevens and Salisbury provide is illuminating.

Using reasoned and dispassionate words to write about a topic that has generated a great deal of heat and passion is not easy. Graham and Harris, however, are the exception, and their words afford readers an understanding of constructivism and whole language. In light of the current imbalance in practice that favors a whole language/process writing approach in general education classrooms, their call for balance is an important one for "remaining responsive" (p. 254) to students with special needs.

Part IV, on Special Groups, consists of three chapters on early intervention and early childhood special education, multicultural teacher education in special education, and antisocial girls. Carta and Greenwood, of the Juniper Gardens Children's Project, describe the barriers to the implementation of effective educational practice for young children with disabilities. The barriers are conspicuous and complicated but representative of all emerging areas of inquiry and practice (à la Kuhn, 1962, and Bruner & Postman, 1949). These barriers include identifying effective practice, gaining consensus on valued and common goals and outcomes, and bridging the chasm between research and practice. As expected, Carta and Greenwood offer a plan of action that gives sufficient promise to overcoming these barriers.

Based on sheer appearances, teacher preparation for *cultural diversity* and *special education* disguises complexities that can only be scaled in orders of magnitude. If the complexity could be scaled numerically, the difference between "traditional" teacher preparation and teacher preparation for cultural diversity and special education would be like the difference between 2 times 100 and 2 times itself 100 times, which is equal to a million trillion trillion, or one followed by 30 zeros (Waldrop, 1992). Artiles and Trent recognize the elusive complexity inherent in multicultural teacher education in special education, as well as the impoverished research in this area. As such, they offer readers a bold and thoughtful "blueprint" to use as either a "rubric to design studies" (p. 282) or as a "framework to guide literature reviews and research syntheses" (p. 282).

Speaking of numbers, it is well accepted in the folklore of behavior disorders that boys dominate in numbers and rule psychologically and physically. As Talbott and Callahan note, boys "dominate classes for students with emotional and behavioral disorders . . . referrals for mental health services . . . and arrests for violent crime" (p. 305). However, thanks to Talbott and Callahan, we also learn that the disorders of girls with a history of disruptive behavior problems are more likely than boys to "co-occur with depression, anxiety, and delinquency during adolescence" (p. 305). Additionally, girls' disruptive behavior disorders are not revealed as early nor as publicly as those of boys. Talbott and Callahan offer readers an interesting and informative rendering of girls' disruptive behavior across development as drawn from studies of community and clinical samples.

Part V, entitled Legislation and Policy, is comprised of three chapters on placement, special education law, and bridging research and practice. In chapter 16, Kauffman and Hallahan extend their penetrating discussion of "place" by considering its meaning in an "ecological perspective" (p. 326). They confront the rhetoric of full inclusion with insight (e.g., "Every environment is inherently restrictive . . . The significance of an environment is not that it is restrictive in a general sense but that it is restrictive of specific things," p. 326), wit (e.g., "Perhaps Mark Twain was right . . . 'To create man was a quaint and original idea, but to add the sheep was tautology,'" p. 328), and reflection (e.g., "For decades, we special educators have found coherence, unity, and mutual support in the notion that we should celebrate the diversity of the characteristics of children and youth," p. 339).

In chapter 17, Huefner readily dispossesses the legalistic clutter of procedural words that often engulf the "legalization and federalization" of special education. Huefner does this with a clarity that is hauntingly Bateman-like. She knows the law and she knows special education, and as a result, her chapter delights without legal intimidation.

Finally, in chapter 18, Carnine examines the detached and promiscuous relationship between research and practice and calls for researchers and practitioners to evaluate research in terms of its "trustworthiness, usability, and accessibility" (p. 364). In addition, he calls for researchers and teachers to work with professional organizations, publishers and developers, legislators, businesses, and advocates to change the marketplace demand for research findings. This is classic Carnine, an eminently clear voice with a message that is compelling and distinctly sensible.

The prologue, 19 chapters, and this introduction complete the Festschrift for Barbara Bateman. While its intent is to honor one person, it bears witness to the contributions of many and reveals the enlarged presence of a field and its leadership. Finally, its message is found in the teacher who tirelessly, creatively, and cleverly teaches students "things they hadn't learned before . . . and what they couldn't learn anywhere else" (Zigmond, chap. 20, p. 379).

REFERENCES

Bruner, J. S., & Postman, L. (1949). On the perception of incongruity: A paradigm. *Journal of Personality, 18*, 206–223.

Carroll, J. B. (1963). A model of school learning. *Teachers College Record, 64*, 723–733.

Kameenui, E. J. (1992). Toward a scientific pedagogy of learning disabilities. In D. W. Carnine & E. J. Kameenui (Eds.), *Higher order thinking: Designing curriculum for mainstreamed students* (pp. 247–267). Austin, TX: PRO-ED.

Kirk, S. A., & Bateman, B. (1962). Diagnosis and remediation of learning disabilities. *Exceptional Children, 26*, 73–78.

Kuhn, T. S. (1962). *The structure of scientific revolutions.* Chicago: University of Chicago Press.

Larrabee, H. A. (1964). *Reliable knowledge: Scientific methods in the social studies.* Boston: Houghton Mifflin.

Thoreau, H. D. (1849). *Walden; or, Life in the woods.* Boston: Ticknor and Fields.

Waldrop, M. M. (1992). *Complexity: The emerging science at the edge of order and chaos.* New York: Simon & Schuster.

DEFINITION OF DISABILITIES

1

DEFINING LEARNING DISABILITIES: CONSONANCE AND DISSONANCE

Kenneth A. Kavale
University of Iowa Division of Special Education

Steven R. Forness
UCLA Neuropsychiatric Hospital

"When I use a word," Humpty Dumpty said, in rather a scornful tone, "it means just what I choose it to mean—neither more nor less."

"The question is," said Alice, "whether you can make words mean so many different things."

"The question is," said Humpty Dumpty, "which is to be master—that's all."

—Lewis Carroll

For a field that was officially recognized only about 25 years ago, learning disabilities (LD) has experienced unprecedented growth and has had significant impact on special education. Besides being the largest category in special education, LD is also among the most problematic because of continuing controversy, conflict, and crisis. Many of the difficulties experienced by the LD field appear to emanate from a failure to answer the seemingly straightforward question, "What is a learning disability?" The vagaries and antagonisms associated with any response has placed the LD field at a critical juncture. The purpose of this chapter is to explore the enduring problem of definition and to suggest positive and rational approaches for resolving many fundamental problems.

THE PROBLEM

On the surface, LD should not be any more problematic than other areas of special education. Although both mild mental retardation (MR) and behavior disorders (BD)—its partners in the large designation "mildly handicapped"—also experience definitional problems, the difficulties experienced by LD appears to take center stage. The problem of defining LD, after so many attempts, appears to defy resolution, and discussion seems only to result in an ever-increasing tangled web from which escape seems impossible. Such language is not mere hyperbole: No other area of special education has ever been called on to defend its very existence. There is ever increasing depiction of LD as myth (McKnight, 1982), questionable construct (Klatt, 1991), or imaginary disease (Finlan, 1993), and, even though usually without merit, require a response defending LD that deflects attention away from more substantive issues. The MR and BD literature does not reveal any similar discussion about their existence, and it is only LD that is referred to as a "phantom category."

For a condition whose reality is continuously challenged, LD is seemingly doing quite well (U.S. Department of Education, 1994). Since the passage of PL 94–142 (now Individuals with Disabilities Education Act [IDEA]), the LD population has increased about 150% to a level where it now represents almost 5% of all students in school and 50% of all students with disabilities. The prevalence ranges from 1.51% (Wyoming) to 6.11% (Alaska) with LD as percent of students with disabilities ranging from 31.9 (Georgia) to 64.5 (Rhode Island). To provide perspective, the prevalence rate for MR is slightly less than 1% across states with the range being from .16% (Wyoming) to 2.52% (Alabama). For BD, the prevalence rate is .69% with a range from .04 (Arkansas) to 1.69 (Connecticut). On average, LD reveals anywhere from 2–3 times more students even in states with the highest prevalence rates for MR and BD. As a percent of students with disabilities, MR ranges from 3.1% (New Jersey) to 28% (Alabama) with an average of 12.3% while BD ranges from .5% (Arkansas) to 20.1% (Georgia) with an average of 8.9%. At about 50%, the LD category includes anywhere from 4–5 times more students than other categories in special education.

The sheer number of students with LD may eventually strain resources, and LD may be trapped by its own "success." Is there any justification for LD being the largest category in special education? Could anyone have anticipated in 1970 that LD would expand to its present proportions? Answers are difficult and may result from a failure to achieve consensus about the nature of LD as manifested in the "problem of definition," the inability to achieve agreement about how best to define LD. Definitions of LD have remained vague and have not presented precise statements (similar to the Supreme Court's definition of pornography: "Individuals know it when they see it"). The result is varying interpretation, and this seems the fate of the LD field: It is known when seen, but accompanied by an inability to bring those views into an exact and unencumbered statement.

HISTORY AND DEFINITION

How did the LD field reach its present chaotic state? In many respects, the LD field appears to have advanced far ahead of itself. The lack of comprehensive and unified definition suggests that LD cannot attain two critical elements: understanding—a clear and unobscured sense of LD, and explanation—a rational exposition of the reasons why a particular student is LD. Without understanding and explanation, statements about LD remain conditional, and this conditionality becomes the source of much debate.

HISTORICAL CONSIDERATIONS

The history of LD is well documented (Cruickshank, Lewandowski, Opp, & Rosenberger, 1993). For example, Weiderholt (1974) conceptualized the historical development of LD along two dimensions: a developmental sequence delineating historical time periods, and a type of disorder analysis. The development phases included foundation (circa 1800–1940), transition (circa 1940–1963), and integration (circa 1963–1974) with Lerner (1989) adding a contemporary phase bringing the field to the present. The types of disorders included spoken language (aphasia), written language (dyslexia), and process disorders (perceptual-motor functioning). Each phase and disorder was placed in a matrix where the work of significant individuals was described to show how their contributions advanced toward the LD concept.

Kavale and Forness (1995) analyzed the development of LD within the context of special education. From clinic-based treatment for aphasia and dyslexia, to classes for neurologically impaired students, to misclassification in special classes for MR and BD, and, finally, to a need for an educational focus—rather than counseling and guidance services—for underachievement, LD filled a void in the spectrum of special education. Previously, there were a variety of LD-like students requiring special education but no provisions except in either nonschool arrangements or inappropriate special education arrangements. The needs of such students were best met through what eventually became LD programs.

Historical analyses point to the fact that there was a need for a category like LD. A variety of pressures led to a convergence on the concept of LD as a foundation for a new category in special education. By bringing disparate elements under a single rubric, there was the potential for more focused diagnosis and treatment.

DEFINITIONAL CONSIDERATIONS

With a need for an LD category established, attention was directed at for-mulating a definition that could describe the parameters of the condition. It is at this point that the definition problem began. The basic problem with LD definitions is the failure to provide insight into the nature of the condition. The most widely used definition is the one found in IDEA that was formalized by the United States Office of Education (USOE, 1977) in the *Federal Register*:

> The term "specific learning disability" means a disorder in one or more of the basic psychological processes involved in understanding or in using language, spoken or written, which may manifest itself in an imperfect ability to listen, speak, read, write, spell, or to do mathematical calculations. The term includes such conditions as perceptual handicaps, brain injury, minimal brain dysfunc-tion, dyslexia, and developmental aphasia. The term does not include children who have learning disabilities which are primarily the result of visual, hearing, or motor handicaps, or mental retardation or emotional disturbance, or of environmental, cultural, or economic disadvantage. (p. 65083)

After reading this definition, it is not at all clear that one could answer the question, "What is LD?" There is some indication about process disorders specifically in the language area that interfere with basic academic achieve-ment but the descriptions and relationships remain vague. There is a state-ment that LD is like other conditions as listed, but definition by analogy introduces much imprecision because indications about how similar and how different the other conditions are from LD is lacking. There is a relatively clear statement about what LD is not (i.e., exclusion), but this is not equiva-lent to stating what LD is—a missing aspect of this definition. The fundamental difficulty is that no sense of LD emerges beyond that of a general and indistinct learning problem even though it is presumably defining "specific learning disability." The definition is marked by a rather nonspecific descrip-tion of the elements contributing to LD.

ANALYSIS AND CRITIQUE OF LD DEFINITIONS

The IDEA definition is widely used, but it is not the only LD definition. To see how the problem of definition emerged, it would be useful to trace their development and determine what they say and don't say.

PRECURSORS TO LD

The seminal work of A. Strauss and H. Werner in the development of the LD field is well documented (Hallahan & Cruickshank, 1973). Their study of brain-injured (exogenous) MR students laid an important foundation for LD. A brain-injured student was defined as one:

> who before, during or after birth has received an injury to or suffered an infection of the brain. As a result of such organic impairment, deficits of the neuromotor system may be present or absent; however, such a child may show disturbances in perception, thinking, and emotional behavior, either separately or in combinations. This disturbance can be demonstrated by specific tests. These disturbances prevent or impede a normal learning process. (Strauss & Lehtinen, 1947, p. 4)

The importance of this definition lies in the fact that it introduced behavioral criteria to diagnose a biophysical phenomenon. Within the context of this definition, brain injury became a rather broad and elastic category spanning gross damage easily documented to slight damage not easily documented but presumed because of the presence of behavioral symptoms. The dilemma created surrounds the tautological reasoning established as suggested by Sarason (1949), "The logically minded may of course object to a reasoning which appears to go like this: Some individuals with known brain damage have certain behavioral characteristics, therefore individuals with these same behavioral characteristics must be presumed to be brain damaged" (p. 415).

The next precursor is found in the concept of minimal brain dysfunction (MBD). Strauss and Lehtinen (1947) recognized a "minor brain damage" where "behavior and learning may be affected by minimal brain injuries without apparent lowering of the intelligence level" (p. 128). The term was formalized by Clements (1966), where MBD was defined as a disorder affecting:

> children of near average, average, or above average general intelligence with certain learning or behavioral disabilities ranging from mild to severe, which are associated with deviations of functions of the central nervous system. These deviations may manifest themselves by various combinations of impairment in perception, conceptualization, language, memory, and control of attention, impulse, or motor function. The aberrations may arise from genetic variation, biochemical irregularities, perinatal brain insults, or other illnesses or injuries sustained during the years which are critical for the development and maturation of the central nervous system or from unknown causes. . . . During the school years, a variety of learning disabilities is the most prominent manifestation of the condition which can be designated by this term. (pp. 9–10)

Although lacking precision with respect to symptomatology and etiology as well as permitting wide latitude with respect to intellectual and severity levels, the definition again affirmed the possibility of diagnosing a biophysical phenomenon on the basis of behavioral characteristics. More specifically, disorders in learning were among the most prominent behavioral characteristics defining MBD.

These two definitions are important because they served to conjoin central nervous system (CNS) dysfunction and LD. There was little question that LD was associated with neurological impairments and that they represented the most prominent etiology of LD.

EARLY DEFINITIONS OF LD

Kirk (1962) offered the first formal definition in the text *Educating Exceptional Children*, which was disseminated further by Kirk and Bateman (1962). The definition reads:

> A learning disability refers to a retardation, disorder, or delayed development in one or more of the processes of speech, language, reading, writing, arithmetic, or other school subjects resulting from a psychological handicap caused by a possible cerebral dysfunction and/or emotional or behavioral disturbances. It is not the result of mental retardation, sensory deprivation, or cultural and instructional factors. (Kirk, 1962, p. 263)

The definition introduced the notion of psychological process disorders as the foundation of LD. The focus was on process problems and how they interfered with academic performance. The actual problem might be either a retardation, disorder, or delay, but the differences among these possibilities was not specified. With respect to etiology, CNS dysfunction was affirmed but some confusion was introduced by suggesting that LD might be caused by emotional or behavioral disturbances (E/BD). The possible confounding with the "emotionally handicapped" category seems apparent. The definition also introduced the exclusion clause, the suggestion that LD cannot be due primarily to some other condition.

The definition offered by Bateman (1965) emphasized underachievement as an important component of LD. The definition reads:

> Children who have learning disorders are those who manifest an educationally significant discrepancy between their estimated intellectual potential and actual level of performance related to basic disorders in the learning process, which may or may not be accompanied by demonstrable central nervous system dysfunction, and which are not secondary to generalized mental retardation, educational or cultural deprivation, severe emotional disturbance, or sensory loss. (p. 220)

The notions about process deficit and exclusion were affirmed and the concept of discrepancy was introduced as a critical factor. A stipulated level for the discrepancy was not provided, however, and no indication of how best to measure estimated intellectual potential or actual level of performance was provided. No etiological statement was included and the CNS dysfunction idea became equivocal with the statement "may or may not."

LEGISLATIVE DEFINITIONS OF LD

The definition offered by the National Advisory Committee on Handicapped Children (NACHC, 1968) provided the basis for federal legislative definitions:

> Children with special (specific) learning disabilities exhibit a disorder in one or more of the basic psychological processes involved in understanding or in using spoken and written language. These may be manifested in disorders of listening, thinking, talking, reading, writing, spelling, or arithmetic. They include conditions which have been referred to as perceptual handicaps, brain injury, minimal brain dysfunction, dyslexia, developmental aphasia, etc. They do not include learning problems that are due primarily to visual, hearing, or motor handicaps, to mental retardation, emotional disturbance, or to environmental disadvantage. (p. 34)

The NACHC introduced the notion of specific LD; the learning failure was not a generalized problem, but rather one predicated on a discrete number of deficits. The specific notion appears to be undermined, however, by the phrase "one or more," because there is no stipulation about the point where, in terms of the number of problems, a disorder is no longer specific. The definition also appears to introduce a hierarchy of processes with language, spoken and written, being most prominent. The range of potential manifestations from process problems was also expanded to include "thinking disorders," which then related LD to a variety of cognitive deficits in addition to basic academic skill problems. Although not as explicit with respect to CNS dysfunction, the assumption that LD is similar to conditions emanating from neurological impairments is clearly indicated. This definition by analogy strategy introduces an inherent vagueness, however, because of the lack of specification about how LD may be similar or different from the conditions noted. No statement about requisite severity levels was included. An exclusion clause was included and appears to have become an integral component in defining LD.

In an effort to halt the proliferation of definitions, the U.S. Office of Education funded an institute whose charge was to resolve the perceived difficulties in existing definitions. Kass and Myklebust (1969) reported the following definition:

- Learning disability refers to one or more significant deficits in essential learning processes requiring special education techniques for remediation.
- Children with learning disability generally demonstrate a discrepancy between expected and actual achievement in one or more areas such as spoken, read, or written language, mathematics, and spatial orientation.
- The learning disability referred to is not primarily the result of sensory, motor, intellectual, or emotional handicap, or lack of opportunity to learn.
- Significant deficits are defined in terms of accepted diagnostic procedures in education and psychology.
- Essential learning processes are those currently referred to in behavioral science as involving perception, integration, and expression, either verbal or nonverbal.
- Special education techniques for remediation refers to educational planning based on the diagnostic procedures and results. (pp. 378–379)

The definition affirmed LD as a condition emanating from process deficits that were deemed "essential." Although statements defining "essential learning processes" and "significant deficits" were included, they were predicated on the assumptions that they are known from "accepted diagnostic procedures" and the way they are "currently referred to in behavioral science." The unarticulated and contentious nature of these statements, both then and now, makes it difficult to perceive how any consensus might be forged with this definition.

An exclusion clause was included and, while incorporating accepted conditions, also suggested an exclusion based on the "lack of opportunity to learn." This is a far less tangible condition that introduces an inherent vagueness because of difficulties in circumscribing boundaries for defining opportunity to learn. With sensory, motor, intellectual, or emotional handicap, classification criteria exist, and the decision becomes a dichotomous one; however, decisions about whether or not a student has had sufficient opportunity to learn are far more subjective.

The definition is noteworthy in two respects. First, the notion of discrepancy was explicitly articulated, thus affirming the relation between LD and underachievement. There was, however, the strange designation of "spatial orientation" as a disorder where a discrepancy might exist. It is unclear why this particular process was included and given equal status with language, reading, and mathematics. Second, the definition emphasized the educational foundation of LD by suggesting that special education techniques are a basic requirement for remediation. By providing an educational focus, no etiology was specified and thus there is no statement about CNS dysfunction. The emphasis was thus on essential learning processes with no presumptions about their origin being some form of neurological impairment.

COMMITTEE DEFINITIONS OF LD

The failure to achieve consensus with respect to defining LD has resulted in repeated efforts to formulate an acceptable definition. An analysis of these efforts reveals many of the difficulties involved in achieving consensus about LD.

As part of the National Project on the Classification of Exceptional Children, Wepman, Cruickshank, Deutsch, Morency, and Strother (1975) proposed the following definition:

> Specific learning disability refers to those children of any age who demonstrate a substantial deficiency in a particular aspect of academic achievement because of perceptual or perceptual-motor handicaps, regardless of etiology or other contributing factors. The term *perceptual* as used here relates to those mental (neurological) processes through which the child acquires his basic alphabets of sounds and forms. (p. 306)

In this definition, the notion of specificity was affirmed by limiting LD to perceptual process-based academic failure. The focus on perceptual or perceptual-motor deficits was introduced because of a concern that too many diverse types of learning failure were being subsumed under the LD rubric. To alleviate this concern, this more restrictive definition was offered but, in all likelihood, would be too limiting. Severity level was not specified but ensconced in the context of "substantial." The definition also eliminated an etiological statement and an exclusion clause.

The National Joint Committee on Learning Disabilities (NJCLD; 1981) was formed by representatives from eight major organizations that had an interest in LD (see Abrams, 1987). Although endorsing the federal definition, it was believed that it could be improved with the following modifications: (a) reinforcing the idea that LD can exist at all ages, (b) deleting the contentious notion of *basic psychological processes*, (c) eliminating spelling as a specific disorder and subsuming it under *writing*, (d) eliminating the list of analogous conditions, and (e) clarifying the "exclusion clause" to indicate that LD may coexist with other handicapping conditions. The resulting NJCLD (1981) definition reads:

> Learning disabilities is a generic term that refers to a heterogeneous group of disorders manifested by significant difficulties in the acquisition and use of listening, speaking, reading, writing, reasoning, or mathematical abilities.

These disorders are intrinsic to the individual and presumed to be due to central nervous system dysfunction. Even though a learning disability may occur concomitantly with other handicapping conditions (e.g., sensory impairment, mental retardation, social and emotional disturbance) or environmental influences (e.g., cultural differences, insufficient or inappropriate instruction, psychogenic factors), it is not the direct result of those conditions or influences. (p. 108)

The NJCLD definition appears to be the antithesis of earlier definitions promoting "specific" LD. Instead, LD is now a general term that is quite likely to manifest a variety of symptoms (i.e., heterogeneity). The notion of discrepancy is not stated explicitly and level of severity is only indicated by "significant." The notion of CNS dysfunction was affirmed as well as the assumption that the disorder emanates from disorders within the individual. Unlike earlier definitions where process deficits were the most direct manifestation of CNS dysfunction, no such relationship is specified, and it is not clear what neurological impairments "cause." The "intrinsic" notion also excludes the possibility of LD being associated with social or educational influences. The focus is on what deficits the individual brings to the situation, and complex environmental interactions and transactions seem not to be recognized. The "exclusion clause" is now modified to move away from an "either–or" dichotomy to one where LD may coexist with other conditions. Although LD is assumed primary, the lack of specification makes it difficult to determine precisely the nature of the relationships with other conditions.

The NJCLD definition was based on the efforts of eight major organizations, and its adoption was predicated on approval by all member organizations. The definition was accepted by all organizations except the Learning Disabilities Association of America (LDA; formerly Association for Children with Learning Disabilities [ACLD]), who chose to write their own definition:

Specific Learning Disabilities is a chronic condition of presumed neurological origin which selectively interfered with the development, integration, and/or demonstration of verbal and/or nonverbal abilities. Specific Learning Disabilities exist as a distinct handicapping condition and varies in its manifestations and in degree of severity. Throughout life, the condition can affect self-esteem, education, vocation, socialization, and/or daily living activities. (ACLD, 1986, p.15)

The notion of specificity is included through the word "selectively," but the possible manifestations span an undefined range of verbal and nonverbal abilities. This introduced considerable imprecision, and it is unclear what type of problems are being defined. For example, are nonverbal abilities primarily social skill deficits? Although verbal abilities would include reading and writing difficulties, what is the status of difficulties in mathematics? The notion of CNS dysfunction as the primary etiology is affirmed, and the most direct problems might be either in the "development, integration, and/or demonstration" of abilities but the differences among these possibilities is not stipulated. The longstanding consequences of LD are recognized through the word "chronic," and a number of possible areas that might be affected adversely, in addition to education, throughout the life span are specified. An exclusion clause is not incorporated and presumably indicates no relationship between LD and other handicapping conditions. This seems to be affirmed through the inclusion of the word "distinct," which suggests LD be perceived as a syndrome, a discrete cluster of symptoms. The "distinct" idea appears to be undermined, however, by phrasing that indicates manifestations may vary as well as severity level.

In an effort to formulate an improved definition, the Interagency Committee on Learning Disabilities (ICLD) was formed from 12 agencies within the federal government. A number of papers were commissioned to determine the state of knowledge (see Kavanagh & Truss, 1988) and, after deliberation, the following definition was proposed:

> Learning disabilities is a generic term that refers to a heterogeneous group of disorders manifested by significant difficulties in the acquisition and use of listening, speaking, reading, writing, reasoning, or mathematical abilities, *or of social skills*. These disorders are intrinsic to the individual and presumed to be due to central nervous system dysfunction. Even though a learning disability may occur concomitantly with other handicapping conditions (e.g., sensory impairment, mental retardation, social and emotional disturbance), with *socio*environmental influences (e.g., cultural differences, insufficient or inappropriate instruction, psychogenic factors), *and especially attention deficit disorder, all of which may cause learning problems*, a learning disability is not the direct result of those conditions or influences. (ICLD, 1987, p. 222)

If the definition looks familiar, it is; the ICLD, rather than formulating a new definition, believed that the NJCLD definition was the best available and required only some modification (the modifications are italicized). Questions about the NJCLD definitions are equally applicable to the ICLD definition but with new points of contention. Most contentious was the addition of social skills to the list of potential primary manifestations. Although recognizing that an individual with LD might also possess social problems, the desirability of including social skill deficits as a primary form of LD was questioned (e.g., Forness & Kavale, 1991; Gresham & Elliott, 1989; Silver, 1988). First and foremost, there is the problem of diagnosing LD without academic deficits; a student without difficulties in reading, writing, or mathematics could be diagnosed as LD and placed in an LD program solely for treatment of social disorders. The confounding with the federal definition for serious emotional disturbance (SED) is substantial given that one of the five diagnostic criteria for SED is an inability to learn that cannot be explained by intellectual, sensory, or health factors. Additionally, the research is unequivocal with respect to the nature, extent, and assessment of social skill deficits in LD. The perceived difficulties led to the Department of Education not endorsing the ICLD definition because including social skills would (a) require a change in IDEA, (b) increase confusion concerning eligibility, and (c) increase the number of students classified as LD. Finally, by stipulating attention deficit disorder (ADD) in the definition, the problematic relationship between ADD and LD comes to the fore (see Silver, 1990).

DEFINITIONS IN PERSPECTIVE

What can be learned from this examination of LD definitions? First, the LD concept has generated a number of definitions. Unlike MR with a single definition, the LD field has generated a number of competing definitions. Second, LD has not been defined with much exactitude; what emerges is a generalized picture of a portion of the school population experiencing academic difficulties. Although many of the same ideas are included either implicitly or explicitly, there exists enough variation so that definitional precision is lost. The consequences are found in the lack of a uniform perspective where LD is viewed differently in different contexts. Some 25 years ago, Cruickshank (1967) described the variegated picture of LD as students moved from state to state and the situation appears not to have changed appreciably.

A variety of issues remain unresolved, and the notion of specificity provides a number of examples. Many definitions included the adjective *specific,* which implied that poor academic performance emanates from a limited number of underlying deficits. The purpose was to differentiate LD from conditions where a wide assortment of processes might be depressed, such as MR, which is viewed as a generalized deficit. The idea that LD results from a circumscribed set of problems that interfere selectively with academic functioning is still acknowledged (e.g., Stanovich, 1986; Swanson, 1988). Assumptions about specificity have, however, been challenged as unrealistic and restrictive (e.g., Siegel, 1988). For example, it is suggested that linguistic and memory deficits might conceivably affect adversely a number of abilities (e.g., reading, writing, listening) and that reading and mathematics are not necessarily independent cognitive abilities.

The notion of specificity is also confounded by the myriad catalogue of potential deficits associated with LD. For example, the areas of linguistic and neuromotor functioning are composed of dozens of discrete skills. Although focusing on the same general function, it is difficult to relate each individual deficit to LD. Why do some students with LD manifest one deficit and not another? Are some deficits more associated with LD than another? Can any single deficit be the major contributor to LD?

A problem also emerges when a large majority of the LD population manifest the same deficit as is the case with reading disability (RD). With about 85% of students with LD revealing primary difficulty in reading (see Kavale & Reese, 1992), differentiating LD and RD becomes problematic. It is not clear whether LD and RD are really similar or whether, because more is known about the established condition, RD, it is easier to explain LD by comparing and contrasting it with RD.

Specificity is also confounded when the basic deficit is termed a "retardation, disorder, or delay," for example, because these imply very different conceptualizations about the nature and origin of LD. For the most part, LD has been viewed as a deficit specifically in the form of a CNS dysfunction intrinsic to the student. This disease model possesses ready appeal but needs to be validated through findings of specific pathology and thus far attempts to specify the neuropathology associated with LD have not received unequivocal support (i.e., Hynd, Marshall, & Gonzalez, 1991). The disease model emphasizes the primacy of biological over psychological and social explanations, but it is difficult to conceive of a behavioral phenomenon like LD being solely the result of neurophysiological determinants.

An alternative explanation may be found in notions about LD as deficiency, the absence of a critical function. The definition offered by Wepman et al. (1975) provides a deficiency explanation of LD in the form of a perceptual deficit. Difficulties are encountered, however, in providing explanations about how a perceptual deficit can result in so specific a problem. For example, the deficiency would have to be selective enough to impair the reading of words, but not the reading of individual letters or numbers. Deficiency explanations fare better with hypotheses linking LD and basic linguistic disorders (see Wagner & Torgesen, 1987) like phonological awareness (Stanovich, 1988) or speed of processing (Lovett, 1987). The problem, however, is the large number of possible deficiencies and the way they may be combined to define LD. Deficiency explanations are limited by their specificity, because any particular deficiency can explain LD in particular, rather than LD in general.

Still another explanation is found in LD as difference; basic abilities differ and create a mismatch between student and environment (especially school). One difference may be related to normal variation and the possibility that LD problems reflect not specific deficits, but the distribution of abilities along the normal curve (Shaywitz, Escobar, Shaywitz, Fletcher, & Makuch, 1992). Difference explanations may also emphasize the problem rather than its source. Brown and Campione (1986), for example, perceived the primary difficulty to be the failure to acquire domain-specific knowledge and skills. Difference explanations, however, lack specificity and may result in tautologies. The generalized character of difference hypotheses permit only a global nature for LD and not an adequate level of explanation for LD functioning.

DEFINING DEFINITION

Many difficulties in defining LD emanate from a failure to understand the nature of definition (see Kavale, Forness, & Lorsbach, 1991). A definition represents an attempt to correlate words with a thing. When words have been agreed on in a logical and rational fashion, a definition is achieved but may not be a real and accurate representation of the thing (Miller, 1980). The "thing" may possess fundamental and basic qualities difficult to capture in words but such qualities are what make the thing real. Aristotle (trans. 1960) termed these qualities *essence* and, to be attained, must not simply describe a thing's physical properties but also the elements that transcend the physical (hence, metaphysical) to make it what it is. Kant (1781/1965) made a distinction between "appearance" and "things in themselves." Appearance represents what has come to be perceived (and believed) about a phenomenon, whereas things in themselves presuppose a more basic level where phenomenon are represented the way they really are. Thus, things in themselves share qualities found in essence and provide a contrast between what we think (believe, suppose) and what actually is.

Definitions come in many forms (Robinson, 1954). *Real definitions* attempt to correlate things with things in a search for essence, but essence is rarely achieved through words. Real definitions are not often attained and, even though LD has operated as if its definitions are real, they are not real in any significant sense. To think otherwise leads to a false sense of closure. *Conceptual definitions* have been assumed to be represented in the LD field (e.g., Hammill, 1990) but their formal meaning is often also difficult to achieve. A *concept*, the basis for conceptual definitions, represents a circumscribed set of characteristics gleaned from the formal activity of concept formation and are theoretically validated (see Hempel, 1952). Too many concepts associated with LD have not been theoretically verified and thus not established firmly enough to be included in a "conceptual" definition of LD (Kavale & Forness, 1985). For example, Kosc (1987) suggested that *LD* need not be defined as such because all that is necessary is "to explain what is to be understood by the component terms 'learning' and 'disabilities' " (p. 36). Kavale and Forness (1987) argued that *learning + disability = LD* is too simplistic and disregards the complex and multivariate nature of LD (see Kavale & Nye, 1991). Furthermore, learning theory is marked by much theoretical diversity (see Hilgard & Bower, 1975), and *disability* becomes very different as evidenced by the earlier discussion about deficit, deficiency, and difference.

The most common form of definition is *nominal*, whose goal is to correlate words with things. One type is *lexical*, as found in a dictionary and representing the customary meaning at a particular point in time; lexical definitions, however, tend to be too general and not very insightful. Most LD definitions may be termed *stipulative*, an explicit and arbitrary adoption of a meaning relation between words. The passage from Lewis Carroll's *Through the Looking Glass* that opened this chapter points to the basic problem with stipulative definitions; they mean whatever a particular individual (or individuals) decide they should mean. Various individuals, groups, and organizations associated with LD have acted like Humpty Dumpty by insisting that *LD* mean what they choose it to mean, based on conventional wisdom about what LD should be.

Stipulative definitions face a fundamental difficulty: They need not be true, only useful (Rantala, 1977). As long as there is consensus about included elements and a perceived heuristic value, the definition is accepted and used. Such definitions never really achieve closure and, as long as consensus is obtained, all theoretical arguments about valid or invalid elements are relative. Stipulative definitions often take the guise of real definitions, but there is no guarantee that they are true; they may be right *or* wrong but still useful. Most available LD definitions have proven useful, but it is necessary to view them as approximations whose validity still needs to be established.

OPERATIONAL DEFINITIONS

Stipulative definitions are, thus, only of generic usefulness, and require transformation to be applied in practice. The most usual transformation is the operational definition, a rule stipulating that the term is to apply to a particular case if specified operations yield certain characteristic results. Any concept has a set of operations that defines it and knowing these operations is to understand the concept fully (see Benjamin, 1955).

Although seemingly unobjectionable, operational definitions possess a number of difficulties. First, they do not meet formal definitional criteria because the operations specified do not really define anything, but merely state the operations required to test for the presence of the thing to which operations refer (Bergmann, 1961). The meaning can be conveyed in a number of ways, depending on the indicators chosen. For example, the concept of discrepancy is defined as the difference between expected and actual achievement, but any number of IQ measures could be used to "define" expected achievement, and an even greater number might be chosen to "define" actual achievement. It is not clear that different measures are operationally, and thus definitionally, equivalent.

A second problem with operational definitions surrounds the fact that LD concepts relate to experience only indirectly (Skinner, 1953). For example, school frustration in an LD student cannot be measured in a way comparable to the direct measurement of heat with a thermometer. School frustration might be defined operationally, but it would be more indirect and require the use of *symbolic operations* to deal with the open terms (i.e., *school, frustration*); symbolic operations, however, introduce metaphysical elements that undermine the operationalist approach.

A final problem surrounds the theoretical validity of operations (Bergmann, 1961). When based on verified theoretical components, operational definitions may be based on a logical and rational foundation. For example, the motion of mercury molecules in a closed tube permits a mathematical interpretation of heat. When the theoretical structure possesses few validated elements as is the case in LD (see Kavale, 1993), operational definitions may not be justified because of the risk of developing spurious procedures. Assume, for example, that there is a proposal for a new *Learning Disability Coefficient* (LDC) defined as the white blood cell count multiplied by body weight in ounces, divided by head circumference in centimeters. Although an LDC could be calculated, it would possess little meaning or significance because a good deal is known about LD and the LDC does not "fit" with any of the existing knowledge. Thus, it is possible to operationalize anything, but whether it "makes sense" is a different matter (Deese, 1972).

OPERATIONAL DEFINITIONS OF LD

The standard definition of LD is the IDEA definition presented earlier and is the official definition under which federal programs are administered. The definition is essentially the NACHC definition that was adopted because of conflicting opinion delivered during Congressional testimony and the conclusion that there was no consensus about definition. Until more definitive and agreed on parameters are forthcoming, no substantive definitional change would be appropriate.

To be useful for practical purposes, however, formal definitions need to be operationalized. The United States Office of Education (1976), in an effort to guide practice, issued the following guidelines:

> A specific learning disability may be found if a child has a severe discrepancy between achievement and intellectual ability in one or more of several areas: oral expression, written expression, listening comprehension or reading com-

prehension, basic reading skills, mathematics calculation, mathematics reasoning, or spelling. A "severe discrepancy" is defined to exist when achievement in one or more of the areas falls at or below 50% of the child's expected achievement level, when age and previous educational experiences are taken into consideration. (p. 52405)

Although appearing to be a useful operational definition, the procedures presented suffer from a fundamental flaw: They bear little resemblance to what was stipulated in the formal definition. Any discussion of operational definition would demand that the proposed operations possess a logical and rational relationship to the elements found in the formal definition in order to avoid meaningless and insignificant procedures (e.g., Benjamin, 1955; Bergmann, 1961; Deese, 1972). The USOE operational definition focuses on discrepancy, but there is no statement about discrepancy in the formal definition. Conversely, the formal definition talks about psychological process deficits and CNS dysfunction but these ideas are not included in the operational definition. Additionally, although stipulated in the formal definition, the exclusion clause is given no specification in the operational definition. Although the vagueness associated with the phrase "one or more" are not clarified in the operational definition, severity level becomes the single aspect better delineated by the stipulation of a 50% figure to define "severe discrepancy."

The lack of correspondence between the formal and operational definition of LD means that two distinct views of LD are being presented. Ideally, the procedures stated in an operational definition should be used to validate the elements stipulated in the formal definition. When there is no correspondence between formal and operational definitions, theoretical verification is not possible, and what remains is simply a low grade of psychometric engineering.

The problems are further exacerbated by the fact that discrepancy itself is a concept and requires an operational definition for implementation. If discrepancy is formally defined as the difference between expected and actual achievement, then it is necessary to define operationally *expected* and *actual achievement*. The usual solution is to define each term with something readily quantifiable. For expected achievement, the prediction is typically based on an IQ score obtained from an intelligence measure. The IQ score, however, is the operational definition of intelligence, and no consideration is given to how or why intelligence tests measure intelligence; it is sufficient to know that intelligence tests can provide an IQ score. Actual achievement may be obtained from any number of standardized achievement measures. Little consideration is given to the fact that the obtained scores in grade equivalents are problematic (Berk, 1982), that Kelley's (1927) "jingle and jangle" fallacy (i.e., the assumption that tests with the same name measure the same thing or that tests with different names measure different things) may be operating, or that scores are dependent on the test used (Jenkins & Pany, 1978). Operationally, discrepancy is simply the difference between expected and actual achievement, and, if the difference meets a stipulated, albeit arbitrary, criterion, then a discrepancy is present. Although simple, this view of discrepancy ignores evidence showing difference scores to be notoriously unreliable (Schulte & Borich, 1984), to be influenced by the measurement model used (e.g., grade equivalent vs. standard score; Reynolds, 1985), and to remain static with respect to a time dimension that may introduce different levels of experience (Thorndike, 1963). Finally, discrepancy itself must be understood as the operational definition of underachievement, not LD. The strongest theoretical link is between underachievement and discrepancy; the linkage between LD and discrepancy is far less robust (Kavale, 1987).

DILEMMAS OF DEFINITION

Hammill (1990) suggested that considerable agreement exists among LD definitions and definers. Although this may be a valid observation, it should provide little comfort. Definitions of LD may show a numbing sameness but do not provide an answer to the question: What is LD? Beyond a vague description about a generalized learning failure, LD definitions are not particularly insightful. To prove this point, it is only necessary to examine actual practice where the primary (and sometimes only) element for determining eligibility (i.e., discrepancy) is not even mentioned in the formal definitions. This is not the hallmark of a tightly structured conceptual system surrounding LD.

Definitions of LD evolved from the seminal work of Strauss and Werner and include many of their paradigmatic assumptions (see Kavale & Forness, 1985). The problem is found in the "softening" of these ideas over time to the point where substantial meaning is lost. The concept of CNS dysfunction provides an example. Brain injury is certainly a valid concept but its modification with adjectives *minimal* and *dysfunction* as well as an emphasis on "soft signs" in diagnosis has made it a behavioral, not physiological, concept with a different meaning. Process deficits share a similar fate. Processes represent hypothetical constructs and, as such, are meaningful only when sufficient construct validity is demonstrated (see Cronbach & Meehl, 1955). Generally, the processes associated with LD (e.g., perceptual-motor) do not achieve sufficient construct validity to demonstrate an independent reality. Thus, two important core concepts of LD are difficult to measure and substantiate.

The difficulties with CNS dysfunction and process disorders have resulted in a movement away from these stipulated core concepts to other important but more peripheral concepts. Exclusion, for example, is a legitimate element but does not really elucidate what LD is; by emphasizing exclusion, LD becomes a residual disorder. Additionally, exclusion is problematic; at a behavioral level, LD reveals more similarities than differences when compared to MR and BD (Hallahan & Kauffman, 1977) which has been demonstrated in diagnostic test data not reliably differentiating among LD, MR, and BD (Gajar, 1979). What remained was academic failure, and it became the primary identification criterion. Unlike CNS dysfunction and process deficits that are hypothetical and unobservable constructs, academic failure as defined by discrepancy is a far more tangible criterion that is both efficient and convenient. However, efficiency and convenience are not good reasons for relying on a single factor. The complex nature of LD demands that more than one variable be included to achieve a comprehensive and unified perspective.

The reliance on a single factor, besides offering a limited view of LD, also leads to a situation where other elements are inferred rather than documented. Once a student is classified on the basis of meeting the discrepancy criterion, the presence of CNS dysfunction and processing disorders are often implied. The reason is that these components are explicitly stated in the formal definition and, when designated LD, it is implicitly assumed that a student then meets all the stipulated parameters. Such an assumption is not justified; you assume something that may not be present and ignore a variety of elements that may be present. Given such circumstances, there is little wonder that LD experiences a "problem of heterogeneity."

PROSPECTS FOR LD DEFINITION

The definitional problem of LD is genuine. It is unlikely that any tinkering with the available definitions will ever result in "the" definition of LD. The reason is that many of the foundation assumptions included, if not invalid, are, at least, questionable (Kavale & Forness, 1985). This problem is exacerbated by the use of operational definitions that exhibit little relationship to whatever is stated in formal definition. The result is a proliferation of LD definitions that have become increasingly obscure and fail to provide insight into the question: What is LD?

Rather than trying to "fix" the present definitions, it seems that resolution can only be achieved if the process starts anew. Kavale and Forness (1995) provided an outline for how this process might proceed. A first step would be laying out a set of foundation principles. Through rational and logical debate, propositions about the nature of LD are formulated and serve as a conceptual framework. Next, although problematic, operational definitions may represent the best means of formalizing the LD definition. They, however, must move beyond finely focused attempts at one-to-one correspondence;

LD is too complex to be captured by a single indicator. The solution would be to move beyond the notion of an operational definition as a single statement to include a number of elements that may be defined operationally. Ennis (1964) termed these *operational interpretations*, and they would possess the advantage of permitting a number of concepts to be given meaning by describing their individual operational definitions. The operational interpretations would then need to be organized into an ordered and sequenced hierarchical arrangement that essentially defines what LD is. With this process complete, attention can be directed to writing a formal definition that needs only be a descriptive rendering of the process and elements included.

The procedures outlined are a radical departure from the way LD definitions have been developed in the past. This seems absolutely necessary if any substantive change is to be accomplished. Historically, LD came into the special education scene as a full-blown entity. It almost immediately became a popular designation, but the popularization resulted in an unsubstantiated "conventional wisdom" driving the system rather than reasoned, albeit slower, scientific wisdom. The increased popularity was accompanied by increased vagueness. Under these circumstances, changes were difficult to achieve, and the almost endless semantic wrangling over LD definition attests to this fact. If nothing else, the procedures outlined might breathe some fresh air into an increasingly stale debate.

REFERENCES

Abrams, J. C. (1987). The National Joint Committee on Learning Disabilities: History, mission, and process. *Journal of Learning Disabilities, 20*, 102–106.

Aristotle. (1960). *Topics* (E. S. Forster, trans.). Cambridge, MA: Harvard University Press.

Association for Children with Learning Disabilities. (1986). ACLD description: Specific learning disabilities. *ACLD Newsbrief, 159*, 15–16.

Bateman, B. D. (1965). An educational view of a diagnostic approach to learning disorders. In J. Hellmuth (Ed.), *Learning disorders* (Vol. 1, pp. 219–239). Seattle, WA: Special Child Publications.

Benjamin, A. C. (1955). *Operationism*. Springfield, IL: Thomas.

Bergmann, G. (1961). Sense and nonsense in operationism. In P. G. Frank (Ed.), *The validation of scientific theories* (pp. 45–56). New York: Collier.

Berk, R. A. (1982). Effectiveness of discrepancy score methods for screening children with learning disabilities. *Learning Disabilities, 1*, 11–24.

Brown, A. L., & Campione, J. C. (1986). Psychological theory and the study of learning disabilities. *American Psychologist, 41*, 1059–1068.

Clements, S. D. (1966). *Minimal brain dysfunction in children: Terminology and identification* (NINDS Monograph No. 3, U.S. Public Health Service Publication No. 1415). Washington, DC: Department of Health, Education, and Welfare.

Cronbach, L. J., & Meehl, P. E. (1955). Construct validity in psychological tests. *Psychological Bulletin, 52*, 281–301.

Cruickshank, W. M. (1967). *The brain-injured child in home, school, and community.* Syracuse, NY: Syracuse University Press.

Cruickshank, W. M., Lewandowski, L. J., Opp, G. H., & Rosenberger, R. B. (1993). *Learning disabilities: An historical perspective.* Ann Arbor: University of Michigan Press.

Deese, J. (1972). *Psychology as science and art.* New York: Harcourt Brace Jovanovich.

Ennis, R. H. (1964). Operational definitions. *American Educational Research Journal, 1,* 3–21.

Finlan, T. G. (1993). *Learning disability: The imaginary disease.* Westport, CT: Bergin & Garvey.

Forness, S. R., & Kavale, K. A. (1991). Social skills deficits as primary learning disabilities. A note on problems with the ICLD diagnostic criteria. *Learning Disabilities Research and Practice, 6,* 44–49.

Gajar, A. H. (1979). Educable mentally retarded, learning disabled, emotionally disturbed: Similarities and differences. *Exceptional Children, 45,* 470–472.

Gresham, F. M., & Elliott, S. N. (1989). Social skill deficits as a primary learning disability. *Journal of Learning Disabilities, 22,* 120–124.

Hallahan, D. P., & Cruickshank, W. M. (1973). *Psychoeducational foundations of learning disabilities.* Englewood Cliffs, NJ: Prentice-Hall.

Hallahan, D. P., & Kauffman, J. M. (1977). Labels, categories, behaviors: ED, LD, and EMR reconsidered. *Journal of Special Education, 11,* 139–149.

Hammill, D. D. (1990). On defining learning disabilities: An emerging consensus. *Journal of Learning Disabilities, 23,* 74–84.

Hempel, C. (1952). Fundamentals of concept formation in empirical science (*International Encyclopedia of Unified Science;* Vol. II, No. 7). Chicago: University of Chicago Press.

Hilgard, E. R., & Bower, G. H. (1975). *Theories of learning* (4th ed.). Englewood Cliffs, NJ: Prentice-Hall.

Hynd, G. W., Marshall, R., & Gonzalez, J. (1991). Learning disabilities and presumed central nervous system dysfunction. *Learning Disability Quarterly, 14,* 283–296.

Interagency Committee on Learning Disabilities. (1987). *Learning disabilities: A report to the U.S. Congress.* Bethesda, MD: National Institutes of Health.

Jenkins, J. R., & Pany, D. (1978). Standardized achievement tests: How useful for special education? *Exceptional Children, 44,* 448–453.

Kant, I. (1965). *Critique of pure reason* (N. K. Smith, trans.; rev. ed.). New York: St. Martin's Press. (Original work published 1781)

Kass, C., & Myklebust, H. (1969). Learning disabilities: An educational definition. *Journal of Learning Disabilities, 2,* 377–379.

Kavale, K. A. (1987). Theoretical issues surrounding severe discrepancy. *Learning Disabilities Research, 3,* 12–20.

Kavale, K. A. (1993). A science and theory of learning disabilities. In G. R. Lyon, D. B. Gray, J. F. Kavanagh, and N. A. Krasnegor (Eds.), *Better understanding learning disabilities: New views from research and their implications for education and public policies* (pp. 171–195). Baltimore: Brookes.

Kavale, K. A., & Forness, S. R. (1985). Learning disability and the history of science: Paradigm or paradox? *Remedial and Special Education, 6,* 12–23.

Kavale, K. A., & Forness, S. R. (1987). How not to specify learning disabilities: A rejoinder to Kosc. *Remedial and Special Education, 8,* 60–62.

Kavale, K. A., & Forness, S. R. (1995). *The nature of learning disabilities.* Hillsdale, NJ: Lawrence Erlbaum Associates.

Kavale, K. A., Forness, S. R., & Lorsbach, T. C. (1991). Definition for definitions of learning disabilities. *Learning Disability Quarterly, 14,* 257–266.

Kavale, K. A., & Nye, C. (1991). The structure of learning disabilities. *Exceptionality, 2,* 141–156.

Kavale, K. A., & Reese, J. H. (1992). The character of learning disabilities: An Iowa profile. *Learning Disability Quarterly, 15,* 74–94.

Kavanagh, J. F., & Truss, T. J. (Eds.). (1988). *Learning disabilities: Proceedings of the national conference.* Parkton, MD: York Press.

Kelley, T. L. (1927). *Interpretation of educational measurements.* New York: World Book.

Kirk, S. A. (1962). *Educating exceptional children.* Boston: Houghton Mifflin.

Kirk, S. A., & Bateman, B. D. (1962). Diagnosis and remediation of learning disabilities. *Exceptional Children, 29,* 73–78.

Klatt, H. J. (1991). Learning disabilities: A questionable construct. *Educational Theory, 41,* 47–60.

Kosc, L. (1987). Learning disabilities: Definition or specification? A response to Kavale and Forness. *Remedial and Special Education, 8,* 36–41.

Lerner, J. (1989). *Learning disabilities: Theories, diagnosis, and teaching strategies* (5th ed.). Boston: Houghton Mifflin.

Lovett, M. W. (1987). A developmental approach to reading disability: Accuracy and speed criteria of normal and deficient reading skill. *Child Development, 58,* 234–260.

McKnight, R. T. (1982). The learning disability myth in American education. *Journal of Education, 164,* 351–359.

Miller, J. W. (1980). *The definition of the thing.* New York: Norton.

National Advisory Committee on Handicapped Children. (1968). *Special education for handicapped children* (First Annual Report). Washington, DC: Department of Health, Education, and Welfare.

National Joint Committee on Learning Disabilities. (1981). Learning disabilities: Issues on definition. Unpublished manuscript. (Available from The Orton Dyslexia Society, 724 York Road, Baltimore, MD 21204. Reprinted in *Journal of Learning Disabilities, 20,* 107–108)

Rantala, V. (1977). *Aspects of definability.* Amsterdam: North-Holland.

Reynolds, C. R. (1985). Measuring the aptitude–achievement discrepancy in learning disability diagnosis. *Remedial and Special Education, 6,* 37–55.

Robinson, R. (1954). *Definition.* Oxford, England: Oxford University Press.

Sarason, S. B. (1949). *Psychological problems in mental deficiency.* New York: Harper & Row.

Schulte, A., & Borich, G. (1984). Considerations in the use of difference scores to identify learning disabled children. *Journal of School Psychology, 22,* 381–390.

Shaywitz, S. E., Escobar, M. D., Shaywitz, B. A., Fletcher, J. A., & Makuch, R. (1992). Evidence that dyslexia may represent the lower tail of a normal distribution of reading ability. *New England Journal of Medicine, 326,* 145–150.

Siegel, L. S. (1988). Definition and theoretical issues and research on learning disabilities. *Journal of Learning Disabilities, 21,* 264–266.

Silver, L. B. (1988). A review of the federal government's Interagency Committee on Learning Disabilities Report to the U.S. Congress. *Learning Disabilities Focus, 3,* 73–80.

Silver, L. B. (1990). Attention deficit–hyperactivity disorder. Is it a learning disability or a related disorder? *Journal of Learning Disbilities, 23,* 394–397.

Skinner, B. F. (1953). The operational analysis of psychological terms. In H. Feigl & M. Brodbeck (Eds.), *Readings in the philosophy of science* (pp. 585–595). New York: Appleton–Century–Crofts.

Stanovich, K. E. (1986). Cognitive processes and the reading problems of learning disabled children: Evaluating the assumption of specificity. In J. K. Torgesen & B. Y. L. Wong (Eds.), *Psychological and educational perspectives on learning disabilities* (pp. 87–131). Orlando, FL: Academic Press.

Stanovich, K. E. (1988). Explaining the differences between the dyslexic and the garden-variety poor reader: The phonological-core variable-difference model. *Journal of Learning Disabilities, 21,* 590–612.

Strauss, A. A., & Lehtinen, L. E. (1947). *Psychopathology and education of the brain-injured child.* New York: Grune & Stratton.

Swanson, H. L. (1988). Memory subtypes in learning disabled readers. *Learning Disability Quarterly, 11,* 342–357.

Thorndike, R. L. (1963). *The concepts of over- and under-achievement.* New York: Teachers College Press.

U. S. Department of Education. (1994). *Sixteenth annual report to Congress on the implementation of The Individuals with Disabilities Education Act.* Washington, DC: Author.

United States Office of Education. (1976). Education of handicapped children (*Federal Register,* 41:52405). Washington, DC: U.S. Government Printing Office.

United States Office of Education. (1977). Definition and criteria for defining students as learning disabled (*Federal Register,* 42:250, p. 65083). Washington, DC: U.S. Government Printing Office.

Wagner, R. K., & Torgesen, J. K. (1987). The nature of phonological processing and its causal role in the acquisition of reading skills. *Psychological Bulletin, 101,* 192–212.

Weiderholt, J. L. (1974). Historical perspectives on the education of the learning disabled. In L. Mann & D. Sabatino (Eds.), *The second review of special education* (pp. 103–152). Philadelphia: JSE.

Wepman, J., Criuckshank, W., Deutsch, C., Morency, A., & Strother, C. (1975). Learning disabilities. In N. Hobbs (Ed.), *Issues in the classification of children* (Vol. 1, pp. 300–317). San Francisco: Jossey-Bass.

2

ATTENTION DEFICIT DISORDERS

Janet W. Lerner
Northeastern Illinois University

Attention deficit disorder (ADD) is a relatively new diagnostic label for children. ADD constitutes a chronic neurobiological condition characterized by developmentally inappropriate attention skills, impulsivity, and, in some cases, hyperactivity (Barkley, 1990). The term is used by many professionals, such as the U.S. Department of Education (1991), to identify these children. An alternative diagnostic term is recommended by the American Psychiatric Association (1994)—namely, *Attention Deficit Hyperactivity Disorder* (ADHD)— and this referent is used in the *DSM–IV* (*Diagnostic and Statistical Manual of Mental Disorders*, 4th ed.). In practice, both ADD and ADHD describe the same disability and are frequently used interchangeably (Rief, 1993). Even though the designations ADD and ADHD are relatively recent, children with the characteristics of ADD have long been recognized and posed a challenge for parents, psychologists, educators, and physicians.

The suspicion that many Americans seem to have ADD may be true. One can speculate that as Americans we inherited the genetic characteristics of our impulsive, hyperactive risk-taking ancestors. After all, we are the descendants of people who made the rash, high-risk decision to leave their native countries and families to start life anew in America. Their peers and family members who remained in the "old country" were the attentive, reflective, conservative people who did not choose to take that impetuous trip to the new world.

BACKGROUND

A conservative estimate is that 3–5% of our school population, or approximately 2 million children and adolescents, are affected by ADD. Further, studies show that approximately 50% of children with ADD grow up to become adults with ADD (Barkley, 1990; Lerner, Lowenthal, & Lerner, 1995).

ADD interferes with many areas of the child's life, disrupting the child's home life, education, behavior, and social adjustment. At home, children with ADD have difficulty accommodating home routines and parent expectations. They may resist going to bed, refuse to eat, or even break toys during play. At school, they have trouble completing their class work, often missing valuable information because of their underdeveloped attention capacity. They speak aloud out of turn and find themselves in trouble for their behavior. Their social lives are undermined by inattention, impulsivity and hyperactivity, hampering their ability to make and keep friends. In terms of gender, more boys than girls are diagnosed as having attention deficit disorders; however, research suggests that the prevalence rate is equal for boys and girls. Boys, however, are more likely to be identified (Shaywitz, Fletcher, & Shaywitz, 1995).

ADD at Different Stages of Life

Symptoms of ADD change over time, and distinctive behaviors are evident at different developmental stages.

Young Children.   Children, ages 2 through 6, who are excessively active, are described as being on the go, or "running like a motor." They exhibit overabundant gross motor activity, with constant running and climbing behavior, and cannot sit still for more than a few minutes at a time. Parents report that it is particularly trying to take their ADD preschoolers to public places, such as supermarkets or restaurants. Young children with ADD may take toys apart to see how they work, but find that they are unable to put them together and end up by destroying the toy.

Elementary-School-Age Students.   Students with ADD at this age are described as restless, fidgety, poorly organized, and haphazard in their behavior. They tend to talk too much in class, get into fights with classmates, and their inattention can impede learning to read. If the child has above-average intelligence, the reading problem may not be noticeable at first (DuPaul, Barkley, & McMurray, 1991; Frick & Lahey, 1991).

Adolescents.   The behavioral problems continue into adolescence. When poor attention and hyperactive behavior add to the turmoil of adolescence itself, deficiencies in academic skills intensify. Many adolescents with ADD also have coexisting conditions, such as learning disabilities, behavior disorders, and social problems. Even though adolescents may appear less hyperactive, they develop other symptoms, such as social disabilities, conduct disorders, low self-esteem, inattentiveness, or even depression (Goldstein, 1993; Shaywitz et al., 1995; Shaywitz & Shaywitz, 1988).

Adults. At one time, ADD was considered a childhood problem; it was thought that ADD symptoms were outgrown when the individual reached adulthood. Now it is recognized that ADD can continue throughout adult life. For many adults, problems related to ADD affect their work and careers, their social lives, marriages, and personal relationships (Barkley, 1990; Mannuzza, Klein, & Bessler, 1993).

COEXISTING DISABILITIES

Frequently, another condition or disability occurs concomitantly with attention deficit disorders. The comorbid or coexisting condition also must be considered in the assessment and treatment. Coexisting conditions are likely to be in the form of learning disabilities, emotional and behavioral disorders, social problems, and traits of gifted/talented children.

Learning Disabilities

ADD is not synonymous with learning disabilities, but many children with attention deficit disorders also display symptoms of learning disabilities, further complicating identification and treatment. Estimates based on research suggest that at least 25% of children with ADD have coexisting learning disabilities (McKinney, Montague, & Hocutt, 1993; Shaywitz et al., 1995; Silver, 1990). Because many students diagnosed with ADD will also be identified and served under the classification of learning disabilities, it is essential that learning disabilities teachers and regular classroom teachers become knowledgeable about ADD.

Emotional and Behavioral Disorders

Another condition that may coexist with ADD is serious emotional disturbance (SED), an existing category of disability in IDEA. In the *Diagnostic and Statistical Manual of Mental Disorders*, fourth edition (*DSM–IV*), the diagnostic classifications are identified as *Conduct Disorder* (CD) and *Oppositional Defiant Disorder* (ODD; American Psychiatric Association, 1994).

Children with coexisting ADD and disruptive behavior disorders often display aggression, oppositional defiance, and conduct problems (McKinney et al., 1993). It is estimated that 40–60% of elementary-age children with ADD have coexisting oppositional defiance disorders, whereas roughly 20–30% develop conduct disorders (Frick & Lahey, 1991).

Social Problems

One of the most consistent findings in the literature on ADD is that children and youth with ADD have significant and persistent problems in social relationships. A social disability is probably the most debilitating problem for a child. Children with ADD often do not relate well to peers and may have few or no friends. Peer rejection can be devastating, leading to feelings of loneliness, poor self-image and low self-esteem. For adolescents, such problems and feelings too often lead to poor school performance, juvenile delinquency, and dropping out of school (Silver, 1993).

Children with ADD and hyperactivity tend to be aggressive and are rejected more often than comparison subjects. Children with ADD not having hyperactivity are more withdrawn and unpopular but not necessarily rejected (McKinney et al., 1993).

Gifted/Talented Students With ADD

It has been observed that many of the characteristics of gifted children are also traits of children with ADD. Gifted children are characterized as spontaneous, inquisitive, imaginative, boundlessly enthusiastic, excitable, and emotional—traits that also describe children with ADD.

The nervous system of gifted children seem to require much activity. Gifted children tend to be immovable when engaged in projects, working persistently and passionately. Gifted children also may find regular classroom environments difficult places in which to maintain engagement because of the slow pace. They may respond by becoming fidgety, inattentive, and even disruptive, because their learning needs are not being met (Webb & Latimer, 1993). Because of the similarity between these two categories, it is suspected that gifted children are sometimes mislabeled as children with ADD (Lind, 1993).

HISTORICAL PERSPECTIVE

The concept of ADD has taken a long time to evolve. Although we have long recognized that these children needed help, they have been identified in the past under other labels, including brain injured, MBD, conduct disordered, hyperkinetic, learning disabled, and emotionally disturbed. A number of historical events shaped the field of attention deficit disorders.

1902: Defects in Moral Control

Early in the 1900s, a physician described the symptoms of a group of hyperactive and inattentive children as aggressive, defiant, resistant to discipline, and lawless (Still, 1902). Reflecting views of that era, Still believed these children lacked the will to control moral behavior and characterized them as having "morbid defects in moral control" (p. 1009).

1947: Brain Damage Syndrome

Paralleling the history of the field of learning disabilities, influential research in the 1930s and 1940s linked the behavioral and hyperactive symptoms of children to brain damage (Strauss & Lehtinen, 1947; Werner & Strauss, 1941). The work of Strauss and his colleagues stressed behavior characteristics more than learning characteristics. Today, many of the behavioral characteristics first identified by Strauss are recognized as key traits of children with attention deficit disorders (Ackerman, Dykman, Oglesby, & Newton, 1994; Dykman & Ackerman, 1991). There was no vigorous follow-up to this early work, and educators and parents instead turned their attention to learning disabilities, where the focus was on children's learning problems rather than on their behavioral characteristics.

1966: Minimal Brain Dysfunction

The term *brain damage* proved to be troublesome for professionals and parents for several reasons, including that it did not differentiate between gross and less severe brain damage. A new term, *minimal brain dysfunction* (MBD), was recommended in a report sponsored by the National Institutes of Health (NIH; Clements, 1966). The symptoms of MBD included specific learning deficits, hyperkinesis, impulsivity, and short attention span.

1968: Hyperkinetic Reaction of Childhood

A significant historical event was the publication of the *Diagnostic and Statistical Manual of Mental Disorders*, second edition (*DSM–II*; American Psychiatric Association, 1968). The DSM publications provide diagnostic criteria for various mental disorders. In the *DSM–II*, the phrase *hyperkinetic reaction of childhood* was first used to describe the hyperactive child.

1980: Attention Deficit Disorder: ADDH and ADD/noH

In 1980, diagnostic guidelines were revised in the third edition of the *Diagnostic and Statistical Manual of Mental Disorders* (*DSM–III*; American Psychiatric Association, 1980). The focus shifted to attention problems rather than hyperactive behavior. The *DSM–III* established the term *attention deficit disorder*, classifying two types: (a) ADD *with* hyperactivity (ADDH), and (b) ADD *without* hyperactivity (ADD/noH). In addition, the *DSM–III* established criteria of onset prior to age 7 and duration of the behavior for at least 6 months.

1987: Attention Deficit Hyperactivity Disorder (ADHD)

Further modification appeared in 1987, with the publication of the *Diagnostic and Statistical Manual of Mental Disorders*, third edition–revised (*DSM–III–R*; American Psychiatric Association, 1987). In the *DSM–III–R*, the term *attention deficit hyperactivity disorder* (ADHD) was recommended. The criteria for the diagnosis of ADHD required that the child exhibit 8 of 14 symptomatic behaviors. In addition, the *DSM–III–R* described a condition referred to as *undifferentiated attention deficit disorder* (U-ADD), which roughly corresponds to the earlier ADD/noH designation.

1994: Attention-Deficit Hyperactivity Disorder (ADHD)

The fourth edition of the *Diagnostic and Statistical Manual of Mental Disorders* (*DSM–IV*) revised the diagnostic criteria for ADHD (American Psychiatric Association, 1994). Because *DSM–IV* criteria is the basis for the diagnosis of ADHD by psychologists, psychiatrists, and other professionals, the *DSM–IV* is discussed in greater detail.

CRITERIA FOR ATTENTION DEFICIT
HYPERACTIVITY DISORDER (ADHD) IN THE *DSM–IV*

The *DSM–IV*, published in 1994, contained new diagnostic criteria for *attention deficit hyperactivity disorder* and has substantial implications for school assessment and for instruction of children with ADD or ADHD. The individual is judged on specific symptomatic behaviors obtained through observation or from informants (such as parents or teachers). The *DSM–IV* continues the terminology of ADHD, but designates three subtypes of ADHD (American Psychiatric Association, 1994; McBurnett, 1995).

ADHD–I: Primarily Inattentive Subtype

In the ADHD–I subtype, the primary problem is that of attention. This subtype is familiar to clinicians as a variant of ADD without hyperactivity. The criteria for the diagnosis of ADHD–I requires that the individual display at least six (of nine) attention symptoms, but fewer than six hyperactivity–impulsivity symptoms.

ADHD–IH: Primarily Hyperactive–Impulsive Subtype

The ADHD–IH subtype is new, as these individuals display behaviors of hyperactivity and impulsivity, but they do not manifest problems with attention. The criteria for the diagnosis of ADHD–IH requires that the individual display at least six (of nine) hyperactivity–impulsivity symptoms, but fewer than six inattention symptoms.

ADHD–C: A Combination of ADHD–I and ADHD–IH

The ADHD–C subtype refers to individuals who have both attention problems and display symptoms of hyperactivity and impulsivity. These individuals have at least six inattention symptoms and six hyperactivity–impulsivity symptoms.

In developing these new criteria for ADHD, researchers conducted field trials with 380 children who were referred to clinics. The study found that 27% of the ADHD population were identified with the subtype ADHD–I, 18% were identified under the subtype ADHD–HI, and 55% were identified under the subtype ADHD–C (Lahey et al., 1994; McBurnett, 1995).

U.S. DEPARTMENT OF EDUCATION CLARIFICATION MEMORANDUM ON ADD

A major step in the recognition of attention deficit disorders in the public schools occurred in 1991, when the U.S. Department of Education issued a memorandum clarifying its policy with regard to eligibility for services for children with ADD. The Department of Education's policy memorandum on ADD was a response to the vigorous lobbying effort of concerned parent groups, particularly CH.A.D.D. (Children and Adults with Attention Deficit Disorder), and by practitioners and researchers in education, medicine, and psychology. This significant policy memorandum was signed jointly by representatives of three offices in the Department of Education: The Office of Special Education and Rehabilitative Services, the Office for Civil Rights, and the Office of Elementary and Secondary Education.

Eligibility Under IDEA

The U.S. Department of Education's (1991) memorandum on ADD states that a child with ADD may qualify for special education and related services under Part B of IDEA, within the category of "other health impaired" if the ADD constitutes "a chronic or acute health problem that results in limited alertness," thus adversely affecting educational performance. As defined in IDEA:

Other health impaired is having limited strength, vitality, or alertness, as a result of chronic or acute health problems, such as heart conditions, tuberculosis, rheumatic fever, nephritis, asthma, sickle cell anemia, hemophilia, epilepsy, lead poisoning, leukemia, or diabetes, that adversely affects educational performance.

The memorandum further states that children with ADD may be eligible for services under Part B of IDEA if they satisfy the criteria applicable to other disability categories, such as learning disabilities or serious emotional disturbance. Thus, children with ADD may be eligible for services under three categories of disability in IDEA: other health impaired, learning disabilities, and seriously emotional disturbance (Lerner et al., 1995; U.S. Department of Education, 1991).

Eligibility Under Section 504 of the Rehabilitation Act of 1973

The U.S. Department of Education policy memorandum on ADD also states that a child with ADD may be eligible for services in the general education classroom under Section 504 of the Rehabilitation Act of 1973, even if that child does not qualify for special education and related services under Part B of IDEA. Under Section 504, if the child is found to have "a physical or mental impairment which substantially limits a major life activity" (e.g., learning), then the school must make an "individualized determination of the child's education needs for regular or special education or related aids and services" (Lerner et al., 1995; U.S. Department of Education, 1991). For the student identified as having ADD under Section 504, "reasonable accommodations" must be provided within the general education classroom. Section 504 states: "No otherwise qualified handicapped individual . . . shall, solely by reason of his/her handicap, be excluded from participation in, be denied the benefits of, or be subject to discrimination under any program or activity receiving federal financial assistance."

ASSESSMENT: SCHOOL PLACEMENT FOR INSTRUCTION

Most students with ADD are served in the general education classroom under the rules and regulations of either IDEA or Section 504. IDEA's provisions for the *least restrictive environment* and a *continuum of alternative placements* mean that many children with ADD who are eligible under IDEA for special education services receive instruction in the regular classroom, with support and collaboration of special education teachers. With the current inclusion movement, even more children with ADD are likely to be placed in general education classrooms. Some students with ADD need other placement options and should receive services in resource rooms or special classrooms. Children with ADD who are eligible for services under Section 504 are served in the regular classroom through appropriate modifications and accommodations.

CH.A.D.D. estimates that about 50% of students with ADD can be appropriately served within the regular classroom, about 35% need resource services, and 15% have severe ADD disabilities and need a special education classroom (Fowler, 1992). Thus, most children with ADD (85%) will be in general education classrooms. Over half will be served solely in general education classrooms. The 35% of the children in resource rooms will be in the general education classroom for a large portion of the day; therefore, the need to offer training for elementary and secondary teachers to work with students with ADD is tremendous. A recent survey of classroom teachers shows that teachers receive virtually no training for working with students with ADD (Yasutake, Lerner, & Ward, 1994).

TEACHING STUDENTS WITH ADD
IN GENERAL EDUCATION CLASSROOMS

Because most children with ADD will be served in the general education classroom, it is important to know about (a) accommodations and modifications in the general education classroom, and (b) promising classroom intervention programs for students with ADD.

Accommodations and Modifications in the General Education Classroom

A number of ways to modify the classroom for children with attention deficit disorders are described in this section (CH.A.D.D., 1992; Lerner et al., 1995; Parker, 1992; Rief, 1993).

Improving Organizational Skills. Students with ADD have difficulty in organizing their lives, and their lack of organization results in uncompleted assignments. The following suggestions are designed to help students learn how to plan ahead, how to gather appropriate materials for school tasks, how to prioritize the steps to complete an assignment, and how to keep track of their work:

1. Provide clear classroom rules to add structure and communicate teacher expectations.

2. Establish routines for placing objects—especially routinely used objects (such as books, assignments, and outdoor clothes)—in designated places so that they can be found easily.

3. Provide the students with a list of materials needed for the task. Limit the list to only those materials necessary to complete the task.

4. Provide a schedule so that the students know exactly what to do for each class period.

5. Make sure the students have all homework assignments before leaving school. Write each assignment on the board and have the student copy it, or write the assignment for a student in a pocket notebook.

6. Provide students with pocket folders to organize materials. For example, place new work on one side and completed work in chronological order on the other.

7. Use a different color folder for each subject.

Increasing Attention. Inattention is a primary characteristic of children with ADD. Because of their short attention span, they may initially attend but their attention soon wanders. The following activities are designed to help students attend and prolong their concentration (Lerner et al., 1995):

1. Shorten the task by breaking a long task into smaller parts. Assign fewer problems; for example, fewer spelling words or mathematics problems.

2. Shorten the homework assignment by giving fewer problems.

3. Use distributed practice. Instead of a few, long, and concentrated practice sessions, set up more short, spaced, and frequent practice sessions.

4. Make tasks more interesting to keep the student's interest. Encourage children to work with partners, in small groups, or in interest centers.

5. Alternate highly interesting and less interesting tasks.

6. Increase the novelty of the task. Tasks that are new or unique are more appealing and will increase attention.

Improving Ability to Listen. Students with ADD frequently miss important instructions and information because they are not actively listening. They may even be unaware that a message is being given. Listening means more than hearing or recognizing the words that are spoken; it means comprehending the message. The following strategies can help students acquire better listening skills:

1. Make instruction simple by using short, direct sentences. Give one instruction at a time. Repeat as often as necessary. Make sure students know the vocabulary being used.
2. Prompt student to repeat instructions after listening to them, then have the students repeat to themselves information they have just heard to build listening and memory skills.
3. Alert the student by using key phrases, such as "this is important" and "listen carefully." (For college students, the phrase "this will be on the exam" is very effective.) Some teachers use prearranged signals, such as hand signals or switching the lights on before giving directions.
4. Use visual aids (such as charts, pictures, graphics, or written key points on a chalkboard or overhead transparencies) to illustrate and support verbal information.

Adapting the Curriculum. Often the curriculum can be changed, modified, or adapted without sacrificing the integrity of the basic curriculum. Even a small change can be beneficial for students with ADD (Lerner et al., 1995):

1. Select high interest materials to reinforce the basic curriculum.
2. Use manipulable, hands-on materials whenever possible. Create activities that require active participation, such as talking through problems and acting out steps. Many students learn better when they actually do something in addition to just listening and observing.
3. Use visual aids to supplement oral and written information. Use learning aids, such as computers, calculators, and tape recorders to increase motivation.
4. Modify tests, allowing the student to take tests orally instead of writing the answers. Teach students how to cross out incorrect answers on multiple-choice tests.

Helping Students Manage Time. A common problem area for many students with ADD is the management of time. They get pulled away from the task at hand and become involved with new challenges and tend to become procrastinators, a trait they retain into their adult lives. The following activities are designed to help students with time management (Lerner et al., 1995):

1. Set up a specific routine and adhere to it. When disruptions occur, explain the situation to the students and appropriate ways to respond.
2. During the school day, alternate activities that are done while sitting and those that involve standing and moving about.

3. Make lists that will help students organize their tasks. Have them check off tasks as they complete them.

4. Use behavioral contracts that specify the amount of time allotted for specific activities.

Promising Classroom Intervention Programs for Students With ADD

The U.S. Department of Education funded a research team at the Research Triangle Institute to conduct an extensive study of effective school-based interventions that teachers can employ in regular classrooms for teaching students with attention deficit disorders (Fiore & Becker, 1994). Although their search found limited studies on teaching students with ADD in school settings, the researchers extrapolated from programs for other difficult-to-teach students. Eight intervention programs are described, which the reseachers consider to be promising classroom interventions for students with attention deficit disorder. The promising programs, which include academic, affect, study skills, behavior, and career programs, are: (a) Classwide Peer Tutoring, (b) Early Literacy Program, (c) Tribes, (d) Self-Regulated Strategy Developing in Writing, (e) Early Science Videodisc Program, (f) Skills for School Success, (g) Aggression Replacement Training, and (h) Life-Centered Career Education. Each is briefly described here.

Classwide Peer Tutoring (CWPT). This is a system in which tutor–tutee pairs work together on a classwide basis (Delquadri, Greenwood, Stretton, & Hall, 1983; Fiore & Becker, 1994; Kamps, Barbetta, Leonard, & Delquadri, 1994). The CWPT research was conducted at schools in Juniper Gardens, a housing project in Kansas City, KS.

In the CWPT program, at the beginning of each week, all students in a class are paired for tutoring, and these tutor–tutee pairs are then assigned to one of two competing teams. Tutees earn points for their team by responding to the tasks presented to them by the tutors. The winning team is determined on the basis of the highest team's point total.

Fuchs, Fuchs, Hamlett, Phillips, and Bentz (1994) enhanced CWPT by combining the procedure of classwide curriculum-based measurement with classwide peer tutoring. The researchers report positive results for children with special needs in regular classrooms.

Early Literacy Program (ELP). This program is a curriculum that promotes student metacognitive awareness of themselves as readers and writers, and promotes students' abilities to self-regulate literacy performance (Englert, Rosendal, & Mariage, 1994a, 1994b; Fiore & Becker, 1994). The students engage in literacy activities that support four literacy principles: (a) literacy instruction must be embedded in meaningful and purposeful activities; (b) instruction should be responsive to the needs, capabilities, and interests of learners and should reflect their zone of proximal development; (c) instruction should promote self-regulated learning; and (d) instruction should be designed to foster student membership in a literacy community.

All of the reading and writing activities are interrelated in thematic units. Students are taught to brainstorm ideas; organize ideas into maps or webs; gather related ideas for expository or narrative texts and revise their maps; read, comprehend, and monitor texts; and use their maps to write, monitor, revise, and publish expository reports using comprehension-monitoring and editing strategies. Activities include choral reading of poems, using predictable texts and other texts related to the thematic units, engaging in sustained silent reading, using partner reading/writing, sharing the chair, having morning news, setting up an author's center, and using story response. The program is designed for nonreaders as well as children who have some reading skills.

Tribes. Tribes is a program that sets up a positive classroom climate. The tribe is a group of five or six children who work together throughout each day throughout the school year. They are seated together in a circle of desks or at the same table in their classroom and each classroom has four to five tribes. The teacher acts as a facilitator, giving time limits and intervening only when necessary. The teacher transfers management responsibilities to the students within the tribes. The program uses cooperative learning, Tribe norms, and group process (Fiore & Becker, 1994; Gibbs, 1987, 1994). The tribe activities fall into three general categories: (a) sharing personal concerns, feelings, and positive regard for one another; (b) planning, problem solving, and maintaining an environment of positive support for all members; and (c) working cooperatively on curriculum as assigned by the teacher.

Self-Regulated Strategy Development in Writing (SRSD). This intervention combines elements of self-regulation with dynamic stages of instruction in order to effectively teach strategies for writing in general, and for writing in different genres (e.g., narrative stories, essays; Fiore & Becker, 1994; Graham & Harris, 1993; Harris & Graham, 1992). Teaching students to self-regulate their behavior helps them become more independent, increases task engagement, and helps students monitor and regulate their own academic performance.

The SRSD program teaches students to write through the following stages:

1. Preskill development (the teacher helps the student develop prerequisite skills).

2. Initial conference—Instructional goals and significance (the teacher and student discuss past performance and goals).

3. Discussion of the strategy (teacher and student discuss the strategy).

4. Modeling (the teacher models the strategy).

5. Memorization of the strategy (the student memorizes the steps of the strategy).

6. Collaborative practice (the student practices the strategy with teacher support).

7. Independent performance (the student performs the strategy independently).

Earth Science Videodisc Program. This is a videodisc-based science program for middle- and high-school students (Fiore & Becker, 1994; Hofmeister, Englemann, & Carnine, 1989). Emphasizing the teaching of science concepts, rather than facts, the visual presentation keeps the attention of the students. The program is based on effective teaching principles: (a) begin each lesson with a review, (b) begin each lesson by stating the goal, (c) present new material in small steps, (d) give clear instructions, (e) provide active practice, (f) ask many questions, (g) guide students during practice, (h) provide systematic feedback, (i) provide explicit instruction and practice for seatwork.

Skills for School Success. This program addresses the organization needs of all students, but especially those with mild disabilities who are being educated in mainstream classroom (Archer & Gleason, 1989, 1992; Fiore & Becker, 1994). The program is designed to teach critical organization skills and study skills systematically to students in grades three through six. *Advanced Skills for School Success* is a similar program for junior-high and middle-school students. This program teaches appropriate school behaviors, organization skills, specific learning strategies, textbook reference skills, graphics skills, and use of classroom reference materials.

Aggression Replacement Training (ART). This program teaches prosocial skills to aggressive adolescents or juvenile delinquents who exhibit acting-out behaviors and have severe problems with prosocial behaviors (Fiore & Becker, 1994; Goldstein & Glick, 1987). There are three components:

1. *Structured learning.* Students learn behaviors such as how to express a complaint, how to respond to anger, how to keep out of fights.

2. *Anger control training.* Students learn how to inhibit anger aggression, and antisocial behavior.

3. *Moral reasoning.* A set of procedures designed to raise the student's level of moral reasoning and have concern with the needs and rights of others.

Life-Centered Career Education (LCCE). This curriculum is designed to promote the development of skills that students will need to succeed in life after graduation (Brolin, 1993; Fiore & Becker, 1994). LCCE instruction is divided into three instruction domains that include 22 competencies in all: *daily living skills, personal-social skills,* and *occupational skills.* Daily living skills refers to learning how to manage a home, family, and finances as effectively as possible. Personal-social skills involves developing independence, self-confidence, socially acceptable behaviors, and maintaining friendships. Occupational guidance and preparation involves becoming aware of diverse job opportunities, developing the necessary skills, and learning to make logical and viable job choices.

SUMMARY

The number of children in our schools who are identified as having attention deficit disorders is rising. The challenge of teaching children with attention deficit disorders and serving them appropriately in schools is increasingly recognized by all who come in contact with these children. Significant issues related to attention deficit disorders from a school perspective reviewed in this chapter include: the characteristics of ADD at difference stages of life, prevalence, coexisting conditions, historical evolution of the field, the *DSM–IV,* the U.S. Department of Education Memorandum on ADD, school placement for students with ADD, accommodations in the general education classroom, and promising programs for intervention.

REFERENCES

Ackerman, P., Dykman, R., Oglesby, D., & Newton, J. (1994). EEG power spectra of children with dyslexia, slow learners, and normally reading children with ADD during verbal processing. *Journal of Learning Disabilities, 27,* 610–630.

American Psychiatric Association. (1968). *Diagnostic and statistical manual of mental disorders* (2nd ed.). Washington, DC: Author.

American Psychiatric Association. (1980). *Diagnostic and statistical manual of mental disorders* (3rd ed.). Washington, DC: Author.

American Psychiatric Association. (1987). *Diagnostic and statistical manual of mental disorders* (3rd ed., rev.). Washington, DC: Author.

American Psychiatric Association. (1994). *Diagnostic and statistical manual of mental disorders* (4th ed.). Washington, DC: Author.

Archer, A., & Gleason, M. (1989). *Skills for school success. Books 5 & 6.* North Billerica, MA: Curriculum Associates.

Archer, A., & Gleason, M. (1992). *Advanced skills for school success. Modules 1, 2, and 3. School behaviors and organizational skills.* North Billerica, MA: Curriculum Associates.

Barkley, R. A. (1990). *Attention deficit hyperactivity disorder: A handbook for diagnosis and treatment.* New York: Guilford.

Brolin, D. E. (1993). *Life centered career education: Trainer's manual* (3rd ed.). Reston, VA: Council for Exceptional Children.

CH.A.D.D. (1992). Testimony to the Senate and U.S. House of Representatives Subcommittee on Appropriations. *CH.A.D.D., 6*(2), 24.

Clements, S. (1966). *Task force one: Minimal brain dysfunction in children* (NINDS Monograph No. 3). Rockville, MD: Department of Health, Education and Welfare.

Delquadri, J., Greenwood, C., Stretton, K., & Hall, F. (1983). The peer tutoring game: A classroom procedure for increasing opportunity to respond. *Education and Treatment of Children, 6,* 225–239.

DuPaul, G., Barkley, R., & McMurray, M. (1991). Therapeutic effects of medication on ADHD: Implications for school psychologists. *School Psychology Review, 20,* 203–239.

Dykman, R., & Ackerman, P. (1991). Attention deficit disorder and specific reading disability: Separate but often overlapping disorders. *Journal of Learning Disabilities, 24,* 96–103.

Englert, C., Raphael, T., & Mariage, T. (1994a). Developing a school-based discourse for literacy learning. A principled search for understanding. *Learning Disability Quarterly, 17,* 2–32.

Englert, C., Raphael, T., & Mariage, T. (1994b). Fostering the search for understanding: A teacher's strategies for leading cognitive development in zones of proximal development. *Learning Disability Quarterly, 17,* 176–204.

Fiore, T. A., & Becker, E. A. (1994). *Promising classroom interventions for students with attention deficit disorder.* Research Triangle Park, NC: Center for Research in Education, Research Triangle Institute.

Fowler, M. (1992). *CH.A.D.D. educators manual: An in-depth look at attention deficit disorders from an educational perspective.* Plantation, FL: CH.A.D.D.

Frick, P., & Lahey, E. (1991). Nature and characteristics of attention-deficit hyperactivity disorder. *School Psychology Review, 20*(2), 163–173.

Fuchs, L., Fuchs, D., Hamlett, C., Phillips, N., & Bentz, J. (1994). Classwide curriculum-based measurement: Helping educators meet the challenge of student diversity. *Exceptional Children, 60,* 518–537.

Gibbs, J. (1987). *Tribes: A process for social development and cooperative learning.* Santa Rosa, CA: Center Source Publications.

Gibbs, J. (1994). *A new way of learning together.* Santa Rosa, CA: Center Source Publications.

Goldstein, A., & Glick, B. (1987). *Aggression replacement training: A comprehensive intervention for aggressive youth.* Champaign, IL: Research Press.

Goldstein, S. (1993). ADHD in the adolescent years. *CH.A.D.D.er Box. 6*(4), 1, 7–9.

Graham, S., & Harris, K. (1993). Self-regulated strategy development. Helping students with learning problems develop as writers. *Elementary School Journal, 94,* 159–182.

Harris, K., & Graham, S. (1992). *Helping young writers master the craft: Strategy instruction and self-regulation in the writing process.* Cambridge, MA: Brookline Books.

Hofmeister, A., Englemann, S., & Carnine, D. (1989). Developing and validating science education videotapes. *Journal of Research in Science Teaching, 26,* 665–667.

Kamps, D. M., Barbetta, P. M., Leonard, B. R., & Delquadri, J. (1994). Classwide peer tutoring: An integrated strategy to improve reading skills and promote peer interactions among students with autism and general education peers. *Journal of Applied Behavior Analysis, 27,* 49–61.

Lahey, B., Applegate, B., McBurnett, K., Biderman, J., Greenhill, L., Hynd, G., Barkley, R., Newcorn, J., Jensen, P., Richters, J., Garfinkel, B., Kerdyke, L., Frick, P., Ollendick, T., Perez, D., Hart,

E., Waldman, I., & Shaffer, D. (1994). DSM–IV field trials for attention deficit/hyperactivity disorder in children and adolescents. *American Journal of Psychiatry, 151*(11), 1673–1685.

Lerner, J. W., Lowenthal, B., & Lerner, S. R. (1995). *Attention deficit disorders: Assessment and teaching.* Monterey, CA: Brooks/Cole.

Lind, S. (1993). Are we mislabeling overexcitable children? *Understanding Our Gifted, 5*(5A), 1, 8–10.

Mannuzza, R., Klein, R., & Bessler, A. (1993). Adult outcomes of hyperactive boys: Educational achievement, occupational rank, and psychiatric status. *Archives of General Psychiatry, 50,* 566–577.

McBurnett, K. (1995). The new subtype of ADHD: Predominantly Hyperactive-Impulsive. *Attention, 1*(3), 10–12.

McKinney, J., Montague, M., & Hocutt, A. (1993). Educational assessment of students with attention deficit disorder. *Exceptional Children, 60,* 125–131.

Parker, H. C. (1992). *The ADD hyperactivity handbook for schools.* Plantation, FL: Impact Publications.

Rief, S. F. (1993). *How to reach and teach ADD/ADHD children.* West Nyack, NY: The Center for Applied Research in Education.

Shaywitz, B., Fletcher, J., & Shaywitz, S. (1995). Defining and classifying learning disabilities and attention-deficit/hyperactivity disorder. *Journal of Child Neurology, 10*(Supplement 1), S50–S57.

Shaywitz, S., & Shaywitz, B. (1988). Attention deficit disorder: Current Perspectives. In J. Kavanagh & J. Truss (Eds.), *Learning disabilities: Proceedings of the national conference* (pp. 359–567). Parkton, MD: York Press.

Silver, L. (1990). Attention-deficit hyperactivity disorder: Is it a learning disability or a related disorder? *Journal of Learning Disabilities, 23,* 394–397.

Silver, L. (1993). *Dr. Larry Silver's advice to parents on attention-deficit hyperactivity disorder.* Washington, DC: American Psychiatric Press.

Still, C. F. (1902). Some abnormal psychical conditions in children. *Lancet, i,* 1008–1012, 1077–1082, 1163–1168.

Strauss, A., & Lehtinen, L. (1947). *Psychopathology and education of the brain-injured child.* New York: Grune & Stratton.

U.S. Department of Education. (1991, September 16). *Clarification of policy to address the needs of children with attention deficit disorders within the general and/or special education* (Unpublished memorandum).

Webb, J., & Latimer, D. (1993). ADHD and children who are gifted. *Exceptional Children, 60*(2), 183–184.

Werner, H., & Strauss, A. (1941). Pathology of the figure-background relation in the child. *Journal of Abnormal and Social Psychology,* 234–248.

Yasutake, D., Lerner, J., & Ward, M. (1994). The need for teachers to receive training for working with students with attention deficit disorder. *B.C. Journal of Special Education, 18,* 81–84.

3

DEFINING EMOTIONAL OR BEHAVIORAL DISORDERS IN SCHOOL AND RELATED SERVICES

Steven R. Forness
UCLA Neuropsychiatric Hospital

Kenneth A. Kavale
University of Iowa Division of Special Education

In special education, the field of emotional or behavioral disorders seems to have considerably more problems in definition than other major categories such as learning disabilities or mental retardation. Although some disagreement remains, both these latter disorders have a much greater consensus as to definitional and diagnostic criteria, not only within special education, but in other related professions such as psychology, pediatrics, or psychiatry. Emotional or behavioral disorders is a subspecialty that, like mental retardation and learning disabilities, has focused on developmental and academic issues yet, at the same time, must give a certain priority to social or emotional issues as well. These are less well understood and enjoy less agreement as to definition, cause, and treatment, both within special education and in its related professional fields. It is also a specialty whose treatments are increasingly seen as dependent on interdisciplinary or interagency services in which a wide variety of professionals must agree on need for service (Koyanagi & Gaines, 1993; McLaughlin, Leone, Warren, & Schofield, 1994; Nelson & Pearson, 1991; Rivera & Kutash, 1994). There has thus been an understandable tendency to identify only the most obviously or seriously disturbed children in this category. The outcomes for children with emotional or behavioral disorders are therefore understandably less optimistic than for children in almost any other category of special education (Knitzer, Steinberg, & Fleisch, 1990; U.S. Department of Education, 1994).

This chapter focuses on the current definition of serious emotional disturbance (SED) used to determine eligibility for special education and on a definition of emotional or behavioral disorders that will replace it in federal law. Because school is not the only agency providing services for such children and eligibility for related services is often largely dependent on other agencies, other definitions of emotional or behavioral disorders are also reviewed briefly. These include a definition used in Head Start programs, an NIMH definition used in a generic sense to determine Baseness, a definition of eligibility used to determine disability in this area under the Social Security administration, the definition used by the American Psychiatric Association, and the definition used in Section 504 of the Rehabilitation Act (1973). The chapter concludes with a discussion of issues related to eligibility under these various definitions.

THE SED DEFINITION

For nearly two decades, the terminology that has been used to determine eligibility of children with emotional or behavioral disorders for special education is serious emotional disturbance (SED). SED is defined in federal law as a:

> Condition exhibiting one or more of the following characteristics over a long period of time or to a marked degree which adversely affects school performance: (a) an inability to learn which cannot be explained by intellectual, sensory, or health factors; (b) an inability to build or maintain satisfactory relationships with peers and teachers (c) inappropriate types of behavior or feelings under normal circumstances (d) a general pervasive mood of unhappiness or depression; or (e) a tendency to develop physical symptoms or fears associated with personal or school problems.

The definition continues by indicating that the term does include children who are schizophrenic, but does not include children who are "socially maladjusted, unless it is determined that they are seriously emotionally disturbed" (Education of the Handicapped Act, 1975). Thus, to qualify, a youngster must have a problem in at least one of the five areas listed here that must further meet all three limiting criteria; that is, severity, duration, and impact on school performance.

Most professionals in special education consider both the term itself and its definition not only problematic but also a primary source of difficulty in underidentification. The principal division of the Council for Exceptional Children, which represents nationally over 9,000 special educators involved in education of children with behavioral or emotional disorders, has published position papers attacking both the terminology and definition (Council for Children with Behavioral Disorders, 1984, 1987). Similar criticism has come from the National Mental Health and Special Education Coalition organized to address the problem of inadequate service delivery for emotionally disturbed children and youth (Forness, 1988). A disclaimer has even come from the person from whose early research the five definitional criteria were adopted. (Bower, 1982).

Use of this particular terminology and definition has led to several problems. For example, the term *seriously* makes this the one special education category in which only the most impaired tend to be considered for eligibility. Of the five criteria, the first, "inability to learn," is often confused with the learning disability (LD) definition. The second, "inability to build or maintain satisfactory relationships with teachers or peers" (i.e., social adjustment problems), confuses matters because children are excluded if their problems are considered merely "social maladjustment." Many children are also excluded because their problems are considered to be "merely" conduct disorders or discipline problems; however, their actual underlying emotional disorders, such as depression or anxiety, are not recognized or identified as such because "social maladjustment" problems become automatic exclusions (Cline, 1990; Forness, 1992a, 1992b). Epidemiologic studies also suggest that symptoms of conduct disorders are inextricably woven into symptoms of other psychiatric disorders, such that very few children are referred to special education with "pure" conduct disorders (Forness, Kavale, King, & Kasari, 1994). The vast majority of states *do not* exclude children with "social maladjustment," as this definition requires, presumably because of the impossibility of reliably distinguishing "social" from "emotional" maladjustment (Gonzalez, 1991).

THE EBD DEFINITION

Responding to these issues, the Council for Children with Behavioral Disorders (CCBD; 1989) drafted a substitute terminology and definition. This draft was submitted to the National Mental Health and Special Education Coalition, which was composed at the time of 30 different education, mental health, advocacy, and parent associations. The Coalition task force on definition further reviewed and revised the draft. This draft was then approved by the full Coalition and subsequently published (Forness & Knitzer, 1992).

This draft terminology and definition was also submitted to relevant House and Senate subcommittees of the U.S. Congress. There were simultaneous contacts with a wide range of other stakeholders in education and mental health, including members from associations or groups representing ethnically diverse populations such as the NAACP and La Raza. Although the terminology and definition change was originally scheduled as an amendment to pending legislation in the summer of 1992 and quick passage was expected, many individuals representing state and local school boards objected at the last minute (National School Board Association, 1992). This was mainly because of fears that large numbers of children previously unserved in this category would now have to be included in special education at great cost to states and local districts.

It was clear, however, that the newly proposed terminology and definition had nonetheless been "vetted" in a historically unique process and that it enjoyed widespread support in the special education and mental health communities. It was also clear that families of children with this disorder had both been included in this process and were supportive of its outcome. For this reason, Congress compromised by directing the U.S. Department of Education to publish a "notice of inquiry" in the *Federal Register* ("Invitation to Comment," 1993) asking for comments on the advisability of changing to the new definition and terminology in IDEA. Approximately 1,200 responses were received, among the largest number of responses ever received from such a notice of inquiry. Although the terminology was originally proposed as "emotional or behavioral disorders" or EBD (Forness & Knitzer, 1992), the terminology currently proposed in the latest House of Representatives proposal to reauthorize IDEA is "emotional disturbance" (Individuals with Disabilities Education Act, 1986/1995). The definition may thus be linked to this terminology, but this is yet be determined. The text of the new definition as published in the *Federal Register* ("Invitation to Comment," 1993) is:

> The term . . . means a disability that is characterized by behavioral or emotional response in school programs that is significantly different from appropriate age, cultural, or ethnic norms to the extent that the responses adversely affect educational performance, including academic, social or vocational skills; more than temporary, expected response to stressful events in the environment; consistently exhibited in two different settings, at least one of which is school related; and unresponsive to direct intervention applied by general education, or the condition of a child is such that general education interventions would be insufficient.
>
> The term includes such a disability that coexists with other disabilities. The term includes a schizophrenic disorder, affective disorder, anxiety disorder, or other mental disorder, affecting a child if the disorder affects educational performance as described in paragraph (1).

There are a number of major advantages and improvements in this new terminology and definition. The core of the definition stresses that emotional or behavioral problems must exist and must have an impact on adaptive behavior, broadly defined. It not only focuses directly on the child's responses in school settings and places these responses in the context of appropriate age and cultural norms but also has several qualifying statements that insure that only children who appropriately qualify will be eligible. The additional qualifying statements indicate that emotional disorder (a) is more than a temporary, expected response to stress; (b) should be based on data gathered in more than one setting; (c) would persist even with prereferral interventions; (d) can coexist with other disabilities; and (e) is referenced to a listing of examples of current mental health diagnoses that *could* make a student eligible, *if* educational performance is also impaired, thus allowing for greater coordination with other agencies that can provide related services in addition to the school. In contrast to the current definition, the definition does not require meaningless distinctions between social and emotional maladjustment, distinctions that often waste diagnostic resources when it is already clear that serious problems exist. It is not at all clear at the time of this writing, however, that the new EBD terminology or definition will be incorporated into IDEA. They have nonetheless been widely accepted as a generic terminology definition for the field (Kauffman, 1997).

THE HEAD START DEFINITION

Even before the first draft of the EBD definition was formally considered in the U.S. Department of Education notice of inquiry, the U.S. Administration on Children, Youth, and Families adopted a version of it for Head Start programs. The Head Start version was used as part of its revised disability regulations ("Head Start Performance Standards," 1993) and is as follows:

(a) An emotional/behavioral disorder is a condition in which a child's behavioral or emotional responses are so different from those of the generally accepted, age-appropriate norms of children with the same ethnic or cultural background as to result in significant impairment in social relationships, self-care, educational progress or classroom behavior. A child is classified as having an emotional/behavioral disorder who exhibits one or more of the following characteristics with such frequency, intensity, or duration as to require intervention:

(1) Seriously delayed social development including an inability to build or maintain satisfactory (age appropriate) interpersonal relationships with peers or adults (e.g., avoids playing with peers);

(2) Inappropriate behavior (e.g., dangerously aggressive towards others, self-destructive, severely withdrawn, noncommunicative);

(3) A general pervasive mood of unhappiness or depression, or evidence of excessive anxiety or fears (e.g., frequent crying episodes, constant need for reassurance); or

(4) Has a professional diagnosis of serious emotional disturbance.

(b) The eligibility decision must be based on multiple sources of data, including assessment of the child's behavior or emotional functioning in multiple settings.

(c) The evaluation process must include a review of the child's regular Head Start physical examination to eliminate the possibility of misdiagnosis due to an underlying physical condition.

As can be seen, the Head Start definition is an amalgamation of the two previous definitions. It borrows the core of the EBD definition and some of its qualifying statements along with considerably revised versions of the SED subtype categories. It adds a provision for medical screening in order to rule out other conditions that might be causing emotional or behavioral symptoms. Because Head Start is perhaps the largest single referral source for children identified for special education in the early years, this represented a significant attempt to make the two agencies more compatible in their eligibility requirements (Forness & Finn, 1993).

THE CMHS DEFINITION

At about the same time that the EBD definition was proposed to Congress, the National Institute of Mental Health (NIMH) reorganized its applied epidemiologic and mental health service efforts into a new Center for Mental Health Services (CMHS). It became clear that several issues in child mental health in particular could not be effectively addressed without a functional definition of childhood emotional or behavioral disorders. CMHS commissioned a panel of experts to draft a definition of caseness that could not only be used in epidemiologic studies but could also be used in planning for child mental health services. The text of this definition became part of the reorganization of child mental health services under the Alcohol, Drug Abuse, and Mental Health Administration (ADAMHA Reorganization Act, 1992) as follows:

Children with serious emotional disturbance are persons:

- from birth up to age 18
- who currently or at any time during the past year
- have had a diagnosable mental, behavioral or emotional disorder of sufficient duration to meet diagnostic criteria specified with *DSM–III–R*, that resulted in functional impairment which substantially interferes with or limits the child's role or functioning in family, school or community activities.

These disorders include any mental disorder (including those of biological etiology) listed in *DSM–III–R* or their *ICD–9–CM* equivalent (and subsequent revisions), with the exception of *DSM–III–R* "V" codes, substance use, and developmental disorders, which are excluded, unless they co-occur with another diagnosable serious emotional disturbance. All of these disorders have episodic, recurrent or persistent features; however, they vary in terms of severity and disabling effects.

Functional impairment is defined as difficulties that substantially interfere with or limit a child or adolescent from achieving or maintaining one or more developmentally appropriate social, behavioral, cognitive, communicative, or adaptive skills. Functional impairments of episodic, recurrent and continuous duration are included unless they are temporary and expected responses to stressful events in the environment. Children who would have met functional impairment criteria during the referenced year without the benefit of treatment or other support services *are* included in this definition.

It should be noted that explanatory footnotes are included in the text of this definition. These note (a) that the definition normally applies up to age 19, but some states currently extend the range to age 22; (b) that the reference to a 1-year period is commonly used both in epidemiologic research and in service planning cycles; (c) that the publication of the *DSM–IV* would cause this to be updated accordingly; and (d) that substantial functional impairment would subsequently be operationally defined as standardized methods are developed.

Beyond the issues of determining prevalence and state planning for Community Mental Health Services Block Grant Awards, it is not yet clear what impact the CMHS definition will have. Perhaps like the proposed school definition of emotional or behavioral disorders, it may only be destined to become a generic definition in the mental health field. Although its dual emphasis on presence of a disorder and on functional impairment render it somewhat compatible with the EBD definition, the SED terminology may continue to pose problems in that only the most severe or obvious cases may be eligible for consideration in service planning (Costello & Tweed, 1994).

THE SSI DEFINITION

Within the U.S. Social Security Administration, the Supplemental Security Income (SSI) program provides funds for people at any age who have severe disabilities and meet requirements for limited income. Most states have a disability determination service that reviews decisions on each child made by a disability examiner and a medical or psychological specialist. This team develops a care record of each child applicant's medical and functional history from a wide variety of sources including parents, caregivers, school staff, and other practitioners as needed. The team uses a sequential evaluation process in which it considers in turn whether the child is not able to engage in gainful activity (generally defined as not earning more than $500 per month), whether the child has a severe impairment, and whether the child's impairment meets an official listing of impairments, or, if not, whether the impairment is comparable in severity to that which would disable an adult.

The childhood mental disorders in which a child might qualify for SSI were first listed in the *Federal Register* in 1990 (Social Security Income Childhood Mental Disorders Listing, 1990) as follows:

112.02 *Organic Mental Disorders*. Abnormalities in perception, cognition, affect or behavior associated with dysfunction of the brain. History and physical examination or laboratory tests, including psychological or neuropsychological tests, demonstrate or support the presence of an organic factor judged to be etiologically related to the abnormal mental state and associated deficit or loss of specific cognitive abilities, affective changes, or loss of previously acquired functional abilities.

112.03 *Schizophrenic, Delusional (Paranoid), Schizoaffective, and Other Psychotic Disorders*. Onset of psychotic features, characterized by marked disturbance of thinking, feeling, and behavior, with deterioration from previous level of functioning or failure to achieve the expected level of social functioning.

112.04 *Mood Disorders*. Characterized by a disturbance of mood (referring to a prolonged emotion that colors the whole psychic life, generally involving either depression or elation), accompanied by a full or partial manic or depressive syndrome.

112.05 *Mental Retardation*. Characterized by significantly subaverage general intellectual functioning with deficits in adaptive functioning.

112.06 *Anxiety Disorders*. In these disorders, anxiety is either the predominant disturbance or is experienced if the individual attempts to master symptoms, e.g., confronting the dreaded object or situation in a phobic disorder, attempting to go to school in a separation anxiety disorder, resisting the obsessions or compulsions in an obsessive compulsive disorder or confronting strangers or peers in avoidant disorders.

112.07 *Somatoform, Eating, and Tic Disorders*. Manifested by physical symptoms for which there are no demonstrable organic findings or known physiologic mechanisms, or eating or tic disorders with physical manifestations. The required level of severity for these disorders is met when functional requirements are satisfied.

112.08 *Personality Disorders*. Manifested by pervasive, inflexible, and maladaptive personality traits, which are typical of the child's long-term functioning and not limited to discrete episodes of illness.

112.09 *Psychoactive Substance Dependence Disorders*. Manifested by a cluster of cognitive, behavioral, and physiologic symptoms that indicate impaired control of psychoactive substance use with continued use of the substance despite adverse consequences.

112.10 *Autistic Disorder and Other Pervasive Developmental Disorders.* Characterized by qualitative deficits in the development of reciprocal social interaction, in the development of verbal and nonverbal communication skills, and in imaginative activity. Often, there is a markedly restricted repertoire of activities and interests, which frequently are stereotyped and repetitive.

112.11 *Attention Deficit Hyperactivity Disorders.* Manifested by developmentally inappropriate degrees of inattention, impulsiveness, and hyperactivity.

112.13 *Developmental and Emotional Disorders of Newborn* and Younger Infants (Birth to Attainment of Age 1). Developmental or emotional disorders of infancy are evidenced by a deficit or lag in the areas of motor, cognitive/communicative or social functioning. These disorders may be related either to organic or functional factors, or to a combination of these factors.

As indicated earlier, each of the listings includes not only a detailed description of various criteria for each disorder but a detailed description of various criteria for functional impairment associated with it. Currently, there would appear to be more than a quarter of a million children or adolescents receiving SSI under these listings (Koyanagi, 1993). The three most common listings used were ADHD (29.5%), personality disorders (21%), and mood disorders (12%). All the remaining disorders were each less than 10%. From the criteria listed in "Personality Disorders," it is possible to conclude that social or conduct disturbances may have accounted for a large proportion of the 21% listed. There is currently no way of determining the extent to which the approximately quarter of a million cases eligible for SSI overlap the approximately 400,000 cases identified as eligible for special education in the SED category (U.S. Department of Education, 1994).

THE *DSM–IV* DEFINITION

Underlying nearly each of the previous definitions is the spectre of psychiatric diagnosis and classification as determined in the current *Diagnostic and Statistical Manual of Mental Disorders*, or *DSM–IV* (American Psychiatric Association, 1994). At least some of the subtypes of the school SED definition appear to correspond with certain psychiatric diagnoses. The EBD definition lists some of the major diagnostic categories. The SED definition used by CMHS refers directly to the *DSM*, and the SSI listings correspond at least approximately to major *DSM–IV* categories. The primary definition of "mental disorder" is not given particular prominence in the *DSM–IV*, but is presented here in order to help define the parameters by which a particular diagnosis is included:

> In the *DSM–IV*, each of the mental disorders is conceptualized as a clinically significant behavioral or psychological syndrome or pattern that occurs in an individual and that is associated with present distress (e.g., a painful symptom) or disability (i.e., impairment in one or more important areas of functioning) or with a significantly increased risk of suffering death, pain, disability, or an important loss of freedom. In addition, this syndrome or pattern must not be merely an expectable and culturally sanctioned response to a particular event, for example, the death of a loved one. Whatever its original cause, it must currently be considered a manifestation of a behavioral, psychological, or biological dysfunction in the individual. Neither deviant behavior (e.g., political, religious, or sexual) nor conflicts that are primarily between the individual and society are mental disorders unless the deviance or conflict is a symptom of a dysfunction in the individual, as described earlier. The core of the *DSM–IV* is a multiaxial system in which various primary and secondary diagnoses are listed on the first axis, presence of personality disorders or mental retardation on the second axis, general medical conditions that may be relevant to understanding a disorder on the third axis, psychosocial and environmental problems that may affect diagnosis or treatment on the fourth axis, and a global assessment of functioning rated from 1 (denoting the severest impairment) to 100 (denoting superior functioning) on the fifth axis.

There are approximately 40 different disorders usually first diagnosed in infancy, childhood, or adolescence and at least 100 other primary disorders with which children or adolescents could be diagnosed, not counting each of the various subtypes of these disorders, substance abuse disorders, dementias, sexual or gender identity disorders, or other conditions that do not constitute a disorder but might be a focus of attention. Examples of major categories include pervasive developmental disorders (autistic disorder, Asperger's disorder), schizophrenia and other psychotic disorders (schizophrenia, schizoaffective disorder, psychotic disorder not otherwise specified), mood disorders (major depressive disorder, dysthymic disorder, bipolar disorder, cyclothymic disorder), anxiety disorders (obsessive–compulsive disorder, posttraumatic stress disorder, generalized anxiety disorder), personality disorders (antisocial personality disorder, schizoid personality disorder, schizotypal personality disorder, borderline personality disorder), feeding and eating disorders (pica, anorexia nervosa, bulimia nervosa), tic disorders (Tourette's syndrome), and attention deficit and disruptive behavior disorders (attention-deficit/hyperactivity disorder, conduct disorder, oppositional defiant disorder). Mental retardation, learning disorders, and communication disorders are also listed, although these each comprise separate categories in special education.

The types of information contained in each listing include primary diagnostic features (usually a minimum threshold number of symptoms chosen from among a list of several that might comprise the disorder); subtypes or specifiers that provide further classification (for example, schizophrenia, paranoid type, or major depressive disorder, single episode); associated features or disorders; specific culture, age or gender features; prevalence; expected course of the disorder; familial pattern; and any differential diagnoses that should be considered.

It should be noted that enormous effort was expended by the American Psychiatric Association in development of the *DSM–IV*. Work groups were assigned to 13 major categories, and the work of each was critiqued by as many as 100 professionals for each group. One of the authors served on the learning disorders subgroup, composed of eight psychiatrists, psychologists, or special educators, and wrote seven different drafts of that section over a 6-year period. Some two dozen other professionals provided specific written or oral input on one or more of the drafts. This was for only *one* of the 40 disorders assigned to the workgroup on disorders with child or adolescent onset. On a dozen of the more prominent disorders, year-long field trials were conducted at 70 sites involving over 6,000 subjects. Psychiatric diagnoses under such a system nonetheless continue to be plagued by problems of validity, reliability, and relevance to treatment (Gresham & Gansle, 1993).

THE 504 DEFINITION

Under Section 504 of the Rehabilitation Act of 1973, discrimination against individuals with handicaps is prohibited by any agency receiving federal financial assistance which obviously includes public schools (Council for Administrators of Special Education, 1992). Thus schools are required to make necessary accommodations for any pupils meeting 504 criteria, even if these pupils do not meet criteria for special education under IDEA. Procedures have been outlined suggesting how 504 accommodations can be made (Zirkel, 1995). Unlike previous definitions, however, the 504 definition is rather broadly defined to refer to any and all conditions of disability. Under this law, an individual with handicaps is defined as "any individual who (a) has a physical or mental impairment which substantially limits one or more of such person's major life activities, (b) has a record of such impairment, or (c) is regarded as having such an impairment" (Rehabilitation Act, 1973).

These terms are further defined in the law. Mental impairment is defined as "any mental or psychological disorder, such as mental retardation, organic brain syndrome, emotional or mental illness, and specific learning disabilities." Major life activities include "functions such as caring for one's self, performing manual tasks, walking, hearing, speaking, breathing, learning and working" (34 C.F.R., Part 104.3).

In effect, any of the disorders in the *DSM–IV* as listed earlier could qualify a pupil for accommodations in the school or classroom. ADHD and even conduct disorders could indeed fall under the purview of these 504 regulations (Cohen, 1994). It is clear, however, that unlike most of the previous definitions for eligibility, 504 does not necessarily bring guaranteed programs, funding, or even, in many cases, substantial accommodations once an individual qualifies. The Council for Administrators of Special Education (1992) mentioned such areas as communication, organization, alternative teaching strategies, or pupil precautions as accommodations in the regular classroom environment. In many cases, these adaptations are relatively minor such as scheduling periodic parent–teacher meetings, networking with other staff, reducing external stimuli in the classroom, individualizing classroom assignments, adjusting level of reading materials, administering medications, and the like. Few accommodations appear to go beyond what one might consider effective teaching or prereferral interventions of mild or moderate intensity.

Most school districts, however, have developed procedures to meet 504 regulations (Zirkel, 1995). These usually include a written individual plan, at least some parental input, procedures for both initial and subsequent evaluations, progress monitoring, and procedural safeguards. Prior notice is required if there is any "significant change" in educational placement, but the law remains relatively vague as to how substantial these procedures must be. Although increased emphasis on 504 definitions and accommodations became apparent largely as a result of increasing attention to children with ADHD, there is considerable evidence that any child with disruptive or troubling behavior could be seen as eligible under this law, especially if he or she fails to qualify under IDEA (Cohen, 1994).

CONCLUSIONS

There are, of course, other definitions under which children with emotional or behavioral disorders could conceivably receive services. The definition of developmental disability in federal law not only encompasses children with coexisting developmental disabilities and mental health disorders, but the state system of protection and advocacy services for persons with developmental disabilities is also responsible for children with mental health needs even when other developmental disabilities are not present (Lubin, Jacobsen, & Kiely, 1982). Various textbook and research definitions have also been used to define eligibility for services in university-based clinics or in the private sector (Kavale, Forness, & Alper, 1986). Other systems used in classification of medical disorders have sections defining various mental illnesses (Koyanagi & Gaines, 1993).

It is quite clear from the aforementioned that a child might be found eligible in one system yet not meet criteria given the definition in another. As noted previously, the SED definition appears to require deficits in academic performance, whereas other definitions tend to define education or adaptive skills much more broadly. Only two definitions, EBD and 504, would seem to target vocational skills as significant determinants of eligibility, an area that becomes increasingly critical as children move into their adolescent years. Most definitions tend specifically to mention social skills among their listings of adaptive skills that could be affected, yet criteria for several *DSM–IV* diagnoses are vague in this area. Relatively few definitions tend to require expression of a disorder across more than one setting. Only the EBD, Head Start, and CMHS definitions mention such a requirement specifically. The EBD, Head Start and *DSM–IV* definitions are the only ones that appear to mention ethnic or cultural considerations.

Only one definition, SED, has a substantial exclusion clause. As noted earlier, this definition excludes children or adolescents with "social maladjustment" unless other emotional disorders are present. Much has been made of this exclusion by proponents who seek to exclude children with oppositional or conduct disorders from receiving special education services under the SED label (Kelly, 1990; Slenkovich, 1992). Nonetheless, it is clear that a variety of disorders may underlie symptoms of social maladjustment or conduct disturbance and that these may require and indeed deserve, both in a legal and a professional sense, special education services (Forness & Kavale, 1994; Forness, Kavale, & Lopez, 1993). The issue of comorbidity is addressed elsewhere in this text and also bears heavily upon the understanding of these issues.

The problem of single eligibility in dual systems is especially significant in the field of emotional or behavioral disorders. It has been demonstrated repeatedly that mental health and special education diagnostic categories are not concordant (Duncan, Forness, & Hartsough, 1995; McGinnis & Forness, 1988; Sinclair, Forness, & Alexson, 1985). This lack of concordance has led to a variety of difficulties both in service delivery (Mattison & Forness, 1993) and in applied research on collaborative treatment systems (Forness & Hoagwood, 1993). Even by conservative estimates in well designed, epidemiologic studies, as many as 1 in 7 children or adolescents may have an emotional or behavioral disorder that both meets a diagnostic threshold and is in need of treatment (Brandenberg, Friedman, & Silver, 1990). Estimates are that fewer than one third of those needing treatment are actually receiving it, and far fewer than that are receiving the interdisciplinary or interagency services that are considered critical to successful outcome (Koyanagi & Gaines, 1993; McLaughlin, Leone, Warren, & Schofield, 1994; Wolford, Nelson, Rutherford, & Forness, 1993). There are a variety of reasons for lack of collaboration among professionals, including disagreement on the nature of emotional or behavioral disorders, different treatment goals or modalities, lack of interdisciplinary training, and lack of resources or systems for coordination (Jensen et al., 1993; Kauffman et al., 1991).

Lack of definitional concordance, however, is clearly a primary cause of underidentification. In a recent study, Duncan, Forness, and Hartsough (1995) demonstrated that parents were aware of their child's emotional or behavioral disorders in the preschool years but that initial services were not provided until early elementary years. Special education within the SED category was not begun until late in the elementary grades. In many cases, services begun in one system such as mental health were inadequate, of and by themselves, without simultaneous efforts in another system such as special education. Although this initial service might have been initiated early enough in some cases, the treatment was clearly inadequate for the problem because collaborative efforts were not simultaneously begun in other systems. It is clear that definitional issues, especially in the school system, were at the root of this problem.

For better or worse, school is the one agency that serves as a mental health screening system (Forness & Kavale, 1989). Teachers in general education classrooms may not recognize a bona fide emotional or behavioral disorder for what it is, but they do have a built-in normative sample of children against which to measure deviance. It is this system that inevitably sets into motion a chain of events that leads to formal or informal prereferral interventions, referral for special education, and ultimately referral procedures for services in other related agencies. This referral process is by no means completely systematic. Walker and his colleagues (Walker & Severson, 1990; Walker, Severson, & Feil, 1995) have developed early identification systems to make school screening much more systematic, with relatively little effort on the part of teachers. Such a system is much more compatible with the EBD and Head Start definitions than it is with the SED definition. It is nonetheless a decided improvement, under any definition, than the relatively haphazard system that we now have.

School is also the one agency with the bulk of responsibility for children with emotional or behavioral disorders because it is the only agency currently with a continuous mandate to serve children regardless of budget cuts, lack of resources, or problems in training personnel. Lack of resources and diminished federal mandates may soon force professionals in this area into a very different mode. Rather than being the lead agency as it now seems to be for children in the school years, school may well begin to assume a role as but one of many collaborating agencies. This school-age model may become similar to that of interagency collaboration under Public Law 99-457 for infants, toddlers, and preschoolers. Instead of an individual family service plan for preschool, an individual educational plan for school, an individual treatment plan for mental health, an individual habilitation plan for employment training, and the like, there may very likely be a comprehensive individual plan that all involved agencies will develop collaboratively. This plan might follow the child not just from agency to agency but from one developmental stage to the next. As these new developments begin to take hold, it seems clear that the school will continue to be an important link in the service system but that other agencies may assume a much greater share in the collaborative network of care for children with mental health needs. This may in turn lead to a generic definition of emotional or behavioral disorders in which a core component defines the disorder and is used throughout every agency, but a list of related skill deficits also becomes part of the definition and triggers the need for services from a particular agency or set of professionals.

REFERENCES

Alcohol, Drug Abuse, and Mental Health Administration Reorganization Act of 1992, Pub. L. No. 102-321, at 201(2), 106 Stat. 378 (1992).

American Psychiatric Association (1994). *Diagnostic and statistical manual of mental disorders* (4th ed.). Washington, DC: Author.

Bower, E. M. (1982). Defining emotional disturbance: Public policy and research. *Psychology in the Schools, 19,* 55–60.

Brandenburg, N. A., Friedman, R. M., & Silver, S. E. (1990). The epidemiology of childhood psychiatric disorders: Recent prevalence findings and methodology issues. *Journal of the American Academy of Child and Adolescent Psychiatry, 29,* 76–83.

Cline, D. H. (1990). A legal analysis of policy initiatives to exclude handicapped/disruptive students from special education. *Behavioral Disorders, 5,* 159–173.

Cohen, M. K. (1994). *Children on the boundaries: Challenges posed by children with conduct disorders.* (Available from National Association of State Directors of Special Education, 1800 Diagonal Road, Suite 320, Alexandria, VA 22314)

Costello, J. E., & Tweed, D. L. (1994). *A review of recent empirical studies linking the prevalence of functional impairment with that of emotional and behavioral illness or disorders in children and adolescents.* (Available from Developmental Epidemiology Program, Duke University Medical Center, Box 3454 DUMC, Durham, NC 27710)

Council of Administrators of Special Education. (1992). *Student access: A response guide for educators on Section 504 of the Rehabilitation Act of 1973.* (Available from Council for Administrators of Special Education, 615 16th Street, NW, Albuquerque, NM 87104)

Council for Children with Behavioral Disorders (1984). Position paper on *substituting "behaviorally disordered" for "seriously emotionally disturbed" as a descriptor term for children and youth handicapped by behavior.* Reston, VA: CCBD. (A Division of the Council for Exceptional Children, 1920 Association Drive, 22901)

Council for Children with Behavioral Disorders (1987). *Position paper on identification of students with behavioral disorders.* Reston, VA: CCBD. (A Division of the Council for Exceptional Children, 1920 Association Drive, 22901)

Council for Children with Behavioral Disorders (1989). *A proposed definition and terminology to replace "serious emotional disturbance" in Education of the Handicapped Act.* Reston, VA: CCBD. (A Division of the Council for Exceptional Children, 1920 Association Drive, 22901)

Duncan, B., Forness, S. R., & Hartsough, C. (1995). Students identified as seriously emotionally disturbed in day treatment classrooms: Cognitive, psychiatric and special education characteristics. *Behavioral Disorders, 20,* 221–237.

Education of the Handicapped Act of 1975 (now known as Individuals with Disabilities Education Act), Pub. L. No. 94-142, 20 U.S.C. 1401 *et seq.* (1978).

Forness, S. R. (1988). Planning for the needs of children with serious emotional disturbance: The national special education and mental health coalition. *Behavioral Disorders, 13,* 127–133.

Forness, S. R. (1992a). Legalism versus professionalism in diagnosing SED in the public school. *School Psychology Review, 21,* 29–34.

Forness, S. R. (1992b). Broadening the cultural-organizational perspective in exclusion of youth with social maladjustment. *Remedial and Special Education, 3*(1), 55–59.

Forness, S. R., & Finn, D. (1993). Screening children in Head Start for emotional or behavioral disorders. *Monographs in Behavioral Disorders, 16,* 6–14.

Forness, S. R., & Hoagwood, K. J. (1993). Where angels fear to tread: Issues in design, measurement, and implementation of school-based, mental-health services research. *School Psychology Quarterly, 8,* 291–300.

Forness, S. R., & Kavale, K. A. (1989). Identification and diagnostic issues in special education: A status report for child psychiatrists. *Child Psychiatry and Human Development, 19,* 279–301.

Forness, S. R., & Kavale, K. A. (1994). The Balkanization of special education: Proliferation of categories for new behavioral disorders. *Education and Treatment of Children, 17,* 215–227.

Forness, S. R., Kavale, K. A., King, B. H., & Kassari, C. (1994). Simple versus complex conduct disorders: Identification and phenomenology. *Behavioral Disorders, 19,* 306–312.

Forness, S. R., Kavale, K. A., & Lopez, M. (1993). Conduct disorders in school: Special education eligibility and co-morbidity. *Journal of Emotional and Behavioral Disorders, 1,* 101–108.

Forness, S. R., & Knitzer, J. (1992). A new proposed definition and terminology to replace "Serious Emotional Disturbance" in Individuals with Disabilities Education Act. *School Psychology Review, 21,* 12–20.

Gonzalez, P. (1991). *A comparison of state policy to the federal definition and a proposed definition of "Serious Emotional Disturbance."* (Available from National Associaton of State Directors of Special Education, 1800 Diagonal Road, Suite 320, Alexandria, VA 22314)

Gresham, F. M., & Gansle, K. (1993). Misguided assumptions of *DSM–III–R*: Implications for school psychological practice. *School Psychology Quarterly, 7,* 79–95.

Head Start Program Performance Standards, 58 Fed. Reg. 5501 (1993) (to be codified at 45 C.F.R. § 1308).

Individuals with Disabilities Education Act of 1995, H.R. 1986, 104th Cong., 1st Sess. (1995).

Invitation to Comment on the Regulatory Definition of Serious Emotional Disturbance, 58 Fed. Reg. 7938 (1993) (to be codified at 34 C.F.R. § 300).

Jensen, P. S., Koretz, D., Locke, B. Z., Schneider, S., Radke-Yarrow, M., Richters, J. E., & Rumsey, J. M. (1993). Child and adolescent psychopathology research: Problems and prospects for the 1990s. *Journal of Abnormal Child Psychology, 21,* 551–580.

Kauffman, J. M. (1997). *Characteristics of emotional and behavioral disorders of children and youth.* New York: Merrill.

Kauffman, J. M., Lloyd, J. W., Cooke, L., Cullinan, D., Epstein, M. H., Forness, S. R., Hallahan, D., Nelson, C. M., Polsgrove, L., Strain, P., Sabornie, E. J., & Walker, H. M. (1991). Problems and prospects in special education and related services for children with emotional and behavioral disorders. *Behavioral Disorders, 16,* 299–313.

Kavale, K., Forness, S., & Alper, A. (1986). Research in behavior disorders/emotional disturbance: A survey of subject identification criteria. *Behavioral Disorders, 11,* 159–167.

Kelly, E. J. (1990). *The differential test of conduct and emotional problems.* Aurora, CO: Slosson.

Knitzer, J., Steinberg, A., & Fleisch, B. (1990). *At the schoolhouse door: An examination of programs and policies for children with behavioral and emotional problems.* New York: Bank Street College of Education.

Koyanagi, C. (1993). *Federal definitions of children with serious emotional disturbance.* (Available from the Bazelon Center for Mental Health Law, 1101 15th Street NW, Suite 1212, Washington, DC 20005)

Koyanagi, C., & Gaines, S. (1993). *A guide for advocates for "All systems failure: An examination of the results of neglecting the needs of children with serious emotional disturbance."* (Available from National Mental Health Association, 1021 Prince Street, Alexandria, VA 22114–2971)

Lubin, R., Jacobson, J. W., & Kiely, M. (1982). Projected impact of the functional definition of developmental disabilities: The categorically disabled population and service eligibility. *American Journal of Mental Deficiency, 87,* 73–79.

Mattison, R. E., & Forness, S. R. (1995). The role of psychiatric and other mental health services in special education placement decisions for children with emotional or behavioral disorders. In J. M. Kauffman, J. W. Lloyd, T. A. Astuto, & D. P. Hallahan (Eds.), *Issues in educational placement of children with emotional or behavioral disorders* (pp. 142–154). Hillsdale, NJ: Lawrence Erlbaum Associates.

McGinnis, E., & Forness, S. R. (1988). Psychiatric diagnosis: A further test of the special education eligibility hypothesis. *Monographs in Behavioral Disorders, 11,* 3–10.

McLaughlin, M. J., Leone, P. E., Warren, S. H., & Schofield, P. F. (1994). *Doing things differently: Issues and options for creating comprehensive school-linked services for children and youth with emotional or behavioral disorders.* (Available from Institute for the Study of Exceptional Children and Youth, University of Maryland, College Park, MD 20742–1161)

National School Board Association. (1992, July). Group urges new definition of emotional disorders. *School Board News, 2.*

Nelson, C. M., & Pearson, C. A. (1991). *Integrating services for children and youth with emotional and behavioral disorders.* Reston, VA: The Council for Exceptional Children.

Rehabilitation Act of 1973, Section 504, 29 U.S.C. § 706 *et seq.* (1973) (Codified at 34 C.F.R. 6 104 et seg.).

Rivera, V. R., & Kutash, K., (1994). *Components of a system of care: What does the research say?* (Available form Research and Training Center for Children's Mental Health, Florida Mental Health Institute, University of South Florida, 13301 Bruce B. Downs Blvd., Tampa, FL 33612)

Sinclair, E., Forness, S. R., & Alexson, J. (1985). Psychiatric diagnosis: A study of its relationship to school needs. *Journal of Special Education, 19,* 333–344.

Slenkovich, J. (1992). Can the language "social maladjustment" in the SED definition be ignored? The final words. *School Psychology Review, 21*(1), 43–45.

Social Security Income Childhood Mental Disorders Listing, 55 Fed. Reg. 51208-51246 (1990) (to be codified at 20 C.F.R. § 404, Subpt. P. Appendix 112 et seq).

U.S. Department of Education (1994). *Sixteenth annual report to Congress on the Implementation of the Education of Individuals with Disabilities Act.* Washington, DC: U.S. Office of Special Education Program.

U.S. Department of Education (1995). *National agenda for achieving better results for children and youth with serious emotional disturbance.* (Prepared for the U.S. Office of Special Education Programs by the Chesapeake Institute, 2030 M Street, N.W., Suite 810, Washington, DC 20036)

Walker, H. M., & Severson, H. H. (1990). *Systematic screening for behavior disorders.* Longmont, CO: Sopris West.

Walker, H. M., Severson, H. H., & Fell, E. G. (1995). *The early screening project.* Longmont, CO: Sopris West.

Wolford, B., Nelson, C. M., Rutherford, R., & Forness, S. R. (1993). *Developing comprehensive systems for troubled youth.* (National Coalition for Juvenile Justice Services, 300 Stratton Building, Eastern Kentucky University, Richmond, KY 40475–3131)

Zirkel, P. A. (1995). *Section 504 and the schools.* Horsham, PA: LRP Publications.

4

CLASSIFICATION FOR CHILDREN

Deborah L. Speece
University of Maryland at College Park

Beth Harry
University of Miami

In this chapter we examine how disability classifications are constructed from the perspectives of society and science. The social and scientific approaches to the construction of disability are not often considered simultaneously, but we believe these perspectives make more understandable the systems used to classify children. We seek to understand the contributions of these approaches to the education of children. The latter point, educating children, is central to our concern in this chapter. That is, the educational and scientific communities often discuss classification *of* children. We propose that another, perhaps more appropriate, emphasis is classification *for* children. This distinction provides a different window from which to view and evaluate classification systems. When classification activities are reified without reference to the original purpose of educating children, it is time to revisit the basis of the system.

SOCIAL CONSTRUCTION OF DISABILITY

The notion that disability is socially constructed is not new (Becker, 1969; Goffman, 1963). The process of social construction means that members of a society identify a point at which an unusual pattern of behavior is seen to be deviant, or beyond acceptable boundaries. Thus, the concept of disability represents a decision made by the society regarding a form of physical or mental deviance, usually thought to be caused by some deficit within the individual. To speak of social construction is not necessarily to argue that the condition does not exist, but to observe that there is a shared understanding that the condition falls outside the norm of what is expected or acceptable.

There is one central question and one subsidiary question relevant to decisions about what constitutes deviance on any particular dimension. The primary question is at what point will a difference in behavior or development be designated as deviant? Secondarily, how will the designated deviance be valued or not valued?

On the first question: Because deviance exists on a spectrum in relation to some accepted norm, the range of what is considered "normal" is decided on either explicitly, by a body given the responsibility for defining deviance, or implicitly, by some mutually arrived at consensus within the community. In either case, it is reasonable to assume that the condition must relate to a human aspect that is seen as important in that society. If the feature were not of importance, it probably would not be noticed or investigated.

Dexter (1964) offered the example of a hypothetical society in which physical awkwardness was seen as a point of deviance, and for which a scale of "normal" to "deviant" was established. A more familiar version of this is the value placed on literacy skills in technological societies where educational equity is a goal. Failing to attain literacy may, thereby, be deviant and certain criteria may be established for the determination of the presence of a "disability" thought to be causing the deviance. We emphasize "where literacy is highly valued" because it is possible to value literacy while expecting it to be the property of a small elite. In such cases, the failure to attain literacy would not be unusual, nor would it be cause for investigation or for the designation "disability."

It is evident, therefore, that if literacy is not an important or expected skill for the majority of a population, it is unlikely that explanations for difficulty in attaining this skill will be sought. Indeed, the concept of a learning disability related to literacy attainment is but a few decades old. This fact could be attributed to previous lack of scientific or pedagogical interest in the question of why some individuals may experience difficulties in this area which may, in turn, relate to the increasing demands of technology. Without such demands, individual variations in literacy acquisition would be of no importance.

Research on culturally diverse parents of children with disabilities indicates how the meaning of disability may vary with culture and acculturation. There is a clear pattern that parents from some minority or working class backgrounds within the United States, or from less technologically developed societies, seem to hold broader parameters of what is normal or acceptable with respect to cognitive development, the attainment of literacy, or both. This has implications for the classifications *mild mental retardation* and *learning disability*. For example, working-class Puerto Rican parents in a study by Harry (1992) did not share the U.S. school system's notion of either of these categories. With regard to mental retardation, a child's daily mental functioning had to be seriously impaired for the term to be used whereas, for learning disability, difficulty in learning to read was seen as a matter for concern "but not necessarily a disability" (p. 157).

In another study by Harry (1995), the following excerpt from an interview with a couple from the Dominican Republic illustrates how the definition of disability differed according to each parent's level of acculturation to U.S. norms. These parents had been asked whether they would use the word "handicapped" or "disabled" to refer to their 13-year-old son who had Down Syndrome. Mother and Father replied simultaneously and respectively "Yes/No!" The father applies the Dominican understanding of "disability," which is used only to refer to the most severe disabilities. On the other hand, the mother uses the U.S. version, explaining that you can be called disabled if you just have "a limp."

Consensus on what constitutes a disability may also vary within a community, according to the acculturation status of an individual belonging to a minority group within that society. This may be particularly so when the condition is perceived as relatively mild and its impact on individual functioning slight. For example, the following excerpt from an interview with a working-class, African American father of a preschooler labeled mildly mentally retarded shows how the view of mental retardation can differ from that of the school (Harry, Allen, & McLaughlin, 1995): "[Mental retardation] to me it means like they're slow; I mean very slow, to the point where they really need some heavy duty attention. But in the school, I guess they use it for any little difference" (p. 370).

It seems the point of view here is affected by the individual's expectations of what is needed for effective and independent functioning. It is likely that people of working-class status and minority groups who have, traditionally, been accustomed to fewer opportunities for advancement, may hold expectations that do not require advanced education and skills. Therefore, like people from less technological cultures, they define the parameters of normalcy more broadly.

It is important to note that cultural change also occurs within a society over time. This is evident in the previously observed point that the concept of learning disability is a recent phenomenon. However, in a matter of 25 years the percentage of school-age children identified as learning disabled grew nearly 300%: from 1.8% in 1976–1977 to 5.2% in 1992–1993 (Moats & Lyon, 1993; U.S. Department of Education, 1994). On the topic of mental retardation, cultural change has wrought equally dramatic effects. The initiation of psychometric measurement coincided with this society's intense concern with eugenics in the early to midyears of this century (Gould, 1982).

During that period, fear of the mentally retarded was reflected in stringent parameters of normal cognitive functioning, by which an IQ of 85 was the definitive cut-off point for mental retardation. In the 1960s, a relaxation of these views, and increasing concerns regarding treatment of persons with retardation, resulted in the American Association on Mental Retardation's change in the criterion for intelligence scores from an IQ of 85 to one of 70 (Grossman, 1973). This decision by the official defining body for mental retardation indicates that the cut-off points are entirely up to society and may, in fact, be quite arbitrary. Obviously, there was no change in the approximately 14% of the population previously defined as mentally retarded, yet they were no longer so classified.

The secondary question identified at the beginning of this section was how an identified disability was valued by the society. There are many societies in which certain physically or mentally handicapping conditions are interpreted in a positive light (Edgerton, 1970; "Hmong Family," 1991). In the United States, it is fair to say that the notion of disability has traditionally connoted deficit and is therefore interpreted negatively. The increasing efforts to diminish this trend and to treat people with disabilities with equity has not yet succeeded in relinquishing stigma. However, not all disabilities are created equal with respect to stigma as seen in the decrease in diagnoses of mental retardation and the corresponding increase in diagnoses of learning disabilities. In documenting this point, MacMillan (1993) commented that this situation is not the result of "mental retardation somehow being cured while an epidemic in learning disabilities occurs" (p. 146), but rather it is due to system identification factors and sociopolitical issues. These factors, of course, pertain to the social construction of disability.

SCIENTIFIC CONSTRUCTION OF DISABILITY

American society has agreed, through legislation and litigation, that there are types of children in school whose behavior does fall outside the bounds of acceptability. This agreement gives license to the scientific study of these types. From perspective of science, classification is regarded as a basic scientific activity that serves to promote understanding of the phenomenon under investigation. Gould (1989) captured the importance of classification in science:

> Taxonomy (the science of classification) is often undervalued as a glorified form of filing . . . but taxonomy is a fundamental and dynamic science, dedicated to exploring the causes of relationships and similarities among organisms. Classifications are theories about the basis of natural order, not dull categories compiled only to avoid chaos. (p. 98)

To address the contribution of science to classification for children, it is necessary to (a) understand terminology, (b) differentiate the purposes of classification, and (c) examine the reciprocal influences between scientific classification and practice. With respect to terminology, it is useful to distinguish the terms *typology* and *taxonomy* as presented by Bailey (1994). Both are classification activities. Construction of typologies is conceptual, whereas taxonomies are empirical. In special education, the typology of children is reflected in concepts such as mental retardation, learning disabilities, and behavioral disorders. Numbers are not required to develop a typology, but they may be required to identify members of the type. Taxonomies, on the other hand, require empirical data and the process of defining "taxons" and their members is simultaneous. Readers familiar with the classification research in special education will recognize that the statistical methods of cluster analysis are associated with the development of taxonomies. Examples are most evident in the field of learning disabilities, as researchers attempt to address the acknowledged heterogeneity of skills in this population of learners (see Lyon & Risucci, 1988, for an overview of this work).

The distinction between typologies and taxonomies is not trivial in special education. Whereas professionals agree, at some level, on the typology, the development of taxonomies is more problematic. Because taxonomies require data, the investigator must select and measure the critical variables as part and parcel of developing a classification. There is little agreement on what the defining variables are (e.g., learning disabilities) leading some to relegate the empirical approach to the back burner until there is consensus on the definition (Kavale & Forness, 1987; see Kavale & Forness, chapter 1, this volume). However, Speece and Cooper (1991) argued that the development of taxonomies can assist the definitional problem through careful analysis of multiple variables and rigorous testing of the validity of the resulting taxonomy. This work has proceeded on a domain by domain basis (e.g., oral language, cognitive processing, classroom behavior) and a single taxonomy of learning disabilities has yet to emerge. It is also true that the typology of atypical learners across the broader spectrum of disability has more conceptual than empirical support. That is, more effort has been placed on classification within a disability category (e.g., mental retardation, learning disabilities) than on distinguishing among the conceptual categories (Fletcher, Francis, Rourke, Shaywitz, & Shaywitz, 1993). This brief review of scientific progress indicates that classification **of** children is the prominent orientation of researchers and that there is still more work to be done in this arena.

The almost exclusive focus on definitional issues, however, need not be the case in scientific classification when we examine the purposes of classification, the second issue to be addressed in this section. The purposes of classification in the social sciences are to enhance prediction and communication (Blashfield & Draguns, 1976). Prediction carries a developmental connotation (e.g., longitudinal outcomes, the stability of a type or taxon) whereas communication is associated with clinical concerns (e.g., response to intervention, enhancing understanding among practitioners). In either case a "good" classification system is one that possesses clear definitional criteria and distinguishes definitional criteria from correlates of the class, leading to reliable identification of entities. Given reliable identification, one assumes homogeneity in which members of the type or taxon resemble each other more than those who are not members. It is at this point that questions concerning long-term outcomes (i.e., prediction) and effectiveness of interventions (i.e., communication) can be entertained. Answering these types of questions provides the basis for determining the validity of the classification scheme. For example, in the realm of prediction, Feagans and Appelbaum (1986) demonstrated that oral language subtypes of children with learning disabilities had differential academic outcomes over a 3-year period such that children with stronger narrative skills outperformed children with stronger semantic and syntactic skills. Cross and Paris (1988) showed, in the domain of metacognition, that subtypes of children with different strengths and weaknesses benefited from different reading instruction. The latter study demonstrates validation from the perspective of communication (also see Lyon, 1985).

From a scientific perspective, then, a worthwhile classification system must pass the tests of reliability and validity. This is true regardless of whether the purpose is prediction or communication. Both purposes are worthy goals in the study of classification in special education. The problem is one of emphasis when we consider this chapter's theme of classification for children. That is, if one is concerned with developing a system that leads to better outcomes for children, then the communication value of the classification is paramount. It is fair to say that the development of taxonomies more often has focused on prediction rather than communication. Validation studies have more often addressed naturally occurring outcomes and not the effects of interventions or the value of a particular classification to practitioners. Thus, classification researchers have little to say to practicing professionals when the issue is educating children.

This state of affairs is troubling, but it is not to say that researchers and practitioners have not influenced each other. This is the third point of this section. Practitioners, valuing the reliability and validity criteria of scientists, proceed as though we have the means of valid classification. In the field of learning disabilities this classification is operationalized primarily through an aptitude–achievement discrepancy. Although this criterion has a scientific "ring," it is rarely noted that discrepancy has its basis in federal regulations rather than science. The resulting muddle between science and practice can be observed either by perusing the description of samples in research studies on "LD" or attending eligibility team meetings in the schools. In the former case, children identified by the schools are used as research subjects with investigators paying scant attention to the tremendous variability across classification systems, thus producing results that are applicable to unknown populations. In the latter case, evaluation teams rely on a standard of aptitude–achievement discrepancy that has uneven scientific support.

What is wrong with this picture? In our view, the fundamental problem on both ends is the *assumption* of validity of classification where none exists. Because there is societal agreement that a type exists (e.g., learning disabilities, mental retardation), there is the assumption of validity *or* simply ignorance of its importance. An examination of statistics on identification rates for each handicapping condition by State shows the folly of this assumption. For example, if classification criteria were valid, why would New York identify 60% of its disabled, school-age population as learning disabled but Georgia identify only 32% (U.S. Department of Education, 1994)?

A second issue is the acceptance by both researchers and practitioners that the disability is the property of the child being classified and that they have no hand in this development other than to apply the "rules." We do not argue that individual differences are unimportant. Rather, we argue that classification efforts **for** children have lost their way by being overly enamored of quantitative over qualitative data and by focusing on the individual to the exclusion of ecological factors (Speece, 1993; Speece & Molloy, 1995). This situation has produced a culture of classification where a score on an intelligence test has more meaning than a child's classroom performance. Gerber and Semmel (1984) captured this phenomenon in the phrase "teacher as imperfect test" (p. 137). That is, when classification decisions are made, a teacher's observations of a child are given less weight than the results of published, standardized tests.

Thus, the science of classification and the practice of classification in the schools have little in common save for a shared but absent value of validity and the assumption that the disability is the property of the child. Professional judgment, not discrepancy formulas, is the legal cornerstone of learning disabilities identification (Bateman, 1992), but scientific study of disability has rarely acknowledged this and it is difficult for practitioners to articulate the multiple variables that lead to an eligibility decision. Any serious attempt to understand classification wreaks havoc with the underlying need for objectivity. To understand disability classifications, one must stir in the context in which scientific and educational classification decisions get made. This is true even in epidemiological studies where unselected samples of children are studied to understand the expression and development of disabilities. Although these types of studies are not "tainted" at the outset by murky professional criteria, someone must decide who has the condition and who does not and, ultimately, the study of children must address the fact that they are in schools, a critical context. Despite what we would like to believe, learning disability and mental retardation are relative conditions: relative to the community (including scientists), relative to who else is in the classroom, relative to the teacher's skills and beliefs, relative to other services in the schools, relative to the school's approach to exclusionary criteria, and relative to researchers' theoretical assumptions. Any discussion of classification needs to confront this messy but fundamental truth.

CONCLUSIONS: CAN WE GET THERE FROM HERE?

We have sketched how classifications are constructed from both social and scientific perspectives. Neither approach appears to serve the goal of providing better educational services for children even though we value the contributions of each perspective in understanding how we go about the business of classification. We are reminded of Annie Mae's response to Heath (1983) in elaborating on why interpersonal relationships and linkages between concepts were more important than knowing a label in the poor, Black community of Trackton: "Whatcha *call* it ain't so important as whatcha *do* with it" (p. 112).

What Annie Mae suggests and what we wish to elaborate is the relative importance of classification. There seems to be no way around the fact that humans, by their very nature, need to classify. Life is too complex to hold in mind all of the individual elements of phenomena. Indeed, when we try to rid ourselves of one classification, another will take its place. A colleague recounted a school-related example: In attempting to implement inclusion practices, children formerly referred to as "LD" or "BD" became the "inclusion kids." No amount of exhortation will reduce our need to classify and we will not argue that classification is unnecessary. The very real dilemma is that there are scarce resources which need to be appropriated and uncertainty in both science and society about who should be served.

The point that we believe requires elaboration is the process by which classification takes place. Both the social and scientific construction of disability classifications reify the condition such that the child *becomes* the condition, as in "He is LD." This reification can be mitigated by changing the classification focus from the child to the nature of instructional interactions and their outcomes. Instead of a preoccupation with measuring individual differences, more effort is devoted to understanding the content and method and response to instruction (see Deno, chapter 5, this volume). As it now stands, instruction is more of an afterthought that follows designation as handicapped rather than a driving force that explicates learning difficulties. We suggest that eligibility discussions take instruction as the primary issue, relegating measurement of a host of individual differences and the naming of the condition to secondary status.

Fuchs (1995) has clearly articulated how this can be accomplished. Thus, our desire to change the focus of classification has empirical backing and does not represent an admirable but unattainable goal. Fuchs proposed that eligibility (i.e., classification) be approached through a treatment validation framework. Her three-phase model that emphasizes collection of curriculum-based data requires (a) documentation of achievement discrepancies relative to local norms that addresses both absolute performance and growth, (b) documentation that instructional changes in the general education setting do not produce adequate growth, and (c) documentation that instruction in a special education setting does result in academic growth. Only when these three requirements are met is a child found eligible for services. That special education services would be provided only if a trial period in special education demonstrated progress is revolutionary in our history of classification. Fuchs carefully detailed feasibility issues and required research, but it is clear that there is both a research and a practice base for implementing these ideas.

A focus on the interactions between children and teachers addresses a number of problems with current classification practices. From the perspective of social construction, emphasis on response to instruction reframes the parent–professional interaction. Instead of discussing labels that have different interpretations among participants, discussion can revolve around what works and what does not. Our prediction is that this type of conversation is both more useful and understandable and does not require professional jargon. From a scientific perspective, valid information is used to identify children who are not progressing, paving the way for the design and implementation of interventions that will accelerate the communicative value of classification. This does not negate the importance of understanding children's characteristics. However, this is a side issue to developing classification practices that serve children.

Finally, and perhaps most importantly, the onus of the problem is shifted from the child to the nature and outcomes of instructional interaction that necessarily involve the child *and* the teacher. We are not so naive as to think this shift will be easy to attain. As Schulte (1996) documented, nativist beliefs about the locus of disability run deep in our culture and teachers may hold these beliefs. We do believe, however, that the shift can occur and that the result will address the issue of classification *for* children.

REFERENCES

Becker, H. S. (1969). *Studies in the sociology of deviance.* New York: The Free Press.
Bailey, K. D. (1994). *Typologies and taxonomies: An introduction to classification techniques.* Thousand Oaks, CA: Sage.

Bateman, B. (1992). Learning disabilities: A changing landscape. *Journal of Learning Disabilities, 25,* 29–36.

Blashfield, R. K., & Draguns, J. G. (1976). Evaluative criteria for psychiatric classification. *Journal of Abnormal Psychology, 85,* 140–150.

Cross, D. R., & Paris, S. G. (1988). Developmental and instructional analyses of children's metacognition and reading comprehension. *Journal of Educational Psychology, 80,* 131–142.

Dexter, L. A. (1964). On the politics and sociology of stupidity in our society. In H. S. Becker (Ed.), *The other side* (pp. 37–49). Glencoe, IL: The Free Press.

Edgerton, R. B. (1970). Mental retardation in non-Western societies: Toward a cross-cultural perspective on incompetence. In H. C. Haywood (Ed.), *Socio-cultural aspects of mental retardation* (pp. 523–559). New York: Appleton–Century–Crofts.

Feagans, L., & Appelbaum, M. I. (1986). Validation of language subtypes in learning disabled children. *Journal of Educational Psychology, 78,* 358–364.

Fletcher, J. M., Francis, D. J., Rourke, B. P., Shaywitz, S. E., & Shaywitz, B. A. (1993). Classification of learning disabilities: Relationships with other childhood disorders. In G. R. Lyon, D. B. Gray, J. F. Kavanagh, & N. A. Krasnegor (Eds.), *Better understanding learning disabilities: New views from research and their implications for education and public policies* (pp. 27–55). Baltimore: Brookes.

Fuchs, L. F. (1995, May). *Incorporating curriculum-based measurement into the eligibility decision-making process: A focus on treatment validity and student growth.* Paper presented at the Workshop on IQ Testing and Educational Decision Making, National Research Council, National Academy of Sciences, Washington, DC.

Gerber, M. M., & Semmel, M. I. (1984). Teacher as imperfect test: Reconceptualizing the referral process. *Educational Psychologist, 19,* 137–148.

Goffman, E. (1963). *Stigma: Notes on the management of spoiled identity.* Englewood Cliffs, NJ: Prentice-Hall.

Gould, S. J. (1982). *The mismeasure of man.* New York: Norton.

Gould, S. J. (1989). *Wonderful life: The Burgess shale and the nature of history.* New York: Norton.

Grossman, H. J. (Ed.). (1973). *Manual on terminology and classification in mental retardation.* Washington, DC: American Association on Mental Deficiency.

Harry, B. (1992). *Cultural diversity, families, and the special education system.* New York: Teachers College Press.

Harry, B. (1995). [Consortium for collaboration research on social relationships]. Unpublished raw data.

Harry, B., Allen, N., & McLaughlin, M. (1995). Communication vs. compliance: African American parents' involvement in special education. *Exceptional Children, 61,* 364–377.

Heath, S. B. (1983). *Ways with words.* New York: Cambridge University Press.

Hmong family prevents forced surgery on son. (1991, January). *Omaha World Herald,* p. 16.

Kavale, K. A., & Forness, S. R. (1987). The far side of heterogeneity: A critical analysis of empirical subtyping research in learning disabilities. *Journal of Learning Disabilities, 20,* 374–382.

Lyon, G. R. (1985). Educational validation studies of learning disabilities subtypes. In B. P. Rourke (Ed.), *Neuropsychology of learning disabilities* (pp. 228–256). New York: Guilford.

Lyon, G. R., & Risucci, D. (1988). Classification of learning disabilities. In K. Kavale (Ed.), *Learning disabilities: State of the art and practice* (pp. 44–70). San Diego: College-Hill Press.

MacMillan, D. L. (1993). Development of operational definitions in mental retardation: Similarities and differences with the field of learning disabilities. In G. R. Lyon, D. B. Gray, J. F. Kavanagh, & N. A. Krasnegor (Eds.), *Better understanding learning disabilities: New views from research and their implications for education and public policies* (pp. 117–152). Baltimore: Brookes.

Moats, L. C., & Lyon, G. R. (1993). Learning disabilities in the United States: Advocacy, science, and the future of the field. *Journal of Learning Disabilities, 5,* 282–292.

Schulte, A. C. (1996). Remediation and inclusion: Can we have it all? In D. L. Speece & B. K. Keogh (Eds.), *Research on classroom ecologies: Implications for inclusion of children with learning disabilities* (pp. 203–210). Hillsdale, NJ: Lawrence Erlbaum Associates.

Speece, D. L. (1993). Broadening the scope of classification research: Conceptual and ecological perspectives. In G. R. Lyon, D. B. Gray, J. F. Kavanagh, & N. A. Krasnegor (Eds.), *Better understanding learning disabilities: New views from research and their implications for education and public policies* (pp. 57–72). Baltimore: Brookes.

Speece, D. L., & Cooper, D. H. (1991). Retreat, regroup, or advance? An agenda for empirical classification research in learning disabilities. In L. V. Feagans, E. J. Short, & L. J. Meltzer (Eds.), *Subtypes of learning disabilities: Theoretical perspectives and research* (pp. 33–52). Hillsdale, NJ: Lawrence Erlbaum Associates.

Speece, D. L., & Molloy, D. E. (1995). *The context–cognition conundrum in early school failure: A case for activity settings.* Manuscript submitted for review.

U.S. Department of Education (1994). *Sixteenth annual report to Congress on the implementation of the Individuals with Disabilities Education Act.* Washington, DC: U.S. Government Printing Office.

ASSESSMENT OF DISABILITIES

5

WHETHER THOU GOEST . . . PERSPECTIVES ON PROGRESS MONITORING

Stanley L. Deno
University of Minnesota

It would be appropriate to begin this chapter with a historical examination of the approaches educators have used to monitor student growth, and, indeed, some attention is given to that issue here. Unfortunately, the history of education is relatively sketchy with respect to the approaches that teachers have used to monitor the progress of individual students within and across their years in school. Although we cannot be sure about why so little work seems to have been directed to developing progress monitoring systems, I believe the reason lies in the emphasis in American schools on making distinctions *between* individuals performing at a particular moment in time, rather than on making distinctions in performance *within* an individual from one occasion to the next. Indeed, even a cursory examination of textbooks on educational and psychological measurement reveals that the primary focus of psychometric methods has been on procedures for reliably establishing an individual's relative position within a group rather than describing changes in individual performance across time.

Why is that we should have emphasized the differences between individuals when assessing performance when improvement in performance by the individual would seem to be the primary concern of education? The answer to this question seems to be that in the United States, as in other countries, the primary function of assessment has been to provide information that could be used to sort individuals into groups for making selection decisions rather than to examine individual growth. If we think about the decisions toward which assessment has been directed we can readily identify that the awarding of grades, admitting students to college, and making job selections have been the primary uses of test data. In addition to these functions, those of us in working in school programs are very much aware that assessments commonly are conducted to classify students as eligible for alternative programs like special education, Title I, and gifted education. In all of these cases, the decision to be made has rested on distinguishing the relative achievements or accomplishments of a subgroup of students within the general student population. Because the economic and social consequences of these decisions are potentially very important, it is not surprising that responsible decision makers would seek assessment procedures that discriminate and quantify differences between individuals as justification for these decisions.

After a very long period in which assessment has been used primarily to aid in sorting and classifying students, interest is now increasing in the ideas that we should examine individual performance to ascertain attainment of "mastery," "competence," and, now, "standards." The significance of the words currently used to describe the goals of assessment is that the reference for all of these terms seems to shift attention from scaling the relative merit or accomplishment of individuals within a group to scaling performance relative to a criterion or standard that is thought to have meaning independent from the group. Performance on particular tasks is gaining prominence in the view of decision makers and, with this new emphasis, the primary purpose of classification and sorting seems is to determine whether the individual can meet or exceed predetermined and independent "standards" for those tasks. Important also in this shift to alternative approaches to performance assessment is not only the increased emphasis on criterion performance, but also on the nature of the tasks selected for assessment purposes. "Authenticity" has become the prime characteristic to be embraced when tasks are selected, and careful consideration must be given to "face validity" in task selection. Indeed, the argument is that authenticity and face validity can take the place of the more traditional reliability and validity criteria of psychometrics. Finally, a major assumption of currently recommended alternative assessment procedures is that, to be useful, they must "inform" or guide instruction. The claim is that teacher behavior should be informed or directed by the results of assessment. Traditional approaches to assessment are viewed as not only lacking the information necessary to improve practice, but also as inimical to best practice. This claim is based on the assumption that the nature of the tasks employed in typical norm-referenced standardized tests is inauthentic and calls for "fractionated" rote learning rather than problem solving and higher-order thinking.

If we are interested in individual student progress monitoring, I think we must see the recommendations associated with alternative approaches to assessment as helpful. Contained in those recommendations is the emphasis on individual growth that is at the basis of progress monitoring. Discriminating growth relative to a performance standard is an important shift in attention away from the emphasis on making distinctions between individuals. At the same time we should not be sanguine about the possibility that the focus will now become individual growth rather than sorting and classifying students. Indeed, those of us concerned with the education and habilitation of people with disabilities have already seen that the emphasis on attaining performance standards has resulted in the tendency to exclude such persons from the assessment process. A second concern is that the race to develop alternatives has resulted in expectations far exceeding reality. Establishing authenticity and instructional utility as characteristics for assessment are admirable ideals, but just as developing a cure for cancer requires more than specifying the goal, developing assessment procedures with particular characteristics requires more than asserting their importance. Contrary to assumptions currently made by advocates of "authentic assessment," the technical knowledge required for accomplishing our goals is neither available nor unnecessary. Any reading of the current literature on the results of efforts to develop and use new alternative approaches to assessment reveals that the effort is fraught with difficulty. Many years ago, Bruner (1965) argued that the achievements in developing instruments that increase our powers of observation was at the basis of most of our greatest scientific achievements. If that is so, then the development of improved procedures for assessing individual growth may well result in breakthroughs that increase our knowledge of human development and our successes in optimizing that development. Most certainly, such breakthroughs in assessment technology will occur as the result of intense research and development efforts rather than from winning social policy battles.

PROGRESS MONITORING: TWO APPROACHES

Approaches to progress monitoring generally are of two types. The first, and more common type, has been referred to elsewhere as *mastery monitoring* (Fuchs & Deno, 1991), or *progress measurement* (Deno & Mirkin, 1977), and is an extension of criterion-referenced testing to monitoring individual growth. The second approach has been termed *general outcome measurement* (Fuchs & Deno, 1991) or *performance measurement* (Deno & Mirkin, 1977).

Mastery Monitoring

Mastery monitoring is based on a task-analytic approach to curriculum wherein the whole is reduced to its component parts. On the basis of this reduction, then, subtasks are identified for both teaching and testing. Inherent in the task-analytic approach is specification of a performance standard for each task that, when attained, is the basis for inferring that task mastery has occurred. Through the process of task analysis, subtasks are specified and an interdependent hierarchical structure is created. This interdependent task structure then serves as the basis for specifying the patterns and orders in which tasks should be mastered for learning to occur most efficiently. To illustrate, the task of "writing a paragraph" could be reduced to subtasks comprising "developing the ideational content," "developing paragraph structure," "writing sentences," and "using formal codes." To complete the task analysis, each of these larger components is reduced to subtasks thought to be prerequisite to successful use of each major component of paragraph composition. A component like "using formal codes" may be analyzed into "capitalization" and "punctuation," whereas "writing sentences" may be reduced to "expressing complete thoughts" and "composing sentences." Because such structures are branching, subordinate relationships among tasks are most clearly identified only within a branch rather than across branches. For the example of paragraph writing, an assumption would be made that "using formal codes" is superordinate to punctuating, but no assumption is made about the relationship between punctuation and sentence content. The result is that the degree of interdependency among tasks within a given structure is usually incomplete or uncertain. Nevertheless, a task analysis inevitably leads to the specification of a set of related tasks that, when mastered, are thought to lay the basis for acquiring proficient performance on the global task that has been analyzed. In the example given, mastery of the component skills is thought to be necessary for acquiring proficiency at writing paragraphs.

Developing a progress-monitoring system based on a task-analytic approach consists of creating measurement procedures for each of the subtasks that generate data on whether the standard or "criterion" for performance on that task has been met. Because the subtasks are qualitatively different from one another, it is common to create measurement procedures that differ from one another in terms of task stimuli and response requirements. For example, the procedures for measuring performance at punctuating sentences would be markedly different from the procedures used to score performance at expressing a complete thought when writing a sentence. Once the process of task analysis and criterion-referenced measurement has been completed for the tasks, it is possible to create a progress-monitoring system that consists of the procedures for measuring performance on each subtask until it has been mastered and then proceeding to the next subtask in the sequence and teaching and testing until mastery on that next task has occurred. In the mastery monitoring approach, a linear sequencing of the subtasks is not necessary, but it is usual to develop linear sequences for teaching and testing based on these analyses and recommend the tracking of progress through those sequences.

Figure 5.1 provides a simple illustration of two types of graphic display that can be used when a student's progress is mastery monitored. As can be seen in the figure, the conventional graph reveals the accuracy of student responding on successive tests of individual skills as a student progresses through the linear sequence of tasks that has been specified. At the point where the mastery criterion for a particular skill is attained, testing on that skill ceases and testing on the next skill begins. In a conventional graph, performance typically drops off as each new skill is introduced and then rises to the criterion level. Whereas on a conventional graph it is possible to see the rate at which individual skills are being mastered by examining individual skill slopes, the rate of progress through the skill sequence is not clearly represented. In contrast, on the cumulative graph the change in accuracy on each task is not shown. Instead, each upward plot of a data point indicates mastery of a new skill in the task sequence. The plot on this graph is cumulative, and the flat segments indicate days when mastery testing occurred on the new skill and the student did not attain criterion. In a cumulative graph of this type, the steepness of the overall slope through any set of skills is the most relevant

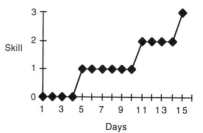

FIG. 5.1. Mastery monitoring progress graphs.

piece of information for progress monitoring because it is indicative of the rate of progress that a student is making through the skill sequence.

Consideration of the graphic images available when plotting progress-monitoring data is important because the pictorial representations of student progress become a powerful instrument in both evaluation and communication of program effectiveness. In the former case, data displays that allow for ease in comparing the student progress effects of a change in instruction are to be preferred. In the latter case, graphs that are easily understood by parents, students, and teachers will be the most helpful.

Roots of Mastery Monitoring

Serious efforts to develop mastery monitoring began in the 1960s with the rise of behavioral objectives, criterion-referenced testing, and competency-based instruction. Each, in its own way, contributed to the idea that both declarative and procedural knowledge consisted of domains that could be operationalized in terms of the discrete components believed to constitute those domains. The general approach is, of course, reductionist, and although reductionism is much out of vogue in the contemporary politics of research in education, neither the current value nor the long-range potential of mastery monitoring should suffer from the constructivist hegemony resulting from this social–political struggle.

Behavioral Objectives. The behavioral objectives movement was based on the argument that instruction and learning would be improved if the specifically desired learning outcomes would be expressed as behavioral descriptions rather than in such abstract terms such as "knowing," "understanding," and "appreciating." Once the "conditions," "behavior," and "criteria" for each objective had been stated, it was assumed that lessons could be carefully designed to produce those behavioral outcomes. In addition, because the lesson objectives had been stated in behavioral terms, it was assumed that assessing student success in attaining the objective was directly accomplished through observing whether the behavior had met the specified criterion. With the advent of behavioral objectives, educators seemed to possess the technology required to create curricula that were defined in terms of specific behavioral outcomes and the move toward building behavioral objective banks began. A center was established at UCLA that was intended to become the national repository of behavioral objectives from which educators everywhere might draw their instructional objectives. Behavioral objectives have been important to the development of progress monitoring systems and they can be found at the heart of the Individual Education Plan (IEP). Indeed, the common approaches to specification of Annual Goals and Short Term Objectives in an IEP, and the requirements for evaluating progress in the IEP perfectly parallels the task-analytic approach described earlier.

Criterion-Referenced Testing. The rise of criterion-referenced tests (CRTs) as an alternative to norm-referenced tests (NRTs) has been important in shifting attention from measurement procedures designed to compare students to measurement procedures designed to determine whether students possess specific knowledge and skills. Briefly, a typical CRT is constructed by (task) analyzing an area of the curriculum in such a way that it is represented by the constituent elements thought to compose that curriculum domain. Once the analysis is completed, a set of equivalent items is created for each of the identified elements and a criterion level of performance on those items is specified that must be exceeded to infer that the student "knows" that part of the domain. The commonalty between CRTs and behavioral objectives is clear. Perhaps the only important difference is that CRT developers are more likely to think of the constituent elements for which they are creating test items in a curriculum domain as knowledge rather than behavior. Whether writing behavioral objectives or developing a CRT, the procedures are functionally equivalent—define the curriculum domain, analyze it into component parts, specify the procedures for measuring each part, and identify the performance criteria required for inferring mastery/attainment of competence. Because these procedures are fundamental to writing IEPs, it is not unusual to see that CRTs are often used in the IEP process to help establish a student's Current Level of Performance, Annual Goals, and sequence of Short-Term Objectives in a particular area of the curriculum.

Competency-Based Instruction. Following closely on the heels of behavioral objectives and CRTs was a movement to design instruction around "competencies." Conceptually, competencies are not different from the elemental knowledge and skills written into behavioral objectives and that are the basis for CRTs. If anything, competencies are behavioral objectives written by people who may not wish to think of themselves as "behavioral" in their orientation to instruction and learning. Within psychology, the term *competence* is usually used with reference to the internal capability that underlies *performance*—the external manifestation of that competence. Thus, someone taking a strictly behavioral position regarding assessment would typically not be directed toward making inferences about what the learner "knows" or "is able to do" from observing performance. Instead, the behaviorist is likely to speak factually about whether the student has met the specified performance criterion, and will leave inferences about the learners generalizable capabilities to the cognitive psychologist who is interested in competence rather than performance. Competency testing became a very popular idea with state education agencies in the 1970s and 1980s, and many states moved to the idea of "minimum" competency testing as a way of assuring attainment of a standard set of learner outcomes for all of their graduates. This approach to ensuring educational quality is currently in favor as part of the "Education 2000" plan advocated by the federal government, and is very much alive in the rush to develop national "standards" of performance in each of the curriculum areas. An unfortunate aspect of the competency testing movement has been the loss of focus on routinely assessing student progress as a part of instruction—mastery monitoring—and an increased emphasis on testing student performance on single occasions such as the end of eighth grade and at high-school graduation. In these cases the political interest has produced a shift from using assessment during learning to using assessment to certify outcomes.

Mastery monitoring is a more familiar approach to progress monitoring in the field of special education. In large part this is because special educators have closely embraced the task analytic approach in efforts to redesign curriculum and instruction for hard-to-teach learners. For students having difficulty learning, the most valued instructional design principle in special education is to simplify the task so that the demands are at a level of difficulty congruent with the learners current level of performance. Generally, this principle has been operationalized through task analysis—breaking the task into simpler parts and teaching the simpler parts in logical order. A good example of this approach is the Direct Instruction approach (cf. Carnine, Silbert, & Kameenui, 1990) that was used in the creation of language, reading, mathematics, and spelling. Despite some criticisms (Hesushius, 1991), this approach is still widely advocated and used in special education and has been fundamental in curriculum analysis and design.

The widespread use of a task analytic approach to instructional redesign for students with disabilities has also resulted in recommendations to conduct criterion-referenced testing and mastery monitoring during instruction. A perusal of the textbooks on assessment with special populations reveals that CRTs and mastery monitoring are fundamental to the training of special education teachers. During this past decade, the mastery monitoring approach has become increasingly popularized in special education as "curriculum-based assessment" (CBA; Tucker, 1985). Although not all forms of CBA are rooted in the task analytic approach, most textbook presentations of CBA describe CBA development consistent with the steps and procedures of task analysis, objectives writing, and criterion-referenced approach previously discussed.

Research on Mastery Monitoring. A variety of research on mastery monitoring is possible; unfortunately, this research has not occurred to the degree that is desirable. For example, interesting research on the reliability and validity of CRTs is important; however, establishing the reliability and validity of mastery monitoring systems is difficult because the typical psychometric procedures used for developing reliable and valid norm-referenced tests (NRTs) do not directly apply to the CRTs used in mastery monitoring. For example, when developing the reliability of an NRT, the primary consideration is the stability of a student's score within the distribution of scores obtained by a sample of students taking the same test. Thus, stability or consistency as the criterial attribute of reliability within the framework of NRTs refers to whether a student's rank order within a distribution remains the same from one occasion to the next (i.e., test–retest reliability) or on randomly created halves of the same test (i.e., internal consistency). On the CRTs used in mastery monitoring, rank-order stability is irrelevant. Because the question to be answered within mastery monitoring is whether the student has attained mastery on the skill being measured, the primary reliability issue is whether the student's performance on the test task is stable from one test occasion to the next. If we wish to infer that the student has attained the criterion level of performance on the task, we must have some confidence that the level of performance attained on that task will not be significantly different on the next occasion of that test. Without this confidence we are left uncertain about whether we can leave instruction on one skill and move to the next. Reliability of this type is typically not addressed by developers of CRTs and mastery monitoring systems, and little research of this type is reported in the literature.

The validity of mastery-monitoring systems is likewise more often assumed than established. In part, this is due to the fact that advocates of mastery-monitoring systems rely primarily on face validity and social validity as the primary criteria for asserting the validity of a mastery monitoring system. "Face validity," of course, refers to the appearance of the measure. If the task "looks like" the skill that has been identified, then it is high in face validity. Social validity is similar in that establishing social validity requires agreement among significant decision makers that the skill is important and measurable through the procedures that have been specified. The effect is that "agreement" is the criterial attribute of validity for most mastery-monitoring systems.

In some respects it is unfortunate that such high reliance is placed on agreement as the source of validity for mastery-monitoring systems because accepting agreement as a sufficient criterion means that very little significant research is conducted on important theoretical assumptions inherent in mastery-monitoring systems. For example, a key assumption of mastery monitoring is that a criterion level of performance can be specified for every task that, when met by the learner, allows important predictions about future performance on that task and on related tasks within the same knowledge and skill domain. This mastery assumption is important when we are seeking an answer to the "Can they do it?" question; that is, "Can they ride a bike?"; "Can they dress themselves?"; "Can they multiply fractions?"; "Can they comprehend narrative text written for 12th-grade students?" Implied in each of these questions is some standard or criterion level of performance that, when met, enables us to answer "yes" or "no." An interesting empirical question seldom if ever addressed is what criterion level of performance provides the evidence base for confidently answering the question.

The empirical validity of "mastery" criteria are also important with respect to the assumption that the acquisition of knowledge and skills is hierarchical and that mastery on one task facilitates acquisition of mastery on the next. If this is true, then it becomes very important to determine the level of performance required for such transfer of learning to be maximized. Unfortunately, the standards of performance that are specified within mastery monitoring systems are almost always arbitrary. In virtually all cases, the criterion for mastery is accuracy (i.e., percentage correct on repetitions of the task). It is common to find specification of doing the task with "90%" accuracy as the criterion despite evidence that accuracy alone can be an insufficient criterion for establishing proficient performance (La Berge & Samuels, 1974).

Ultimately, the validity of mastery-monitoring systems is dependent on the validity of the task hierarchy on which the monitoring system is based. It makes sense to monitor progress through a task sequence if mastery of the elements in that task sequence reflects incremental growth in the curriculum domain represented by that task hierarchy. If competence in a domain can or does develop without successive mastery of the individual elements—or, if a particular task sequence is not generally applicable—then requiring all learners to proceed through a mastery sequence will be inefficient or unsuccessful. One important reason why advocates of task-analytic approaches to learning and instruction have had difficulty in refuting the criticisms of constructivists is that very little empirical evidence has been developed to demonstrate the effectiveness of task hierarchies in learning. The reason for this is that, to this point, task analysis has been treated more as "art" than science. The assumption seems to be that anyone who is competent in a knowledge domain is capable of task analyzing that domain for purposes of curriculum design. This somewhat casual assumption about the competence needed to accomplish curriculum design has, no doubt, contributed to both the plethora of untested and potentially harmful materials that have been commercially produced and to the massive failure of national curriculum reform efforts that have been directed by leading academics. Perhaps the only exception to task-analytic approach as art is the systematic approach to curriculum design that has been developed by advocates of Direct Instruction. A reading of the principles of curriculum design used by this group makes it clear that they view the role of knowledge organization in learning as neither trivial nor arbitrary, and believe that major differences in curriculum effectiveness obtain when appropriate analysis and sequencing of curriculum elements occurs. Despite the rigor of their work, however, a body of empirical evidence cannot be identified that establishes how a curriculum hierarchy can be developed which is either necessary for developing proficiency in a curriculum domain or that results in more effective instruction when used by a teacher. The result of this failure to demonstrate empirically the necessity of specific task sequences in learning has been that many "scopes and sequence" exist for the same curriculum domain. In the face of these limitations, then, mastery-monitoring systems developed to track student progress in the curriculum typically report no information on the reliability of the assessment procedures and only "expert" judgment as the basis for validity claims.

As previously suggested, a critically important type of research to be done on any progress-monitoring system is its effectiveness in improving instructional decision making. Evidence should be sought demonstrating that teachers are more effective in teaching when they use mastery-monitoring systems than when they are not using such systems. A primary value attributed to mastery monitoring is that the data obtained inform the teacher about both the effectiveness and content of instruction. Thus, successive mastery of tasks should provide information on whether to change an instructional approach and what to teach at any stage in the program. Certainly, alterations in the students program can be made when adequate progress is not occurring. Further, decisions to continue teaching a task when mastery has not been demonstrated or what task to move to when mastery occurs can be based in mastery-monitoring data as well. The testable assumption is, of course, that teachers so informed by the data from mastery monitoring will be more effective.

Reflecting on the validity of mastery approaches to progress monitoring, then, at least three types of questions can be identified that need to be addressed:

1. *Growth validity*—Does measured progress through the hierarchy of tasks or skills correspond to growth in generalized proficiency in the curriculum domain in which progress is being measured?

2. *Instructional efficiency*—Is mastery of each element included in the progress-monitoring system necessary, and are the mastery criteria appropriate?

3. *Instructional effectiveness*—Can teachers use the mastery-monitoring system to improve their instructional effectiveness?

Although these three questions are related to one another, it is possible to produce evidence in answer to one question without establishing the answer to another. For example, it is entirely possible that teachers could improve their effectiveness by using a mastery-monitoring system (Question 3) despite the fact that evidence of growth validity is negative and instructional efficiency is low. The reason for this, of course, is that a mastery-monitoring system might well provide teachers with some heuristic advantage in the analysis and selection of what to teach, or that using a "small-steps" approach to teaching might prove to be successful with students irrespective of the steps that are used for instruction. Indeed, a good bit of speculation exists that students who are struggling to learn content can overcome their barriers to learning only if the task is sufficiently simplified.

Unfortunately, the available literature does not contain research directly testing the instructional efficiency of alternative mastery-monitoring systems. Several reasons may account for this fact. First, the mastery-monitoring systems that exist are embedded in commercially developed curricula. Thus, for example, many reading and math curriculum series include "end of unit/lesson" tests in the materials available for teachers to use for instruction. In addition, the explicit or implicit assumption is that students should demonstrate mastery on these curriculum embedded tests before they progress to the next unit or lesson. Indeed, in some cases, decision rules are provided to teachers in regard to the performance criterion students are to meet before the teacher moves to the next lesson. However, curriculum publishers do not provide evidence on the increased efficiency in learning that occurs when teachers use these curriculum embedded tests in a mastery learning format because no such evidence exists. Curriculum publishers do not conduct research on the growth validity, instructional efficiency, or instructional effectiveness of the curriculum-embedded mastery tests that they provide because, in the current sales and purchasing environment it is unnecessary. School personnel who decide what curricula to purchase simply do not demand data on the effects or the effectiveness of curricula. Thus, it is not in the best economic interests of a curriculum publishing company to use its resources to conduct empirical research addressing these issues.

Advantages and Disadvantages

Conceptually, the criterion-referenced mastery monitoring (MM) approach has much to recommend it as an approach to monitoring student progress. Perhaps the most appealing aspect of MM is that it is very specific and prescriptive with respect to the scope, sequence, and mastery criteria for the skills that constitute what is to be learned in a given domain. This specificity and prescriptiveness create a basis for teachers to (a) assess and describe a student's current level of functioning within the scope and sequence, (b) establish the starting point for instruction, (c) specify the sequence of tasks/objectives through which the student should progress to attain competence in that domain, and (d) determine when to shift instruction from one skill to the next. It is important to recognize that the assessment procedures associated with mastery monitoring enable teachers to plan proactively so that they design instructional programs that should minimize student failure. In addition, however, these mastery monitoring procedures can be used remedially to diagnose problems when students are having difficulty in learning within a given domain.

The specific and prescriptive nature of mastery monitoring appeals to teachers who must decide what to teach a particular student at any particular time. In providing direction to this decision, mastery monitoring meets what is currently one of the most highly desired characteristics of an assessment procedure; that is, it should inform teacher decision making.

As has been discussed earlier, criterion-referenced mastery monitoring is an approach to progress monitoring that is both widely used and relatively untested. The technical questions that have been raised thus far, however, are answerable through empirical research. At the same time, those technical questions do not exhaust the potential problems of using MM. For example, a good progress monitoring system should allow teachers to determine not only what to teach, but also whether they should change their instructional approach with a student. The primary data for deciding that a change in instructional approach is necessary are those bearing on rate of growth in the curriculum domain. In the case of MM, these data are the rate at which a student is mastering skills in the task sequence. If the rate of progress through the sequence is judged to be inadequate, then two primary options are available to the teacher—change the content of instruction ("what to teach") or change tactics and strategies ("how to teach"). A moment's reflection reveals that MM is an approach which is not flexible with respect to changing the content of instruction—at least insofar as content is defined as teaching different skills. This inflexibility derives from the fact that the MM data are based on a particular skill sequence that directs instruction. If a change in content occurs, a new skill sequence is introduced that makes all previous data on rate of acquisition irrelevant. This means that the effect of changing what to teach cannot be evaluated by contrasting the rate of acquisition of the skill sequence before and after the content change occurs, because this would be tantamount to contrasting growth using two different measurement systems. It should be noted that this problem is especially acute when a teacher would like to try a new set of curriculum materials with a student. If, as is typical, the new curriculum materials include a different skill sequence, or if, as is common nowadays, the approach is "holistic" rather than analytic, then it is not sensible to use the data from the original MM system to evaluate the effects of changing the curriculum materials. In sum, MM data can be used to evaluate changes in instructional tactics only when the skill sequence is maintained.

General Outcome Measurement

A second approach to progress monitoring involves repeated sampling of performance on the same task to assess change in proficiency at doing that task. Over the past decade, this approach to progress monitoring has been widely applied in Curriculum-Based Measurement (Deno, 1985). More recently, Fuchs and Deno (1991) referred to this approach as *General Outcome Measurement* (GOM) because it is characterized by assessing performance on a general outcome, or goal, that represents proficiency in a given curriculum domain.

The contrast between MM and GOM is quite clear and straightforward. As described earlier, development of a MM system is based on a task analysis that begins by specifying a major desired curriculum outcome. Where in MM the major outcome is then reduced to the subskills presumed be the constituents of that outcome, in GOM procedures for direct and repeated sampling of performance on the desired outcome are created. Presumably, these sampling procedures for repeated sampling of performance on the desired outcome—often referred to as "probes"—are the same procedures that would be used to assess performance on the final (or terminal) task in a MM approach. Thus, the point of intersection of these two approaches is at the level of measuring the degree of proficiency on the outcome. Although the two approaches intersect at outcome measurement, they differ markedly with respect to the information that is collected regarding progress toward the goal. With MM the information obtained is the rate of acquisition of a series of qualitatively different subskills, whereas in GOM the information is rate of increase in performance on the desired outcome.

The contrast between MM and GOM can be clarified if we refer to the earlier example of "paragraph writing" that served as an illustration of how task analysis would be used to develop a MM approach. Recalling that in the MM approach progress monitoring consisted of measuring performance on each successive element identified as a subskill of paragraph writing, a GOM approach to monitoring student performance would consist of repeatedly sampling performance at the level of paragraph writing itself. This repeated sampling of performance would occur throughout the course of instruction on the assumption that, although student performance on the terminal task is very low at the outset of instruction, improvement in the student's performance is revealed in the data obtained through repeated sampling across time. Within GOM, therefore, progress monitoring consists of directly measuring the rate of a student's growth on a valued outcome, rather than the rate of acquisition of those subskills thought to be the critical constituents of that outcome. In this respect, GOM is similar to the measurement of height and weight in a developing child, and, indeed, the growth curves developed through GOM are similar in appearance to height and weight charts (Deno, 1985).

Perhaps the earliest systematic examples of the GOM approach can be found in the single case intervention studies of Applied Behavior Analysis (ABA). ABA is typically viewed as an approach to developing social behavior intervention programs rather than to developing academic skills instruction. Nevertheless, the seminal work by Lindsley (1971) in developing Precision Teaching and the work of Lovitt (1976) describing the application of ABA to academic skills provided a framework for using a direct and repeated measurement approach to monitor individual progress and evaluate the effectiveness of interventions. Although most of the measurement systems based on ABA have been influenced by the assumptions of a task analytic approach to teaching, it is possible to find clear case examples of GOM in the data displays (cf. White & Haring, 1980). More recently, the development of Curriculum-Based Measurement (CBM; Deno, 1985; Shinn, 1989) has illustrated the potential for using the same types of observational methods employed in ABA to create a standardized set of assessment procedures for monitoring individual student growth on generalized outcomes.

All GOM approaches have a common focus on creating graphic records of performance across time that are used to evaluate the effects of instructional interventions that are intended to effect changes in dimensions of performance. Graphic display of progress monitoring data collected through GOM is illustrated in Fig. 5.2. The graph in this figure displays the percentage of correct word sequences contained in paragraphs written by a student across 25 school days. At the outset, the student was writing paragraphs wherein only 30–40% of the two-word sequences consisted of correctly spelled words that were also semantically and syntactically acceptable within the context of the phrases where they were written. As instruction and practice at paragraph writing occurred, the performance in writing correct word sequences increased until, at the end of this series of samples, 80–100% of the word sequences written by the student were correct. In this conventional graph of the student's performance, the rate of improvement in writing paragraphs is represented by the overall slope of the data. When the graph from Fig. 5.2 is

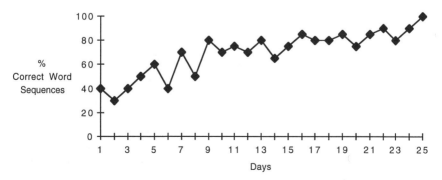

FIG. 5.2. General outcome measurement progress graph.

compared with the graphs in Fig. 5.1, the connection between MM and GOM become apparent. The progress monitoring graph for GOM is like the conventional graph in Fig. 5.1, except that all of the data displayed on the GOM graph are derived from measurements of performance on the final integrative skill—the general outcome—in the task-analytic sequence.

In essence, all GOM approaches share the use of single-case research designs as the method for attempting to identify environmental variables that significantly effect performance, and to improve student programs through formative evaluation. Single-case research methods are very flexible and can be used with many types of measurement. In their most basic form, however, single-case research designs are based on a time series data record created through repeated measurement of performance on the same, rather than successively different, tasks. Thus, analysis of the environmental variables effecting behavioral change is more easily conducted when the data record is produced through GOM rather than MM.

Recent research on the GOM approach to progress monitoring has attempted to address three key questions: (a) "What are the global outcome tasks on which performance should be measured?" ("What to measure"), (b) "How should the measurement activities be structured to produce technically adequate data?" ("How to measure"), and (c) "How can the data be used to improve educational programs?" ("How to use").

What to Measure. Because GOM rests on repeated measurement of performance on the same task, the value of the progress-monitoring data produced through using this approach will depend on the significance of the task to be performed for purposes of obtaining performance samples. Historically, task selection has been accomplished through the judgment of curriculum specialists and test developers. In such cases, curriculum specialists thought to be able to identify key outcomes have been asked to identify those skills or competencies that are at the top of the hierarchy in a particular curriculum domain and test developers have set about designing ways to test that performance. With the move toward developing alternative approaches to assessment, the emphasis in task selection has been on the so-called "authenticity" of the tasks that have been specified and the measurement procedures used. Although the meaning of the term *authenticity* has not been precisely operationalized, the essence of the referent seems to be that the task should be perceived as "real" and "meaningful" to the learners within the context of their lives. To be authentic, tasks should not be a contrivance of the teacher or test maker that is remote from the learner's interest and experience. From this perspective, then, "authentic" seems to refer to whether the task is something typical of what an individual might do in applying the subject matter either academically or practically. This emphasis on the meaningful application of knowledge is accompanied by a concern for the substance of tasks rather than the formal or procedural aspects of performance. Thus, writing an alternative conclusion to a story is thought to be more authentic than answering comprehension questions as a task for assessing a student's reading proficiency, and the focus in appraising performance on this task will be the substance of the alternative conclusion rather than the mechanics of paragraph composition and grammar.

As might be expected, the selection of authentic tasks for measuring learner outcomes has been associated with considerable difference of opinion among groups with differing investments in educational outcomes. As a result, the selection of critical outcomes too often is a political struggle where educators with differing theoretical orientations "win" the outcomes argument by relying on their political power rather than on the available empirical evidence. As might be expected under such circumstances, the outcome tasks that have been selected, although rich and creative in design, are of uncertain value to use a basis for assessing progress toward, and attainment of, those outcomes. Political struggles over outcomes abound, and a useful example was provided in the August 31, 1995, *Star Tribune* newspaper of Minneapolis where the new "content standards" were presented for the 1995–1996 school year (Duchesne, 1995). The article describing the State of Minnesota's approach to developing "standards" that all students would have to attain in order to receive a diploma. Included as an example was an outcome for students across all ages in language arts stating that they should be able to "demonstrate understanding of cause-and-effect relationships," and one for physical science that 14–18-year-olds could "collect, synthesize, and document evidence that supports the laws of thermodynamics" (p. 4B). Reading such statements of outcomes should clarify that little or no prior work has been done to establish the "reasonableness" of these outcomes for the children who will be held accountable for their attainment. Indeed subsequent articles in the same newspaper have quoted measurement experts as stating that reliable assessments of many of the outcomes "may not be possible." Despite requests from their own State administrators to lengthen the time schedule for the development and implementation of procedures for assessing progress toward these outcomes, the Minnesota State Board of Education has insisted on maintaining the original schedule. In explaining their position, one Board member was quoted as saying that "they didn't want to appear to be 'going soft' or 'backing down' on commitments made to legislators" (Smetanka, 1996, p. A15). His statement was reminiscent of Richard Nixon's famous comment in the face of proposals to withdraw from Vietnam that he wasn't going to be the first American President to "lose a war."

In large part, the issue of reasonableness or feasibility does not have to be addressed in these politically based identifications of outcomes because the actual tasks that will be used for assessing performance are not specified. Thus, the outcomes are approved "in spirit" and the operational procedures for assessing those outcomes are either left for later work by a different group, or left to the teacher's discretion. This is generally an agreeable solution for all involved because we have learned from politics that when operationalizing policy that "the devil is in the detail." Unfortunately, the result of this "we'll-figure-out-how-to-do-this-later" approach is too often that the measures do not work for either political or educative purposes. Thus, policy makers are enraged and educators are embarrassed to find in pilot implementations that large proportions of students cannot successfully demonstrate attainment of what look like basic skill outcomes that are assessed with instruments of unknown reliability and validity.

As mentioned previously, social validation is a version of using consensus as a basis for selecting outcomes on which to monitor progress that is often used and recommended by special educators. Social validation of objectives has been much advocated by applied behavior analysts as a basis for selecting target behaviors. This is not surprising in that although the behavioral system is functional and pragmatic, it does not include a theory of development from which theory-based outcomes might be derived. Although behavioral intervention typically assumes that skills are hierarchically organized, a behavioral task analysis can only proceed after outcomes have been selected. While "political" differences may occur when attempting social validation in behavioral programs, the number of people who must come together to establish consensus is at least manageable when compared to massive state or national efforts to identify outcomes. The risk still exists, however, that the political interests of all parties can be met without assuring good developmental outcomes for students. The reason is twofold: First, political interests tend to be time limited and situational, and second, our knowledge of what might be the best short-, intermediate-, and long-term developmental outcomes for a learner at any time is often inadequate. Knowledge is a precious thing that is always difficult to secure; thus, although consensus satisfies individual desires it does not assure empirical outcomes.

Ultimately, an empirical science for identifying tasks that can be used for assessing progress toward outcomes will have to rely primarily on what Cronbach and Meehl (1955) termed *relational fertility* in their seminal article on construct validity. In that article they proposed that the validity of any measure of a construct rests on the degree to which it enters into sensible empirical relationships with other theoretical and empirical criteria. Cronbach and Meehl rooted the concept of relational fertility in the idea that a measure demonstrating construct validity would correlate with other "criteria" in directions and degrees that were theoretically consistent. Most often these criteria have been interpreted to be measured levels of performance on other educational and psychological tests. Recently, however, the concept of relational fertility has been expanded to include criteria such as the practical and ethical consequences of any assessment (Messick, 1995).

For the present discussion, the expanded concept of relational fertility as a basis for empirically selecting outcomes for measurement necessarily leads to considerations of the degree to which systematic research on construct validity has been conducted. We must wonder about the extent to which evidence exists on the empirical relations between measures that have been created for particular outcomes and the relative benefits (and costs) accruing when using those measures. To the extent that educators and policy makers identify ad hoc or idiosyncratic outcomes it is, of course, impossible to address the construct validity of any procedures used to measure progress toward the outcome. In the case of outcomes like those specified by ambitious state boards of education, however, we can hope that the construct validity of outcome measures will be systematically examined. At the same time, researchers in the special education community need not wait for political decisions regarding key educational outcomes before undertaking empirical development of generalized outcome measures. As in medicine, where measures of vital functioning (the so-called "vital signs") did not follow from political decisions, measures of the vital signs of developmental progress in education are a feasible and worthy goal for research and development.

Examples of an empirical approach to selecting tasks and developing valid measures for GOM can be found in the special education literature. Thus far, applications have focused on reading, spelling, written expression, and arithmetic in the elementary grades (cf. Fuchs & Fuchs, 1992; Germann & Tindal, 1985; Marston & Magnusson, 1988; Shinn, 1989). Extensions of this research have been made to monitoring growth in early literacy (Kaminski & Good, in press; Priest, Spicuzza, Haseth, Peterson, & McConnell, 1992), secondary reading and writing (Espin & Deno, 1993) and middle-school math (Foegen, 1995). The validity criteria examined in research on these measures include teacher judgment of student proficiency, developmental growth, and sensitivity to that growth across short and long time periods, utility in increasing instructional effectiveness, utility in instructional diagnosis, utility in evaluating program entry and exit, placement in special and compensatory educational programs, and performance on norm-referenced standardized achievement tests. The value of examining this body of research is that it illustrates that a construct validation approach can be used to create workable progress monitoring procedures with known empirical properties.

How to Measure. If anything has been learned from the history of psychometrics, it is that standardization of assessment procedures creates opportunities to make performance comparisons between individuals on the same occasion, and within individuals from occasion to the next. As mentioned at the outset of this chapter, the use of assessment to discriminate between individuals has predominated; thus, standardization has been necessary to legitimate statements of difference. Standardization of progress monitoring procedures in GOM is no less important. Progress monitoring data are used to both ascertain growth over baseline performance and to make judgments about goal attainment. Making these comparative judgments requires that the data produced be reliable and that the conditions of administration of the progress measures be consistent. Casualness in assessing progress can only contribute to measurement error and to erroneous conclusions regarding program success. In such cases, programs that are not succeeding may be continued and programs that are successful in moving a student to goal attainment may be abandoned. Further, many advantages accrue when progress-monitoring procedures are standardized. For example, if standardized procedures are used, it becomes possible to gather normative performance data that can serve as a basis for establishing reasonable empirical goals. Seldom does any empirical basis exist for goal selection. As has already been mentioned with respect to specifying mastery criteria, the specification of criterion levels of performance—standards—is usually quite arbitrary. In the face of insufficient empirical information, therefore, we rely on specifying high levels of accuracy as if doing so somehow guarantees sufficiency.

In contrast, when progress-monitoring procedures are standardized, normative peer sampling within classrooms can be conducted by teachers to assist them in making judgments about whether a students might be able to successfully function in the classroom and about what levels of performance are typical for students of the same age and grade (Fuchs, Fuchs, Hamlett, Walz, & Germann, 1993; Shinn, Baker, Habedank, & Good, in press). More ambitious undertakings have involved developing school and district norms for performance on standardized GOMs (cf. Marston & Magnusson, 1988). We should keep in mind, of course, that the purpose of progress monitoring is to be able to empirically determine our success in developing the individual student program. At the same time, we would be foolish if we failed to recognize the efficiency of using progress-monitoring procedures that can produce data for reporting to parents and school personnel that enable our evaluations of programs and groups as well. We need to recognize, too, that the political consequences of our choices of assessment procedure. If we use only nonstandardized and ad hoc progress-monitoring procedures, than it is inevitable that different assessment procedures will be used to generate the information for the decision makers who are the source of funds. We can predict with some confidence that those decision makers will be more likely to value and use the data that can be aggregated across individuals to enable judgments about group and program success.

How to Use the Data. No aspect of progress monitoring can be more important than how the data are used to improve educational outcomes for students. Indeed, the broader conception of validity articulated by Messick

(1995) is based on a consideration of the social consequences of assessment. Messick's view is that for a test to be validated it is necessary to demonstrate that using the test properly results in benefit to the individual and society. A significant aspect of the recent research on GOM is the focus on how the data obtained through progress monitoring are used by professionals as a basis for educational decision making. This research has demonstrated the consequences of using GOM data to make decisions during prereferral screening, eligibility for services, instructional evaluation, reintegration evaluation, and program effectiveness (Marston & Magnusson, 1988; Shinn, 1995). Among these decisions, evaluating instructional effectiveness is most central to the purpose of progress monitoring. If progress monitoring is to function as a dynamic in the development of improved instructional programs, teachers must be able to use the information generated to determine when a program is effective and when to make changes in the program. Fortunately, evidence exists that teachers can use GOM to increase their effectiveness (Fuchs, Deno, & Mirkin, 1984; Fuchs & Fuchs, 1986).

CONCLUSION

Monitoring student progress is an activity included in any conceptualization of teaching—no matter how informal. The issues that confront us when considering progress monitoring seem not to surround whether teachers should monitor progress; rather, they surround the degree of formalization and the nature of the progress-monitoring procedures used. Evidence exists that progress-monitoring approaches can be highly structured and precise, and that using such approaches can produce benefits in terms of increased student achievement and improved communication. Despite this evidence, the use of highly structured and empirically validated progress-monitoring procedures is not widespread. How long it will take for systematic progress-monitoring procedures to be adopted by state education agencies and school districts is difficult to estimate. Perhaps the greater pressure for accountability with respect to student outcomes will result in policies that require the availability of progress-monitoring data. We can hope that the adoption of such beneficial practices will occur more rapidly than was true of the British Navy when it waited more than 200 years after discovering that fresh fruit prevented scurvy to require that its ships carry such food.

REFERENCES

Bruner, J. S. (1965). *On knowing: Essays for the left hand.* New York: Atheneum.

Carnine, D., Silbert, J., & Kameenui, E. J. (1990). *Direct instruction reading* . (2nd ed.). Columbus, OH: Merrill.

Cronbach, L. J., & Meehl, P. E. (1955). Construct validity in psychological tests. *Psychology Bulletin, 52,* 281–302.

Deno, S. L. (1985). Curriculum-based measurement: The emerging alternative. *Exceptional Children, 52,* 219–232.

Deno, S. L., & Mirkin, P. K. (1977). *Data-based program modification: A manual.* Reston, VA: Council for Exceptional Children.

Duchesne, P. D. (1995). Schools get new content criteria. *Star Tribune, XIV(149),* 1B, 4B.

Espin, C., & Deno, S. L. (1993). Performance in reading from content area text as an indicator of achievement. *Remedial and Special Education, 14(6),* 47–58.

Foegen, A. (1995). *Reliability and validity of three general outcome measures for low-achieving students in secondary mathematics.* Unpublished doctoral dissertation, University of Minnesota, Minneapolis, MN.

Fuchs, L. S., & Deno, S. L. (1991). Paradigmatic distinctions between instructionally relevant measurement models. *Exceptional Children, 57,* 448–501.

Fuchs, L. S., Deno, S. L., & Mirkin, P. K. (1984). The effects of frequent curriculum-based measurement and evaluation on pedagogy, student achievement, and student awareness of learning. *American Educational Research Journal, 21(2),* 449–460.

Fuchs, L. S., & Fuchs, D. (1986). Effects of systematic formative evaluation: A meta-analysis. *Exceptional Children, 53,* 199–208.

Fuchs, L. S., & Fuchs, D. (1992). Identifying an alternative measure for monitoring students' reading growth. *School Psychology Review, 21,* 45–58.

Fuchs, L. S., Fuchs, D., Hamlett, C. L., Walz, L., & Germann, G. (1993). Formative evaluation of academic progress: How much growth can we expect? *School Psychology Review, 22(1),* 27–48.

Germann, G., & Tindal, G. (1985). An application of curriculum-based assessment: The use of direct and repeated measurement. *Exceptional Children, 52,* 244–265.

Hesushius, L. (1991). Curriculum-based assessment and direct instruction: Critical reflections on fundamental assumptions. *Exceptional Children, 57,* 315–328.

Kaminski, R., & Good, R. H. (in press). Towards a technology for assessing basic early literacy skills. *School Psychology Review.*

La Berge, D., & Samuels, S. J. (1974). Toward a theory of automatic information processing in reading. *Cognitive Psychology, 6,* 293–323.

Lindsley, O. R. (1971). Precision teaching in perspective: An interview with Ogden Lindsley. *Teaching Exceptional Children, 3,* 114–119.

Lovitt, T. C. (1976). Applied behavior analysis techniques and curriculum research: Implications for instruction. In N. G. Haring & R. L. Schiefelbush (Eds.), *Teaching Special Children* (pp. 112–155). New York: McGraw-Hill.

Marston, D., & Magnusson, D. (1988). Curriculum-based measurement: District level implementation. In J. Graden, J. Zins, & M. Curtis (Eds.), *Alternative educational delivery systems: Enhancing instructional options for all students* (pp. 137–172). Washington, DC: National Association of School Psychologists.

Messick, S. (1995). Validity of psychological assessment. *American Psychologist, 50,* 741–749.

Priest, J., Spicuzza, R., Haseth, M., Peterson, C., & McConnell, S. (1992, December). *Developing a continuous progress monitoring tool for preschoolers with disabilities.* Poster presented at the national conference of the Division for Early Childhood, Washington, DC.

Shinn, M. R. (1989). *Curriculum-based measurement.* New York: Guilford.

Shinn, M. R. (1995). Best practices in curriculum-based measurement and its use in a problem solving model. In A. Thomas & J. Grimes (Eds.), *Best practices in school psychology* (pp. 547–567). Washington, DC: The National Association of School Psychologists.

Shinn, M. R., Baker, S., Habedank, L., & Good, R. (in press). The effects of classroom reading performance data on general education teachers' and parents' attitudes about reintegration. *Exceptionality.*

Smetanka, M. J. (1996). Test results have schools hustling to boost learning. *Star Tribune, XVI(56),* A1, A15.

Tucker, J. A. (1985). Curriculum-based assessment: An introduction. *Exceptional Children, 52,* 199–204.
White, O., & Haring, N. G. (1980). *Exceptional teaching.* Columbus, OH: Merrill.

6

PROGRAMMING: ALIGNING TEACHER THOUGHT PROCESSES WITH THE CURRICULUM

Kenneth W. Howell
Marcia R. Davidson
Western Washington University

A few years ago Ken Howell bought a boat and took it out in the ocean off of the San Juan Islands in northwest Washington state. At one point the boat stopped and started leaking. Recognizing these occurrences as problems, Howell tried to figure out exactly what to do to correct the situation. At that time, he knew little about boats, which presented a completely different problem.

The story of Howell's boat, and his lack of knowledge about boats, serves as a good metaphor for the fix one finds oneself in while trying to develop a program for students with mild learning problems. First of all, given the current political context, and the increasing dissension regarding mildly disabled students within special education (Zigmond et al., 1995), the image of a sinking ship seems uniquely applicable. Second, however, and more befitting to the theme of this part of this text, it raises certain propositions one must consider when discussing the topic of programming. These include: (a) the nature of need; (b) the nature of helping; (c) the general nature and purpose of problem solving; and (d) the quality of the various programming procedures and actions one must employ to recognize need, solve problems, and provide help for students with disabilities.

Students who need help should receive programs that supply quality services. These are developed through the process of problem definition and problem solving that we call *Programming*. Programming for students with mild disabilities (or even those with severe disabilities) involves a set of activities which, in order to be effective, must be grounded in the consideration of the core propositions listed earlier. Programs are plans. They have goals and procedures for meeting these goals. However, as we illustrate shortly, not all of the programs developed for students are good. They may be missing meaningful outcomes, effective instructional procedures, or both.

Before we continue, it is important to avoid confusion by noting that Programming is not synonymous with IEP development and that confusion of the two may lead to difficulties with both activities. For example, the specificity of IEP requirements in relation to goals and objectives far exceeds the IEP requirements related to the specification of the instructional techniques to meet these outcomes. Consequently, it is not uncommon to find what Bateman (1996) referred to as "empty" IEPs. These are IEPs that contain goals and objectives but no information about the services which will be delivered to meet these goals and objectives. Although the failure to thoroughly consider instructional interventions is antithetical to the concept of programming, it is allowed by the regulations governing IEP development. (In fact, in some states the requirement for describing service interventions on IEPs has been reduced to a simple blank where one writes in the percent of time—or number of minutes—to be spent in a special education class. In these cases there may be nothing included on the IEP that tells what will be done during those minutes.) IEP development is an important topic that is *related* to programming, but the regulatory definition of a legally correct IEP provides little insight into good instructional programming.

EVALUATION AND PROGRAMMING: OR, "HOW WE SHOULD THINK SO WE DON'T SINK."

Programming

A program is a plan for teaching the student what he or she needs to know. A completed program will contain "what" statements and "how" statements. The "what" is the curriculum, the goals, and objectives to be learned. The "how" is instruction, the materials and teacher actions to be used to teach the objectives. Because the quality of a program will be judged according to how well it assures that the student learns the goals and objectives, decisions about *what* to teach (i.e., decisions about the curriculum) are preeminent.

The process of programming follows certain basic steps as outlined by Howell (in press) in Fig. 6.1. The reader will want to take a close look at that figure, as we will not explain each of its steps in sequence. However, each of the topics represented in the figure are addressed in this chapter.

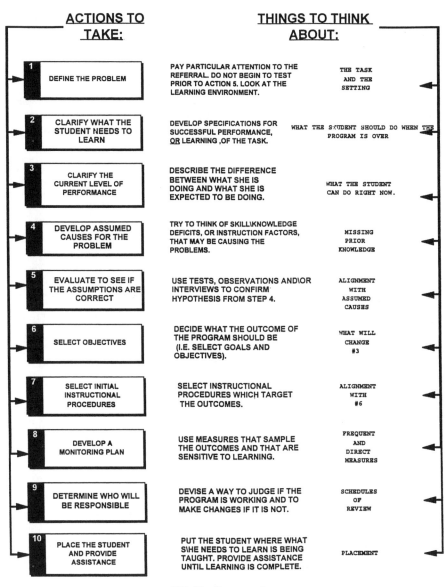

FIG. 6.1. Programming.

Certain themes link the components in Fig. 6.1 and this chapter. One of these is the emphasis on teacher thought process. Programming is a thoughtful activity that leads to different outcomes depending on the way the programmer thinks about it. Another theme is the central role of curriculum and the need to think of it in expanded terms. Then, finally, there is the theme of alignment (Dixon & Carnine, 1992; Kameenui, 1991; Spady, 1988), this being the idea that what we think about, test, and teach should all complement each other.

The pivotal place of curriculum within the process of programming can be illustrated in many ways. For example, the tenth action in the programming sequence presented in Fig. 6.1 deals with the placement decision. This involves deciding where on the continuum, from institutionalization to inclusion, a student should be sent to receive the program that is developed. Placement, in our minds, is not a central theme in the process of good programming. However, we realize that there is considerable turmoil regarding placement options in the field today (Renick, 1995), so it seems appropriate to single it out for this example.

It is our position that placement options should generally be selected on the basis of the curricular elements (i.e., goals and objectives) that need to be taught, not necessarily the assistance (i.e., teaching staff and instructional modifications) that needs to be provided to teach these goals and objectives. That is because assistance, in the form of consultation, modified books, teacher aides, cooperative learning groups, or even team teaching can appropriately be provided within any setting. However, it is not appropriate for special educators to go into any setting, particularly a general education classroom, and change what is being taught (i.e., the curriculum). This means that full inclusion is not appropriate if a student needs to be taught content not taught in the inclusive setting.

Students should go where things they need to learn are taught, and they should move when they have learned them. For some students, particularly those with extreme social skills deficits (Kauffman, Lloyd, Baker, & Riedel, 1995), and those without the skills to learn in a particular setting, this may require temporarily leaving the general classroom to acquire content not taught there (Zigmond et al., 1995).

Aligning Evaluation With Curriculum

Within special education, evaluation activities are undertaken for a variety of reasons and the techniques one uses often depend on the purpose of the activity. In Fig. 6.2, Howell, Fox, and Morehead (1993) have separated these activities and purposes into general categories defined by the kind of decision the evaluator is trying to make. The two major categories of evaluation and decision making are "Eligibility" and "Teaching."

Eligibility Decisions. These decisions focus on the assignment, or sorting, of students into groups (e.g., at risk/not at risk, referred/not referred, learning disabled/not learning disabled), which should help professionals decide if students are eligible, or not eligible, for some type of special education program, a compensatory educational program, or both. Eligibility decisions have instructional utility only in that they allow students access

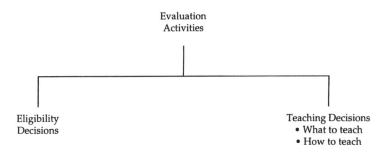

FIG. 6.2. Types of decisions.

to the locations, professionals, or funds which are designated to provide service. These decisions characteristically depend on instrumentation designed to discriminate between the groups of interest.

The evaluation tools used to inform eligibility decisions tend to be norm-referenced in nature and attempts at validating them usually focus on their power as sorting devices. In many cases, these measures sample domains that are more relevant to ideas about disabilities (e.g., Auditory Processing, Attention Deficit, Emotional Disturbance) than about education (Carnine & Woodward, 1988; Kameenui, 1991). As a consequence, such measures tend to have limited programming utility.

The current evaluative focus on eligibility is largely the result of a pattern in resource allocation known as categorical funding (Ysseldyke, Algozzine, & Thurlow, 1992). However, the categorical model also reflects the Aristotelian tradition of organizing knowledge through classification. In this tradition, classification is a necessary prerequisite to the definition of concepts and terms (Korzybski, 1948). Therefore, the process of classification helps in communication and the accumulation of information. It also helps make information both cohesive and accessible. As a result, the labels and definitions associated with eligibility decisions have a place in the conversation about special education and the research on the needs of its clients. Beyond this, however, it is hard to argue that the prevailing classification/eligibility function of decision making, which has occupied the major focus of formal evaluation in special and remedial education for decades (Deno, 1989), has many redeeming qualities.

It seems that the "legitimate" drive to classify, which was based on the way our developing profession organized information, was overwhelmed long ago by waves of categorical advocacy and funding. Today, for every student who is classified as learning disabled to define a research population, there must now be thousands who are classified to gain access to the educational funding that comes with that label (whereas thousands of others, having the same needs, are not classified because of the imposition of funding caps and discrepancy formulas). Although we have little more to say about the eligibility process in this chapter, it is important to note that disability labels have little to do with programming, and may even confuse teacher thought processes.

   Teaching Decisions. These decisions directly influence the actions of teachers and the learning of students. In this chapter, these will be divided into two subgroups: *what-to-teach* decisions and *how-to-teach* decisions. Decisions about what-to-teach focus on selection of the outcomes, in the form of skill and knowledge, that are to be achieved through instruction, and are the products of lessons. In contrast, decisions about how-to-teach focus on the selection of the instructional materials and teacher actions that are meant to bring about learning outcomes. These are the processes of instruction.

   As a general rule, what-to-teach decisions are made by comparing student performance to expectations in order to find out which things a student might need to learn or is expected to have learned, but has not yet acquired. Such decisions cannot be made if the outcomes have not been defined or if the evaluation procedures employed are not aligned with these outcomes. However, when the outcomes have been defined and measures have been aligned with them, comparisons of the student's performance to these outcomes yields results that can be used to select goals and objectives (i.e., desired products) for instruction.

   Although selecting objectives is a critical aspect of programming, it is not the only one. Teachers must also make decisions about how to teach. Unfortunately, this is one area where decision making in special education seems to break down (Fuchs & Fuchs, 1995; Swanson, 1988).

   At some global level, decisions about what to teach also have how-to-teach implications. Recognition that the student needs to be taught to read, for example, implies a need to use books during instruction. However, as one becomes more specific in attempts to designate how instruction should take place, the decision maker may be forced into one of three pathways. The first is to identify instructional techniques that are generally better than others and to use these techniques with the student. This approach, which attempts to find the "best" instructional program for most students, is ordinarily not valued by special educators because it is not "individualized" and flies in the face of the commonly accepted platitude that "the best method for one cannot be the best method for all" (Thorndike, 1917, p. 67). Although this doctrine may be true, it is a mistake for special educators to routinely ignore the literature on instructional effectiveness while fixating on information about student differences. After all, student differences are not the only causes of failures to learn. There are many qualitative differences between instructional techniques and the ways different teachers deliver instruction (Howell & Evans, 1995), which can also account for variability in student learning.

We believe that until there is evidence that students have actually been given validated instructional approaches, efforts at individualization through special education should be avoided. That is because such efforts often end up producing expensive distractions for teachers while occasionally erecting barriers between students and the "mainstream." (We are not talking about the routine personalization of teaching that occurs in any caring and effective classroom, but rather about sending students to special education.) We also believe that the quality of the teaching environment should receive as much attention as the student. These are not new ideas (Malouf & Schiller, 1995), but somehow they never seem to catch on.

The second approach to deciding how to teach is to collect information that can be used to adjust instruction by matching student characteristics to particular instructional procedures. This is what most special educators think of when they think of "individualization." This approach has historically led to the efforts to recognize "styles of learners" who do better in certain types of instructional processes (Mann & Sabatino, 1985). These efforts have, in turn, produced some of the most genuinely disappointing work done in measurement and educational decision making (Arter & Jenkins, 1979; Snider, 1992).

The third path one might follow when trying to decide how to teach is the path of formative evaluation through curriculum-based measurement (Deno & Espin, 1991). In this process, the evaluator gives up some of the hope that one can decide how to teach before instruction begins and moves to fine tuning the instructional selections that are available (see Actions 8 and 9 in Fig. 6.1). This is accomplished by collecting formative information about the impact various teaching actions have as the student is learning. The formative approach uses information on the emerging products of instruction to inform decisions about the quality of instruction. Efforts along this path have produced some of the most impressive work in measurement and decision making (Fuchs & Fuchs, 1995). Of the first two options, number one (i.e., picking the technique that is generally the "best") is not very popular in special education rhetoric, but number two (i.e., picking a technique by matching it to the processing style of the learner) is. Therefore, the most direct contrast is between options two and three and the most obvious difference between these two is that the learning style approach requires the decision maker to "front load" the how-to-teach decision-making process. In other words, the approach encourages the collection of data prior to instruction and it encourages the making of long-term predictions from these data. In contrast, the formative approach requires the decision maker to use data from measures that are aligned with the curriculum to see if learning is occurring. Under this option, long-term prediction is de-emphasized in favor of flexibility in program planning and modification.

There are plenty of ways to explain why trying to make predictions about instructional preferences based on measures given before instruction does not seem to work, whereas techniques for monitoring and adjusting instruction during teaching do work (Reschly, 1992). However, we believe that the most basic reason for this difference can be found in the focus of the measures applied. Front-end measures designed to predict how students will learn have tended to focus on the summary and interpretation of data about noncurricular student characteristics (e.g., information-processing style, perceptual modality preference, cerebral dominance). In contrast, formative alternatives have tended to focus on measurements of skill and knowledge. The latter procedures, therefore, are simply extensions (or even repetitions) of the techniques used to make the original determinations about what the student should be taught. Formative techniques ask the "what-to-teach" question over and over again and are predicated on the assumption that, if the answer to that question begins to show signs of positive changing, learning must be occurring. These measures constantly reorient the program planner to the curriculum because they are aligned with it. Another critical part of formative evaluation is the visual display of learning. Charts are often used to illustrate progress and facilitate decision making. These charts have dots on them which, if they reflect what the student needs to learn, will illustrate important trends in goal acquisition. If, however, the dots do not reflect what the student needs to learn, the trends will have no implications for programming.

The main point of this brief review of evaluation categories is that the most productive procedures for deciding about *both* what a student needs to be taught, and how that student should be taught, are grounded in the measurement of instructional outcomes. However, as we are about to explain, efforts to define these outcomes have not always appeared important to special educators. It is as though members of the field have preferred to think about who they are working with, not what kind of work they are doing.

THE STRUCTURE AND USE OF THE CURRICULUM: OR, "NOW THAT I KNOW THIS BOAT ISN'T WORKING RIGHT, WOULDN'T IT BE NICE IF I KNEW SOMETHING ABOUT THE ONES THAT DO."

The curriculum is generally defined as a set of learning outcomes (Howell & Evans, 1995; Johnson, 1967; Marx & Walsh, 1988), whereas instruction is the set of actions designed and delivered to bring about these outcomes (Cooper, 1990; Engelmann & Carnine, 1982). Therefore, the curriculum is *what* one teaches and instruction is *how* one teaches it.

Effective program planning hinges on the planner's knowledge of instructional outcomes (Stiggins, 1994). In addition, there is considerable information that the effectiveness of instruction depends on the teacher's skill at maintaining a focus on these outcomes by aligning the activities of instruction with them (Bloom, 1980). However, there is confusion about exactly what the curriculum of special education should be.

Special Education's Historical Noninterest in Curriculum

For years, what is now recognized as "special education" has tended to give the back seat to both curriculum and instruction in favor of discussions of causation and etiology (Carnine & Woodward, 1988). Prior to the 1970s, the students identified as handicapped (now disabled) tended to have severe impairments in sensory, physical, or intellectual functioning, or any combination thereof. During this period, which continued roughly into the mid 1960s, disabled individuals were defined by their congenital symptoms, not by what they had, or had not, learned. Because the field focused almost exclusively on procedures for mapping the sensory, physical, and mental peculiarities of the students, there was little, if any, popular discussion of what curriculum the students needed to be taught (Blanton, 1976). In that context, a special educator was a person who worked with a "type" of student, not a person who engaged in a "type" of instruction and decision making. "Inclusion" was not a "hot" topic at the time, and ideas like "normalization" and "mainstreaming" were not commonly accepted.

Interestingly, although most of special education remained committed to the idea that the disabled had permanent and physical incapacities, during the 1970s the proof of these incapacities gradually shifted from the use of medical examinations to the use of psychometric testing (Mercer, 1973). In addition, the regulatory criteria for inclusion into special education, most notably for the categories of learning disabilities and severe emotional disturbance, evolved an achievement component. The evolution of the achievement deficit eventually gained such standing that, when Public Law 94–142 was passed in 1975, a distinction was made between the *existence* of a disability and the *need* for special education services.

This distinction made it clear that a student who was progressing adequately through the school curriculum, regardless of evidence that he or she had a disability, did not qualify for federally supported special education services (*Hendrick Hudson Central School District Board of Education v. Rowley*, 458 U.S. 176, 1982). At this point, and apparently without much acknowledgment within the emerging field of special education, things began to change. As soon as the existence of a personal defect became subordinate to school achievement, special educators could no longer ignore the curriculum. It was also at this point that the work of persons who were interested in the nature of tasks became important to the people who were interested in the nature of learning.

"Prior Knowledge" Becomes Respectable. By the late 1970s, dissatisfaction with the functional implications of traditional views of ability, combined with new information about the effectiveness of teachers (and what Bloom, 1980, termed *alterable variables*), led many researchers in special education to become interested in curriculum and instruction. This interest and its implications for practice was nicely summarized in Bateman's (1971) book *The Essentials of Teaching.* Bateman asserted, among other things, that:

> Thousands of thick volumes have been devoted to the philosophy of education and the role of schools in our society. The issues are complex and changing, no doubt. However, many believe that until school people clearly articulate measurable objectives, chaos may continue to reign. (p. 3)

This new interest in tasks did not replace interest in students. Instead, it had the effect of changing the way the learning of students was viewed. Whereas the traditional view held that students failed at tasks because of innate limitations, the new view held that students failed at tasks simply because they did not know how to do them. This variable, student prior knowledge, has rapidly became *the* topic of interest in psychology (Chinn & Brewer, 1993; Kulik, Kulik, & Bangert-Drowns, 1990; Marx & Walsh, 1988; Tobias, 1994) and its emergence has affected the understanding of many common problems faced by special educators. Examples of changes in thinking are:

1. The difficulty of a task was no longer seen as fixed; rather, it was understood to vary with the prior knowledge of the person attempting to do it.

2. The acquisition of new knowledge was no longer thought of simply in terms of storage; it came to be understood in terms of how it was actively linked, and related to what was already known.

3. The success of instruction itself was found to depend on what a student had learned about learning, rather than student ability.

4. The single best predictors of success in learning situations were found to be not things like IQ scores, but direct measures of things teachers teach.

These ideas, and others, all had the effect of forcing educators to recognize that what a student already knows is a powerful determinant of future learning. Therefore, finding out what the student knows, both about content being taught and the learning process itself, is necessary for adequate program planning.

PROGRAM PLANNING: OR, "IF I'M GOING TO FIX THE BOAT I NEED A PLAN."

Teacher Decision Making

Clark and Peterson (1986), in their review of teacher thought processes, divide the deliberations of teachers into two categories: planning and inter-active decision making. In this model, planning comes before instruction begins and interactive decision making occurs within the lessons itself (IEP development is a "planning" activity). One conclusion reached in that review was that whereas planning often focuses on the intended outcomes of the lesson (i.e., the curriculum), interactive decisions tend to be based more on the teacher's perceptions of the students. As a result, the alignment between the planned lesson and the lesson which is actually delivered, is sometimes lost. This loss of alignment has been viewed as the major threat to effective instruction (Kameenui, 1991), and seems to be illustrated by the finding that the content of the lessons provided to special education students often has little relation to the content of their IEPs (Dudley-Marling, 1985; Lynch & Beare, 1990; Smith, 1990; Weisenfeld, 1987).

An Example of How Alignment Can Be Lost. Earlier in the chapter we said programming is a thoughtful process. This means that teachers who think differently will make different programming decisions. In the next few paragraphs, we expand on the idea of programming by presenting an illus-tration of lost alignment.

Consider a classroom with a teacher and students. We continue to refer to the particular problems of this teacher and one of his students through-out the remainder of the chapter. All of the characters in this illustration are in trouble: the teacher, a student (Peg), and (just in case you have forgotten) an author who is by now drifting roughly in the direction of Japan. This example also makes frequent reference to "student interest" (although many other variables, such as the examples the teacher uses or the mate-rials he employs, also impact the character of lessons).

In our illustration, the teacher, perceiving that Peg's attention to the lesson is slipping, chooses to present examples that are thought to be of interest to her, rather than those that best delineate the targeted concept of the lesson (Clark & Peterson, 1986). This "error" in presentation is similar to an error that Peg herself makes when she reads. Peg, a fifth grader, has trouble with reading comprehension even though she decodes just fine, knows what the words in the passages mean, and knows quite a bit about the topics she is studying. Her biggest problem is that she selectively fo-cuses on the vivid portions of passages and ignores the portions containing critical information (Grossen & Carnine, 1991). She also seems to be unmotivated because, once she realizes that she is having difficulty with an assignment, she stops working on it (Dweck, 1986). To compound matters, she makes these same mistakes in classification and perseverance while listening to classroom discourse. As a result, she ends up missing important points and failing tests.

Peg's teacher has made a programming error similar to Peg's studying errors by letting the critical information in his lesson slide in order to spice things up for his student. During instruction it is most productive to present examples that are both interesting to the student *and* relevant to the intended outcome of the lesson. However, that is not an easy thing to do because it requires a teacher to have extensive knowledge of the content as well as accurate perceptions about student interest. In addition, the problem is compounded by the reality that some students find some things boring whereas other students do not. Given this reality, a teacher wishing to maintain a group's focus on planned outcomes seems to have three available programming solutions:

1. Find an example relevant to the outcome *and* of interest to every student in the class.
2. Periodically abandon the goal and move to topics that are likely to be of the greatest interest to the most students.
3. Abandon the interests of some students while continuing to focus on the goal of the lesson using examples that are of interest to the majority of the class.

There are problems with each of these solutions. The first is most likely impossible to carry out (at least on a routine basis) because it requires extraordinary knowledge of content, infallible awareness of student interest, superhuman teacher flexibility, and a group of students who just happen to all be interested in the same thing. The problem with the second solution is that it results in a loss of alignment and, assuming that the preselected goal was important, a loss in instructional effectiveness. The problem with the third solution is that, when carried out, it has the effect of causing students in the class (in this case Peg) to be disenfranchised.

As provided earlier, teachers can really only pick the second or third solution (or, more realistically, a combination of the two). The degree to which teachers in general opt for the second is probably reflected in the data on low teacher effectiveness (e.g., Rosenshine & Stevens, 1986). The degree to which they select the third is revealed in the information on drop-out rates, teacher "write-offs," and referrals to special education (Ysseldyke et al., 1984). That is because option three, the programming decision to abandon the interests of some students in order to tailor examples to the instructional goal while maintaining the interests of other students, appears to be employed selectively. In other words, some students are more apt to have their interests ignored than others (Anderman & Maehr, 1994).

Regardless of the variable used (we could have substituted "student interest" with "academic skill level"), the point of this example is that students like Peg are routinely marginalized because they cannot stick with instruction tailored for the majority. These students fall behind and leave us trying to figure out what form of instructional support (i.e., modification of programming) we can use to help them catch up. Unfortunately, the problem is not just one of instructional delivery (Zigmond et. al., 1995), but is also a problem of what is being taught. As we explain shortly, the content of IEPs seems to indicate that academic skills (particularly basic academic skills) are the *only* things that appear in many special education student programs because they are the only skills many special educators think about when trying to solve problems for students like Peg. As we illustrate through the IEP analysis, this preoccupation with basic skills, although justified for many students, fails to meet the needs of others. There are several possible reasons for this fixation:

1. Many special educators may think basic academics are the most important skills in a student's education.
2. Basic skills are the only things many special education teachers believe they are supposed to teach.
3. The evaluative tools used to guide the thinking of most special educators only provide functional information (i.e., information about things teachers can actually alter through instruction) in the area of basic skills.

Each of these three reasons for fixating on basic skills can be accounted for by the absence of a thoroughly defined special education curriculum. Without a richer set of learning outcomes to think about, teachers must think about and evaluate basic skills, and that is all their IEPs reflect.

Task-Related Knowledge. Peg is failing to comprehend what she reads because she selectively attends to only one type of information (i.e., vivid descriptions) while ignoring information that is relevant. Apparently she does not need instruction in basic reading skills because, if she lacked decoding proficiency or knowledge of the vocabulary in the passage, she would be just as unprepared to deal with vivid descriptors. She needs to be taught something else—how to discriminate relevant information from vivid text— but that is not a skill commonly found within the general education curriculum, or on IEPs. Nevertheless, if Peg should be taught how to obtain information from text, then it appears that there is a fourth programming solution available to the teacher in our example.

A QUICK SUMMARY: OR, "LET ME SEE IF I'VE GOT THIS STRAIGHT. WE HAVE AN AMERICAN-MADE BOAT, BUT A SET OF METRIC TOOLS."

It is time for a summary. So far we have talked about the history of special education, the evolution of the concept of disabilities, changes in the way learning is conceptualized, the problems of Peg and her teacher, and a boat.

Current thinking about success and failure in school accentuates the role of prior knowledge and de-emphasizes the influence of fixed (i.e., unalterable) impairments, abilities, or both of the student. In some cases, the prior knowledge in question is knowledge of the task being taught. However, in other cases success, or failure, to learn may depend on prior knowledge of task-related skills. Task-related skills have not typically appeared in the curriculum and such skills are not routinely taught to most students in a formal, that is intentional, fashion. Therefore, task-related skills are often ignored during evaluation and are often missing when teachers try to think of programming solutions for student problems. This oversight may be attributed in part to the failure to adequately define the curriculum of special education.

COMMON OUTCOMES IN SPECIAL EDUCATION: OR, "ALL RIGHT, EXACTLY WHAT ISN'T WORKING?"

We examine the content of typical IEPs in order to find out if shifts in the thinking about learning problems and curriculum have affected programming in special education.

The IEP is intended to serve as the basis for providing a remedy for educational deficits identified in the assessment process. The IEP should provide a blueprint of what to teach and at what rate progress should occur in the identified areas of deficit. However, in reality, the IEP frequently lacks congruence with diagnostic information (Fiedler & Knight, 1986; Reiher, 1992; Smith & Simpson, 1989). Furthermore, the IEP frequently emphasizes academic goal areas to the exclusion of other deficit areas identified in the assessment process (Lynch & Beare, 1990). Thus, it cannot be automatically assumed that the IEP reflects appropriate instructional interventions for individual students.

There is further evidence that questions our assumptions regarding the contribution of diagnostic/assessment data to instructional recommendations, and thus, to the importance of congruence between diagnosis and IEP goals and objectives. The diagnostic information on which IEP current levels of performance are based frequently consists of data from psychometric measures that are not useful in instructional planning (Arter & Jenkins, 1979; Reschley, 1992). The IEP process as currently defined may not provide the critical data needed to develop appropriate instructional programs.

The development of the IEP and instructional programming, then, may not necessarily be the same things. To further compound the difficulties with the IEP process, procedural compliance requirements can diminish the utility of the IEP. It is possible to have a "legally correct" IEP that meets the minimal stipulations of law, but is educationally frivolous. Unfortunately, there seems to be a tendency to take what is called for in the regulations and to convert these into the image of best practice (when in fact they may be far from that). For example, the 30 days allowed between evaluation and IEP development becomes the time it usually takes, not the maximum time that is permitted. Similarly, the description of special education services becomes a check mark next to "resource room" and a blank for "minutes of service per week." Those may be minimum requirements allowed by law, but they do not represent good programming.

EXTENDING THE SCOPE OF CURRICULUM: OR, "WAIT A MINUTE. HERE'S AN IDEA."

Figure 6.3 (Howell, in press) illustrates a view of curriculum that is expanded to include task-related content. The figure depicts the idea that students have learning problems because they are missing one or more elements of the essential knowledge that they need to succeed in class. Figure 6.3 also illustrates various categories of knowledge, and provides references to student behavior that might lead a teacher to focus on objectives from one or more of those categories. It also indicates what sort of instruction might be needed given the category targeted. Here is what all of these categories, references, and indications mean.

Task-Specific Knowledge

This is the stuff that most people think is taught in school. About the only surprise here might be the inclusion of *social skills* as a category of content equivalent in status to *academic skills*. This may seem out of place, because social-skill objectives do not appear on IEPs with the frequency that concern about social skills would seem to predict. However, we are placing social skills under the task-specific heading because students who fail to perform as expected in that domain are referred to special education not unlike those

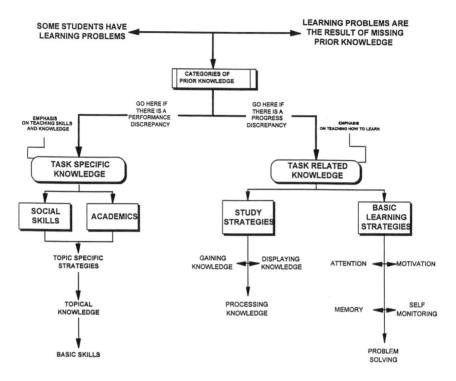

FIG. 6.3. An expanded view of curriculum.

who fail to comprehend text. Additionally, we have no information to indicate that the task-related knowledge required for the processing of social skills lessons is any different from that required for the processing of academic lessons.

Under the headings of academics and social skills three subheadings appear. These are *topic-specific strategies, topical knowledge,* and *basic skills.* Basic skills are those things that students must use over and over in order to carry out particular tasks. They are the fundamental tools for task completion and typically need to be learned to automaticity so that, during their use, they do not occupy students' working memory (Frederiksen, 1984; Rigney, 1980). Topical knowledge refers to the set of concepts and principles that a student must learn in order to understand a topic. These are the things that define a topic and they are often referred to as "higher level" knowledge (Nuthall & Alton-Lee, 1995). Topic-specific strategies are the rules and procedures that students follow to combine their proficiency at basic skills with topical knowledge in order to carry out operations. Without topic-specific strategies, a student may understand a task and have all of the prerequisite skills needed to carry it out, but still fail to perform because he or she does not know how to go about doing the work.

The headings and subheadings in Fig. 6.3 do not refer to set domains of content. For example, because Peg is in the fifth grade, decoding is considered a basic skill for her. However, when she was in the first grade she was taught topical knowledge of, and topic specific strategies for, decoding. This means that the same content may fall within any of these three subheadings depending on where the student is in the process of knowledge acquisition.

Task-Related Knowledge

This domain of skills and knowledge is seldom taught in the same systematic way that one might teach academics. As represented in Fig. 6.3, it is composed of two categories: *study strategies* and *basic learning strategies*. Study strategies are those skills needed to learn from classroom presentations and activities designed by teachers and delivered in schools (Gleason, Colvin, & Archer, 1991). They are often specific to particular modes of presentation (e.g., lecture, discussion, reading) and particular modes of display (e.g., multiple-choice testing, essay exams).

Strategies for *gaining knowledge* are used to get information from a source, whereas *processing-knowledge* strategies are used to organize and treat information. These include techniques that students use to actively process the information they have already gained (e.g., by reviewing previously taken notes prior to a new class meeting, or by writing summaries of chapters read). The strategies used to *display knowledge* communicate what a student knows.

Under *basic learning strategies* in Fig. 6.3 you will find another set of subheadings referring to skills that are often brought up by teachers and school psychologists, but which are seldom directly included in programs of instruction. This category of skills is so large that we deal with it here by briefly running through the definition of each subheading and then using one of them in the continuation of our three ongoing examples (i.e., the teacher, Peg, and the boat). Before defining the subheadings, however, there is an important point that needs to be made about this domain of content: It can be learned!

Students learn how to use basic learning strategies (Alexander, Kulikowich, & Jetton, 1994). They may have learned adaptive patterns for attending, remembering, persevering, monitoring, and problem solving or they may have learned nonadaptive patterns, but the patterns they use are the result of their experiences and are determined by the knowledge they have acquired. This domain, at least in this chapter, is not comprised of fixed and unalterable student abilities and disabilities. It does not refer to patterns of use determined by congenital and structural processing impairments. It may refer to the same patterns, but here the determination of these patterns is attributed to prior knowledge, rather than fixed ability.

Attention skills are those students use to selectively focus on one thing while ignoring others. *Memory* skills are those related to the storage and recall of information. *Motivation* skills provide students with interest in a topic and assure that they persevere in the face of difficulty in order to finish work. *Self-monitoring* skills allow students to be aware of their circumstances and their own behavior. *Problem-solving* skills allow students to generate and select solutions in order to overcome obstacles.

Once again, these subheadings do not designate fixed bodies of content. These basic learning strategies are interrelated. For example, without attention, a student's self-monitoring skills will not alert him or her to the need for problem solving. Similarly, neither study strategies nor basic learning strategies can exist apart from some aspect of task-specific knowledge. This means that a student cannot attend without something to attend to, and a student cannot display knowledge without some knowledge to display. Consequently, the domains of task-related knowledge and task-specific knowledge must merge whenever evaluation and instruction occur (i.e., talking about teaching attention without referencing what the student should attend to is meaningless). However, they may be thought about separately during the planning process and programs can be developed to teach them.

PROGRAMMING WITHIN THE EXTENDED CURRICULUM: OR, "I MAY NOT KNOW ANYTHING ABOUT BOATS, BUT I DO KNOW HOW TO YELL FOR HELP."

Students are referred for special or remedial instruction because they are failing to perform adequately in the academic arena, social-skill arena, or both of task-specific knowledge (for example, in Peg's case her referral would be for performance deficits in reading comprehension). When a student has a performance deficit, the standard way to begin programming for that student is to evaluate his or her status on the skills (i.e., prior knowledge) required to succeed on the task of interest. If topic-specific strategies, topical knowledge, basic skills, or any combination thereof are found missing or deficient, these are selected as goals and objectives. Once the goals and objectives are identified, methods for teaching them are also selected. So where does task-related knowledge come in?

Students are not referred if they have deficits exclusively in the domain of task-related knowledge such as failure to use study skills or basic learning strategies. That is because if a kid can do academics and get along with others (i.e., is competent at anticipated levels of task-specific knowledge) it never occurs to anyone to check and see how she studies or learns. One should not tamper when things are working! However, when a student *is not* succeeding in an area of task-specific knowledge, there is always the possibility that this failure may be related to problems with task-related skills.

The easiest way to explain the difference between a student who is only deficient in task-specific knowledge and one who is also deficient in task related knowledge is to show how they learn. Figures 6.4a and 6.4b show the charts of two students as they acquired reading comprehension skills. Initially, both of the students were missing important knowledge of the comprehension process, so special programs were developed, the students were taught, and both of them improved in their performance. After the intervention, Jimmy continued to perform as expected by improving his skills. However, Peg fell behind again. Why? Apparently Jimmy knew how to learn within a general educational program and without the continued assistance of a specially designed program. However, Peg only had enough

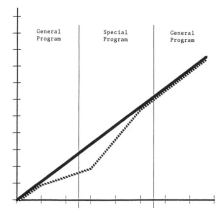

4A – Jimmy

FIG. 6.4A. Jimmy's progress.

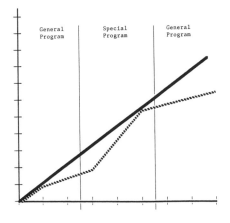

4B – Peg

FIG. 6.4B. Peg's progress.

skill in the task-related area to learn with the level of assistance provided by the special program. (You may be wondering why Jimmy fell behind in the first place. Several possibilities occur to us, including the possibility that no one ever taught him how to comprehend.)

In the case of a student like Peg it is necessary to do more than map out the sequence of task-specific knowledge that needs to be learned and to focus instruction on that. It is also necessary to determine what task-related skills she needs to acquire in order to progress adequately with the least amount of special programming. It can be seen in Fig. 6.4b that Peg can learn, as long as she is receiving the level of assistance provided by the special intervention. However, to fully address her needs, it is necessary to teach her how to learn without such assistance. In the section that follows, we offer general guidelines for productively thinking through problems in the domains of task-related knowledge:

1. Do not rely on performance data to identify and solve problems in the task-related domain. These problems are indicated by the failure to improve (i.e., progress) in a given setting or under a given set of instructional conditions. Consequently, you will need information on how students progress over time, not on how well they perform on a particular task.

2. Begin with the assumption that students "learn how to learn" and that failures to learn are the result of missing knowledge, not structural pathology.

3. Believe that learning problems are alterable and can be fixed through instruction.

4. Only attempt to evaluate and describe task-related knowledge within the content of the academic skills, social skills, or both that the student needs to learn. If you do not do this, you may end up off in the periphery somewhere trying to teach "note taking" for its own sake or trying to teach students to "be motivated." One way to stay grounded in task-specific knowledge is to avoid making statements about things like "motivation" without tying these constructs to content and behavior (e.g., "It looks to me like Peg isn't motivated to *focus on the important parts of stories* because she only *repeats* the parts that seem exciting to her").

5. Develop a clear understanding of the content of task-related knowledge.

6. Once you have a clear understanding of the content in each domain, try to separate your thinking about study strategies from your thinking about basic learning strategies (but do not fall into the trap of believing the domains can actually exist without each other). Think about one of them and *then* think about the other.

7. A focus on study strategies may be indicated if poor progress is associated with classes where the demands for good study skills are very high.

It may also be indicated when the student does well in classes where the teacher and the texts are considerate.

8. Focus on the content of basic learning strategies if the student fails to progress in both school and nonschool settings, or in contexts where "studying" is not required. (Be careful here; the need to gain, process and display knowledge comes up plenty of times outside of school.)

9. If the problem seems to be in the domain of basic learning strategies, understand that things like memory and attention cannot be isolated from each other, or from content (i.e., there is no attention without something to which one can attend).

10. Do not limit evaluation to the student. Base your efforts at programming on an analysis of the differences between those tasks and situations in which the student learns effectively, and those in which she does not. Some high-impact differences to look for include: the level of structure; the grouping arrangements; the degree of autonomy allowed to students; the clarity of goals, assignments, and explanations; and the general quality of classroom discourse (Rueda, Goldenberg, & Gallimore, 1993; Ysseldyke & Christenson, 1987).

11. Emphasize teaching the student *how* to learn.

12. Teach task-related strategies to a high level of proficiency. This is necessary because most students will already be using nonadaptive strategies for task completion (such as guessing, cheating, and using known strategies that work on the wrong skills), task avoidance (such as inventing excuses, disrupting the class, trying to negotiate their way out of the requirement, or any combination thereof), or both. Therefore, programs for teaching task-related objectives must include sufficient opportunities for practice to allow the student to build proficiency. High levels of proficiency and comfort are needed in order for the new adaptive skills to compete with previously practiced, nonadaptive patterns of attention, motivation, memory, self-monitoring, problem solving, or any combination of these.

AN EXAMPLE OF CONTENT CLARIFICATION: OR, "THE FIRST TIME I TRIED CALLING TO A PASSING BOAT EVERYONE WAVED. MAYBE I NEED TO THINK ABOUT HOW TO LOOK DESPERATE."

Guideline number 5 in the previous list recommends that you become thoroughly familiar with the content of task-related knowledge before you try to program interventions for that particular domain. To give you an idea of how that may be done, we show you how objectives can be generated for a domain such as motivation.

Figure 6.5 is a table of specifications for the domain of motivation. It has content statements (e.g., Interest) listed down the left side and behav-

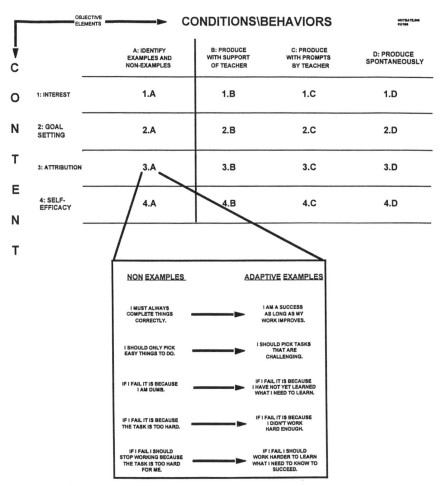

FIG. 6.5. Table of specifications for motivation.

ior/condition statements running across the top (e.g., Produce with teacher support). At the intersections within the table, objectives are indicated with numbers and letters. For example, the objectives related to attribution might read as follows:

3.a. "The student will accurately discriminate between adaptive and maladaptive statements of attribution modeled by peers."

3.b. "The student will correctly repeat adaptive statements of attribution supplied by the teacher."

3.c. "Every time the student is prompted to do so the student will replace nonadaptive statements of attribution with those which are adaptive."

3.d. "The student will use adaptive statements of attribution, in the same proportion as successful students, to explain classroom successes and failures."

(To help clarify what is meant by maladaptive and adaptive attributional statements, a list of them is supplied at the bottom of the Fig. 6.5.)

It is possible to elaborate on each of the objectives generated in Fig. 6.5 by attending to the literature that supports their relationship to motivation. For example, the relationship of "interest" to motivation has been discussed by Alexander, Kulikowich, and Schulze (1994), the importance of "goals" to reinforcement has been investigated by Cameron and Pierce (1994) and the impact of a student's "definition of success" has been described by Dweck (1986) and Anderman and Maehr (1994). The critical role of student attributions relative to success and failure (the source for the content of objectives 3.a–3.d) has also been described extensively (Dweck, 1986; Graham, 1994; Skaalvik & Rankin, 1995; Weiner, 1994).

Tables of specifications, like the one in Fig. 6.5, can be used to generate objectives, plan tests, and monitor student progress. However, one final point about this example needs to be made. As presented in Fig. 6.5, the domain of motivation is defined only by its content and the conditions under which behaviors will be displayed. Although these elements of objectives are important, even defining, they are not the only elements (Popham, 1995). Objectives must also have statements of criteria that specify the level of competency a student will obtain (these are present in the sample objectives given earlier, e.g., ". . . will *correctly* repeat . . ." but they do not appear in the table). When setting criteria it is important to aim for high levels of proficiency. This is because the new skills you may be teaching will often need to compete with existing nonadaptive skills. In some cases, students will have practiced these nonadaptive skills to the point of automaticity.

SOLUTIONS TO THE PROBLEMS: OR, "I THINK SOUNDING THE HORN, WAVING A WHITE T-SHIRT, AND SETTING THE ICE CHEST ON FIRE SHOULD GET THEIR ATTENTION."

Peg's Teacher

As you recall, the teacher's problem was trying to figure out how to maintain task focus while also maintaining student interest. Prior to the introduction of Fig. 6.2, the teacher had three programming solutions: (a) finding an example of interest to every student in the class; (b) abandoning the goal; or (c) abandoning the interests of some students (e.g., Peg) while continuing to focus on the goal of the lesson. Consideration of task-related knowledge, and the belief that it can be taught, introduced a fourth option, namely, (d) to teach uninterested students the skills they need to learn in spite of their disinterest.

Expanding the view of curriculum to include task-related knowledge allows the teacher who is having trouble providing equivalent learning to the members of a heterogeneous class to abolish some of the heterogeneity by teaching all of the students how to survive in that class. For example, Cohen and Lotan (1995) have concluded that "it is possible to produce equal-status behavior in heterogeneous classrooms as well as significant gains in achievement" (p. 118), by altering the nature and frequency of teacher talk to low-status students.

To some extent, every teacher does things to prepare students for success, just as every student makes some efforts to figure out what his or her teachers demand. However, it is sometimes impossible to go beyond such common efforts when there are students in the class who need to be taught skills that almost everyone else has already acquired. In these cases, evaluation and remediation should occur following the sequence in Fig. 6.1. This means, in part, comparing the demands of the classroom to the task-related skills of the individual student. If such comparisons reveal that the student only lacks the competence to learn in this one particular setting, then the student should stay there and be taught whatever specific skill he or she is missing. However, if the student exhibits problems learning across a variety of contexts, general programming may be needed to teach the set of task-related skills the student lacks.

Peg

As you recall, Peg was mistaking vivid information for important information in both reading and lecture/discussion. This means that she needs to be taught skills in selective attention for both reading comprehension and general class presentation. For the sake of our example let us assume that the comprehension portion of this goal is in keeping with the instructional activities of her current class. That means she should continue to receive the same comprehension program that everyone else is getting because selective attention to relevant information is being taught to everyone in her class. However, it is not likely that she will benefit from that program, even though its focus is correct, without learning how to understand the teacher's presentations (and we saw evidence of that in Fig. 6.4b). Therefore, she needs a special program to teach her how to subordinate (i.e., selectively attend) within the flow of information presented in class. Because, in our example, this is not a skill taught in Peg's class, she needs a specially designed program to teach it to her. She does not need the objectives in basic skills or comprehension specific strategies that would commonly appear in a program for someone with her difficulties. She needs objectives from the domains of study skills and attention, and she may need assistance beyond what her general education teacher can supply to learn these objectives. This is a result of the fact that what she needs to be taught is not currently being taught by that teacher.

Dr. Howell

After some attempts at marine engine repair, our author remembered and employed one of the most basic of all problem-solving strategies. He asked for help and was towed to the marina by another boat. He is now working on building proficiency at the strategy so that he will ask for help earlier—possibly even before buying a boat.

SUMMARY

This chapter includes a discussion of the role of task-related knowledge in school success, which was defined in general terms, and specific portions of it were represented through examples and illustrations. The argument was made that many of the weaknesses present in current efforts at programming, as revealed through an analysis of IEPs, can be avoided if the present view of special education curriculum is expanded to include task-related knowledge. It was asserted that this expansion, once incorporated into the model of programming presented in Fig. 6.1, will lead to more productive thinking by professionals interested in finding solutions for students who have not yet learned how to learn.

REFERENCES

Alexander, P. A., Kulikowich, J. M., & Jetton, T. L. (1994). The role of subject-matter knowledge and interest in the processing of linear and nonlinear texts. *Review of Educational Research, 64*(2), 201–252.

Alexander, P. A., Kulikowich, J. M., & Schulze, S. K. (1994). How Subject-matter knowledge affects recall and interest. *American Educational Research Journal, 32*, 313–337.

Anderman, E. M., & Maehr, M. L. (1994). Motivation and schooling in the middle grades. *Review of Educational Research, 64*(2), 287–309.

Arter, J. A., & Jenkins, J. R. (1979). Differential diagnosis prescriptive teaching: A critical appraisal. *Review of Educational Research, 49*, 517–555.

Bateman, B. D. (1971). *The essentials for teaching.* Sioux Falls, SD: Dimension.

Bateman, B. D. (1996). *Better IEPs* (2nd ed.). Longmont, CO: Sopris West.

Blanton, R. L. (1976). Historical perspectives on classification of mental retardation. In N. Hobbs (Ed.), *Issues in the classification of children* (Vol. 1, pp. 164–193). San Francisco: Jossey-Bass.

Bloom, B. S. (1980). The new direction in education research: Alterable variables. *Phi Delta Kappan, 61*, 382–385.

Cameron, J. C., & Pierce, W. D. (1994). Reinforcement, reward, and intrinsic motivation: A meta-analysis. *Review of Educational Research, 64*(3), 363–423.

Carnine, D., & Woodward, J. (1988). Paradigms lost: Learning disabilities and the new ghost in the old machine. *Journal of Learning Disabilities, 21*(4), 233–243.

Chinn, C. A., & Brewer, W. F. (1993). The role of anomalous data in knowledge acquisition: A theoretical framework and implications for science instruction. *Review of Educational Research, 63*(1), 1–49.

Clark, C. M., & Peterson, P. L. (1986). Teachers' thought processes. In M. C. Wittrock (Ed.), *Handbook of research on teaching* (3rd ed., pp. 255–296). New York: Macmillan.

Cohen, E. G., & Lotan, R. A. (1995). Producing equal-status interaction in the heterogeneous classroom. *American Educational Research Journal, 32*, 99–120.

Cooper, J. M. (1990). *Classroom teaching skills* (4th ed.). Lexington, MA: D. C. Heath.

Deno, S. L. (1989). Curriculum-based measurement and special education services: A fundamental and direct relationship. In M. R. Shinn (Ed.), *Curriculum-based measurement: Assessing special children* (pp. 1–17). New York: Guilford.

Deno, S. L., & Espin, C. A. (1991). Evaluation strategies for preventing and remediating basic skill deficits. In G. Stoner, M. Shinn, & H. Walker (Eds.), *Interventions for achievement and behavior problems* (pp. 79–97). Silver Springs, MD: National Association of School Psychologists.

Dixon, R., & Carnine, D. (1992). A response to Heshusius' "Curriculum-based assessment and direct instruction: Critical reflections on fundamental assumptions." *Exceptional Children, 58*(5), 461–463.

Dudley-Marling, C. (1985). Perceptions of the usefulness of the IEP by teachers of learning disabled and emotionally disturbed children. *Psychology in the Schools, 22*, 65–67.

Dweck, C. (1986). Motivational processes affecting learning. *American Psychologist, 41*(10), 1040–1048.

Engelmann, S., & Carnine, D. (1982). *Theory of instruction: principles and applications.* New York: Irvington.

Fiedler, J. F., & Knight, R. R. (1986, November). Congruence between assessed needs and IEP goals of identified behaviorally disabled students. *Behavioral Disorders*, 22–27.

Frederiksen, N. (1984). Implications of cognitive theory for instruction in problem solving. *Review of Educational Research, 54*, 363–407.

Fuchs, D., & Fuchs, L. (1995, March). What's "special" about special education. *Phi Delta Kappan*, 522–530.

Gleason, M. M., Colvin, G., & Archer, A. L. (1991). Interventions for improving study skills. In G. Stoner, M. Shinn, & H. Walker (Eds.), *Interventions for achievement and behavior problems* (pp. 130–167). Silver Springs, MD: National Association of School Psychologists.

Graham, S. (1994). Motivation in African Americans. *Review of Educational Research, 64*(1), 55–117.

Grossen, B., & Carnine, D. (1991). Strategies for maximizing reading success in the regular classroom. In G. Stoner, M. Shinn, & H. Walker (Eds.), *Interventions for achievement and behavior problems* (pp. 333–355). Silver Springs, MD: National Association of School Psychologists.

Hendrick Hudson Central School District Board of Education v. Rowley, 458 U.S. 176, 203, 102 S. Ct. 3034, 3049, 73 L.Ed. 2d 690 (1982).

Howell, K. W. (in press). *Curriculum-based evaluation: Teaching and decision making* (3rd ed.). Monterey, CA: Brooks/Cole.

Howell, K. W., & Evans, D. G. (1995). A comment on "Must instructionally useful performance assessment be based in the curriculum?" *Exceptional Children, 64*(4), 394–396.

Howell, K. W., Fox, S. L., & Morehead, M. K. (1993). *Curriculum-based evaluation: Teaching and decision making* (2nd ed.). Monterey, CA: Brooks/Cole.

Johnson, M. (1967). Definitions and models in curriculum theory. *Educational Theory, 7*, 127–140.

Kameenui, E. J. (1991). Toward a scientific pedagogy of learning disabilities: A sameness in the message. *Journal of Learning Disabilities, 24*(6), 364–372.

Kauffman, J. M., Lloyd, J. W., Baker, J., & Riedel, T. M. (1995). Inclusion of all students with emotional or behavioral disorders? Let's think again. *Phi Delta Kappan, 76,* 542–546.

Korzybski, A. (1948). *Science and sanity: An introduction to non-Aristotelian systems and general semantics* (3rd ed.). Lakeville, CT: Institute of General Semantics.

Kulik, J. A., Kulik, C. C., & Bangert-Drowns, R. L. (1990). Is there better evidence on mastery learning? A response to Slavin. *Review of Educational Research, 60*(2), 303–307.

Lynch, E. C., & Beare, P. L. (1990). The quality of IEP objectives and their relevance to instruction for students with mental retardation and behavioral disorders. *Remedial and Special Education, 11,* 48–55.

Malouf, D., & Schiller, E. (1995). Practice and research in special education. *Exceptional Children, 61*(5), 414–424.

Mann, L., & Sabatino, D. A. (1985). *Foundations of cognitive process in remedial and special education.* Rockville, MD: Aspen Systems Corp.

Marx, R. W., & Walsh, J. (1988). Learning from academic tasks. *The Elementary School Journal, 88*(3), 207–219.

Mercer, J. R. (1973). *Labeling the mentally retarded: Clinical and social system perspectives on mental retardation.* Berkeley: University of California Press.

Nuthall, G., & Alton-Lee, A. (1995). Assessing classroom learning: How students use their knowledge and experience to answer classroom achievement test questions in science and social studies. *American Educational Research Journal, 32,* 185–223.

Popham, W. J. (1995). *Classroom assessment: What teachers need to know.* Boston: Allyn & Bacon.

Reiher, T. (1992). Identified deficits and their congruence to the IEP for behaviorally disordered students. *Behavioral Disorders, 17,* 167–177.

Renick, P. R. (1995). Inclusion: An ethical perspective. *National Forum of Applied Educational Research Journal, 8*(1), 44–47.

Reschly, D. J. (1992). Special education decision making and functional/behavioral assessment. In W. Stainback & S. Stainback (Eds.), *Controversial issues confronting special education* (pp. 127–128). Needham Heights, MA: Allyn & Bacon.

Rigney, J. W. (1980). Cognitive learning strategies and dualities in information processing. In R. Snow, P. A. Federico, & W. Motaguel (Eds.), *Aptitude, learning and instruction* (Vol. 1, pp. 27–63). Hillsdale, NJ: Lawrence Erlbaum Associates.

Rosenshine, B., & Stevens, R. (1986). Teaching functions. In M. C. Wittrock (Ed.), *Handbook of research on teaching* (3rd ed., pp. 376–391). New York: Macmillan.

Rueda, R., Goldenberg, C., & Gallimore, R. (1993). *A Manual for the use of the instructional conversion rating scale.* National Center on Cultural Diversity. Second Language Learning and Center for Applied Linguistics. Santa Cruz: University of California.

Skaalvik, E. M., & Rankin, R. (1995). A test of the internal/external frame of reference model at different levels of math and verbal self-perception. *American Educational Research Journal, 32,* 161–184.

Smith, S. W. (1990). Individualized education programs (IEPs) in special education—from intent to acquiescence. *Exceptional Children, 57,* 6–14.

Smith, S. W., & Simpson, R. L. (1989). An analysis of individualized education programs (IEPs) for students with behavior disorders. *Behavioral Disorders, 14,* 107–116.

Snider, V. E. (1992). Learning styles and learning to read. *Remedial and Special Education, 13*(1), 6–18.

Spady, W. G. (1988). Organizing for results: The basis of authentic restructuring and reform. *Educational Leadership, 46,* 4–8.

Stiggins, R. J. (1994). *Student-centered classroom assessment.* New York: Macmillan.

Swanson, H. L. (1988). Toward a metatheory of learning disabilities. *Journal of Learning Disabilities, 21*(4), 196–209.

Thorndike, E. L. (1917). *Education: A first book.* New York: Macmillan.

Tobias, S. (1994). Interest, prior knowledge, and learning. *Review of Educational Research, 64*(1), 37–54.

Weiner, B. (1994). Integrating social and personal theories of achievement striving. *Review of Educational Research, 64*(1), 557–573.

Weisenfeld, R. B. (1987). Functionality in the IEPs of children with Down Syndrome. *Mental Retardation, 25,* 281–286.

Ysseldyke, J. E., Algozzine, B. J., & Thurlow, M. L. (Eds.). (1992). *Critical issues in special education.* Boston: Houghton Mifflin.

Ysseldyke, J. E., & Christenson, S. L. (1987). *TIES: The instructional environment scale.* Austin, TX: Pro-Ed.

Ysseldyke, J. E., Thurlow, M. L., Mecklenburg, C., & Graden, J. (1984). Opportunity to learn for regular and special education students during reading instruction. *Remedial and Special Education, 5,* 29–37.

Zigmond, N., Jenkins, J., Fuchs, L. S., Deno, S., Fuchs, D., Baker, J. N., Jenkins, L., & Couthino, M. (1995). Special education in restructured schools: Findings from three multi-year studies. *Phi Delta Kappan, 76*(4), 531–540.

7

Assessment of Social Competence in Students With Learning Disabilities

Diane Haager
California State University, Los Angeles

Sharon Vaughn
University of Miami

For the past two decades, research has addressed critical issues related to the social competence of individuals with learning disabilities (LD). A significant body of literature highlights the social difficulties of youngsters with LD as compared to typically achieving, nondisabled peers (see, for reviews, Hazel & Schumaker, 1988; Pearl, Donahue, & Bryan, 1986). Studies have also examined the social development of individuals with LD relative to normal developmental patterns (e.g., Vaughn, Haager, Hogan, & Kouzekanani, 1992) and the extent to which within-individual differences occur over time (Vaughn & Hogan, 1994). According to Killen (1989), the ongoing, active, social processes of interpretation, evaluation, and coordination of social events are central to understanding social development in general. Indeed, most of the social competence research related to individuals with LD could be viewed as examining how individuals with LD interpret, evaluate, or coordinate social events.

Killen (1989) also identified three dimensions key to understanding these social processes: context, conflict, and coordination. According to Killen, context influences the type and structure of social interactions. Thus, youngsters behave differently in various social settings, such as their own home, the homes of others, school, and community settings. The issue of context is particularly important when considering the social competence of individuals with LD. We would expect that the context of school would not be particularly "comfortable" for students with LD given their significant academic difficulties in this context and, thus, they may not demonstrate their best social behaviors. In fact, with few exceptions, most of what we know about individuals with LD we know from their behavior, peer reports, and self-reports at school which are largely about school. Therefore, we believe that comprehensive social assessment of individuals with or without LD must consider relevant contextual factors at school and outside of school.

A second dimension, conflicts, provides an understanding of how an individual negotiates and interprets events and behaviors across settings. Assessment in this area is largely dependent on observation and interpretation, self-reports, or reports from others. Because the collection of observation data is time consuming and expensive, we have relied on the perceptions of others, such as teachers, parents, and peers, to interpret and judge the social negotiations of individuals with LD and on self-reports to understand social interpretations. How an individual interprets events and behaviors is perhaps the most difficult area to assess and interpret, particularly for students with LD who have communication or memory problems. A consistent concern with self-reports is the extent to which individuals are able to tell you what and why a behavior occurred or their interpretation of what they or other individuals have done. This problem is exacerbated when a student has communication difficulties that inhibit retell or a memory problem that interferes with recall.

Third, the process of social coordination, how one interacts with and responds to others, can be assessed through observation, self-report, or reports from others, often peers and teachers. A limited number of observational studies have examined the interactions of students with LD as compared to students without LD (NLD) and have demonstrated less positive interactions with peers as well as teachers (McIntosh, Vaughn, Schumm, Haager, & Lee, 1993).

Although academic difficulties, by definition, characterize students with LD, there is little question that many students with LD also demonstrate significant difficulties with social relationships or display inappropriate social behaviors (see, for reviews, Hazel & Schumaker, 1988; Pearl et al., 1986). Researchers and practitioners are quick to point out, however, that not all youngsters with LD have significant social difficulties. In fact, for some students with LD, the social domain is their area of strength, as evidenced by the testimony of an adult with severe reading disabilities: "I could talk my way out of anything. I couldn't read in high school but I always managed to do 'OK' because I could get the teachers to believe anything I told them."

Significant social difficulties are known to characterize students with other types of disorders such as behavior disorders, attention deficit hyperactive disorder, and social maladjustment. Many of these disorders overlap with LD, making identification of individuals with LD difficult. It is the overlap of these related disorders with LD that has contributed to controversy and debate regarding definitional issues and has made the construct of LD the most difficult disorder to define (Fletcher, Francis, Rourke, Shaywitz, & Shaywitz, 1993; Lyon & Moats, 1993). This issue is important as we consider the social assessment of students with LD, because social problems are often more pronounced when students have other disabilities as well.

When the Interagency Committee on Learning Disabilities was established to determine the state of knowledge regarding LD and to consider the formal definition of LD, they reviewed assessment in the social domain and provided several recommendations (Interagency Committee on Learning Disabilities, 1987). They indicated that optimal social assessment of individuals with LD would be done with an instrument that demonstrates the following characteristics:

1. It is based on empirically validated social skills problems of individuals with LD.
2. It must be psychometrically sound.
3. It could be used in school settings.
4. It must be able to assess individuals across the developmental age range from preschool through adulthood.
5. It must allow for the assessment of all social competence skills.

We agree with Gresham and Elliott (1989) that it is highly unlikely that a single measurement tool could adequately demonstrate all of the recommended qualities for social assessment and that multiple assessment tools will need to be used. There are many tools that generate relevant information about the social functioning of individuals. Peer ratings, observational measures, ratings by teachers and parents, and self-reports each provide an important piece of the social competence puzzle.

In both research and practice, social assessment has typically provided a simplistic overview of readily observable social behaviors of a target student from the perspective of a single person (most often a classroom teacher) and in one setting (the classroom). We believe that optimal social assessment should be more comprehensive than that. The process of determining what factors related to social functioning need to be assessed and how these factors are related should be based on a comprehensive model of social competence. This chapter is organized around a theoretical model of social competence developed by Vaughn and Hogan (1990) and provides information on assessment tools and practices that best represent this model. Here we discuss the best practices for social assessment for both identification and research purposes. Discussion emphasizes the importance of comprehensive assessment of social competence from a contextual perspective, that is, considering assessment data within the context in which behaviors and events occur.

Although the assessment tools discussed here may be relevant for a wide range of ages, we focus primarily on their use with elementary-age children because that is the age range in which most students with LD are identified. To the extent that it is possible, we discuss their use with younger and older children but refer the reader to other sources for specific information regarding preschool and adolescent populations.

SOCIAL COMPETENCE AS A MULTIFACETED CONSTRUCT

We think of social competence as a multifaceted construct analogous to intelligence in that it is a higher order, elusive construct that cannot be measured or observed directly (Vaughn & Hogan, 1990). This model assumes four dimensions of social competence: effective use of social skills, absence of maladaptive behavior, positive relations with others, and accurate/age-appropriate social cognition. Although we define and measure social competence in terms of its separate components, it is not only the presence of the components but also their interaction that yields social competence. For the purposes of assessment and research, the components must be isolated and measured separately, but it is important in terms of interpretation and understanding of social competence that each component be considered in consort with the others.

For the past few years, we have conducted a number of studies in which we have applied this model of social competence with school-age students with LD to better understand the nature and implications of their social difficulties (e.g., Haager & Vaughn, 1995). Our findings have exemplified the importance of considering multiple factors of social competence (e.g., self-concept, relationships with others), multiple reporters (peers, parents, self), and multiple settings (e.g., home, school, play). Our findings have also highlighted the importance of considering the context in which we measure social competence. For example, although most of our studies have reported lower peer acceptance for students with LD than for NLD students (e.g., Haager & Vaughn, 1995; Vaughn, Hogan, Kouzekanani, & Shapiro, 1990), one study in which subjects were selected from classrooms where teachers were highly accepting of students with LD yielded no significant differences in the peer acceptance of students with LD and typically achieving students across elementary and secondary grade levels (Vaughn, McIntosh, Schumm, Haager, & Callwood, 1993). Examinations of social competence across school and nonschool settings is valuable to assist in determining the extent to which behavior that is reported at school corresponds with behavior in other settings. In another study, we found that, although classroom teachers rated students with LD and other low achievers as less competent in terms of social skills than their typically achieving peers, parents (who view their children in the home setting) did not see their LD or low achieving children as less socially skilled than the parents of typically achieving students (Haager & Vaughn, 1995).

There are several correlates of social competence that need to be considered as relevant to the measurement of social competence. We are not suggesting that a comprehensive evaluation of social competence should include formal assessment of all related factors. Rather, we feel that such factors are often highly relevant and should be considered when interpreting results of social assessments. Athletic ability, academic ability, physical appearance, and various classroom behaviors are highly related to peer acceptance in school-age children (Dodge, 1983; Wiener, Harris, & Shirer, 1990). We know less about the extent to which these factors relate specifically to the social competence of students with LD. It may be relevant to consider these factors and their influence on students' peer acceptance when conducting and interpreting social assessments.

Achievement difficulties are another important factor related to social competence. It is often assumed that when students with LD demonstrate social difficulties it is a function of their learning disabilities. That is, the learning processes that interfere with their ability to effectively read and write also interfere with their ability to effectively interact with others. There is increasing evidence that there is a subgroup of students for whom this is true (Rourke & Fuerst, 1991), however, there is also evidence that social difficulties may be concomitant with low achievement in general rather than causally related to LD (Gresham, 1992). Indeed, our studies have shown that, for four components of social competence (i.e., peer relations, behavioral adjustment, social skills, and self-perceptions), students with LD are very similar to other low achievers who have not been referred or identified as having LD (e.g., Haager & Vaughn, 1995; Vaughn, Zaragoza, Hogan, & Walker, 1993). Thus, we have substantial evidence of the general co-occurrence of achievement difficulties and social difficulties.

The following sections describe each component of the model of social competence (Vaughn & Hogan, 1990) as well as what we consider to be the current best practice for assessment within each area. We discuss assessment tools in relation to their purposes and potential uses as well as needs for further research and measure development.

ASSESSING SOCIAL SKILLS AND MALADAPTIVE BEHAVIORS

Although social skills and maladaptive behaviors represent two different areas of social competence, we have converged them in this chapter, because many of the issues regarding measurement of these two areas are similar. Social skills refer to the pro-social and responding skills demonstrated across settings and persons. These include language, nonverbal reactions, and attitudes a person conveys to others. Social skills involves appropriate initiation and responsiveness to others. The *absence* of maladaptive behaviors is another component of social competence. Absence of maladaptive behaviors refers to the ability to refrain from engaging in behaviors considered by societal norms to be inappropriate. Naturally, the frequency and setting in which the behaviors occur influences the extent to which behaviors are viewed as maladaptive.

Maladaptive behaviors are not the opposite of social skills, although they are likely to be highly related. Maladaptive behavior is not necessarily the ineffective use of or lack of effective social skills, but rather behaviors that would be considered to be inappropriate or maladaptive. For example, hitting another person is not considered to be the ineffective use of a social skill nor is it the absence of an effective social behavior. It is an inappropriate behavior. Crying is another example. Although there are situations in which crying would be an appropriate response, a child repeatedly crying in response to normal social situations—such as lining up to go to lunch or another child speaking to him or her—would be considered to exhibit maladaptive behavior. There are individuals who are capable of demonstrating appropriate social skills and demonstrating maladaptive behavior. For example, a student with conduct disorders may be able to display highly appropriate social behaviors in selected settings and also display acting out and aggressive behaviors in other settings.

Social skills measures, largely rating scales, assess the extent to which the target youngster demonstrates age-appropriate social behaviors with peers and adults across a range of settings (Vaughn & Haager, 1994a). The existing social skills rating measures report better than adequate reliability and validity (e.g., Gresham & Elliott, 1990; Matson, Rotatori, & Helsel, 1983; Walker & McConnell, 1988). For the most part, measures of social skills are designed for teachers to rate the social behaviors of selected students in their class. However, some of these social skills rating scales do not distinguish between school-related social behaviors (e.g., completing homework, following teacher's directions) and social behaviors related to adequate social functioning (e.g., greeting peers, solving one's own interpersonal problems). Social skills measures have also been designed to assess parents' perceptions of their child's social skills (Gresham & Elliott, 1991).

Although considerable emphasis has been placed on peer assessments of friendship and likability, few measures that ask peers to assess the social skills of other peers have been developed (see Vaughn & Haager, 1994a, for an example of such a measure). We feel that peers' assessment of the social skills of students is a promising area for several reasons. First, peers witness behaviors of others their own age that are not demonstrated to adults. Thus,

they can provide unique insights into social behaviors. Second, social behaviors are not viewed the same by adults and children and, therefore,
peers' perceptions of the social skills of their classmates could assist in the
interpretation of why some students are not well liked by peers despite their
high ratings of social skills by parents and teachers. Third, peers' perceptions of classmates are formed across multiple settings (e.g., in the classroom and on the playground) and could provide a more accurate perception
of a student's social skills outside of the classroom. In a study conducted
by Lancelotta and Vaughn (1989), peer ratings of three subtypes of aggression (i.e., provoked, outburst, and verbal) did not correspond with teacher
ratings. However, teachers' and students' perceptions of unprovoked aggression were highly related. One likely explanation is that teachers have
little opportunity to observe some types of aggressive behavior.

School-age youngsters with LD have consistently been found to have
higher incidence of behavioral difficulties in comparison to non-LD peers,
including higher levels of aggression, distractibility, internalizing or withdrawn behavior, and externalizing behavior (e.g., Bender, 1985; Bender &
Smith, 1990; Vaughn & Haager, 1994b). Teacher ratings have consistently
identified problematic classroom behavior for children with LD as compared
to non-LD peers, such as more off-task behavior (McKinney & Feagans, 1983;
McKinney & Speece, 1983) and low rates of responding during instruction
(McIntosh et al., 1993). Typically, students with LD have lower rates of
behavior problems than students identified as having behavior disorders
(Thompson & Kronenberger, 1990). Some evidence suggests that behavior
problems accompany achievement difficulties in general, rather than being
associated with LD per se. In a limited number of studies comparing the
behavior problems of students with LD, low achievers, and average/high
achievers, both low-achieving groups (i.e., students with LD and low achievers) have demonstrated similarly high incidence of behavior problems relative to average and high achievers (Haager & Vaughn, 1995; Vaughn,
Zaragoza, et al., 1993). Thus, at least when teacher ratings are used as an
index of maladaptive behavior, achievement difficulties and behavioral difficulties often co-occur.

Although teacher ratings of social skills and behavior problems are usually
considered quite reliable (Bailey, Bender, & Montgomery, 1983), we have three
concerns regarding the use of most standardized teacher rating scales for
either research or identification purposes. First, we have found that most
teacher rating scales of social skills and behavior problems focus on class-
room-oriented behavior, which is a context-specific view of social skills and
maladaptive behaviors. For example, the Social Skills Rating Scale for Teachers (Gresham & Elliott, 1990), which has social skills and behavior problems
subscales, includes such items as "Finishes class assignments within time
limits," and "Keeps desk clean and neat without being reminded" in the social

skills subscale. Although these are important behaviors in the social context of the classroom, they are really more related to issues such as compliance or organization within this particular setting. Students with LD who often display disorganization and difficulty with school work score low on these items, which may not reflect overall social skills difficulties. When using behavioral assessment for research purposes, it is important for researchers to be confident that the measure selected identifies true, generalized social skills or behavioral difficulties rather than school-oriented behaviors such as compliance and work habits. We believe that a comprehensive assessment of behavioral difficulties would include assessment of behaviors considered to be socially unacceptable in the classroom as well as in other contexts.

Our second concern is that the behavior of students with LD in the school context may not be representative of their behavior in other contexts. Most teacher rating scales are limited to use in the classroom context and provide the perspective of the classroom teacher. Because these measures are designed to be completed by classroom teachers, setting-specific items that are particularly relevant to teachers make sense. However, this may not provide adequate evidence to identify significant behavioral difficulties. This is particularly problematic when studying students with LD who by definition fail to thrive in school settings. We would expect the classroom to be an environment in which students with LD experience frustration or anxiety— feelings that often lead to anger, aggression, or withdrawal. If a student with LD has behavioral difficulties in the general education classroom, but there is no indication of difficulties at home or in a special education classroom, it is highly possible that the difficulties are an indication of frustration relative to the context. Negative teacher ratings may also indicate frustration on the part of the teacher who finds the child difficult to teach. This has very different implications for intervention than when the difficulties occur consistently across settings. It may be possible in some instances to work with the context as well as with the student's context-specific behaviors, whereas implementing an intensive behavioral intervention may be warranted in other cases. For research purposes, it may be helpful to obtain ratings of students' behaviors both in and out of the classroom context, using multiple raters, thus providing cross-validation of results. The Social Skills Rating System (Gresham & Elliott, 1991), for example, includes parallel forms for parent, teacher, and self-report ratings of social skills and parent and teacher ratings of behavior problems. In addition, the items are specific to the different contexts in which the raters know the target students. The Child Behavior Checklist (Achenbach, 1991a), a parent report measure, also has a corresponding Teacher Report Form (Achenbach, 1991b) as well as a self-report form (Achenbach, 1991c) to assess behavior problems.

Third, we suggest the use of independent observations in addition to rating scales to minimize the bias inherent in rating scales. Although teachers are knowledgeable of students within the classroom context, they may not always differentiate behavioral difficulties from other concerns, such as social or academic concerns (Vaughn & Haager, 1994b), whereas parents either may not have an awareness of developmental norms for behavior or may not be willing to rate their child negatively. Few studies have compared teacher or parent ratings with actual observations regarding students with LD. However, in one of our studies, parent and teacher ratings of the behavioral difficulties of youngsters with LD were only moderately correlated (Haager & Vaughn, 1995). We might not expect teacher and parent ratings to converge because their knowledge of the child involves different settings and experiences (Achenbach, McConaughy, & Howell, 1987). Thus, observation provides a third perspective on children's behavioral difficulties. Best practice for identification purposes might involve observation in and out of the structured classroom context. Although it is probably unrealistic for school personnel to conduct observation in the home setting, it is important to seek information from the family regarding the child's functioning in the home setting. It might also be possible when considering a child for placement in special education to observe the student during a class lesson as well as on the playground or other social context with peers.

For research purposes, observation provides several advantages for assessing behavioral difficulties. First, observation offers an assessment of children's behavior independent of teacher or parent bias, although observer bias is a potential risk (Repp, Nieminen, Olinger, & Brusca, 1988). Reliability is enhanced in observation studies by careful training of observers, interrater reliability checks, and the use of a well-defined data-coding system for either qualitative and quantitative analysis. Probably the greatest advantage is the opportunity to simultaneously observe the child's behavior and contextual factors such as the reactions or initiations of teachers or peers and contextual events.

Although direct observation has been widely used in developmental research with non-LD subjects, studies using observation techniques with LD subjects are limited in number. Previous studies have examined the frequency and quality of the interactions between LD students and teachers (e.g., McKinney & Speece, 1983) or peers (e.g., McIntosh et al., 1993) or have investigated the correlates of various social variables such as peer acceptance (e.g., Wiener et al., 1990). Vaughn and Haager (1994a) provided a review of observational studies of social competence with students with LD.

Methods of observing include naturalistic observation—using either anecdotal recording, time sampling, frequency counts, checklists, or other recording techniques—and analogue or simulated situations designed to elicit specific responses or behaviors, often through role-playing techniques. Naturalistic observation has the advantage of providing an assessment of a child in a naturally occurring environment. However, simulated situations are often selected when the behavior of interest generally occurs with low frequency or in nonschool contexts. Observation is potentially a rich source of information regarding the maladaptive behavior of individuals with LD. However, both naturalistic and analogue or role-play techniques are costly in terms of personnel and time, which limits the number of observations, length of observations, or both. Comprehensive instruction on implementing observational assessment for both identification and research purposes is beyond the scope of this chapter. Entire university courses, textbooks, and reference materials are devoted to observational methodology. For the purpose of identifying youngsters for special education programs, we refer the reader to assessment texts (e.g., Salvia & Ysseldyke, 1995) and other reviews (e.g., LaGreca, 1990; Vaughn & Haager, 1994a).

ASSESSING POSITIVE RELATIONS WITH OTHERS

The measures that provide perhaps the most relevant insight into the overall social functioning of individuals with LD are those that assess their relationships with others. In particular, the quality and number of friendships and how target students are perceived by peers provides an excellent index of overall social competence. How youngsters are perceived by their peers has been linked to such outcomes as later adjustment, success in the workplace, and school completion (see, for review, Parker & Asher, 1987). Peers' perceptions also influence self-perceptions and overall adjustment (Cowen, Pederson, Babigian, Izzo, & Trost, 1973). These implications are particularly relevant for individuals with LD who are more frequently rejected by their peers and are less well accepted (e.g., Haager & Vaughn, 1995; Stone & La Greca, 1990; Wiener, 1987).

Sociometry is the most commonly used method of assessing peer acceptance. Developed by Moreno (1934), sociometry is the study of peer rankings in a group. Most frequently this is done with peer rating scales or nomination techniques. Peer rating scales yield a measure of a target student's likability within a peer group or peer acceptance, whereas peer nominations indicate social status within a peer group, that is, popularity (Gresham, 1981). Examining the nature, patterns, and numbers of friendships among peers is also an important avenue for assessing students' relations with others. This section of the chapter identifies measures and techniques for assessing peer acceptance, social status, and friendship qualities.

Peer Acceptance

Rating scales are the most accepted form of assessing peer acceptance for the purpose of identifying individuals in need of intervention or for research purposes. Because assessing individual students' peer groups would be difficult outside the school setting, peer ratings are most frequently obtained in the classroom. All students within the target student's class are asked to rate on a Likert-type scale each student in the class including the target child. Although different formats such as an easel or card format could be used, we have found the use of a roster of names followed by rating indicators to be most convenient. See Fig. 7.1 for a sample rating scale.

In our own work, we use a 3-point scale with youngsters preschool through first grade then convert to a 4-point scale for youngsters second grade and older, through high school (e.g., Vaughn et al., 1992; Vaughn,

How Well Do You Like?

Your Name _____   School _____

Male _____ Female _____   Age _____   Teacher _____

Directions: Please circle the number that indicates how well you like each of the classmates listed. Cross out your own name.

1 = Do not like at at all   2 =Do not like very much   3 = Like a little   4 = Like a lot

Student's Name		How well do you like?			
1.	Student A	1	2	3	4
2.	Student B	1	2	3	4
3.	Student C	1	2	3	4
4.	Student D	1	2	3	4
5.	Student E	1	2	3	4
6.	Student F	1	2	3	4
7.	Student G	1	2	3	4
8.	Student H	1	2	3	4
9.	Student I	1	2	3	4
10.	Student J	1	2	3	4
11.	Student K	1	2	3	4
12.	Student L	1	2	3	4

FIG. 7.1. Sample of a peer rating form using a roster of names followed by rating indicators.

McIntosh, et al., 1993). We also individually assess children through second grade and conduct small-group or whole-class assessment thereafter. With young children, we use a visual prompt of three faces: a happy face, a neutral face, and an unhappy face. They are instructed that there is no right or wrong answer and that they should indicate how they truly feel. They are also assured their responses will be kept confidential and told that they should not tell others how they have responded. We then provide some examples of the rating procedures and ask the children to point to the face which indicates how they feel about such familiar items as eating pizza, going swimming, cleaning their room, eating cake or spinach. Each face is assigned a point value from 1 for *least positive* to 3 for *most positive*. For older children in a group or class setting, we recommend using similar examples but numbers instead of faces for the ratings, with 1 indicating *Don't like at all*, 2 indicating *Don't like very much*, 3 indicating *Sort of like*, and 4 indicating *Like a lot*. We demonstrate how to circle the numbers on a sample paper. For the younger children, the examiner holds and marks the roster of names, whereas the older children are given the roster and asked to mark it themselves. Once children of both age groups grasp the procedures, they are asked to rate each child in their class, excluding themselves, by indicating how much they like each individual according to the instructions. It should be noted that, even if one is only interested in particular target students such as the students with LD, it is important to obtain whole-class ratings for two reasons. First, the larger the number of raters, the higher the reliability of the ratings (Asher & Hymel, 1981; Gresham & Elliott, 1989; Singleton & Asher, 1977). Second, there is potential harm to an individual's self-esteem when including some but not all students in the class in the roster of names. The reliability and validity of peer ratings is moderately high for preschool and elementary students (Asher & Hymel, 1981; Asher, Markell, & Hymel, 1981; Drewry & Clark, 1983; Hayvren & Hymel, 1984; Sainato, Zigmond, & Strain, 1983) and, overall, are higher than for peer nominations (Thompson & Powell, 1951).

Typically, the mean score for each target student is calculated and scores can then be used in a comparative analysis or merely examined in relation to those of others. The mean score is indicative of how well a student is liked or accepted by peers. However, mean scores should not be used alone. A list of all the ratings for an individual student will indicate if there are students in the class who like this student a lot (perhaps despite a low mean score) or very little or whether the student is universally liked, viewed neutrally, or disliked. We have found the use of a grid to provide a convenient scoring system as demonstrated in Fig. 7.2.

Despite the ease and usefulness of peer rating information, there are several issues to consider in their use. First, the "stem" that is used to request the ratings should be chosen carefully. The most frequently used

Peer Rating Scoring Grid

	A	B	C	D	E	F	G	H	I	J	K	L
Student A	X	3	4	4	3	3	1	3	4	3	2	3
Student B	3	X	4	3	2	1	1	4	3	3	1	2
Student C	4	3	X	3	3	1	2	4	3	2	1	2
Student D	4	2	4	X	3	2	1	3	4	3	2	3
Student E	3	3	4	4	X	1	2	4	3	4	3	4
Student F	4	2	3	2	3	X	2	3	2	4	2	3
Student G	3	2	4	2	4	2	X	3	2	3	3	4
Student H	2	3	3	3	3	2	3	X	3	3	1	4
Student I	3	4	3	3	4	1	2	4	X	2	1	2
Student J	3	1	4	4	3	2	3	4	4	X	3	3
Student K	3	2	3	3	3	3	2	4	3	3	X	4
Student L	4	2	3	4	2	2	2	3	3	3	1	X
4's rec'd	4	1	6	4	2	0	0	6	3	2	0	4
3's rec'd	6	4	5	5	7	2	2	5	6	7	3	4
2's rec'd	1	5	0	2	2	5	6	0	2	2	3	3
1's rec'd	0	1	0	0	0	4	3	0	0	0	5	0

FIG. 7.2. Sample of a grid used to score peer ratings. Going from left to right, the numbers indicate the scores given by an individual. Going from top to bottom, the numbers indicate the scores received by an individual. Note that subjects do not rate themselves, thus an "X" is placed in the box where the individual's scores given and scores received intersect. The number of 4s, 3s, 2s, and 1s received are tallied at the bottom of the form. The mean peer rating for each individual is computed using the scores received as follows: (#4's × 4) + (#3's × 3) + (#2's × 2) + (#1's × 1) / # raters.

stem is "How much do you like . . ." each name on the list. However, other possibilities include "How much would you like to work with . . ." and "How much would you like to play with . . ." or "How much would you like ___ to come to your birthday party?" We would not expect participants to respond similarly using these different stems, due to the fact that they must appraise their classmates on different features for each. For example, a student with LD may be viewed as limited in reading ability and, therefore, might not be rated positively using the "work with" stem whereas they may be athletically skilled and rated more positively using the "play with" stem. In a study conducted by Gresham and Reschly (1986) in which non-LD students and students with LD were rated using both "work with" and "play with" stems, the largest statistically significant difference between the groups was obtained with the "work with" stem. The "play with" stem may be influenced by age, sex, athletic ability, or temperament. Our recommendation is that, if you are most interested in assessing how well a student is *accepted* by peers, the best stem is "How much do you like. . . ." If other stems are used, they should be carefully selected to represent the desired factor to be assessed.

Social Status

Social status is determined by the number of positive and negative nominations received from classmates. Although there are several methods of obtaining nominations (e.g., name the person you think of as the funniest, smartest), the procedure that yields positive and negative nominations, which then can be used to compute social status categories, is as follows: First, students are asked to write or tell the examiner up to three classmates who they "like most" or would consider to be their "best friends" in the class. These are referred to as positive nominations. Next, students are asked to write or name up to three classmates who they "least like" or would "not want to be friends with." These are considered negative nominations. Using the nominations of the whole class, the number of positive and negative nominations for each target student are computed. These scores can then be used in statistical analyses or for diagnostic purposes. For either purpose, social impact and social preference scores are computed. Social impact is indicative of the extent to which the target student influences the group and is obtained by adding the number of positive and negative nominations. Social preference is the extent to which a target child is highly liked by peers and is obtained by subtracting the number of negative nominations from the number of positive nominations. Note that this could be a negative number if a student receives a high number of negative nominations. For diagnostic purposes, the scores could be compared informally with those of peers. For research purposes, however, the scores are standardized by class by conversion to z-scores and yield social status categories using analysis procedures outlined by Coie, Dodge, and Coppotelli (1982). Using these procedures, students are categorized as popular (high positive social impact, high social preference), rejected (high social impact, low social preference), controversial (high positive and negative nominations), and neglected (low social impact). This system of classification provides information about social structure and specific behavior patterns associated with different status groups (Coie & Kupersmidt, 1983; Dodge, Coie, & Brakke, 1982) and has demonstrated adequate test–retest reliability (Bukowski & Newcomb, 1984; Wasik, 1987) and criterion-related validity (Vosk, Forehand, Parker, & Rickard, 1982).

Peer rejection is not only associated with interpersonal difficulties, low levels of cooperation and friendliness, and high levels of aggression (Coie, Dodge, & Kupersmidt, 1990; Dodge, 1983; Dodge, Coie, & Brakke, 1982; Dodge, Pettit, McClaskey, & Brown, 1986), but is also thought to be predictive of negative later life outcomes such as poor adult adjustment, criminal involvement, and dropping out of school (Parker & Asher, 1987). Thus, the consistent finding that students with LD are more likely to be rejected than non-LD students is alarming and warrants further investigation. In a recent study, however, we found that low achieving students (not referred or identified as having LD) were overrepresented in the rejected category, whereas a smaller proportion of students with LD and typically achieving students were classified as rejected, thus indicating that low achievement status may be an important factor.

Friendship Qualities

In addition to considering how the target student is perceived by the group as a whole, it is important to understand the quality of the student's friendships. We know surprisingly little about the nature of friendships of students with LD (Vaughn & Haager, 1994b; Vaughn, McIntosh, et al., 1993), but we have hypothesized that, for students with social difficulties, having at least one or two strong friendship bonds may serve as a "buffer" to the ill effects of low peer acceptance and rejection. Bukowski and Hoza (1989) presented several key questions to consider that provide a conceptual framework for assessing the quality of children's friendships:

1. Does a child have at least one mutual friend?
2. How many mutual friends does the child have?
3. What is/are the quality of that child's mutual friend?

One way of examining friendship bonds is through identifying *reciprocal* friendships, in which two students name each other as "best friends." This can be done easily through the positive nomination procedure described earlier by examining the nomination forms of those named as "best friends" by the target student to see if they also named the target student. If they did, it is a "hit," if not, a "miss." According to Howes (1987), rejected children had an easier time with peer group entry if they had reciprocal friendships than if they did not. In a recent study examining the reciprocal friendships of students with LD in inclusion settings, overall peer acceptance of students with LD did not increase from fall to spring; however, their number of reciprocal friends increased (Vaughn, Elbaum, & Schumm, in press).

Other measures that assess the quality of friendships are self-reports or interviews. These might be used to answer Bukowski and Hoza's (1989) third question related to the quality of mutual friendships. Bierman and McCauley

(1987) have developed the Friendship Questionnaire to specifically assess youngsters' peer relations and friendships outside of the school setting. This is a 32-item scale that has three subscales: positive interactions, negative interactions, and extensive peer network. Berndt and Perry (1986) adapted the Friendship Survey from a structured interview. This 18-item questionnaire was designed to investigate dimensions of children's friendships. Items consist of such questions as, "Do you and your friends get together on weekends or after school?" to which children respond "yes," "sometimes," or "no." The authors identified six dimensions of friendship: play/association, pro-social behavior, intimacy, loyalty, attachment/self-esteem, and absence of conflicts. However, according to Berndt and Perry (1986), for second, fourth, and sixth graders, the ratings for all six dimensions loaded on a single factor. We, therefore, suggest using the total score on the friendship survey as a measure of the quality of a student's friendships. Whereas peer ratings and reciprocal friendship nominations address only those relationships that occur among classmates, the Friendship Survey gives an index of perceived support from friends irrespective of context and can provide information not tapped by classroom peer measures. We encourage further research regarding the friendships of students with LD.

ASSESSING SOCIAL COGNITION

Social cognition refers to the ability to understand and interpret social events and the behaviors of self and others. This requires an understanding of an individual's cognitive processes, an area that is difficult to assess directly. With some academic situations such as math problem solving and writing, researchers have attempted to examine students' cognitions by having them "think aloud" while performing the task (e.g., Graham & Harris, 1989). However, this technique is not particularly useful in assessing social cognition, because the act of thinking aloud would interfere with the social interaction and alter the situation. Furthermore, even if it were possible to accurately assess an individual's cognition, it would be difficult to know whether the particular cognitions assessed are general to all environments or limited to specific environmental situations (Swanson, 1993).

Until social assessment is further refined, we have concluded that it is not possible to assess social cognition directly. Therefore, we suggest the use of self-report assessments that measure some aspect of social cognition, such as self-concept, using measures that require reflective thinking about events or interpretations of events in an individual's experience, to better understand social cognition.

Examining the self-perceptions of students with LD is one way of determining the impact of academic and social difficulties on students' emotional well-being and sense of self. Because students with LD experience repeated academic (and often social) difficulties, we would expect their self-concepts to reflect negative self-perceptions. Although numerous studies have demonstrated that students with LD have less positive self-concepts than NLD students (for review, see Chapman, 1988b), this is an oversimplified interpretation of years of research. Several other studies have found no differences in self-concepts of students with LD and NLD students (e.g., Vaughn et al., 1992; Winne, Woodlands, & Wong, 1982). Several factors may help us to understand this apparent contradiction in findings.

First, how self-concept is defined is an important factor. Self-perceptions appear to be domain-specific and results may vary depending on whether the measure used assesses the student's feelings of general self-worth or self-perceptions within specific developmental domains (e.g., academic or social; Harter, 1985; Harter & Pike, 1984; Winne et al., 1982). Harter and her colleagues described six domains of self-perception: scholastic competence, social acceptance, athletic competence, physical competence, behavioral competence, and global self-worth. Several studies have found students with LD to have lower academic-related self-perceptions than NLD students, whereas self-perceptions in other domains did not differ (Chapman, 1988b). It is important, then, for the self-concept assessment tool to measure not only general self-worth, but also specific developmental domains.

Age is a second factor that may explain the contradictory findings of previous self-concept research comparing students with LD and NLD. Self-perceptions tend to become more differentiated and refined with age and, generally, self-concept declines through the childhood years (Marsh, 1989; Marsh, Byrne, & Shavelson, 1988; Ruble, 1983). Although we might assume that the self-concept development of youngsters with LD would follow a normal developmental pattern, few studies have provided a developmental perspective. Two longitudinal studies indicated negative self-perceptions for youngsters with LD as compared to NLD peers over time (Battle & Blowers, 1982; Chapman, 1988a). In contrast, our research following a cohort of children from kindergarten through fifth grade demonstrated that the domain-specific and global self-perceptions of youngsters with LD did not differ significantly at any time from those of typically achieving youngsters (Vaughn & Haager, 1994b; Vaughn, Haager, et al., 1992; Vaughn & Hogan, 1994). The self-perceptions of the children with LD appeared to follow the same developmental trends of other youngsters. Because we had a small number of LD subjects who remained in the study through the fifth grade, we caution against overinterpretation of our findings and encourage further longitudinal research in order to better understand such developmental issues.

A third issue that complicates the interpretation of previous self-concept research is that of setting. As children develop a sense of self and become self-evaluative around the age of 7 or 8 years, they also begin to engage in social comparison, that is, seeing themselves in relation to others (Harter,

1983; Ruble, 1983). Renick and Harter (1989) have proposed that social comparison processes are important to consider when examining the self-perceptions of youngsters with LD. Youngsters with LD who are served primarily in a general education classroom have a different social comparison group than those served in pull-out settings. Coleman (1983) and Renick and Harter (1989) found that when students with LD use the regular classroom as a comparison group they tend to rate themselves lower academically than their NLD peers, but when they are considering themselves in relation to others in pull-out or self-contained special classes they rate themselves more positively.

The three factors discussed earlier also provide some guidelines for best practice for assessment of self-perceptions. It is important to select an assessment tool that differentiates and measures the specific domain(s) of interest. Several published rating scales provide domain-specific assessment. Harter has been a leader in this area with the development of several rating scales that have primarily been used for research purposes. The Self-Perception Profile for Children (ages 8–13; Harter, 1985) and Self-Perception Profile for Adolescents (ages 14–18; Harter, 1986) as well as the Self-Perception Profile for Learning Disabled Students (ages 8–18; Renick & Harter, 1988) and the Pictorial Scale of Perceived Competence and Social Acceptance for Young Children (ages 4–7; Harter & Pike, 1984) provide domain-specific self-ratings. Norms have been developed for each of these measures, thus making it possible to compare an individual's score with normative data that might be helpful for assessment related to identification as well.

We also suggest that care be taken to select assessment tools that are developmentally appropriate. Children with LD younger than 7 or 8 years may not have well-defined self-perceptions (Priel & Leshem, 1990). The issues that are salient in the formation of self-perceptions vary at different ages. For example, having a large social network may be more critical to the positive self-perceptions of preadolescent and adolescent youngsters than it would be to primary-grade children. Therefore, it is important when selecting or developing self-concept measures to look for a good match between the age of the youngster and the issues included in specific items.

Another important issue in selecting an appropriate measure for use with youngsters with LD is the dependence of self-rating measures on language and cognitive abilities to complete the measures. Instruments that require a great deal of reading or listening may be influenced by the youngster's ability to maintain attention and to process the language involved. A measure with a large number of items may be cumbersome and it may be necessary to take frequent breaks during administration. The examiner should be prepared to explain any item that the individual student does not understand and may have to rephrase or elaborate on specific items. This poses a threat when standardization of administration procedures is desired. It also provides an argument for individual administration even when the instructions indicate the instrument could be given in a group.

CONCLUSION

The purpose of this chapter is to provide an overview of issues related to assessment of social competence with students with LD. Additionally, four factors related to social competence (i.e., social skills, absence of maladaptive behaviors, relationships with others, and social cognition) are defined and discussed. Measures that have been developed to assess each of these four factors are described and their use for assessment and research purposes presented. The use (and misuse) of measures designed to assess the social competence of students with LD is explained.

There are several reoccurring themes in this chapter regarding the assessment of social competence of individuals with LD. They are summarized in the following.

Comprehensive Assessment

We have gathered significant evidence to conclude that social assessment from the narrow perspective of one rater (e.g., teachers) or in a single setting (e.g., the classroom) provides an incomplete picture of the social competence of individuals with LD. Furthermore, assessment along a single dimension of social competence (e.g., social skills) provides a limited view of social competence. Whether the assessment is conducted for identification or research purposes, it is critical to obtain a comprehensive measurement of social competence, considering multiple perspectives, settings, dimensions, and other related factors.

Context

The setting in which the student is assessed is critical and must be considered both prior to assessment and in the interpretation of the assessment. This is particularly important for students with LD, because most assessments of social competence occur in the school setting. Thus, it is possible that students' social behavior in the school context is not representative of their social behavior in other settings. We advocate the use of measures that tap students' behavior across multiple settings as well as measures that rate school behaviors and other behaviors.

Rater

Who rates the social competence of students with LD largely influences the score. Even when the same measure is used and ratings are completed by the special education teacher and the general education teacher, outcomes will differ. Multiple raters provide multiple perspectives; however, first consideration should be given to selecting a rater that matches the goal of the study or the purpose of the assessment.

Content

The purpose of the measure, content of its factors, and content of relevant items must be carefully considered in the selection and interpretation of social measures. It is important to determine that the measure taps the dimension of interest and that items are worded appropriately.

Characteristics

The characteristics of students with LD may interfere with their completion of or responses on the social measure. For example, students with LD who have attention problems may incorrectly complete measures, thus altering their scores in significant ways that are not related to their social competence. Memory and communication problems, frequently associated with students with LD, often interfere with their performance on social measures and need to be considered when interpreting their responses.

REFERENCES

Achenbach, T. M. (1991a). *Child behavior checklist for ages 4–16.* San Antonio, TX: The Psychological Corporation.

Achenbach, T. M. (1991b). *Teacher's report form (TRF).* Burlington: University of Vermont Department of Psychiatry.

Achenbach, T. M. (1991c). *Youth self-report (YSR).* Burlington: University of Vermont Department of Psychiatry.

Achenbach, T. M., McConaughy, S. H., & Howell, C. T. (1987). Child/adolescent behavioral and emotional problems: Implications of cross-informant correlations for situational specificity. *Psychological Bulletin, 101,* 213–232.

Asher, S. R., & Hymel, S. (1981). Children's social competence in peer relations: Sociometric and behavioral assessment. In J. D. Wine & M. D. Smye (Eds.), *Social competence* (pp. 124–159). New York: Guilford.

Asher, S. R., Markell, R. A., & Hymel, S. (1981). Identifying children at risk in peer relations: A critique of the rate-of-interaction approach to assessment. *Child Development, 52,* 1239–1245.

Bailey, D. B., Bender, W. N., & Montgomery, D. L. (1983). Comparisons of teacher, peer, and self-ratings of classroom and social behavior. *Behavior Disorders, 8,* 153–160.

Battle, J., & Blowers, T. (1982). A longitudinal comparative study of the self-esteem of students in regular and special education classes. *Journal of Learning Disabilities, 15,* 100–102.

Bender, W. N. (1985). Differences between learning disabled and non-learning disabled children in temperament and behavior. *Learning Disability Quarterly, 8,* 11–18.

Bender, W. N., & Smith, J. K. (1990). Classroom behavior of children and adolescents with learning disabilities: A meta-analysis. *Journal of Learning Disabilities, 23,* 298–306.

Berndt, T. J., & Perry, T. B. (1986). Children's perceptions of friendships as supportive relationships. *Developmental Psychology, 22,* 640–648.

Bierman, K. L., & McCauley, E. (1987). Children's descriptions of their peer interactions: Useful information for clinical child assessment. *Journal of Clinical Child Psychology, 55,* 194–200.

Bukowski, W. M., & Hoza, B. (1989). Popularity and friendship: Issues in theory, measurement, and outcome. In T. J. Berndt & G. W. Ladd (Eds.), *Peer relationships in child development* (pp. 15–45). New York: Wiley.

Bukowski, W. M., & Newcomb, A. F. (1984). Stability and determinants of sociometric status and friendship choice: A longitudinal perspective. *Developmental Psychology, 20,* 941–952.

Chapman, J. W. (1998a). Cognitive-motivational characteristics and academic achievement of learning disabled children: A longitudinal study. *Journal of Educational Psychology, 80,* 357–365.

Chapman, J. W. (1988b). Learning disabled children's self-concepts. *Review of Educational Research, 58,* 347–371.

Coie, J. D., Dodge, K. A., & Coppotelli, H. (1982). Dimensions and type of social status: A cross-age perspective. *Developmental Psychology, 18,* 557–570.

Coie, J. D., Dodge, K. A., & Kupersmidt, J. B. (1990). Peer group behavior and social status. In S. R. Asher & J. D. Coie (Eds.), *Peer rejection in childhood* (pp. 17–59). Cambridge, England: Cambridge University Press.

Coie, J. D., & Kupersmidt, J. B. (1983). A behavioral analysis of emerging social status in boys' groups. *Child Development, 54,* 1400–1416.

Coleman, J. M. (1983). Self-concept and the mildly handicapped: The role of social comparisons. *The Journal of Special Education, 17,* 37–45.

Cowen, E. L., Pederson, A., Babigian, H., Izzo, L. D., & Trost, M. A. (1973). Long-term follow-up of early detected vulnerable children. *Journal of Consulting and Clinical Psychology, 41,* 438–446.

Dodge, K. A. (1983). Behavioral antecedents of peer social status. *Child Development, 54,* 1386–1399.

Dodge, K. A., Coie, J. D., & Brakke, N. P. (1982). Behavior patterns of socially rejected and neglected preadolescents: The role of social approach and aggression. *Journal of Abnormal Child Psychology, 10,* 389–410.

Dodge, K. A., Pettit, G. S., McClaskey, C. L., & Brown, M. (1986). Social competence in children. *Monographs of the Society for Research in Child Development, 51*(1, Serial No. 213).

Drewry, D. L., & Clark, M. L. (1983). Factors important in the formation of preschoolers' friendships. *Journal of Genetic Psychology, 146,* 37–44.

Fletcher, J. M., Francis, D. J., Rourke, B. P., Shaywitz, S. E., & Shaywitz, B. A. (1993). Classification of learning disabilities: Relationships with other childhood disorders. In G. R. Lyon, D. B. Gray, J. F. Kavanagh, & N. A. Krasnegor (Eds.), *Better understanding learning disabilities: New views from research and their implications for education and public policies* (pp. 27–55). Baltimore: Brookes.

Gresham, F. M. (1981). Validity of social skills measures for assessing social competence in low-status children: A multivariate investigation. *Developmental Psychology, 17,* 390–398.

Gresham, F. M. (1992). Social skills and learning disabilities: Causal, concomitant, or correlational? *School Psychology Review, 21,* 348–360.

Gresham, F. M., & Elliott, S. N. (1989). Social skills assessment technology for LD students. *Learning Disability Quarterly, 9,* 23–32.

Gresham, F. M., & Elliott, S. N. (1990). *Social skills rating system manual.* Circle Pines, MN: American Guidance Service.

Graham, S., & Harris, K. R. (1989). Components analysis of cognitive strategy instruction: Effects on learning disabled students' compositions and self-efficacy. *Journal of Educational Psychology, 81,* 353–361.

Gresham, F. M., & Reschly, D. J. (1986). Social skills deficits and low peer acceptance of mainstreamed learning disabled children. *Learning Disability Quarterly, 9,* 23–32.

Haager, D., & Vaughn, S. (1995). Parent, teacher, peer, and self-reports of the social competence of students with learning disabilities. *Journal of Learning Disabilities, 28*(4), 205–215, 231.

Harter, S. (1983). Developmental perspectives on the self-system. In P. H. Mussen (Ed.), *Handbook of child psychology: Vol. IV, Socialization, personality, and social development* (pp. 275–385). New York: Wiley.

Harter, S. (1985). *Manual for the self-perception profile for children.* Denver: University of Denver, Department of Developmental Psychology.

Harter, S. (1986). *Manual for the self-perception profile for adolescents.* Denver: University of Denver, Department of Developmental Psychology.

Harter, S., & Pike, R. (1984). The pictorial scale of perceived competence and social acceptance for young children. *Child Development, 55,* 1969–1982.

Hayvren, M., & Hymel, S. (1984). Ethical issues in sociometric testing: The impact of sociometric measures on interaction behavior. *Developmental Psychology, 20,* 844–849.

Hazel, J. S., & Schumaker, J. B. (1988). Social skills and learning disabilities: Current issues and recommendations for future research. In J. F. Kavanagh & T. J. Truss, Jr. (Eds.), *Learning disabilities: Proceedings of the national conference* (pp. 293–344). Parkton, MD: York Press.

Howes, C. (1987). Peer interaction of young children. *Monographs of the Society for Research in Child Development, 53*(1, Serial No. 217).

Interagency Committee on Learning Disabilities. (1987). *Learning disabilities: A report to the U.S. Congress.* Bethesda, MD: National Institutes of Health.

Killen, M. (1989). Context, conflict, and coordination in social development. In L. T. Winegar (Ed.), *Social interaction and the development of children's understanding* (119–146). Norwood, NJ: Ablex.

LaGreca, A. M. (1990). Issues and perspectives on the child assessment process. In A. M. LaGreca (Ed.), *Through the eyes of the child: Obtaining self-reports from children and adolescents* (pp. 3–17). Boston: Allyn & Bacon.

Lancelotta, G. X., & Vaughn, S. (1989). Relation between types of aggression and sociometric status: Peer and teacher perceptions. *Journal of Educational Psychology, 81*(1), 86–90.

Lyon, G. R., & Moats, L. C. (1993). An examination of research in learning disabilities: Past practices and future directions. In G. R. Lyon, D. B. Gray, J. F. Kavanagh, & N. A. Krasnegor (Eds.), *Better understanding learning disabilities: New views from research and their implications for education and public policies* (pp. 1–13). Baltimore: Brookes.

Marsh, H. W. (1989). Age and sex effects in multiple dimensions of self-concept: Preadolescence to early adulthood. *Journal of Educational Psychology, 81,* 417–430.

Marsh, H. W., Byrne, B. M., & Shavelson, R. J. (1988). A multifaceted academic self-concept: Its hierarchical structure and its relation to academic achievement. *Journal of Educational Psychology, 80,* 366–380.

Matson, J. L., Rotatori, A. F., & Helsel, W. J. (1983). Development of a rating scale to measure social skills in children: The Matson Evaluation of Social Skills with Youngsters (MESSY). *Behavioral Research and Therapy, 21,* 335–340.

McIntosh, R., Vaughn, S., Schumm, J. S., Haager, D., & Lee, O. (1993). Observations of students with learning disabilities in general education classrooms. *Exceptional Children, 60*(3), 249–261.

McKinney, J. D., & Feagans, L. (1983). Adaptive classroom behavior of learning disabled students. *Journal of Learning Disabilities, 16,* 360–367.

McKinney, J. D., & Speece, D. L. (1983). Classroom behavior and the academic progress of learning disabled students. *Journal of Applied Developmental Psychology, 4,* 149–161.

Moreno, J. L. (1934). *Who shall survive? A new approach to the problem of human interrelations.* Washington, DC: Nervous and Mental Disease Publishing Co.

Parker, J. G., & Asher, S. R. (1987). Peer relations and later personal adjustment: Are low-accepted children at risk? *Psychological Bulletin, 102,* 357–389.

Pearl, R., Donahue, M., & Bryan, T. (1986). Social relationships of learning-disabled children. In J. K. Torgesen & B. Y. L. Wong (Eds.), *Psychological and educational perspectives on learning disabilities* (pp. 193–224). Orlando, FL: Academic Press.

Priel, B., & Leshem, T. (1990). Self-perceptions of first- and second-grade children with learning disabilities. *Journal of Learning Disabilities, 23,* 637–642.

Renick, M. J., & Harter, S. (1988). *Manual for the self-perception profile for learning disabled students.* Denver, CO: University of Denver.

Renick, M. J., & Harter, S. (1989). Impact of social comparisons on the developing self-perceptions of learning disabled students. *Journal of Educational Psychology, 81,* 631–638.

Repp, A. C., Nieminen, G. S., Olinger, E., & Brusca, R. (1988). Direct observation: Factors affecting the accuracy of observers. *Exceptional Children, 55,* 29–36.

Rourke, B. P., & Fuerst, D. R. (1991). *Learning disabilities and psychosocial functioning: A neuropsychological perspective.* New York: Guilford.

Ruble, D. N. (1983). The development of social comparison processes and their role in achievement-related self-socialization. In E. T. Higgings, W. W. Hartup, & D. N. Ruble (Eds.), *Social cognition and social development: A sociocultural perspective* (pp. 134–157). New York: Cambridge University Press.

Sainato, D. M., Zigmond, N., & Strain, P. S. (1983). Social status and initiations of interactions by learning disabled and nonhandicapped students. *Exceptional Children, 56*(4), 314–323.

Salvia, J., & Ysseldyke, J. E. (1995). *Assessment* (6th ed.). Boston: Houghton Mifflin.

Singleton, L. C., & Asher, S. R. (1977). Peer preferences and social interaction among third-grade children in an integrated school district. *Journal of Educational Psychology, 69,* 330–336.

Stone, W. L., & La Greca, A. M. (1990). The social status of children with learning disabilities: A reexamination. *Journal of Learning Disabilities, 23,* 32–37.

Swanson, H. L. (1993). Learning disabilities from the perspective of cognitive psychology. In G. R. Lyon, D. B. Gray, J. F. Kavanagh, & N. A. Krasnegor (Eds.), *Better understanding learning disabilities: New views from research and their implications for education and public policies* (pp. 197–228). Baltimore: Brookes.

Thompson, R. J., & Kronenberger, W. (1990). Behavior problems in children with learning problems. In H. L. Swanson & B. Keogh (Eds.), *Learning disabilities: Theoretical and research issues* (pp. 156–174). Hillsdale, NJ: Lawrence Erlbaum Associates.

Thompson, G. G., & Powell, M. (1951). An investigation of the rating scale approach to the measurement of social status. *Educational and Psychological Measurement, 11,* 440–445.

Vaughn, S., Elbaum, B. E., & Schumm, J. S. (in press). Are students with learning disabilities in inclusion classrooms better liked and less lonely? *Journal of Learning Disabilities.*

Vaughn, S., & Haager, D. (1994a). Social assessments of students with learning disabilities: Do they measure up? In S. Vaughn & C. Bos (Eds.), *Research issues in learning disabilities: Theory, methodology, assessment, and ethics* (pp. 276–311). New York: Springer-Verlag.

Vaughn, S., & Haager, D. (1994b). Social competence as a multifaceted construct: How do students with learning disabilities fare? *Learning Disability Quarterly, 17,* 253–256.

Vaughn, S., Haager, D., Hogan, A., & Kouzekanani, K. (1992). Self-concept and peer acceptance in students with learning disabilities: A four- to five-year prospective study. *Journal of Educational Psychology, 84,* 43–50.

Vaughn, S., & Hogan, A. (1990). Social competence and learning disabilities: A prospective study. In H. L. Swanson & B. K. Keogh (Eds.), *Learning disabilities: Theoretical and research issues* (pp. 175–191). Hillsdale, NJ: Lawrence Erlbaum Associates.

Vaughn, S., & Hogan, A. (1994). Social competence of students with LD over time: A within-individual examiniation. *Journal of Learning Disabilities, 27*(5), 292–303.

Vaughn, S., Hogan, A., Kouzekanani, K., & Shapiro, S. (1990). Peer acceptance, self-perceptions, and social skills of learning disabled students prior to identification. *Journal of Educational Psychology, 82*(1), 101–106.

Vaughn, S., McIntosh, R., Schumm, J. S., Haager, D., & Callwood, D. (1993). Social status, peer acceptance, and reciprocal friendships revisited. *Learning Disabilities Research and Practice, 8,* 82–88.

Vaughn, S., Zaragoza, N., Hogan, A., & Walker, J. (1993). A four-year longitudinal investigation of the social skills and behavior disabilities. *Journal of Learning Disabilities, 26,* 404–412.

Vosk, B., Forehand, R., Parker, J. B., & Rickard, K. (1982). A multimethod comparison of popular and unpopular children. *Developmental Psychology, 18,* 571–575.

Walker, H. M., & McConnell, S. R. (1988). *Walker–McConnell scale of social competence and school adjustment.* Austin, TX: Pro-Ed.

Wasik, B. H. (1987). Sociometric measures and peer descriptors of kindergarten children: A study of reliability and validity. *Journal of Clinical Child Psychology, 16,* 218–224.

Wiener, J. (1987). Peer status of learning disabled children and adolescents: A review of the literature. *Learning Disabilities Research, 2,* 62–79.

Wiener, J., Harris, P. J., & Shirer, C. (1990). Achievement and social–behavioral correlates of peer status in LD children. *Learning Disability Quarterly, 13,* 114–127.

Winne, P. H., Woodlands, M. J., & Wong, B. Y. L. (1982). Comparability of self-concept among learning disabled, normal, and gifted students. *Journal of Learning Disabilities, 15,* 470–475.

8

COMORBIDITY OF EMOTIONAL AND BEHAVIORAL DISORDERS

Melody Tankersley
Kent State University

Timothy J. Landrum
University of Nebraska–Kearney

Current classification schemes and empirical research have held that there are two dimensions of behavior: internalizing and externalizing (e.g., Achenbach, 1985). Internalizing behaviors are those that are directed inwardly, toward the self, and externalizing behaviors are directed outwardly, toward the environment. Emotional and behavioral disorders, then, are also delineated along these lines; internalizing disorders include anxiety, depression, fearfulness (or phobia), and social withdrawal, whereas externalizing disorders include those associated with conduct, hyperactivity, delinquency, and aggression.

In practice, assessment of emotional and behavioral disorders typically occurs for one of four reasons: screening, classification, identification for services, or intervention. Assessment is also an important component of research surrounding the emotional and behavioral disorders of children, as samples are typically chosen based on specific behavioral characteristics. Assessing the emotional and behavioral disorders of children and youth at each of these levels, however, has been problematic for educators and researchers for several reasons. One of the major frustrations regarding assessment in this area is that the federal definition of emotional and behavioral disorders (referred to as Serious Emotional Disturbance in federal regulations) is ambiguous and inconsistent (see Forness & Knitzer, 1990, for an in-depth discussion and analysis of problems associated with the federal definition). Other problematic issues of assessment of the emotional and behavioral disorders of children and adolescents involve the person pro-

viding the information (e.g., child, parent, teacher, clinician) or the characteristics associated with the disorder (e.g., cognitive, affective, behavioral,
physiological). With increased attention on identifying the emotional and
behavioral disorders of children and youth has come increased interest in
the methodological and conceptual issues of assessment.

A particularly complex issue that has received attention recently in the
areas of mental health and psychiatry, and that may further complicate the
assessment of emotional and behavioral disorders of children and youth in
school settings, is the phenomenon of comorbidity. Although assumptions
underlying assessment in mental health and psychiatry may differ from those
underlying the assessment of children and youth with behavioral disorders
as identified through educational criteria, it is important to consider the ways
in which comorbidity might influence assessment in the educational arena for
the purposes of screening, classification, identification for services, and
intervention. In addition, the issue of comorbidity may have serious implications for educational research with children and youth who have emotional
and behavioral disorders. Because the overwhelming majority of comorbidity
research has been conducted with clinical samples (i.e., samples identified
through clinical diagnostic criteria such as those found in the *Diagnostic and
Statistical Manual of Mental Disorders*, or *DSM*, currently in its fourth revision;
American Psychiatric Association, 1995), rather than samples identified
through school criteria, it is by necessity that we have focused our review and
framed our discussion on findings and conclusions drawn from clinical
samples. Our purpose in this chapter is to discuss several issues surrounding
the relation of comorbidity to assessment.

DEFINITION OF COMORBIDITY

Comorbidity refers to the co-occurrence of two or more conditions in the
same individual. Initially, the term was used in the medical literature to
describe the presence of two or more disease states (Feinstein, 1970). More
recently, the term has been applied to the field of mental health to describe
the co-occurrence of emotional and behavioral disorders. Although emotional and behavioral disorders can co-occur with other identified disabilities, such as learning disabilities (e.g., Forness, 1988; Hodges & Plow, 1990),
the term comorbidity has yet to be applied formally, or technically, to this
distinction. That is, the term is not used, for example, to describe the student
who has both an emotional or behavioral disorder and a learning disability,
or the student who has a learning disability and a speech disorder, although
we know with certainty that such disabilities do co-occur. Therefore, for the
purpose of this chapter, we restrict our discussion to the co-occurrence of
more than one specific emotional and behavioral disorder of children and
youth.

Research has demonstrated quite clearly that specific syndromes associated with emotional and behavioral disorders do not always exist in isolation; rather, for many individuals, syndromes exist concurrently (see reviews by Anderson & McGee, 1994; Munir & Boulifard, 1995). In fact, the research has been so convincing that many argue that the comorbidity of disorders is the rule, rather than the exception (e.g., Caron & Rutter, 1991). In the following section, we provide a brief overview of the literature that has examined the prevalence of comorbidity among emotional and behavioral disorders of children and adolescents.

PREVALENCE OF COMORBIDITY

The prevalence of comorbidity among groups of children and youth with emotional and behavioral disorders has been documented consistently in the literature. In particular, many studies have found comorbid conditions among specific internalizing disorders (e.g., anxiety and depression), among specific externalizing disorders (e.g., conduct disorder and attention deficit disorder), and among specific internalizing and specific externalizing disorders (e.g., depression and conduct disorder). In Table 8.1 we summarize several studies that have addressed the prevalence of comorbidity among specific emotional and behavioral disorders.

Although researchers have identified the presence of comorbid conditions consistently, several issues related to prevalence of comorbid disorders can be gleaned from Table 8.1. First, it is important to note the wide range of comorbid conditions summarized from research presented. The comorbidity of specific internalizing disorders such as depression and anxiety (e.g., Alessi & Magen, 1988; Kovacs, Feinberg, Crouse-Novak, Paulauskas, & Finkelstein, 1984), depression and phobia (e.g., Last & Strauss, 1990; Last, Strauss, & Francis, 1987), and anxiety and phobia (e.g., Bernstein & Garfinkel, 1986; Kashani & Orvaschel, 1990) are strongly supported through research. Likewise, the comorbidity of externalizing disorders such as attention deficit disorder and conduct disorder (e.g., Munir, Biederman, & Knee, 1987; Tankersley & Lloyd, 1993) has been firmly established in the literature.

In addition to specific disorders of a behavioral dimension (internalizing or externalizing) coexisting, researchers have also shown that specific internalizing disorders often co-occur with specific externalizing disorders (e.g., McGee & Williams, 1988; Munir et al., 1987; Puig-Antich, 1982). For example, Marriage, Fine, Moretti, and Haley (1986) found that 18% of the youth in their study had comorbid depression and conduct disorder. Moreover, many researchers have found that emotional and behavioral disorders can exist in combination with several other disorders concurrently; that is, comorbidity can occur among three or more disorders (e.g., Tankersley,

TABLE 8.1

Summaries of Studies in Which Rate of Comorbidity of Emotional and Behavioral Disorders was Assessed With Children and Adolescents

Authors	Sample Description	Age of Subjects (Years)	Method for Identification of Disorders	Findings Relative to Comorbidity
Alessi & Magen (1988)	Clinically identified as depressed ($n = 25$)	Mean 10-7	Clinician interviews with children	25% of depressed children met DSM-III criteria for anxiety as well
Anderson, Williams, McGee, & Silva (1987)	Clinically identified with a DSM diagnosis of ($n = 219$)	11	Clinician interviews with children; parent report; teacher report	55% showed one or more comorbid conditions among conduct, oppositional defiant, attention deficit, anxiety, and phobic disorder
Bernstein & Garfinkel (1986)	Referred from schools and juvenile court systems for school phobia ($n = 26$)	Range 9-17	Clinician interviews with children; self-report from children	69% also met DSM-III criteria for depression; 62% also met criteria for anxiety disorder; 50 % evidenced both depression and anxiety disorder
Kashani & Orvashel (1990)	Nonclinically identified with anxiety ($n = 44$)	8, 12, and 17	Clinician interviews with parents; clinician interviews with children	9 children evidenced both separation anxiety and over-anxious disorder; 3 children evidenced both separation anxiety and simple phobia; 2 children evidenced both phobia and overanxious disorder; 2 children evidenced separation anxiety, phobia, and overanxious disorder
Kolvin, Berney, & Bhate (1984)	Clinically identified as school phobic ($n = 51$)	Range 9-15	Clinician interviews with parents; clinician interviews with children	45% of school phobics were rated as depressed as well

Study	Sample	Age	Method	Findings
Kovacs, Feinberg, Crouse-Novak, Paulauskas, & Finkelstein (1984)	Clinically identified as depressed (n = 65)	Range 8-13	Clinician interviews with parents; clinician interviews with children	25% of depressed children had anxiety disorders as well
Kovacs, Gatsonis, Paulauskas, & Richards (1989)	Clinically identified as depressed (n = 142)	Range 8-13	Clinician interviews with parents, clinician interviews with children	41% of depressed children also had anxiety disorders
Last, Hersen, Kazdin, Finkelstein, & Strauss (1987)	Clinically identified as school phobic (n = 63)	Range 7-17	Clinician interviews	Coexisting diagnoses: 25% overanxious disorder, 13% social phobia, 13% simple phobia, 13% major depression, 11% avoidant disorder
Last, Strauss, & Francis (1987)	Total of 73 children clinically identified with separation anxiety disorder (33%); overanxious disorder (15%; social phobia (15%); major depression (15%)	Range 5-18	Clinician interviews with children	33% of the separation anxiety group met DSM-III criteria for overanxious disorder; 36% of the overanxious disorder group met criteria for social phobia and 27% for avoidant disorder, 55% of the major depression group met criteria for social phobia, 45% for separation anxiety disorder, 27% for avoidant disorder
Marriage, Fine, Moretti, & Haley (1986)	Referred for assessment of depression (n = 60)	Range 11-15	Clinician interviews; DSM-III symptoms checklist	18% had comorbid depressive disorders and conduct disorders
McConaughy & Achenbach (1994)	Matched general population (n = 2705) and clinical sample (n = 2705)	Range 4-18	Parent ratings; self-ratings; teacher ratings	Using parent ratings, comorbidity for 2 or more syndromes was 12% in general population & 60% in clinical sample; using teacher ratings, comorbidity was 12% in general population and 29% in clinical sample; using self-ratings, comorbidity was 12% in general population and 41% in clinical sample

(Continued)

TABLE 8.1
(Continued)

Authors	Sample Description	Age of Subjects (Years)	Method for Identification of Disorders	Findings Relative to Comorbidity
McGee & Williams (1988)	Clinically identified as depressed ($n = 40$)	9, 11, 13	Clinician interviews; parent report; self-report; teacher report	9-year-old children with depressive disorders also displayed high levels of worrying-fearful behavior and antisocial behavior (boys only) and as reported by parents; 13-year-old boys with depressive disorders also displayed high levels of antisocial behavior as reported by parents and teachers
Mitchell, McCauley, Burke, & Moss (1988)	Children ($n = 45$) and adolescents ($n = 50$) clinically identified with major depression	Range 7-17	Clinician interviews with parents; clinician interviews with children	42% of children, 44% of adolescents exhibited concurrent separation anxiety; 18% of children and 8% of adolescents exhibited concurrent generalized anxiety; 11% of children and 20% of adolescents exhibited concurrent phobia
Munir, Biederman, & Knee (1987)	Clinically identified males with attention deficit disorder (ADD; $n = 22$)	Mean 11-7	Clinician interviews with parents; clinician interviews with children	96% of ADD males had more than one diagnosis or 82% had three or more diagnosis; 36% had conduct disorder; 59% had oppositional disorder; 32% had affective disorder
Norvell, Brophy, & Finch (1985)	Children hospitalized for emotional and behavioral disorders ($n = 30$)	Mean 11-6	Self-report	Significant relationship between anxiety and depression
Ollendick & Yule (1990)	Nonclinical sample ($n = 663$)	Range 8-10	Self-report	Children who reported high levels of depression also reported high levels of anxiety and high levels of social evaluative fear
Puig-Antich (1982)	Males clinically identified as depressed ($n = 43$)	Prepubertal	Clinician interviews with parents; clinician interviews with children	One-third of males clinically identified as depressed also fit diagnostic criteria for conduct disorder

Study	Sample	Age	Measure	Findings
Rohde et al. (1991)	Clinically identified as depressed (n = 50)	Range 14-18	Clinician interviews	18% had concurrent anxiety disorders; 8% had concurrent disruptive behavior
Ryan et al. (1987)	Children (n = 95) and adolescents (n = 95) clinically identified as depressed	Range 6-18	Clinician interviews with parents; clinician interviews with children	Separation anxiety evident in 58% of children and 11% of adolescents; overanxious disorders evident in 20% of children and 20% of adolescents; phobias evident in 45% of children and 17% of adolescents
Seidman et al. (1995)	Males clinically identified with attention deficit hyperactivity disorder (ADHD; n = 65)	Range 9-20	Clinician interviews	55% of ADHD males had comorbid depression, anxiety, or conduct disorders (specific patterns and rates of comorbidity not provided)
Stavrakaki, Vargo, Boodoosingh, & Roberts (1987)	One group (n = 33) clinically identified as anxious; one group (n = 51) clinically identified as depressed	Range 6-16	Self-report; parent report; clinician report	Depressed children (the majority of whom were older) evidenced symptoms of concurrent anxiety; anxious children (the majority of whom were younger) were not rated as manifesting concurrent depressive symptoms
Strauss, Last, Hersen, & Kazdin (1988)	Clinically identified as anxious (n = 106)	Range 5-17	Self-report; clinician interviews with children	28% also met DSM-III criteria for concurrent major depression
Tankersley (1992)	Nonclinical, regular education 4th and 5th graders (n = 148) nominated by teachers as most evident of internalizing behaviors when compared to remaining class members	Range 9-11	Teacher report	12% of sample evidenced elevated scores (above one standard deviation of sample scores) on subscales Fear, Anxious/Depressed, and Anxiety-Withdrawal

(Continued)

159

TABLE 8.1
(Continued)

Authors	Sample Description	Age of Subjects (Years)	Method for Identification of Disorders	Findings Relative to Comorbidity
Tankersley & Lloyd (1993)	Nonclinical, regular education 4th- and 5th-grade females (n = 15) nominated by teachers as most evident of internalizing or externalizing behaviors when compared to remaining class members	Range 9-11	Teacher report	26% of the females had elevated scores (at least one standard deviation above mean for the instrument) on subscales of Anxiety-Withdrawal and Anxious/Depressed; 21% elevated scores on subscales Attention Problems and Conduct Disorder; 15% elevated scores on subscales Anxiety-Withdrawal, Anxious/Depressed, Attention Problems, and Conduct Disorder
Verhulst & van der Ende (1993)	General population (n = 1117)	Range 4-11	Parent ratings	Among the highest odds ratio calculated for a group scoring in the deviant range (above the 90th percentile) were the following: subjects who were deviant on the Attention Problems scale were 18.9 times more likely than nondeviant subjects to have deviant score on Social Problems scale; deviant on Anxious/Depressed 7.2 times more likely to be deviant on Withdrawn; deviant on Attention Problems 9.1 times more likely to be deviant on Aggressive Behavior; deviant on Somatic Complaints 6.1 times more likely deviant on Anxious/Depressed
Woolston et al. (1989)	Psychiatrically hospitalized children (n = 35)	Mean 9-5	Clinician interviews and observations; parent report	51% of children had at least one behavioral diagnosis (conduct disorder, oppositional-defiant disorder, or ADHD) and one affective/anxiety diagnosis (depression, dysthymia, anxiety disorders)

1992). Indeed, Munir et al. (1987) found that over 82% of the males identified with attention deficit disorder in their study fit diagnostic criteria for two or more other disorders as well.

Second, it is important to note that in the sample of studies summarized in Table 8.1, the majority of the researchers have calculated the rate of comorbidity based on clinical samples. Using clinical samples to identify comorbidity might overrepresent the true rate of occurrence in the general population. The likelihood of children with comorbid disorders being included in clinical samples is great because (a) research has shown that children who have concurrent disorders are more likely to demonstrate a greater severity of disorder than children who evidence only one disorder (e.g., Bernstein, 1991), (b) children who demonstrate the greatest severity of problems are the most likely to receive services, and (c) clinical samples are drawn from individuals who are currently receiving services. Therefore, researchers are likely to identify disproportionately more comorbid conditions in clinical samples than in general population samples (Caron & Rutter, 1991).

Even though the majority of studies reviewed have used clinical samples to estimate prevalence, comorbidity has also been found in studies that have assessed the general population (see review in McConaughy & Achenbach, 1994). The prevalence of comorbidity in the general population, however, is much less than in the clinical population. Indeed, McConaughy and Achenbach found that the rate of comorbidity for particular syndrome pairs assessed by parents on the Child Behavior Checklist (Achenbach, 1991) for children aged 4 to 18 years ranged from 10.5 to 30.2% in the general population and 21.1 to 51.9% in clinical samples. Although the rate of comorbidity is significantly lower in the general population, the importance if its occurrence should not be overlooked. That syndromes associated with emotional and behavioral disorders of children and youth may be present in 10 to 30% of the general population suggests a substantial rate of occurrence of comorbidity.

The high rates of prevalence of comorbidity and the wide range of comorbid conditions provide a strong rationale for further examination of comorbidity. In the following section, we discuss the present and long-term implications of comorbidity for children and youth with emotional and behavioral disorders.

IMPLICATIONS OF COMORBIDITY

Perhaps the most important implication of comorbidity of emotional and behavioral disorders is the severity of problem behavior and the poor long-term prognosis associated with it (e.g., Verhulst & van der Ende, 1993). Children and youth who demonstrate comorbid conditions typically display more severe levels of both conditions than children with only one identified disorder (e.g., Bernstein, 1991). For example, Harrington, Fudge, Rutter, Pickles, and Hill (1991) found that children identified clinically with comorbid depression and conduct disorder had significantly lower degrees of recovery and demonstrated significantly higher degrees of disability than did children with depression alone. Moreover, children with comorbid depression and conduct disorder also had significantly higher degrees of disability than did children with conduct disorder. Although it seems logical that two disorders would cause more problems than one, the fact is that comorbid conditions may interact or exacerbate one another to the degree that the combined effect of more than one disorder may not be additive but exponential (e.g., Verhulst & van der Ende, 1993).

That children with comorbid conditions display the most severe of behaviors is important in assessing comorbidity among children and youth identified as emotionally and behaviorally disordered in school settings. Leaders in the field of emotional and behavioral disorders contend that we are currently identifying and providing educational services to fewer children than would be expected by chance to have an emotional and behavioral disorder in schools (e.g., Kauffman, 1993). In fact, even conservative estimates of the prevalence of emotional and behavioral disorders of the school-age population range from 3 to 6% (e.g., Brandenburg, Friedman, & Silver, 1990), yet schools currently serve less than one percent of children and youth under the federally designated label of serious emotional disturbance (U.S. Department of Education, 1992). Therefore, over half of the students who should be receiving services under the designation of this category are not being identified. Because fewer children are identified and served through schools than should be, it seems reasonable to assume that the children and youth who are being served are those with the most troublesome or unmanageable behaviors. Given that individuals with comorbid conditions often display the most severe behavioral problems, it is likely that they are the children and youth whom schools identify to receive services.

Not only might students with comorbid emotional and behavioral disorders display more severe forms of behavioral problems, they might also display these disorders over longer periods of time than students with singular disorders. For example, Anderson, Williams, McGee, and Silva (1987) studied the persistence of disorders by assessing a sample of youth with internalizing disorders (i.e., depression, dysthymia) at age 11 years and again at age 15 years. The results showed that 11-year-old youth with comorbid disorders were more likely to continue having disorders at age 15 than were 11-year-olds who presented single internalizing disorders.

In addition, children and youth with comorbid conditions also may be at greater risk for problems in later life than children and youth with one disorder. For example, Harrington et al. (1991) found that clinically referred children with comorbid depression and conduct disorder had a higher risk of adult criminality and adult substance abuse or dependence than depressed children without conduct disorder.

Because of the serious implications of comorbidity for the life course and identification for services of such individuals, it is important to discuss how comorbidity may influence the process of assessment of emotional and behavioral disorders in schools. In the following sections, we discuss issues of comorbidity in assessment of emotional and behavioral disorders. In particular, we focus on issues that could be related to the ways we screen, classify, identify, and intervene with students who have emotional and behavioral disorders.

ISSUES OF COMORBIDITY IN ASSESSMENT

Comorbidity creates interesting dilemmas for assessing emotional and behavioral disorders of children and youth. For example, professionals might debate the extent to which one should assess for disorders whose symptoms may not be readily apparent. In practice, comorbidity might have implications for how we screen for emotional and behavioral disorders, how we classify emotional and behavioral problems, who is identified to receive services, and the type of intervention they receive. In the following sections, we discuss the implications comorbidity might have for assessment for the following purposes: screening for emotional and behavioral disorders, classification, identifying students for services, and intervention.

Implications for Screening

Screening is a difficult task that is often not exercised for identifying the emotional and behavioral disorders of children and youth. Because schools have limited resources, and evaluation and services are expensive, few school systems actively seek to identify students who would qualify for services within this category of special education (Peacock Hill Working Group, 1991). Instead, most wait on teacher-initiated referral for screening of emotional and behavioral disorders of children and youth. Therefore, screening for emotional and behavioral disorders is typically a first step in preventing existing problems from worsening, rather than the prevention of the occurrence of the disorder (see Kauffman, 1993, for a discussion on issues surrounding the screening of emotional and behavioral disorders in schools).

The presence of comorbidity, however, is important to consider in screening for emotional and behavioral disorders. Procedures that rely foremost on teacher referral may ensure that only students with behaviors that are most disruptive to the educational process and environment get identified for screening. Students who display few behaviors that are disruptive to the environment may not come to the attention of teachers as readily as students who engage in disruptive behaviors. For example, students with internalizing behavioral patterns (comorbid or pure, singular internalizing patterns) may not be referred by teachers for screening at the same rate as students with externalizing behavioral patterns or students with comorbid externalizing and internalizing behavioral patterns. Indeed, many researchers have found that the majority of students who do receive special education services under the designation of serious emotional disturbance display patterns that include externalizing behavioral characteristics (e.g., Mattison, Humphrey, & Kales, 1986).

Because of the complications associated with screening, it seems critical that we employ a combination of methods designed to assess behavior for screening purposes. Empirically based assessment tools that consider students' gender and age in relation to behaviors exhibited present a wide scope of behavior, provide ratings from a variety of informants (e.g., self, parent, teacher), and allow for a range of behavior occurrence (e.g., never–frequently) might be the best alternative for screening and assessing emotional and behavioral disorders. Screening instruments such as the Systematic Screening for Behavior Disorders (Walker & Severson, 1990) and assessment tools such as the Child Behavior Checklist (Achenbach, 1991) and the Revised Behavior Problem Checklist (Quay & Peterson, 1987) allow for identifying not only the dichotomous classification of internalizing and externalizing behavioral dimensions, but also provide for identifying specific behavior disorders and the co-occurrence of those disorders as well. Looking at the results of such assessment tools should permit detection of not only the symptoms of many types of pure disorders, but also the detection of comorbid disorders (Caron & Rutter, 1991), which may then warrant the study of the individual's behavior in greater depth.

Implications for Classification

The classification of emotional and behavioral disorders of children and youth involves ordering behavior into meaningful groups that delineate similarities within groups of behaviors and differences across groups of behavior. Perhaps the greatest utility of classification for special education lies in the provision of some general categories or groups of behavior that can aid discussion and communication among professionals.

Two types of classification systems are currently used in practice: psychiatric systems and behavioral dimension systems. Psychiatric, or clinical psychological, systems of classifying the emotional and behavioral disorders of children and youth rely on primarily unstructured interviews (with parents, the child, or other significant adults) for assessing presenting problems. Information gathered from such interviews is matched to a set of qualifying criteria (e.g., must exhibit three out of the following nine indicators) for specific diagnoses of disorder. The most widely used psychiatric system for classifying emotional and behavioral disorders is the *DSM–IV* (American Psychological Association, 1995).

Dimensional classification schemes are based on the results of multivariate techniques (factor analysis, cluster analysis) that have assessed the observed behavioral characteristics of large samples of children and youth. Parents, teachers, and the children being assessed rate the occurrence of specific behaviors on a scale (e.g., the behavior happens frequently, sometimes, never). Behaviors that tend to be associated with one another as assessed through such methods identify syndromes of behavior. Two of the most widely used assessment instruments designed through a multivariate approach to classification are the Child Behavior Checklist (with versions for parent-, self-, and teacher report of behavior; Achenbach, 1991) and the Revised Behavior Problem Checklist (Quay & Peterson, 1987).

Although there is strong evidence of congruence in the identification of syndromes between psychiatric and dimensional classification techniques (e.g., Biederman et al., 1993), educators tend to rely on the dimensional classification systems for several reasons. First, the syndromes associated with psychiatric classification systems have no useful meaning for educators. In other words, psychiatric diagnoses provide little information on which educators can base interventions.

Second, dimensional systems allow for the classification of a wide variety of behaviors concurrently. Children referred to clinicians who use psychiatric classification systems may be assessed primarily in the areas identified by the referring person or may be restricted to the observations made during interviews. This practice could decrease the likelihood of identifying all behavior problems present. A dimensional approach to assessment, on the other hand, may have greater probability of identifying less obvious syndromes of behavior because a wide variety of behavior is evaluated. Moreover, dimensional systems allow for assessment of the extent to which behaviors occur rather than recording their mere occurrence or non-occurrence.

For this reason, the dimensional approach might also have a greater probability for identifying comorbid emotional and behavioral problems. Regardless of the classification system used, however, it seems important that any clinician or educator charged with the assessment of the emotional and behavioral disorders of children and youth must attend specifically to the possibility of comorbidity and take active steps to assess the broad range of behaviors.

Implications of Identification for Special Education Services

Determining who is eligible for services as a student with serious emotional disturbance under the federal regulations requires multiple sources of data and assessment from multiple professional perspectives. The task of identification is arduous, confounded by such variables as inconsistent judgments of professionals and the appropriateness of evaluation methods. Perhaps the most critical confounding variable in assessing the emotional and behavioral disorders of students is the eligibility criteria for receiving services.

The federal definition of serious emotional disturbance (SED) includes many behaviors that could be associated with specific dimensions of behavior and specific conditions of behavior. For example, the definition includes in its criteria the following characteristics (enumerated here with the corresponding federal designations):

> (B) an inability to build or maintain satisfactory interpersonal relationships with peers and teachers; (C) inappropriate types of behavior or feelings under normal circumstances; (D) a general, pervasive mood of unhappiness or depression; or (E) a tendency to develop physical symptoms or fears associated with personal or school problems. (Individuals with Disabilities Act, IDEA; 34 C.F.R. §300.7 [b] [9])

Taken together, these criteria specifically identify problems associated with the internalizing dimension of behavior. Separately, the characteristics could refer to specific disorders of behavior such as social withdrawal (characteristic B), anxiety (characteristic C), depression (characteristic D), phobia (characteristic E), or somatic complaints (also characteristic E).

In addition to identifying problems associated with the internalizing dimension of behavior, the characteristics listed in the federal definition of SED also point to problems associated with the externalizing dimension of behavior. For example, characteristics B and C (as outlined in the previous paragraph) could also refer to conduct disorder, oppositional defiance, or attention deficit disorder. However, as the definition currently stands, an exclusion clause of the definition states that "the term does not include children who are socially maladjusted unless it is determined that they are seriously emotionally disturbed" (EHA, 1978; amended in IDEA). The implications of the exclusion clause (see Cline, 1990; Forness & Knitzer, 1990) are critical for students with conduct disorder because they may be judged to be socially maladjusted and thereby be denied special education services. Indeed, several states have already begun to exclude students who have been identified as having a conduct disorder from receiving special education services under the SED designation (e.g., Cheney & Sampson, 1990).

Past research has shown that, although the majority of the criteria in the federal definition are inclusive of internalizing behavioral patterns, and only two characteristics could qualify as externalizing behavioral patterns, most students who have received services under the definition of SED would be classified as having an attention deficit disorder or a conduct disorder (Mattison, Humphrey, Kales, Hanford, et al., 1986). In fact, Mattison, Humphrey, Kales, Hanford, et al. found that 70% of their sample of 6- to 12-year-old males receiving SED services could be identified as having an externalizing disorder and only 25% could be identified as having an internalizing disorder.

Moreover, students who are identified with an internalizing disorder might not receive special education services unless they are also identified with an externalizing disorder. From a sample of 111 elementary and junior-high students diagnosed with an internalizing disorder (i.e., depression or dysthymia), Forness (1988) found that the students who had comorbid externalizing disorders (e.g., conduct disorder, attention deficit disorder) were more likely to be eligible for and receive special education services than students with an internalizing disorder alone. Specifically, 44% of the students with the comorbid conditions and 21% of students with internalizing disorders alone received services. The group of students who were practically guaranteed of special education services, however, were students with comorbid behavioral disorders and learning disabilities. Indeed, 85% of students with comorbid behavioral disorders and a diagnosed learning disability received special education services. Although these students were receiving special education services, these services were targeted for their learning disabilities rather than for their emotional and behavioral problems. Because they were identified as having a learning disability instead of an emotional and behavioral disorder, it may be very likely that their emotional and behavioral problems were not being addressed fully.

Assessment of comorbidity among disorders may be one way to facilitate the identification of some students for SED services. Students who may be excluded from services because they have been identified as having conduct disorders could actually have comorbid emotional and behavioral disorders; the coexisting disorders could identify them as eligible for services. To illustrate, if a student has comorbid conduct disorder and depression, he could still meet current criteria for SED under characteristic D in the federal definition (i.e., a general, pervasive mood of unhappiness or depression). Until changes are made in the definition of SED, assessing comorbidity of emotional and behavioral disorders might offer students their only opportunity to become eligible for special education services and interventions in states that practice exclusion of conduct disorder (Forness, Kavale, & Lopez, 1993).

Implications for Intervention

School-based interventions for students with emotional and behavioral disorders typically are prescribed based on the identified problems exhibited by the students. Externalizing behavioral problems involve excess behavior (such as aggression, disruption, noncompliance, overactivity) and intervention techniques designed to reduce or eliminate the frequency or intensity of specific behavioral displays are needed. Techniques such as time out from positive reinforcement, response cost, and differential reinforcement are among those that might be employed in the classroom to replace or reduce the frequency of the inappropriate displays of acting-out behavioral problems. In contrast, internalizing behavioral problems (such as social isolation, depressive affect, anxiety, immaturity) often signify the need to teach skills that are not displayed or that are displayed at an insufficient rate. Techniques such as social skills training and positive reinforcement for specific displays of behavior are among those that might be employed in the classroom to build the skills or facilitate the acquisition and use of the skills that are necessary to be successful in that environment.

In order to improve intervention and properly evaluate its effectiveness, we must use assessment procedures that tap a wide range of behavior problems if we are to be fully informed and responsive to the patterns of comorbidity (Achenbach, 1995). Attending to the array of disorders evidenced by an individual enables educators and other professionals to be more proficient in selecting and implementing appropriate interventions; failing to attend to the possibility of comorbidity may mean providing less effective interventions.

ISSUES OF COMORBIDITY FOR RESEARCHERS

As the phenomenon of comorbidity appears increasingly in the professional literature, it is important to discuss the implications of comorbidity for researchers. From a research perspective, comorbidity may influence the inferences researchers draw regarding behavioral displays and risk or causal factors. Moreover, the presence of comorbidity may affect the methods and course of intervention recommended for students with emotional and behavioral disorders.

Caron and Rutter (1991) identified two specific ways in which researchers could draw inaccurate conclusions if comorbidity is not taken into account. First, a failure to assess comorbidity in samples may lead to inferences about the course, features, or correlates of a particular behavior disorder that may be related to a nonidentified disorder or the combined effects of disorders. For example, if a researcher is interested in identifying the familial characteristics of children identified as depressed, but does not assess the co-occurrence of anxiety in their sample, the results might be attributable to the presence of anxiety rather than a characteristic of depression.

Second, a failure to take comorbidity into account in research may lead to assumptions that the nature of a disorder is the same, regardless of the presence of other disorders (Caron & Rutter, 1991). This assumption could also lead to erroneous conclusions. For example, if a researcher seeks to identify risk factors for conduct disorder, but does not assess the presence of other disorders in the sample, the risk factors identified could be inaccurate or at least fundamentally different. In fact, because children with pure disorders may actually represent a minority of individuals with emotional and behavioral disorders, drawing conclusions about the nature of a disorder without considering comorbidity of the sample could prove misleading and, thus, make findings tenuous at best.

In terms of research associated with educational intervention, comorbidity of disorders could result in researchers recommending inappropriate interventions. If researchers assess their sample only for the occurrence of a specific disorder, or a classification of disorders (i.e., internalizing or externalizing), their recommendations for the use of intervention strategies may not be appropriate for samples with singular occurrences of the disorder.

Moreover, the manner in which we identify our samples, and the conclusions we draw from our research, has an overarching effect on our profession. Categories or classifications of behavioral disorders of children and youth not only shape our identification of samples for research, but also dictate agendas for funding, the services provided, and the training of professionals (Achenbach, 1995).

DISCUSSION AND SUMMARY

There can be little doubt that students with emotional and behavioral disorders present among the greatest challenges that educators face. The idea that professionals have estimated that at least two to three times as many SED students as are currently served may actually have emotional and behavioral disorders further suggests that the task of assessment and intervention for this population is formidable. In this chapter we have addressed the concept of comorbidity and its importance as we consider assessment for screening, classification, identification for services, and intervention.

The suggestion that children and youth with emotional and behavioral disorders may more often than not have comorbid disorders may be particularly important to consider as we examine the role and function of schools and professional educators in serving these students. In special education we have a tradition of designating students' "primary handicapping conditions" when one or more disabilities are present. For students who display comorbid emotional and behavioral disorders, the process may be much more complex. Although we may only extrapolate from the clinical samples described in the bulk of published studies addressing comorbidity, we believe that comorbidity may be as much the rule among students identified as SED as this literature suggests. As Kauffman (1993) and others have argued, it seems clear that schools identify as SED only those students with the most severe cases of emotional and behavioral disorders—precisely those most likely to experience comorbid conditions.

How must practice change to address these issues? First, we advocate a more thorough approach to assessment, with attention to a greater depth and range of behavioral disorders at all stages of the assessment process. From screening, the initial point at which most students should be identified as potentially having problems that require specialized services, educators must attend as much to internalizing as to externalizing behavior disorders. Even when students come to our attention due to their behavioral excesses, we must not overlook the potential that comorbid conditions are present.

Second, an increased focus on interventions that teach new skills and behaviors must replace an overreliance on behavior reductive strategies. These interventions obviously must be derived from careful assessments that provide information about not only a student's obvious (i.e., externalizing) behavior problems, but also about potential comorbid disorders that may be less obvious (e.g., depression, anxiety, social withdrawal).

Finally, and ultimately, we advocate for a concentrated reexamination of the definition of serious emotional disturbance that continues to drive educational practice. We believe that an open, inclusive definition, such as the definition proposed by the National Mental Health and Special Education Coalition (Forness & Knitzer, 1990), may provide practitioners with more guidance than the current restrictive, exclusive definition. Indeed, the worrisome trend in our field toward excluding from services those students who are socially maladjusted warrants our closer attention to the likelihood that these students also display comorbid conditions. For example, the student who can be said to be socially maladjusted may be quite likely to have at least one other, generally less obvious, comorbid emotional and behavioral disorder. For these students, greater attention to the broad range of possible comorbid conditions on the part of professionals may be the only means by which they receive the services they need.

In summary, we believe that the very concept of comorbidity, which has received limited attention in the educational literature, may ultimately play a significant part in such basic decisions for students with emotional and behavioral disorders as determinations of eligibility and intervention prescription. At the least, comorbidity should become a common consideration for any professional involved in assessing students with potential emotional and behavioral disorders.

REFERENCES

Achenbach, T. M. (1985). *Assessment and taxonomy of child and adolescent psychopathology*. Beverly Hills: Sage.

Achenbach, T. M. (1991). *Manual for the child behavior checklist/4–18 and 1991 profile*. Burlington: University of Vermont, Department of Psychiatry.

Achenbach, T. M. (1995). Empirically based assessment and taxonomy: Application to clinical research. *Psychological Assessment, 7*, 261–274.

Alessi, N. E., & Magen, J. (1988). Comorbidity of other psychiatric disturbances in depressed, psychiatrically hospitalized children. *American Journal of Psychiatry, 145,* 1582–1584.

American Psychiatric Association. (1995). *Diagnostic and statistical manual of mental disorders* (4th ed.). Washington, DC: Author.

Anderson, J. C., & McGee, R. (1994). Comorbidity of depression in children and adolescents. In W. M. Reynolds & H. F. Johnson (Eds.), *Handbook of depression in children and adolescents* (pp. 581–601). New York: Plenum.

Anderson, J. C., Williams, S., McGee, R., & Silva, P. A. (1987). DSM–III disorders in preadolescent children: Prevalence in a large sample from the general population. *Archives of General Psychiatry, 44,* 69–76.

Bernstein, G. A. (1991). Comorbidity and severity of anxiety and depressive disorders in a clinical sample. *Journal of American Academy of Child and Adolescent Psychiatry, 30,* 43–50.

Bernstein, G. A., & Garfinkel, B. D. (1986). School phobia: The overlap of affective and anxiety disorders. *Journal of American Academy of Child and Adolescent Psychiatry, 25,* 235–241.

Biederman, J., Faraone, S. V., Doyle, A., Lehman, B. K., Kraus, I., Perrin, J., & Tsuang, M. T. (1993). Convergence of the Child Behavior Checklist with structured interview-based psychiatric diagnoses of ADHD children with and without comorbidity. *Journal of Child Psychology and Psychiatry and Allied Disciplines, 34,* 1241–1251.

Brandenburg, N. A., Friedman, R. M., & Silver, S. E. (1990). The epidemiology of childhood psychiatric disorders: Prevalence findings from recent studies. *Journal of American Academy of Child and Adolescent Psychiatry, 29,* 76–83.

Caron, C., & Rutter, M. (1991). Comorbidity in child psychopathology: Concepts, issues and research strategies. *Journal of Child Psychology and Psychiatry, 45,* 1063–1080.

Cheney, C. O., & Sampson, K. (1990). Issues in identification and service delivery for students with conduct disorders: The "Nevada solution." *Behavioral Disorders, 15,* 174–179.

Cline, D. H. (1990). A legal analysis of policy initiatives to exclude handicapped/disruptive students from special education. *Behavioral Disorders, 15,* 159–173.

Feinstein, A. R. (1970). The pre-therapeutic classification of comorbidity in chronic disease. *Journal of Chronic Diseases, 23,* 455–468.

Forness, S. R. (1988). School characteristics of children and adolescents with depression. *Monographs in Behavioral Disorders, 10,* 117–203.

Forness, S. R., Kavale, K. A., & Lopez, M. (1993). Conduct disorders in school: Special education eligibility and comorbidity. *Journal of Emotional and Behavioral Disorders, 1,* 101–108.

Forness, S. R., & Knitzer, J. (1990). *A new proposed definition and terminology to replace "Serious Emotional Disturbance" in Education of the Handicapped Act.* Alexandria, VA: National Mental Health and Special Educational Coalition, National Mental Health Association.

Harrington, R., Fudge, H., Rutter, M., Pickles, A., & Hill, J. (1991). Adult outcomes of childhood and adolescent depression: II. Links with antisocial disorders. *Journal of the American Academy of Child and Adolescent Psychiatry, 30,* 434–439.

Hodges, K., & Plow, J. (1990). Intellectual ability and achievement in psychiatrically hospitalized children with conduct, anxiety, and affective disorders. *Journal of Consulting and Clinical Psychology, 58,* 589–595.

Kashani, J. H., & Orvaschel, H. (1990). A community study of anxiety in children and adolescents. *American Journal of Psychiatry, 147,* 313–318.

Kauffman, J. M. (1993). *Characteristics of emotional and behavioral disorders of children and youth* (5th ed.). New York: Macmillan.

Kolvin, I., Berney, T. P., & Bhate, S. R. (1984). Classification and diagnosis of depression in school phobia. *British Journal of Psychiatry, 145,* 347–357.

Kovacs, M., Feinberg, T. L., Crouse-Novak, M., Paulauskas, S. L., & Finkelstein, R. (1984). Depressive disorders in childhood: I. A longitudinal prospective study of characteristics and recovery. *Archives of General Psychiatry, 41,* 229–237.

Kovacs, M., Gatsonis, C., Paulauskas, S. L., & Richards, C. (1989). Depressive disorders in children: IV. A longitudinal study of comorbidity with and risk for anxiety disorders. *Archives of General Psychiatry, 46,* 776–782.

Last, C. G., Hersen, M., Kazdin, A. E., Finkelstein, R., & Strauss, C. C. (1987). Comparison of DSM-III separation anxiety and overanxious disorders: Demographic characteristics and patterns of comorbidity. *Journal of American Academy of Child and Adolescent Psychiatry, 26,* 527–531.

Last, C. G., & Strauss, C. C. (1990). School refusal in anxiety-disordered children and adolescents. *Journal of American Academy of Child and Adolescent Psychiatry, 29,* 31–35.

Last, C. G., Strauss, C. C., & Francis, G. (1987). Comorbidity among childhood anxiety disorders. *The Journal of Nervous and Mental Disease, 175,* 726–730.

Marriage, K., Fine, S., Moretti, M., & Haley, G. (1986). Relationship between depression and conduct disorder in children and adolescents. *Journal of the American Academy of Child Psychiatry, 25,* 687–691.

Mattison, R. E., Humphrey, F. J., & Kales, S. N. (1986). An objective evaluation of special class placement of elementary schoolboys with behavior problems. *Journal of Abnormal Psychology, 14,* 251–262.

Mattison, R. E., Humphrey, F. J., Kales, S. N., Hanford, H. A., Finkenbinder, R. L., & Hernit, R. C. (1986). Psychiatric background and diagnosis of children evaluated for special class placement. *Journal of the American Academy of Child and Adolescent Psychiatry, 25,* 514–520.

McConaughy, S. H., & Achenbach, T. M. (1994). Comorbidity of empirically based syndromes in matched general population and clinical samples. *Journal of Child Psychology and Psychiatry and Allied Disciplines, 35,* 1141–1157.

McGee, R., & Williams, S. (1988). A longitudinal study of depression in nine-year-old children. *Journal of American Academy of Child and Adolescent Psychiatry, 27,* 342–348.

Mitchell, J., McCauley, E., Burke, P. M., & Moss, S. J. (1988). Phenomenology of depression in children and adolescents. *Journal of American Child and Adolescent Psychiatry, 27,* 12–20.

Munir, K., & Boulifard, D. (1995). Comorbidity. In G. P. Scholevar (Ed.), *Conduct disorders in children and adolescents* (pp. 59–80). Washington, DC: American Psychiatric Press.

Munir, K., Biederman, J., & Knee, D. (1987). Psychiatric comorbidity in patients with attention deficit disorder: A controlled study. *Journal of American Child and Adolescent Psychiatry, 26,* 844–848.

Norvell, N., Brophy, C., & Finch, A. J. (1985). The relationship of anxiety to childhood depression. *Journal of Personality Assessment, 49,* 150–153.

Ollendick, T. H., & Yule, W. (1990). Depression in British and American children and its relation to anxiety and fear. *Journal of Consulting and Clinical Psychology, 58,* 126–129.

Peacock Hill Working Group. (1991). Problems and promises in special education and related services for children and youth with emotional and behavioral disorders. *Behavioral Disorders, 16,* 299–313.

Puig-Antich, J. (1982). Major depression and conduct disorder in prepuberty. *Journal of the American Academy of Child Psychiatry, 21,* 118–128.

Quay, H. C., & Peterson, D. R. (1987). *Manual for the revised behavior problem checklist.* Coral Gables, FL: Author.

Rohde, P., Lewinsohn, P. M., & Seeley, J. R. (1991). Comorbidity of unipolar depression: II. Comorbidity with other mental disorders in adolescents and adults. *Journal of Abnormal Psychology, 100,* 214–222.

Ryan, N. D., Puig-Antich, J., Ambrosini, P., Rabinovich, H., Robinson, D., Nelson, B., Iyengar, S., & Twomey, J. (1987). The clinical picture of major depression in children and adolescents. *Archives of General Psychiatry, 44,* 854–861.

Seidman, L. J., Biederman, J., Faraone, S. V., Milberger, S., Norman, D., Seiverd, K., Benedict, K., Guite, J., Mick, E., & Kiely, K. (1995). Effects of family history and comorbidity on the neuropsychological performance of children with ADHD: Preliminary findings. *Journal of the American Academy of Child and Adolescent Psychiatry, 34,* 1015–1024.

Stavrakaki, C., Vargo, B., Boodoosingh, & Roberts, N. (1987). The relationship between anxiety and depression in children: Rating scales and clinical variables. *Canadian Journal of Psychiatry, 32,* 433–439.

Strauss, C. C., Last, C. G., Hersen, M., & Kazdin, A. E. (1988). Association between anxiety and depression in children and adolescents with anxiety disorders. *Journal of Abnormal Child Psychology, 16,* 57–68.

Tankersley, M. (1992). *Classification and identification of internalizing behavioral subtypes.* Unpublished doctoral dissertation, University of Virginia, Charlottesville, VA.

Tankersley, M., & Lloyd, J. W. (1993, October). *Teacher ratings of preadolescent girls with internalizing or externalizing behavior dimensions.* Paper presented at the 3rd Annual Conference on Children and Adolescents with Emotional and Behavioral Disorders, Virginia Beach, VA.

U.S. Department of Education. (1992). *Fourteenth annual report to Congress on the implementation of the Individuals with Disabilities Act.* Washington, DC: U.S. Office of Special Education.

Verhulst, F. C., & van der Ende, J. (1993). "Comorbidity" in an epidemiological sample: A longitudinal perspective. *Journal of Child Psychology and Psychiatry and Allied Disciplines, 34,* 767–783.

Walker, H. M., & Severson, H. H. (1990). *Systematic screening for behavior disorders: Users guide and administration manual.* Longmont, CO: Sopris West.

Woolston, J. L., Rosenthal, S. L., Riddle, M. A., Sparrow, S. S., Cicchetti, D., & Zimmerman, L. D. (1989). Childhood comorbidity of anxiety/affective disorders and behavior disorders. *Journal of the American Academy of Child and Adolescent Psychiatry, 28,* 707–713.

INSTRUCTION

9

THEORY OF MASTERY AND ACCELERATION

Siegfried Engelmann
Engelmann-Becker Corporation

The theory of mastery holds simply that children's learning performance and motivation or responses to new learning are affected by the extent to which children master material. This orientation is suggested in the *Theory of Instruction* by Engelmann and Carnine (1982). The basic assumption is that children learn about learning and how to learn just as they learn other skills. Initial examples require more time and a greater number of trials to learn than later examples. If we present a naive learner with the task of learning different "classes," such as the class of things that are furniture, the class of vehicles, the class of zoo animals, the class of common containers, and others, we will discover that the number of trials required for the naive learner to master the first class presented is far greater than the number required to master the sixth class presented or the ninth. This pattern obtains regardless of which class is presented first and which is presented sixth. This pattern further confirms that the learner learns how to learn.

According to the *Theory of Instruction*, this acceleration occurs because the learner has learned what is the same about all the instances. In addition to learning about the specific content presented (e.g., the names of the things in the class of appliances, and the fact that these things are not in the class of animals), the learner learns the structural details that are the same from one class to another. Once the learner learns this structure, the learning of subsequent classes requires less learning than the first class, because the learner is not required to relearn the common structural details. Other savings in what is logically required to learn the various classes occur because the learner learns the strategies needed to remember the various details of each class. The learning of a new class, therefore, has "familiar" details. This accelerated learning trend is not observed if the learner does not achieve mastery on the various classes that are presented. Learning only some aspects of the content is actually mislearning the content and, therefore, cannot serve to greatly accelerate the learner's performance on later examples that are similar.

The effect that mastery has on the child's capacity to learn how to learn implies that acceleration of intellectual performance in any subject is possible by teaching to mastery. This type of acceleration is rarely observed in traditional educational settings, however, because lower performers rarely master material when it is taught and, therefore, have a poorly developed and inefficient mental schema for learning to mastery (e.g., poor memory, large number of trials required to induce mastery, tendencies to mislearn, low tolerance for failure, low level of motivation).

Often, attempts to help lower performers do not provide help. For example, "inclusive" practices that place the child in the same classroom as the average performer are supposed to make the lower performers feel good about themselves because they are not stigmatized by being in the special classroom. The assumption of these practices is that somehow the lower performer will be able to perform better in this setting and will be able to keep pace with the others. A logical analysis of what is required for the lower performer to do this, however, shows how preposterous the practice is. The basic problem is that the amount of new learning required for the lower performer to achieve mastery in this setting is significantly greater than this learner can achieve. Not only does the lower performer require more practice than the average performer needs to achieve mastery, the lower performer has fewer skills and less information than the average performer. Therefore, if the amount of new learning an average performer must achieve for mastery of a "lesson" is represented by the length of this line segment, ___ , the amount of learning required by the lower performer may be this much _____ . However, the expectation of the setting is that the learning will occur during the same period of time that the average performer masters the material (or will occur by providing a little more help and practice for the lower performer). This expectation is somewhat incredible, in that the lower performer must learn approximately two times the amount of material the average performer is to master and at two times the rate of the average performer. Historically, however, the lower performer has mastered material at only about .7 the rate of the average performer (Abt Associates, 1977). The cycle repeats itself, with the same expectations for each new lesson. The net result is that the lower performer never learns the foundation skills needed for new learning, and never learns the associated strategies for learning new material to mastery—never learns how to apply them appropriately, never learns the precise relationships they have to other concepts and skills.

Performance of children can be viewed as the ratio of mastery over time (which is what an IQ score is—the mental age or content that has been mastered over the chronological age, or the amount of time the learner has been exposed to content). Within this context, acceleration is simply a more efficient use of time. If what is learned is induced in half the time, the learner is accelerated. (The learner is growing at twice the rate of the average learner.) If what is learned requires an "average" amount of time, no acceleration is achieved (although the learner becomes "smarter," the learner is not improving relative to norms of "intellectual development," or relative rate of mastering new skills and concepts). If a below-average learning rate continues over an extended period of time, the learner becomes relatively retarded.

For mastery and concomitant acceleration of learning to occur across an entire population of children (from very low normal or mildly retarded to above average), three conditions must be met: (a) The instructional material must be appropriate, (b) the ongoing placement of children must be appropriate, and (c) the details of an operating system and plan of implementation (from the daily schedule to training of teachers and monitoring of student performance) must be designed to assure that mastery is occurring at reasonable rates.

APPROPRIATE MATERIAL

The curriculum and instructional programs used to teach skills and academic content should be engineered so they are capable of inducing learning. The material should be capable of being correlated with the clock and calendar so that expectations of student progress can be expressed precisely; the material should be clear and present new concepts or discriminations in a way that cannot be misinterpreted by the naive learner; the material should be efficient; and the program should be validated to be effective with the population of children to be taught and the population of teachers to teach them. Such validation occurs only through field testing and revision of the program on the basis of problems with the field-test version.

Relationship of Expectations and Program

Some of the more serious problems that teachers have in trying to induce mastery is that they have no clear idea of what sort of progress or performance to expect from different children. How long should the teacher work on something before it is mastered? If the instructional material is tightly designed, the material can provide the teacher with benchmarks for the mastery of different children. The material should be divided into lessons that are capable of being presented in a specified period of time (such as 30 minutes). Given that the material is capable of inducing mastery of the content if properly presented to children who are properly placed in the program, the structure of the program makes it possible to engineer a management system that has fairly precise expectations for the performance of different children and is capable of identifying any "problems" of children not being taught on schedule. If the expectations for an average performer are to master one lesson during a period, and the periods are presented daily, the number of school days should provide a precise indication both of where the teacher should be teaching in the program, and what skills the child should have mastered. For example, if 80 contact days have occurred, the teacher should be teaching lesson 80 and the child should be perfectly firm on all the skills and content that have been presented in the first 80 lessons.

The expectation for lower performers would initially be lower, perhaps .7 lessons a day (or 7 lessons in 10 contact days). This expectation is appropriate for the naive learner and would suggest that in 100 school days the child would be at lesson 70 and would have mastered all the content in the first 70 lessons. Given that the learner has mastered the content, the expectation for future learning is that the learner's rate of learning will tend to increase—possibly not much during the remainder of the year, but substantially over the next several years. The expectations for how well the material is learned, however, are the same for the lower performer as for the average or higher performer. There is no assumption that because a particular learner is a low performer, the level of mastery should be any lower than it is for a very high performer. All are expected to master the material to the same minimum criterion of performance.

Clarity of Communication

The material should be designed so it provides teaching demonstrations that are consistent with one and only one interpretation. In beginning reading, for instance, there would be no guessing on the basis of syntax or context, no using pictures to provide clues for the words to be read. There would be no "sight words" that are identified as global units, no memorizing of the stories that are to be "read," and there would be no exercises that encourage children to look at the general shape of the word or try to figure out the word on the basis of the first letter. All these "techniques" are used in traditional teaching of reading, but they are based on a serious misunderstanding of the learner's mental mechanism and what the learner is to learn. Basically, two misconceptions underpin these practices. The first is that the young learner is incapable of learning "fine" discriminations and must therefore first learn "global" ones. The second is that the learner is capable of learning things that are logically impossible. Techniques like trying to figure out words by looking at pictures or guessing on the basis of the first letter of the word require the learner to attempt what is logically impossible. The only way the naive learner will be capable of learning the difference between any two words that are similar is by reference to the sequence of letters that compose the words. Given that it is logically impossible to identify a word by reference to the first letter or identify it from a picture, the techniques are clearly problematic. The corrective reader—the reading failure—is a product of these spurious clues. The corrective reader is the one who guesses, who makes up narratives on the basis of the picture, who uses the syntax of the sentence as a basis for trying to identify words, and who "reads in synonyms," which reveals a complete lack of understanding of what the reading code is and how it works. To read in synonyms, the learner must be able to recognize the word but be completely confused about the relationship of the written word to how it is pronounced. For this learner, the word is associated with a meaning, not with a spelling. The learner recognizes the symbols as meaning, searches for the pronunciation of the meaning, and is surprised when the teacher points out that the learner did not identify the correct word.

In a well-designed program, the learner would only be exposed to demonstrations and practices that are consistent with a single interpretation. The learner would receive no exposures that suggested anything other than each word is a unique series of letters and is identified by the order of the letters.

Adequacy

The teaching material should provide for the mastery of all the skills that the child will need later in the sequence. The complex applications that occur later in the program dictate the nature and extent of the earlier skills that are needed. All that the child needs for the later applications should be taught before the child is required to perform these applications. Anything that is not needed for future applications is not taught. For the initial teaching of reading, for instance, the program would teach all the varieties of phonemic awareness that are needed for the child to decode accurately. The child would know the sound for each of the letter in the initial set of words to be decoded; the child would know the relationship between the order of sounds in the spoken word and the order of letters for the word (i.e., /mmm/ is the first sound in *mat* and presented to the left of the other letters in the word); the child would know two basic transformations for the sequence of sounds in a spoken word—how to say the sounds slowly and how to say them fast; and the child would understand the various instructions the teacher would present in directing the decoding of a new word ("Touch the first letter. What sound? Touch and say all the sounds. Get ready. What word?").

The teaching should be as direct as possible, with sufficient practice to assure that the skills are mastered and retained. The practice provided should generally occur over three consecutive lessons, should be immediately applied to other contexts, and should be tested.

Efficiency

The program should have "tracks" each of which provides training in a particular skill. During each period, children learn material from possibly five tracks, with each track receiving 3–6 minutes of instruction. This design is preferable to the traditional "object lesson" design, which devotes a period to one topic or skill. The multitrack design does not overload the children with an undue amount of learning on various lessons; it allows three consecutive lessons for teaching any new skill, and permits ongoing reviews. An efficient program should also have multiple entry points to accommodate children of different levels of initial skill.

Reliability

The material should be field tested, revised on the basis of field-test observations (particularly the mistakes that children make), and generally validated so that it is capable of serving as an implied and detailed time table for the initial expectations that we should have for the performance of children. Given that the program is capable of inducing the various skills for the appropriately placed child, the program provides a timetable of "developmental" skills the children will learn. Basically, if the program is executed correctly, the children will learn everything that is taught. The time of learning will correspond to the lessons during which the skill is taught. Therefore, consulting the program should provide an accurate reference to the observed development of the children's skills.

APPROPRIATE PLACEMENT OF CHILDREN

The properties of the program make it possible to accommodate a wide range of children who meet the placement requirements for entering the program: the goal is for all children to master the content in the most time-efficient manner possible. Achieving this goal implies that not all children will start at the same point or progress through the program at the same rate. As noted earlier, a general rule for the initial performance of children is that higher performers are expected to progress through the program sequence at about 1.3 lessons per period; average performers, about one lesson per period; lower performers, about .7 lessons per period. These are initial performance rates. The theory of mastery suggests that the child's performance will change as a function of the child's mastery experiences.

For the maximum effects to be observed, children should be of kindergarten age and should receive acceleration experiences for at least 4 years (ideally through the elementary grades, which would provide 6 or 7 years of mastery learning).

Given that the performance of children will change as they progress through the program, the following general criteria for appropriate placement must be applied to assure that the children are neither overwhelmed nor placed so they proceed far slower than ideal.

Four criteria provide fairly tight guidelines for placing children in any subject or skill that is to be taught:

1. The child's performance should be 70% first-time correct on material that is being taught.
2. The child should be at least 90% first-time correct on material that had been taught earlier and is assumed to have been mastered.
3. The child should be able to go through a "lesson" in the anticipated amount of time and should not require great amounts of additional practice.
4. At the end of each lesson, the child should be virtually 100% firm on everything presented in the lesson.

There is a logical or analytical basis for these criteria:

Achieves 70% first-time correct on material being taught. If the learner has not previously mastered 70% or more of the material, the learner is being required to learn an inordinate amount of new material. The learning does not take because of the excessive processing and memory requirements. For example, one of the tendencies of conscientious teachers in working with lower-performing students in Grade 6 is to try to drag them through the lessons of a sixth level program by giving them additional practice. If the same children are placed according to the 70% first-time correct criterion, they may be placed in the third level of the program. Note, however, that over a 2-year period, the student placed in the third level will, almost without exception, pass up the student who is being dragged through the sixth level of the program. It is not uncommon for students to finish the third and part of the fourth level of the program the first year and complete the fourth and most of the fifth during the next year. Their performance tends to be close to mastery. During the same period of time, the student placed in the sixth level of the program repeats parts and progresses slowly through the program, but not at mastery.

Achieves 90% correct on earlier taught material. If the learner is not 90% correct on material that is assumed to have been mastered, the learner does not have a sufficiently solid understanding of the material to proceed at an optimum rate. For this learner to master the current lesson, the learner would have to learn all the foundation concepts and skills that had not been mastered plus the new material presented in the current lesson. If the earlier taught material has been learned to mastery, the amount of new learning presented in the lesson is manageable and will not overwhelm the learner.

Completes the lesson in a reasonable amount of time. If the learner is physically disabled and incapable of performing some of the motor tasks called for in the lesson, the learner's performance will understandably be slowed. As a general practice, however, the learner who cannot go through the lesson in a reasonable amount of time (the time suggested by the daily schedule) is not adequately prepared. Possibly the learner's rate of writing, copying, or working is not sufficiently fast. Possibly the learner is not adequately practiced in following the directions the teacher provides. Possibly the learner is not at mastery on some of the concepts or skills assumed by the new learning.

Achieves close to 100% correct on everything in the lesson. The test of this criterion is for the teacher to present questions or assign anything taught earlier in the lesson. The learner should be able to perform perfectly.

These criteria are virtually never met in a public-school setting because they demand either individual instruction or homogeneous placement of children during the lessons. Homogeneous grouping is preferable because it provides motivational features and challenges not possible in the one-on-one setting. Also, it is far more cost efficient. The major problem in maintaining groups is to assure that the composition of the group is consistent with the four placement criteria. It is not legitimate for a group to have four children placed appropriately and two who are being dragged through the lessons (with extra firming and practice). The two lower children do not meet the placement criteria and should be placed in a lesson range that is more commensurate with their abilities.

OPERATING PLAN AND STRUCTURE

For acceleration to occur uniformly, there must be coordination of effort from one teacher to another, from one grade to the next. The teachers should be well trained in what they are to do, and the school must have some sort of mechanisms that flag possible problems of teacher or student performance. During the initial implementation, when teachers and building administrators are learning the game of mastery immersion, the operating plan and the structure must be very "compulsive" and very little should be left to chance.

The Progress of Each Student Should Be Recorded

Criterion-referenced tests or simply performance on the lessons in the program provide evidence of progress. Such progress measures should be recorded regularly. Also, the progress of the group should be recorded. For example, the average performing group should be on lesson 80 after 80 days of instruction and all children in the group should be able to perform adequately on all tasks or discriminations presented in lesson 80. Deviations from the expected performance imply problems that should be addressed immediately. For instance, the children are placed on lesson 80 but are not able to pass some of the skill items that should have been mastered by lesson 60. This is a problem of teaching fidelity because the teacher is not inducing mastery and children need further training.

If a group is on lesson 80 after 80 contact days, but only some of the children in the group perform adequately on the content of lesson 80, there may be a placement problem for some of the children in the group. These children should be moved to a group that is on an earlier lesson and that moves at a rate commensurate with their current rate of learning.

The Site Should Have an Adequate Schedule
for the Teaching of the Various Subjects

An adequate schedule provides precise times for the teaching of the various skills, firm-up periods that permit teachers to address problems of performance not adequately handled during the period. Firm-up periods are initially needed to make sure that each child is firm on the material, and to provide for possible acceleration of children who may be more appropriately placed in a higher group. Note: Without an appropriate schedule, which is to be honored by all teachers, serious problems of mastery occur; projections of student performance are not met; and practices like dragging students through the material, rather than following the specified criteria for mastery, occur frequently. The schedules should be coordinated so that several grades teach particular subjects at the same time, thereby permitting cross-class grouping of students.

The final feature of the schedule is that it should not have a great deal of loose time scheduled for minor subjects or questionable activities. Good activities include art, music, computer science, social studies, and science. Questionable activities include time-consuming projects, field trips, and other activities that have no close tie to what students learn in the primary subjects.

A Training, Monitoring, and Management System Is Needed

This operating system ensures that teachers are adequately prepared and their problems are identified and solved in a timely manner. The system should assure that teachers meet performance criteria in presenting the instructional programs and responding to students. Their progress (number of lessons presented per week, student performance on the in-program tests) should be monitored, and each classroom should have posted data that make the progress of the various instructional groups accessible.

To help teachers solve problems of teaching, grouping children appropriately, and generally meeting expectations for the instructional groups, some mechanism is needed. A very workable plan is to use peer coaches who are freed up a sufficient amount of time to observe the teachers assigned to them, to identify problems, and to give feedback. The coaches should be superior teachers, who are released for possibly 8 hours a week to coach and follow up. In addition to this time, the coaches should meet with the building administrator or training supervisor once a week to report on problems and progress. Identifying problems is the main responsibility of the coaches. In a well-designed implementation, responses to problems occur in a timely manner. (Problems of child performance in grades K–2 must be responded to and corrected within 1 week of their identification. More lag time is permissible for the higher grades, but, ideally, remedies would be implemented within a few days of the identification of the problem.)

The principal and assistant principal would be responsible for seeing to it that the projections for student performance are met, that teaching problems, grouping problems, and scheduling problems are resolved in a timely manner, and that the school celebrates academic success. The responsibilities of the administrators should be articulated in detail. A good plan requires the principal to give a weekly report to a supervisor on all the problems that have not been solved and an indication of what progress is being made with these problems.

Outside consulting help during the first years of the implementation is needed to assure that teachers, coaches, administrators learn their roles and recognize that proper execution of the roles makes a great difference in the performance of students. The help consists of these facets: Training of coaches; preservice training of teachers, aides, substitutes, and all others who will be teaching; regularly scheduled ongoing in-class assistance to teachers, coaches, and administrators; regular feedback on the decisions coaches and administrators are making.

During the first year of a program's implementation, outside help is needed on a regular basis. After year two of the implementation, the site should be solidly established and should need outside consulting only occasionally.

After the site has reached the point of near self-sufficiency, the site may be used as a training vehicle for other sites. The teachers and coaches will be capable of providing consulting to new implementations.

EVIDENCE OF EFFECTIVENESS

The theory of mastery holds that if a site adequately meets the three requirements outlined in the preceding section (providing appropriate instructional material, providing proper placement of students, and adopting a well conceived operating plan), the student performance will accelerate. Several Direct-Instruction sites have followed the acceleration plan and have realized predicted outcomes. One site is Kreole School in Moss Point, MS, which is virtually 100% Black and 85% "at-risk." The per capita level of funding is low (around $3,300 compared to the U.S. average of over $5,000)—low enough for some critics to suggest that the principal cause of poor performance in states like Mississippi is low funding. The level of expected performance for the Kreole population is around the 20th percentile, which means that a large percentage of the children are serious academic failures.

Kreole first introduced Direct Instruction in 1979 and dropped it in 1985. In 1991, Kreole later became a Follow Through site sponsored by the Direct Instruction model (University of Oregon), and was able to implement Direct Instruction better than it had in the early 1980s. Kreole became a full-school Chapter One implementation (1015) and implemented Direct Instruction in all grades.

Figure 9.1 shows the performance of fourth graders on the Stanford Achievement Test in reading and language during two periods in which the school provided Direct Instruction and two periods in which it did not. The performance of the children in 1978 and 1990 show that baseline performance is slightly below the 20th percentile in reading and close to the 20th percentile in language.

In 1985, after 7 years of Direct Instruction that was self-implemented, the data reveal a large increase in reading performance in the two subjects—43rd percentile in reading and 34th in language. However, in 1994 students' per-

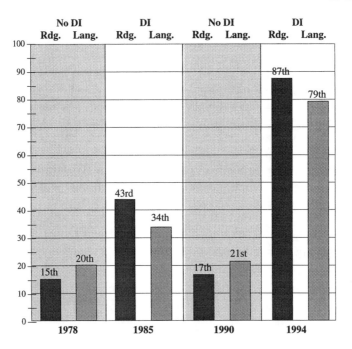

FIG. 9.1. Moss Point, Kreole Elementary School 4th grade reading and language performance (percentiles).

formance was much higher–87th percentile in reading and 79th percentile in language. In 1994, Kreole fourth graders achieved the second highest reading performance in the state and the eighth highest in language. (Mississippi has 149 school districts.)

The differences between the two Direct Instruction periods are largely differences in teaching. During the Follow-Through period, the teaching was more effective, more uniform throughout the early grades, and there were more quality-control measures in place to assure that children's progress was accelerated. This is not to say that the performance of the children during the self-implemented period was not good. The achievement of the children showed that for a self implemented site, Kreole did a remarkable job during this period.

Another project that provided for acceleration of students through Direct Instruction is ASAP (Accelerated Student Achievement Project), which comprises three low-income Title One schools in Utah. The schools provide school-wide 100% implementation of Direct Instruction as specified in the first section of this chaper. In 1994–1995, the schools were implemented in all grades and all subjects, for all students and all teachers. Title One and special education children were completely integrated so that each school had a single instructional sequence that was designed to accommodate all students.

The ASAP schools have produced data during their first year that suggest acceleration in teaching. Historically, one of the ASAP schools used its Title One funds to support 80 to 100 of the lowest Title One students. The performance of the students over the years prior to 1994–1995 remained stable: curve equivalent scores (NCEs) for reading were close to zero in both basic skills and more advanced skills. Figure 9.2 shows the end-of-year gains in NCEs for the period of 1991 through 1995. The unprecedented gains (about ⅔ of a standard deviation) occurred for both basic skills and more advanced skills in the 1994–1995 school year.

As Table 9.1 indicates, the gains occurred on every grade level. The smallest average gain for any grade was 9.1 NCE on basic skills (grade 5). The smallest average gain for more advanced skills was 10.4, which also occurred in grade 5.

Table 9.1 shows that the baseline level of the children was quite low. Children in grades K and 1 performed below the 15th NCE in reading. The preimplementation pattern of scores from grade to grade suggests that the school had actually been doing a relatively good job with these students. With well-implemented Direct Instruction, however, the gains were much larger than they had been historically.

Other data that suggest a shift in achievement as a function of Direct Instruction comes from the K–1 end-of-year evaluation of children in all ASAP

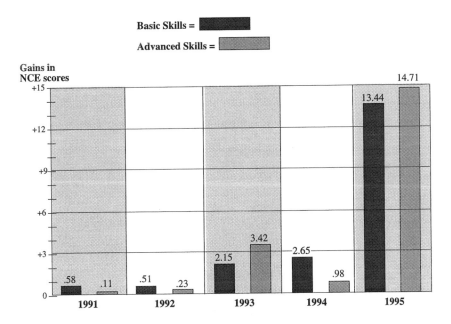

FIG. 9.2. Title 1 students' average NCE reading gains—Gunnison Elementary, 1991–1995.

TABLE 9.1
1994-1995 Gunnison Chapter 1 Students Average NCE Performance*

| | | Basic Skills | | | More advanced Skills | | |
Grade	Total Number Students	Average Pretest	Average Posttest	Difference	Average Pretest	Average Posttest	Difference
K	5	8.2	23.2	15	22.6	36.4	13.8
1	13	14.7	36.2	21.5	22.4	36.5	14.2
2	17	36.6	51.7	15.1	37.9	51.9	14
3	16	31.3	43.7	12.5	29	44.3	15.3
4	16	25.6	34.8	9.2	22.3	40.4	18.1
5	13	20.1	29.2	9.1	16.7	28.4	11.7
total	80			13.4			14.7

Note. *Stanford Achievement Test

schools.[1] These data compare the performance of the ASAP schools with control schools. All control sites were higher than their ASAP counterparts on pretest measures, but for school 1, the match was quite good. The end-of-year test measured the performance of the children on two of the Woodcock Johnson subtests—passage reading and the oral reading of nonsense words. The Woodcock Johnson was individually administered to all ASAP children, including special education and Title One children, and a random sample of 50 children from each grade (K and 1) of each comparison school.

The comparison for the passage comprehension shows a shift in the ASAP population, both in K and in 1. Figures 9.3 and 9.4 display the percentage of children scoring in the various percentile ranges. Each display shows a pair of schools (labeled 1–3), the ASAP school on the left and the control on the right.

If the distribution shown were a "normal distribution" it would have the largest percentage of children scoring in the 40–59 percentile range, and the number of children in other ranges decreasing with distance from the normative midpoint. A skewed distribution is shown by a range other than the midrange having the largest percentage of children.

Figure 9.3 shows extreme skewing for the kindergartens of the three ASAP schools, with Schools 1 and 3 having the highest percentage of students in

---

[1]The K to 1 testing program was conducted by Timothy Slocum, of Utah State University, Logan, Utah, who trained the testers, monitored the testing, analyzed the data, and designed the data displays.

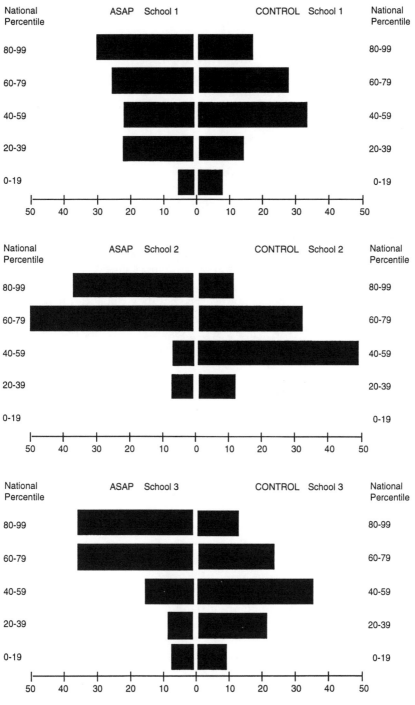

FIG. 9.3. Test: passage comprehension. Grade level: kindergarten.

the 80–99 percentile range. School 2 has over 35% of its students in the highest range and has almost all the rest of them in the 60–79 percentile range. (This school has no students in the 0–19 percentile range, and neither does the control, which suggests that the control does an excellent job of working with the lowest performers.)

School 1 was new to Direct Instruction. It was the lowest school in a district of 24 schools. Although its performance in kindergarten is not as skewed as the other two ASAP schools, it shows great progress for the faculty, which historically did not teach reading in K and did a relatively ineffective job in Grades 1 and above.

Figure 9.4 shows passage-reading-comprehension performance for the first grades. Skewing for school 1 is minimal, and the percentage of students in the lowest two ranges (0–39 percentile) is much larger than it is for the other ASAP schools. This is an artifact caused by the lack of reading instruction in K during the preceding school year. A prediction is that during the 1995–1996 school year School 1 will perform more closely to the pattern of the other two ASAP schools' performance in the 1994–1995 school year. (The prediction for these schools, however, is that they will perform better than they did during the 1994–1995 school year.)

The skewing for ASAP schools 2 and 3 is extreme. More than 50% of the students are in the 80–99 percentile range, and less than 15% of the students perform below the 40th percentile. The distributions for the comparison schools tend to be more normal than those of the ASAP schools.

IMPLICATIONS

The data from the ASAP schools and from Kreole elementary suggest that significant acceleration of student performance is possible. Mississippi and Utah are the two lowest funded states in the United States.

Although any single table or figure may be disregarded on the basis that data may not accurately show what happened and may just be a glitch, the remaining figures and table show consistent changes in student achievement. The same trends seem to occur in all the ASAP schools, and these trends are not explicable in terms of history or the current population of students or teachers. These trends provide a substantial challenge to popular nostrums and slogans of current reform, including the following:

1. *You cannot use the same approach for all children.* The same program and the same sequence were used for all students in the accelerated schools.

2. *Direct Instruction does not teach higher order skills, only rote or basic skills.* The data lavishly demonstrate the acceleration of the children in higher order skills. The largest gains in School 2's Title One program were

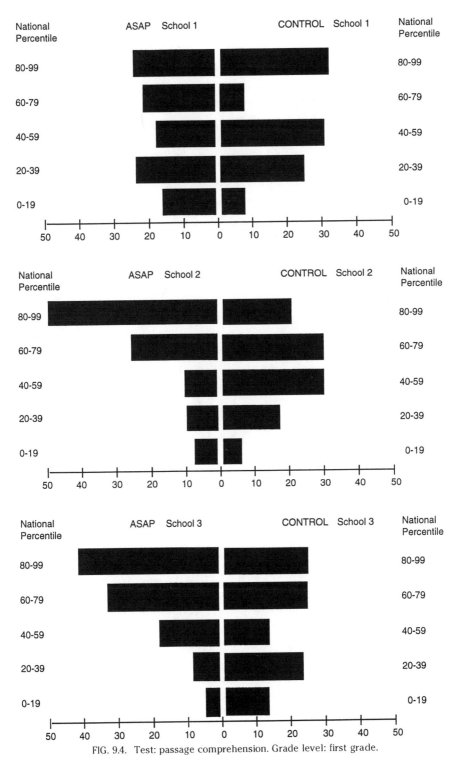

FIG. 9.4. Test: passage comprehension. Grade level: first grade.

in higher order skills. Passage reading is considered a higher order endeavor; for Kreole to score at the 87th percentile on the Stanford Achievement test, the students would have to be very facile in higher order skills.

3. *Direct Instruction programs work only for lower performing children.* This slogan, although popular, defies all data and all logic of learning. If it works for lower performers, it would clearly work faster and easier with higher performers. The only differences would be that the higher performers would move through the sequences faster and may have different initial placements than lower performers of the same age. In any case, the data show that the approach apparently works for the full range of students.

4. *It takes a long time to implement a program so it produces positive results.* The gains in ASAP were achieved—and predicted—in the first year of the implementation. The gains in Kreole occurred over a 4-year period. This performance is in stark contrast to the reforms for Education 2000, which occurred in the early 1990s and have produced no overall positive data.

5. *Schools need to recruit better teachers and need to pay teachers more money than they currently receive.* Not only were these schools from communities that have low funding levels for education; there was no recruitment of teachers for the project. The same teachers were utilized before and after the Direct Instruction implementations occurred.

6. *Decisions should be based on a school-council model, not a top-down model.* None of the schools made up its own procedures for training and monitoring, for the schedule, curricula, or coaches. All were specified as part of a top-down implementation. This is not to say that the sites did not personalize and institutionalize the practices in different ways, nor is it to say that there is an absence of on-site decisions based on current observation of student performance. The format and details, however, do not correspond to the more popular model of "site-based decision making."

7. *It is not possible to measure success of programs using standardized measures.* This assertion is paradoxical because the problems that sparked the reforms were clearly identified through performance deficiencies on standardized measures. It would seem to follow that the solutions to the problems should also be apparent through changes in performance on standardized measures. In any case, the success of the ASAP implementations is documented rather dramatically through the use of standardized measures.

8. *Exemplary projects are ephemeral, unpredictable, and tend not to be exemplary when measured at a later time.* This assertion is quite true of traditional projects, but may not be true of projects like ASAP, where complete implementation is achieved and should manifest itself in correlated student success. A prediction is that the students will perform better on each grade level 2 years from now than they did in 1994–1995.

The final chapters for the students in ASAP will be written during the upcoming years. If students perform according to predictions made before the implementation of the project, the population of ASAP students who go through the instructional sequence (from K or 1) will be accelerated at least 2 years in all subjects. If this prediction is realized, it will further substantiate the reliability and potential of Direct Instruction when it is implemented properly. The confirmation will also provide benchmark achievements for entering children of varying abilities. Hopefully, the level of achievement will show that the achievements possible for even the lowest performers (the special-education and Title One students) is far higher than is realized by currently popular school practices and patterns.

REFERENCES

Abt Associates. (1977). *Education as experimentation: A planned variation model* (Vol. IV). Cambridge, MA: Author.

Engelmann, S., & Carnine, D. W. (1982). *Theory of instruction: Principles and applications.* New York: Irvington.

10

ADVANCES IN RESEARCH ON INSTRUCTION

Barak Rosenshine
University of Illinois at Urbana

This chapter discusses what I regard as some of the most important instructional advancements of the last 30 years. These advancements came from three bodies of research: (a) research on cognitive processing; (b) research on teacher effects, that is, studies of teachers whose classes made the highest achievement gain compared to other classes; and (c) intervention studies in which students were taught cognitive strategies they could apply to their learning. Although I would not advocate converting these ideas into another evaluation form, I suggest that the ideas represented by this research can and should be used to discuss and improve instruction.

FINDINGS FROM RESEARCH ON COGNITIVE PROCESSING: THE IMPORTANCE OF WELL-CONNECTED KNOWLEDGE STRUCTURES

A major area of research, one with important implications for teaching, has been the research on cognitive processing—research on how information is stored and retrieved. This research has shown us the importance of helping students develop a well-connected body of accessible knowledge.

It is currently thought that the information in our long-term memory is stored in interconnected networks called *knowledge structures*. The size of these structures, the number of connections between pieces of knowledge, the strength of the connections, and the organization and richness of the relationships are all important for processing information and solving problems.

It is easier to assimilate new information, and easier to use prior knowledge for problem solving, when one has more connections and interconnections, stronger ties between the connections, and a better organized knowledge structure. When the knowledge structure on a particular topic is large and well connected, new information is more readily acquired and prior knowledge is more readily available for use. Having a well-connected network means that any one piece of information can serve to help retrieve the entire pattern. Having strong connections and a richness of relationships enables one to retrieve more pieces of the pattern. When information is "meaningful" to students, they have more points in their knowledge structures to which they can attach new information. Education is a process of developing, enlarging, expanding, and refining our students' knowledge structures.

Helping students to organize information into well-connected patterns has another advantage. When a pattern is unified, it only occupies a few bits in the working memory. Thus, having larger and better connected patterns frees up space in our working memory. This available space can be used for reflecting on new information and for problem solving. For example, when U.S. history is organized into well-connected patterns, these patterns occupy less space in the working memory and the learner has additional space in the working memory to use to consider, assimilate, and manipulate new information. A major difference between an expert and a novice is that the expert's knowledge structure has a larger number of knowledge items, the expert has more connections between the items, the links between the connections are stronger, and the structure is better organized. A novice, on the other hand, is unable to see these patterns, and often ignores them. This development of well-connected patterns and the concomitant freeing of space in the working memory is one of the hallmarks of an expert in a field.

To summarize, well-connected and elaborate knowledge structures are important because (a) they allow for easier retrieval of old material, (b) they permit more information to be carried in a single chunk, and (c) they facilitate the understanding and integration of new information.

There are three important instructional implications that follow from this research: (a) the need to help students develop background knowledge, (b) the importance of student processing, and (c) the importance of organizers.

Help Students Develop Their Background Knowledge

What can be done to help students develop well-connected bodies of knowledge? One important instructional procedure is providing for extensive reading, review, practice, and discussion. These activities serve to help students *increase* the number of pieces of information that are the long-term memory, *organize* those pieces, and *increase* the strength and number of these interconnections. The more one rehearses and reviews information, the stronger these interconnections become. Thus, the research on cognitive processing supports the need for a teacher to assist students by providing for extensive reading of a variety of materials, frequent review, testing, and discussion and application activities.

Provide for Student Processing

New material is stored in the long-term memory when one processes it. The quality of storage can depend on the "level of processing." For example, if we were told to read a passage and count the number of times the word "the" appeared, the quality of storage would not be as strong as if we read the same passage and focused on its meaning. Similarly, the quality of storage would be stronger if one summarized or compared the material in the passage rather than simply reading it.

Processing of new material takes place through a variety of activities such as rehearsal, review, comparing and contrasting, and drawing connections. Thus, the research on cognitive processing supports the importance of a teacher initiating activities that require students to process and apply new information. Such processing strengthens the knowledge network that the student is developing. Asking students to organize information, summarize information, or compare new material with prior material are all activities that require processing and should help students develop and strengthen their cognitive structures. In addition, Brown and Campione (1986) wrote:

> Understanding is more likely to occur when a child is required to explain, elaborate, or defend his position to others; the burden of explanation is often the push needed to make him or her evaluate, integrate, and elaborate knowledge in new ways. (p. 1061)

Other examples of such processing activities include asking students to do any of the following:

Read a variety of materials extensively.

Explain the new material to someone else.

Write questions/answer questions.

Develop knowledge maps.

Write daily summaries.

Apply the ideas to a new situation.

Give a new example.

Compare and contrast the new material to other material.

Study for an exam.

All these activities are useful in helping students develop, organize, strengthen, and expand their knowledge structures.

Help Students Organize Their Knowledge

As has been noted, new information is organized into knowledge structures. Without these structures, new knowledge tends to be fragmented and not readily available for recall and use. However, students frequently lack these knowledge structures when they are learning new material. Without direction, students might develop a fragmented, incomplete, or erroneous knowledge structure. Therefore, the research suggests that it is important for teachers to help students organize the new material.

One way to do this is to provide students with "graphic organizers," that is, organizing structures for expository material. An outline is an example of such an organizer, concept maps are another example. These structures help students organize the elements of the new learning and such organization can serve to facilitate retrieval. In addition, having such organizers can enable the student to devote more working memory to the content.

Another approach is to teach students how to develop their own graphic organizers for new material. This process is facilitated by providing students with a variety of graphic organizer structures that they can use to construct their own graphic organizers. When teaching students to develop a graphic organizer, it is useful for the teacher to model the process and also provides models of thinking and thinking aloud as she or he constructs the maps.

In summary, the research on cognitive processing identified the importance of developing a well-connected knowledge structures. Such structures might be developed by encouraging extensive reading and practice, student processing of new information, and helping students organize their new knowledge.

RESEARCH ON TEACHER EFFECTS

A second important body of research is the teacher effects studies. The teacher effects research represents a line of studies in which attempts were made to identify those teacher behaviors that were related to student achievement gain. The focus was on observing and recording classroom instruction and identifying those instructional procedures associated with the most successful and the least successful teachers.

In this research, the investigators first identified a number of instructional procedures to study. About 20 to 30 procedures would be selected, and these included a teacher's use of praise, a teacher's use of criticism, the number and type of questions that were asked, the quality of the student answers, and the responses of a teacher to a student's answers. Then achievement tests were given to the students in 20 to 30 classrooms. After the achievement tests, the investigators observed the classrooms and recorded the frequency with which the teachers used instructional behaviors such as those mentioned earlier. After 3 to 6 months, a second achievement test was given to the same 20 to 30 classrooms.

After all the data were collected, the investigators used correlational statistics to specify the "adjusted gain" for each classroom. That is, the raw gain for each class, from pretest to posttest, was adjusted for the entry level of each classroom. In the final step, the investigators looked to instructional behaviors they had recorded for each class and correlated those behaviors with the measure of each class' adjusted achievement gain. Through the use of these procedures, the investigators were able to identify which instructional behaviors were associated or correlated with student achievement gain.

In many cases, these correctional results were tested in subsequent experimental studies in which one group of teachers were trained and helped to use these behaviors in their teaching and another group of teachers was told to continue their regular teaching. All the teachers were observed, and classes of all teachers were given achievement tests before the experiment began and at the end of the experiment. In most cases, students in the classes of the teachers who received the training had higher posttest achievement scores than those of students of teachers in the control classes.

Although a number of studies of this type were conducted by Barr (1948) and his associates, the modern era of this research began with the work of Medley and Mitzel (1959) and Flanders (1960). The largest number of teacher effects studies were conducted during the 1970s. The earliest studies were summarized by Rosenshine in 1971 and the studies that were conducted between 1973 and 1983 were summarized by Brophy and Good (1986) and by Rosenshine and Stevens (1986). The experimental studies have been summarized by Gage and Needles (1989).

I suggest that the teacher-effects era, between 1955 and 1980, was an impressive run of cumulative research. During this period, over 100 correlational and experimental studies were conducted using a common design and the different observation instruments shared many common instructional procedures, and it was cumulative: Researchers cited and built on the instructional findings of others.

Rosenshine and Stevens (1986) summarized this research and concluded that across a number of studies, when effective teachers taught well-structured skills and expository material, the teachers used the following procedures:

- Begin a lesson with a short review of previous learning.

- Begin a lesson with a short statement of goals.
- Present new material in small steps, providing for student practice after each step.
- Give clear and detailed instructions and explanations.
- Provide a high level of active practice for all students.
- Ask a large number of questions, check for student understanding, and obtain responses from all students.
- Guide students during initial practice.
- Provide systematic feedback and corrections.
- Provide explicit instruction and practice for seatwork exercises and, where necessary, monitor students during seatwork.

Rosenshine and Stevens (1986) further grouped these instructional procedures under six teaching "functions" as shown in Table 10.1. These teaching functions appear to be relevant today for teaching students skills that they can use to independently complete well-structured tasks.

Two findings from that research that are most relevant to teaching are (a) the importance of teaching in small steps and (b) the importance of guiding student practice. In addition, a third finding, the importance of extensive practice, is shared with the research on cognitive processing.

Present New Material in Small Steps

We learned, in the teacher-effects research, that the least effective teachers would present an entire lesson, and then pass out worksheets and tell students to work the problems. However, the most effective teachers taught new material in small steps. That is, they only presented small parts of new material a single time, and after presenting the material the teachers then guided students in practicing the material that was taught.

This procedure of teaching in small steps fits well with the findings from cognitive psychology on the limitations of our working memory. Our working memory, where we process information, is small. It can only handle five to seven bits of information at once; any additional information swamps it. The procedure of first teaching in small steps and then guiding student practice represents an appropriate way of dealing with the limitation of our small working memories.

Guide Student Practice

A second major finding from the teacher effects literature was the importance of guided practice. The concept of guided practice was developed by Hunter (1982), and it first appeared in the teacher-effects literature in an experimental study by Good and Grouws (1979).

TABLE 10.1
Functions for Teaching Well-Structured Tasks

---

1. Review

Review homework.
Review relevant previous learning.
Review prerequisite skills and knowledge for the lesson.

2. Presentation

State lesson goals or provide outline.
Present new material in small steps.
Model procedures.
Provide positive and negative examples.
Use clear language.
Check for student understanding.
Avoid digressions.

3. Guided Practice

Spend more time on guided practice.
High frequency of questions.
All students respond and receive feedback.
High success rate.
Continue practice until students are fluent.

4. Corrections and Feedback

Provide process feedback when answers are correct but hesitant.
Provide sustaining feedback, clues, or reteaching when answers are incorrect.
Reteach material when necessary.

5. Independent Practice

Students receive overview and/or help during initial steps.
Practice continues until students are automatic (where relevant).
Teacher provides active supervision (where possible).
Routines are used to provide help for slower students.

6. Weekly and Monthly Reviews

In the teacher-effects research we learned that it was not sufficient to present a lesson and then ask students to practice on their own. The least effective teachers—those teachers whose classes made the smallest gains—would present an entire lesson, and then pass out worksheets and tell the students to work the problems. When this happened, it was observed that many students were confused and made errors on the worksheets. One reason for these errors was the aforementioned limitation of the working memory. For many students, particularly those who had not learned the previous material well, the amount of material presented in the lesson was too large, and therefore swamped the working memory.

The most effective teachers—those teachers whose classes made the greatest gains—taught differently. First, as noted, the most effective teachers presented only some of the material at a time; that is, they taught in small steps. After presenting a small amount of material, these teachers then guided student practice. This guidance often consisted of the teacher working a few problems at the board and discussing the steps out loud. This instruction served as a model for the students. This guidance also included asking students to come to the board, work problems, and discuss their procedures. Through this process the students at their seats would see additional models.

The process of guiding practice also includes checking the answers of the entire class in order to see whether some students need additional instruction. Guided practice has also included asking students to work together, in pairs or in groups, to quiz and explain the material to each other. Guided practice may occur when a teacher questions and helps a class with their work before assigning independent practice.

Another reason for the importance of guided practice comes from the fact that we construct and reconstruct knowledge. We do not, we cannot, simply repeat what we hear word for word. Rather, we connect our understanding of the new information to our existing concepts or "schema" and we then construct a "gist" of what we have heard. However, when left on their own, many students make errors in the process of constructing this gist. These errors occur particularly when the information is new and the student does not have adequate or well-formed background knowledge. These constructions are not errors so much as attempts by the students to be logical in an area where their background knowledge is weak. These errors are so common that there is a literature on the development and correction of student misconceptions in science (Guzzetti, Snyder, & Glass, 1992). When students are left on their own, without the guidance of someone who understands the new area, there is a danger that they will develop misconceptions. Providing guided practice, after teaching small amounts of new material, and checking for student understanding, are ways to limit the development of misconceptions.

Guiding practice also fits the cognitive processing findings on the need to provide for student processing. Guided practice is the place where the students—working alone, with other students, or with the teacher—engage in the cognitive-processing activities of organizing, reviewing, rehearsing, summarizing, comparing, and contrasting. However, it is important that *all* students engage in these activities. The least effective teachers often asked a question, called on one student to answer, and then assumed that everyone had learned this point. In contrast, the most effective teachers attempted to check the understanding of *all* students and to provide for processing by *all* students.

In summary, the most effective teachers differed from the others in that they (a) presented smaller amounts of material at any time and (b) guided student practice as students worked problems, (c) provided for student processing of the new material, (d) checked the understanding of all students, and (e) attempted to prevent students from developing misconceptions.

Provide for Extensive Practice

The most effective teachers also provided for extensive and successful practice. As noted in the cognitive-processing research, students need extensive practice in order to develop well-connected networks. The most effective teachers made sure that such practice took place *after* there has been sufficient guided practice, so that students were not practicing errors and misconceptions.

THE TEACHING OF COGNITIVE STRATEGIES

The third, major instructional development in the last 30 years has been the concept of cognitive strategies. Cognitive strategies are guiding procedures that students can use to help them complete less structured tasks such as those in reading comprehension and writing. The concept of cognitive strategies and the research on cognitive strategies represent the third important advance in instruction.

There are some academic tasks that are "well structured." These tasks can be broken down into a fixed sequence of subtasks and steps that consistently lead to the same goal. The steps are concrete and visible. There is a specific, predictable algorithm that can be followed, one that enables students to obtain the same result each time they perform the algorithmic operations. These well-structured tasks are taught by teaching each step of the algorithm to students. The results of the research on teacher effects are particularly relevant in helping us learn how teach students algorithms they can use to complete well-structured tasks.

In contrast, reading comprehension, writing, and study skills are examples of less structured tasks—tasks that cannot be broken down into a fixed sequence of subtasks and steps that consistently and unfailingly lead to the goal. Because these tasks are less structured and difficult, they have also been called higher level tasks. These types of tasks do not have the fixed sequence that is part of well-structured tasks. One cannot develop algorithms that students can use to complete these tasks.

Until the late 1970s, students were seldom provided with any help in completing less structured tasks. In a classic observational study of reading-comprehension instruction, Durkin (1979) noted that of the 4,469 minutes she observed in reading instruction in grade 4, only 20 minutes were spent in comprehension instruction by the teacher. Durkin noted that teachers spent almost all of the instructional time *asking* students questions, but they spent little time *teaching students comprehension strategies* they could use to answer the questions. Duffy, Lanier, and Roehler (1980) noted a similar lack of comprehension instruction in elementary classrooms:

> There is little evidence of instruction of any kind. Teachers spend most of their time assigning activities, monitoring to be sure the pupils are on task, directing recitation sessions to assess how well children are doing and providing corrective feedback in response to pupil errors. Seldom does one observe teaching in which a teacher presents a skill, a strategy, or a process to pupils, shows them how to do it, provides assistance as they initiate attempts to perform the task and assures that they can be successful. (p. 4)

As a result of these astonishing findings, and as a result of emerging research on cognition and information processing, investigators began to develop and validate procedures that students might be taught to aid their reading comprehension. In the field of reading, the research consisted of developing and teaching students to use specific cognitive strategies that help them to perform higher level operations in reading. Other research focused on developing, teaching, and testing cognitive strategies that are specific to writing, mathematical problem solving, and science comprehension.

The research design usually consisted of the investigator locating or developing a cognitive strategy such as teaching students to generate questions about the material they have read. Then one group of students would be taught this strategy and would practice using this strategy; they would practice generating questions and answering other students' question. Another group of similar students continued with their regular lessons. After a period of 4 to 20 weeks, both groups would take a comprehension test and the scores of the two groups were compared. This section focuses on the results of those intervention studies in which cognitive strategies were developed and taught.

Cognitive strategies are heuristics. A cognitive strategy is not a direct procedure; it is not an algorithm to be precisely followed. Rather, a cognitive strategy is a heuristic or guide that serves to support or facilitate the learner as she or he develops internal procedures that enable them to perform the higher level operations. Teaching students to generate questions about their reading is an example of a cognitive strategy. Generating questions does not directly lead, in a step-by-step manner, to comprehension. Rather, in the process of generating questions, students need to search the text and combine information, and these processes serve to help students comprehend what they read.

In the late 1970s, investigators began to teach students specific cognitive strategies such as question generation and summarization that could be applied to reading comprehension (Alvermann, 1981; Paris, Cross, & Lipson, 1984; Raphael & Pearson, 1985). Cognitive strategy procedures have also been developed and taught in mathematics problem solving (Schoenfeld, 1985), physics problem solving (Larkin & Reif, 1976), and in writing (Englert & Raphael, 1989; Scardamalia & Bereiter, 1985).

The concept of cognitive strategies represents at least two instructional advances. First, when teachers are faced with difficult areas they can now ask "What cognitive strategies might I develop that can help students complete these tasks?" The concept of cognitive strategies provides us with a general approach that can be applied to the teaching of higher order tasks in the content areas. Second, researchers have completed a large number of intervention studies in which students who were taught various cognitive strategies obtained significantly higher posttest scores than did students in the control groups. The cognitive strategies that were taught in these studies and the procedures by which these cognitive strategies were taught can now be used as part of regular instruction. These intervention studies, in reading, writing, mathematics, and science, together with a description of the cognitive strategies and the instructional procedures were used, has been assembled in an excellent volume by Pressley et al. (1995).

We can be proud of our progress as a profession. In place of Durkin's observation that there was little evidence of cognitive strategy instruction in reading, we now have a large number of intervention studies, studies that have been successful in providing instruction in cognitive strategies in a number of domains.

INSTRUCTIONAL ELEMENTS IN THE TEACHING OF COGNITIVE STRATEGIES

How have cognitive strategies been taught? This section attempts to identify and discuss the instructional elements that have been used to teach cognitive strategies. It is hoped that a knowledge of these elements might add to our knowledge of instruction and might be applied to the teaching of other cognitive strategies. Such information might serve as an aid that teachers can use to help teach cognitive strategies to their students.

Scaffolds

Cognitive strategies cannot be taught directly, as one teaches an algorithm. Rather, cognitive strategies are taught by providing students with a variety of support structures or *scaffolds* (Palincsar & Brown, 1984; Wood, Bruner,

& Ross, 1976). Many of the instructional elements to be described here serve as scaffolds for the learner. A scaffold is a temporary support used to assist a learner during initial learning. This support is usually provided by the teacher to help students bridge the gap between current abilities and the goal. Examples of scaffolds include simplified problems, modeling of the procedures by the teacher, thinking aloud by the teacher as he or she solves the problem, prompts, suggestions, and guidance as students work problems. Scaffolds may also be tools, such as cue cards or checklists. A model of the completed task against which students can compare their work is another example of such support (Collins, Brown, & Newman, 1990; Palincsar & Brown, 1984). *Cognitive apprenticeship* (Collins et al., 1990) is a term for instructional process by which teachers provide and support students with scaffolds as the students develop cognitive strategies.

Scaffolds operate to reduce the complexities of the problems and break them down into manageable chunks that the child has a real chance of solving (Bickhard, 1992). "The metaphor of a scaffold captures the idea of an adjustable and temporary support that can be removed when no longer necessary" (Brown & Palincsar, 1989, p. 411). The scaffolds assist the learner in learning a cognitive process and are gradually withdrawn or faded as learners become more independent, although some students may continue to rely on scaffolds when they encounter particularly difficult problems.

Scaffolds can be applied to the teaching of all skills, but they are particularly useful, and often indispensable, for teaching higher level cognitive strategies. A number of investigators (Collins et al., 1990; Pressley et al., 1995; Rosenshine & Meister, 1995) have studied the intervention studies and identified instructional procedures that teachers might use to teach cognitive strategies. Through this process, 13 major instructional elements were identified. These are listed in Table 10.2.

The search of this literature, in which we looked for the instructional procedures that were used to teach cognitive strategies, led to the identification of scaffolds, such as cue cards, as well as the identification of other instructional procedures such as extensive independent practice. These elements are described and discussed in the following.

Provide Procedural Prompts or Facilitators

In these studies, the first step in teaching a cognitive strategy was the development of a *procedural prompt.* These procedural prompts (or procedural facilitators, a term used by Scardamalia & Bereiter, 1985) supply the students with specific procedures or suggestions that facilitate the completion of the task. Learners can temporarily rely on these hints and suggestions until they create their own internal structures. For example, the words "who," "what," "why," "where," "when," and "how" are procedural prompts that

TABLE 10.2
Instructional Elements Used in the Teaching of Cognitive Strategies

---

1. Provide procedural prompts specific to the strategy being taught.
2. Teach the cognitive strategy using small steps.
3. Provide models of appropriate responses.
4. Think aloud as choices are being made.
5. Anticipate potential difficulties.
6. Regulate the difficulty of the material.
7. Provide a cue card.
8. Guide student practice.
9. Provide feedback and corrections.
10. Provide and teach a checklist.
11. Provide independent practice.
12. Increase student responsibilities.
13. Assess student mastery.

---

help students learn the cognitive strategy of asking questions about the material they have read. These prompts are concrete references on which students can rely for support as they learn to apply the cognitive strategy.

Another example of procedural prompts comes from a study by King (1990), where students were provided with and taught to use a list of question stems that served to help the students form questions about a particular passage:

How are _____ and _____ alike?
What is the main idea of _____?
What do you think would happen if _____?
What are the strengths and weakness of _____ ?
In what way is _____ related to _____ ?
How does _____ affect _____?
Compare _____ and _____ with regard to _____.
What do you think causes _____?
How does _____ tie in with what we have learned before?
Which one is the best _____ and why?
What are some possible solutions for the problem of _____?
Do you agree or disagree with this statement: _____? Support your answer.
What do I (you) still not understand about . . . ? (p. 667)

Procedural prompts are scaffolds that are specific to the cognitive strategy. Procedural prompts have been used, successfully, in a variety of content areas. Prompts have been used to assist teaching the strategy of summarization (Alvermann, 1981; Baumann, 1984) and writing (Englert & Raphael, 1989; Scardamalia & Bereiter, 1985). Procedural prompts have also been used to assist college students to solve problems in physics (Hiller &

Hungate, 1985; Larkin & Reif, 1976) and mathematical problem solving (Schoenfeld, 1985). Pressley et al. (1995) have compiled a summary of research on instruction in cognitive strategies in reading, writing, mathematics, vocabulary, and science, and in almost all of these studies, the student learning was mediated through the use of procedural prompts.

Procedural prompts are an important concept that might be applied to the teaching of a variety of cognitive strategies. Procedural prompts are discussed in more detail in a later section.

Teach the Cognitive Strategy Using Small Steps

An earlier idea that came from the teacher-effects literature, the importance of teaching new material in small steps, also appears in the research on teaching cognitive strategies. When teaching cognitive strategies, it is easier for the learner if cognitive strategy is taught in small steps because teaching too much of the cognitive strategy at once would swamp the working memory. This idea of teaching in small steps, therefore, has extensive support. It fits the research on cognitive processing on the limitations of the working memory, was derived from studying the classrooms of the teachers who obtained the highest achievement gain, and was also an instructional procedure that was used in intervention studies to teach students cognitive strategies.

Provide Models of the Appropriate Responses

Modeling is particularly important when teaching cognitive strategies because we cannot specify all the steps in these strategies. Therefore, models provide an important scaffold for the learner. Almost all of the researchers in these studies provided models of how to use the procedural prompt they had selected or developed. Models, modeling, or both were used at three different places in these studies: (a) during initial instruction, before students practiced; (b) during practice; and (c) after practice. Each approach is discussed here.

Models During Initial Instruction. In some studies, the teachers began by modeling responses based on the procedural prompts. Nolte and Singer (1985), for example, provided students with questions based on elements of the story grammar (e.g., What action does the leading character initiate? What do you learn about the character from this action?). Then they began by modeling questions based on this story grammar. In other studies, students received models of questions based on the main idea and then practiced generating questions on their own (Andre & Anderson, 1978–1979; Dreher & Gambrell, 1985).

Models Given During Practice. Models were also provided *during* practice. Such modeling is part of reciprocal teaching (Palincsar, 1987; Palincsar & Brown, 1984). In reciprocal teaching, the teacher first models asking a question and the students answer. Then the teacher guides students as they develop their own questions, to be answered by one of their classmates, and the teacher provides additional models when the students have difficulty. Other studies also provided models during practice (Helfeldt & Lalik, 1976; Labercane & Battle, 1987; Manzo, 1969).

Models Given After Practice. In studies on question generation, teachers also provided models of questions for the students to view *after* they had written questions relevant to a paragraph or passage (Andre & Anderson, 1978–1979; Dreher & Gambrell, 1985). The intent of this model was to enable the students to compare their efforts with that of an expert (Collins, Brown, & Newman, 1990).

Think Aloud as Choices Are Being Made

Another scaffold, similar to modeling, is *thinking aloud,* that is, the vocalization of the internal thought processes one goes through when using the cognitive strategy. For example, when teaching students to generate questions, the teacher describes the thought processes that occur as a question word is selected and integrated with text information to form a question. A teacher might think aloud while summarizing a paragraph, illustrating the thought processes that occur as the topic of the passage is determined and then used to generate a summary sentence.

Anderson (1991) provided illustrations of thinking aloud for several cognitive strategies in reading:

> *For clarifying difficult statements or concepts*: I don't get this. It says that things that are dark look smaller. I know that a white dog looks smaller than a black elephant, so this rule must only work for things that are about the same size. Maybe black shoes would make your feet look smaller than white ones would.
>
> *For summarizing important information*: I'll summarize this part of the article. So far, it tells where the Spanish started in North America and what parts they explored. Since the title is "The Spanish in California," the part about California must be important. I'd sum up by saying that Spanish explorers from Mexico discovered California. They didn't stay in California, but lived in other parts of America. These are the most important ideas so far.
>
> *For thinking ahead*: So far this has told me that Columbus is poor, the trip will be expensive, and everyone's laughing at his plan. I'd predict

that Columbus will have trouble getting the money he needs for his exploration.

As individual students accepted more responsibility in the completion of a task, they often modeled and thought aloud for their less capable classmates. Not only did student modeling and think alouds involve the students actively in the process, but it allowed the teacher to better assess student progress in the use of the strategy. Thinking aloud by the teacher and more capable students provided novice learners with a way to observe "expert thinking," which is usually hidden from the student. Indeed, identifying the hidden strategies of experts so that they can become available to learners has become a useful area of research (Collins et al., 1990).

"Thinking aloud" by the teacher while solving problems is an important scaffold that has been used when teaching students higher level cognitive strategies. Garcia and Pearson (1990) referred to this process as the teacher "sharing the reading secrets" (p. 4) by making them overt. Thinking aloud is also an important part of a cognitive apprenticeship model (Collins, Brown, & Newman, 1990). Thinking aloud was only described in one study, that of Richey (1985), who had "the teacher model the thinking involved in each step for finding the main idea" (p. 3).

Anticipate and Discuss Potential Difficulties

Another instructional scaffold found in these question-generation studies was anticipating the difficulties a student is likely to face. In some studies, the instructor anticipated common errors that students might make and spent time discussing these errors *before* the students made them. For example, in a study by Palincsar (1987) the teacher anticipated the inappropriate questions that students might generate. The students read a paragraph followed by three questions one might ask about the paragraph. The students were asked to look at each example and decide whether or not that question was about the most important information in the paragraph. In one choice, the children were shown a question that could not be answered by the information provided in the paragraph, and the students discussed why it was a poor question. In another choice, the students were shown a question that was too narrow, that focused only on a small detail, and the students discussed why it was a poor question. The students continued through the exercise discussing whether each question was too narrow, too broad, or appropriate.

Another example of anticipating problems occurred in the study by Cohen (1983) where the students were taught specific rules to discriminate (a) a question from a nonquestion and (b) a good question from a poor one:

A good question starts with a question word.

A good question can be answered by the story.

A good question asks about an important detail of the story.

Although only two studies discussed this scaffold of anticipating student difficulties (Cohen, 1983; Palincsar, 1987), this technique seems potentially useful and might be used for teaching other skills, strategies, and subject areas.

Regulate the Difficulty of the Material

Some of the investigators attempted to regulate the difficulty of the material. Some did this by having the students begin with simpler material and then gradually move to more complex materials. For example, when Palincsar (1987) taught students to generate questions, the teacher first modeled how to generate questions about a single *sentence*. This was followed by class practice. Next, the teacher modeled and provided practice on asking questions after reading a *paragraph*. Finally, the teacher modeled and then the class practiced generating questions after reading an entire *passage*.

Similarly, in studies by Andre and Anderson (1978–1979) and Dreher and Gambrell (1985) the students began with a single paragraph, then moved to a double paragraph, and from there to a 450-word passage. Another example comes from the study by Wong, Wong, Perry, and Sawatsky (1986). Here, students began by generating questions about a single, simple paragraph. When the students were successful at that task, they moved to single, complex paragraphs and, lastly, to 800-word selections from social studies texts.

In another study (Wong & Jones, 1982), the researchers regulated the difficult of the task by *decreasing* the prompts. First, students worked with a paragraph using procedural prompts. After they were successful at that level, they were moved to a passage with prompts and finally to a passage *without* prompts.

Provide a Cue Card

Another scaffold was the provision of a cue card containing the procedural prompt, which might support a student during initial learning by reducing the strain on the working memory. With a cue card, students can put of their limited short-term memory into the application of the strategy instead of having to use some short-term memory to store the procedural prompts. One example appeared in a study by Billingsley and Wildman (1984), who provided students with cue cards listing the signal words (e.g., who, what, why…) which could be used as prompts for generating questions. Singer and Donlan (1982) presented a chart listing the five elements of a story grammar that the students were taught to use as prompts for generating questions. Wong and Jones (1982) and Wong et al. (1986) gave each student a cue card that listed the steps in developing a question about the main idea. In all four of these studies, the investigators modeled the use of the cue card.

Cue cards were also used in studies where students were provided with generic questions. In these studies (Blaha, 1979; Wong et al., 1986) students were provided with cue cards listing specific questions to ask after they had read paragraphs and passages (e.g., "What's the most important sentence in this paragraph?"), and King (1990) provided students with question stems (e.g., How are ＿＿ and ＿＿ alike?; What is a new example of . . . ?).

Guide Student Practice

In many of these studies, the teacher guided the students during their initial practice. Typically, after the modeling, the teacher guided students during their initial practice. As they worked through the text, the teacher gave hints, reminders of the prompts, reminders of what was overlooked, and suggestions of how something could be improved (Cohen, 1983; Palincsar, 1987; Wong et al., 1986). This guided practice was often combined with the presentation, as in the study by Blaha (1979) where the teacher first taught a part of a strategy, then guided student practice in identifying and then applying the strategy, then taught the next part of the strategy, and then guided student practice. This type of guided practice is the same as the guided practice that emerged from the teacher effects research (Rosenshine & Stevens, 1986).

The reciprocal teaching setting is another example of guided practice. As noted earlier, in reciprocal teaching the teacher first models the cognitive process being taught and then provides cognitive support and coaching (scaffolding) for the students as they attempt the task. As the students become more proficient, the teacher fades the support and students provide support for each other. Reciprocal teaching is a way of modifying the guided practice so that students take a more active role, eventually assuming the role of coteacher.

A third form of guided practice occurred when students met in small groups of two to six, without the teacher, and practiced asking, revising, and correcting questions and provided support and feedback to each other (King, 1990; Nolte & Singer, 1985; Singer & Donlan, 1982). Such groupings allow for more support when revising questions and for more practice than can be obtained in a whole-class setting. Nolte and Singer (1985) applied the concept of diminishing support to the organization of groups. Here, students first spent 3 days working in groups of five or six, then 3 days working in pairs, and eventually working alone.

Provide Feedback and Corrections

Providing feedback and corrections to the students most likely occurred in all studies, but was explicitly mentioned in only a few. In these studies, there were three sources of feedback and corrections: the teacher, other students, and a computer.

Teacher feedback and corrections occurred during the guided practice as students attempted to generate questions. Feedback typically took the form of hints, questions, and suggestions. A second form of feedback—group feedback—was illustrated in the three studies by King (1990) and in a study by Richey (1985). In the King studies, after students had written their questions, they met in groups, posed questions to each other, and compared questions within each group. The third type of feedback—which was computer-based—occurred in the computer-based instructional format designed by MacGregor (1988). In this study, students asked the computer to provide a model of an appropriate question when they made an error.

Provide and Teach a Checklist

In some of the studies, students were taught to use another scaffold—a self-evaluation checklist. In a study by Davey and McBride (1986), a self-evaluation checklist was introduced in the fourth of five instructional sessions. The checklist listed the following questions:

How well did I identify important information?

How well did I link information together?

How well could I answer my questions?

Did my "think questions" use different language from the text?

Did I use good signal words? (p. 259)

Wong and Jones (1982) wrote that students in their study were furnished with the "criteria for a good question" (p. 235), although these criteria were not described in the report. In the three studies by King (1990), students were taught to ask themselves the question "What do I still not understand?" after they had generated and answered their questions.

There were differences between the studies with regard to when checklists were introduced into a lesson. Wong and Jones (1982) and King (1989, 1990, 1992) presented checklists during the presentation, whereas Davey and McBride (1986) presented them during the guided practice, and Richey (1985) presented them after initial practice.

Provide Independent Practice With New Examples

Independent practice refers to student practice in applying the cognitive strategy with diminishing help from the teacher and other students. One goal of independent practice is to develop automatic responding so the students no longer have to recall the strategy, and thus more of their limited working memory can be applied to the task. Another goal of independent practice is to achieve "unitization" of the strategy, that is, the blending of elements of the strategy into a unified whole. This unitization is usually the result of extensive practice—practice that helps students develop an automatic, unified approach. This extensive practice, and practice with a variety of material, also decontextualizes the learning. That is, the strategies become free of their original "bindings" and can now be applied easily and unconsciously to various situations (Collins et al., 1989).

Another purpose of independent practice is to facilitate transfer to other content areas. One hopes that the reading comprehension skills that are taught in one content area, such as social studies, might also be applied to another content areas, such as science. Such transfer might be facilitated if students receive guided practice in applying their skills to *different* content areas. For example, in a study by Dermody (1988) the last phase of the study involved application of cognitive strategy to a different content area that was used for the original instruction.

Increase Student Responsibilities

As students become more competent during guided practice and independent practice, the scaffolds are diminished and student responsibilities are increased. Thus, with greater competency, the teacher diminishes the use of models and prompts and other scaffolds, and diminishes the support offered by other students. In addition, the complexity and difficulty of the material is gradually increased. In reading, for example, one begins with well-organized, reader-friendly material and then increases the difficulty of the material. That way, students receive practice and support in applying their strategies to the more difficult material they can expect to encounter in their regular reading.

Assess Student Mastery

After guided practice and independent practice, some of the studies assessed whether students had achieved a mastery level, and provided for additional instruction when necessary. On the fifth and final day of instruction, Davey and McBride (1986) required students to generate three acceptable questions for each of three passages. Smith (1977) stated that student questions at the end of a story were compared to model questions, and reteaching took place when necessary. Wong et al. (1986) required that students achieve mastery in applying the self-questioning steps and students had to continue doing the exercises (sometimes daily for 2 months) until they achieved mastery. Unfortunately, the other studies cited in this review did not report the level of mastery students achieved in generating questions.

Fitting Things Together

How might the results from these three areas of research fit together? First, the research allows us to articulate a major goal of education: helping students develop well-organized knowledge structures. In well-developed structures, the parts are well organized, the pieces are well connected, and the bonds between the connections are strong.

We also know something about how to help students acquire these structures.

1. Present new material in small steps to that the working memory does not become overloaded.
2. Help students develop an organization for the new material.
3. Guide student practice by (a) supporting students during initial practice, and (b) providing for extensive student processing.
4. When teaching higher level tasks, support students by providing them with cognitive strategies.
5. Help students learn to use the cognitive strategies by providing them with procedural prompts and modeling the use of these procedural prompts.
6. Provide for extensive student practice.

SUMMARY

Thirty years ago, particularly with the publication of the first *Handbook of Research on Teaching* (Gage, 1963) and the investment of public and private funds into research, we began an extensive program of research and development in education. This chapter is an attempt to highlight some of the major results that have been obtained in the area of instruction, results which have relevance for today's teachers and students.

REFERENCES

Alvermann, D. E. (1981). The compensatory effect of graphic organizers on descriptive text. *Journal of Educational Research, 75,* 44–48.

Anderson, V. (1991, April). *Training teachers to foster active reading strategies in reading-disabled adolescents.* Paper presented at the annual meeting of the American Educational Research Association, Chicago.

Andre, M. D. A., & Anderson, T. H. (1978–1979). The development and evaluation of a self-questioning study technique. *Reading Research Quarterly, 14,* 605–623.

Barr, A. S. (1948). The measurement and prediction of teaching efficiency: A summary of the investigations. *Journal of Experimental Education, 16,* 203–283.

Baumann, J. F. (1984). The effectiveness of a direct instruction paradigm for teaching main idea comprehension. *Reading Research Quarterly, 20,* 93–115.

Bickhard, M. H. (1992). Scaffolding and self-scaffolding: Central aspects of development. In L. T. Winegar & J. Valsiner (Eds.), *Children's development within social context* (Vol. 2, pp. 33–52). Hillsdale, NJ: Lawrence Erlbaum Associates.

Billingsley, B. S., & Wildman, T. M. (1988). Question generation and reading comprehension. *Learning Disability Research, 4,* 36–44.

Blaha, B. A. (1979). *The effects of answering self-generated questions on reading.* Unpublished doctoral dissertation, Boston University School of Education.

Brophy, J., & Good, T. (1986). Teacher-effects results. In M. C. Wittrock (Ed.), *Handbook of research on teaching* (3rd ed., pp. 328–376). New York: Macmillan.

Brown, A. L., & Campione, J. C. (1986). Psychological theory and the study of learning disabilities. *American Psychologist, 41,* 1059–1068.

Brown, A. L., & Palincsar, A. S. (1989). Guided, cooperative learning and individual knowledge acquisition. In L. B. Resnick (Ed.), *Knowing, learning, and instruction: Essays in honor of Robert Glaser* (pp. 393–451). Hillsdale, NJ: Lawrence Erlbaum Associates.

Cohen, R. (1983). Students generate questions as an aid to reading comprehension. *Reading Teacher, 36,* 770–775.

Collins, A., Brown, J. S., & Newman, S. E. (1990). Cognitive apprenticeship: Teaching the crafts of reading, writing, and mathematics. In L. Resnick (Ed.), *Knowing, learning, and instruction: Essays in honor of Robert Glaser.* Hillsdale, NJ: Lawrence Erlbaum Associates.

Davey, B., & McBride, S. (1986). Effects of question-generation on reading comprehension. *Journal of Educational Psychology, 78,* 256–262.

Dermody, M. (1988). *Metacognitive strategies for development of reading comprehension for younger children.* Paper presented at the annual meeting of the American Association of Colleges for Teacher Education. New Orleans, February, 1988. (Louisiana State Department of Education, New Orleans Adolescent Hospital, New Orleans). ERIC ED 292070

Dreher, M. J., & Gambrell, L. B. (1985). Teaching children to use a self-questioning strategy for studying expository text. *Reading Improvement, 22,* 2–7.

Duffy, G., Lanier, J. E., & Roehler, L. R. (1980). *On the need to consider instructional practice when looking for instructional implications.* Paper presented at the Conference on Reading Expository Materials, Wisconsin Research and Development Center, University of Wisconsin–Madison.

Durkin, D. (1979). What classroom observations reveal about reading comprehension. *Reading Research Quarterly, 14,* 581–544.

Englert, C. S., & Raphael, T. E. (1989). Developing successful writers through cognitive strategy instruction. In J. Brophy (Ed.), *Advances in research on teaching, Vol. 1* (pp. 105–151). Greenwich, CT: JAI Press.

Flanders, N. A. (1960). *Teacher influence, pupil attitudes and achievement.* Minneapolis: University of Minnesota. (Also published under this title as FS 5.225:25040 U.S. Department of Education, U.S. Government Printing Office).

Gage, N. L. (Ed.). (1963). *Handbook of research on teaching.* Chicago, IL: Rand McNally.

Gage, N. L., & Needles, M. C. (1989). Process-product research on teaching: A review of criticisms. *Elementary School Journal, 89,* 253–300.

Garcia, G. E., & Pearson, P. D. (1991). Modifying reading instruction to maximize its effectiveness for all students. In M. S. Knapp & P. M. Shields (Eds.), *Better strategies for the children of poverty: Alternatives to conventional wisdom.* Berkeley, CA: McCutchan. Also (Tech. Rep. #489). Champaign, IL: Center for the Study of Reading, University of Illinois.

Good, T., & Grouws, D. (1979). The Missouri teacher effectiveness program. *Journal of Educational Psychology, 71,* 355–362.

Guzzetti, B. J., Snyder, T. E., & Glass, G. V. (1992). Promoting conceptual change in science: Can texts be used effectively? *Journal of Reading, 35,* 642–649.

Helfeldt, J. P., & Lalik, R. (1976). Reciprocal student-teacher questioning. *Reading Teacher, 33,* 283–287.

Hiller, J. I., & Hungate, H. N. (1985). Implications for mathematics instruction of research on scientific problem solving. In E. A. Silver (Ed.), *Teaching and learning mathematical problem solving: Multiple research perspectives.* Hillsdale, NJ: Lawrence Erlbaum Associates.

Hunter, M. (1982). *Mastery teaching.* P.O. Box 514, El Segundo, CA.: TIP Publications.

King, A. (1990). Enhancing peer interaction and learning in the classroom through reciprocal peer questioning. *American Educational Research Journal, 27,* 664–687.

Labercane, G., & Battle, J. (1987). Cognitive processing strategies, self-esteem, and reading comprehension of learning disabled students. *Journal of Special Education, 11,* 167–185.

Larkin, J. H., & Reif, F. (1976). Analysis and teaching of a general skill for studying scientific text. *Journal of Educational Psychology, 72,* 348–350.

Manzo, A. V. (1969). *Improving reading comprehension thorugh reciprocal teaching.* Unpublished doctoral dissertation, Syracuse University.

Medley, D. M., & Mitzel, H. E. (1959). Some behavioral correlates of teacher effectiveness. *Journal of Educational Psychology, 50,* 239–246.

Nolte, R. Y., & Singer, H. (1985). Active comprehension: teaching a process of reading comprehension and its effects on reading achievement. *The Reading Teacher, 39,* 24–31.

Palincsar, A. S. (1987, April). *Collaborating for collaborative learning of text comprehension.* Paper presented at the annual conference of the American Educational Research Association, Washington, DC.

Palincsar, A. S., & Brown, A. L. (1984). Reciprocal teaching of comprehension-fostering and comprehension-monitoring activities. *Cognition and Instruction, 2,* 117–175.

Paris, S. C., Cross, D. R., & Lipson, M. Y. (1984). Informed strategies for learning: A program to improve children's reading awareness and comprehension. *Journal of Educational Psychology, 76,* 1239–1252.

Pressley, M., Burkell, J., Cariglia-Bull, T., Lysynchuk, L., McGoldrick, J. A., Schneider, B., Symons, S., & Woloshyn, V. E. (1995). *Cognitive strategy instruction* (2nd ed.) Cambridge, MA.: Brookline Books

Raphael, T. E., & Pearson, P. D. (1985). Increasing student awareness of sources of information for answering questions. *American Educational Research Journal, 22,* 217–237.

Richey, P. (1985). The effects of instruction in main idea and question generation. *Reading Canada Lecture, 3,* 139–146.

Rosenshine, B. (1971). *Teaching behaviors and student achievement.* Slough, England: National Federation for Educational Research.

Rosenshine, B., & Meister, C. (1995). Scaffolds for teaching higher-order cognitive strategies. In A. C. Ornstein (Ed.), *Teaching: Theory into practice* (pp. 134–153). Boston: Allyn & Bacon.

Rosenshine, B., & Stevens, R. (1986). Teaching functions. In M. C. Wittrock (Ed.), *Handbook of research on teaching* (3rd Ed., pp. 745–799). New York, Macmillan.

Scardamalia, M., & Bereiter, C. (1985). Fostering the development of self-regulation in children's knowledge processing. In S. F. Chipman, J. W. Segal, & R. Glaser (Eds.), *Thinking and learning skills: Research and open questions.* Hillsdale, NJ: Lawrence Erlbaum Associates.

Schoenfeld, A. H. (1985). *Mathematical problem solving.* New York: Academic Press.

Singer, H., & Donlan, D. (1982). Active comprehension: Problem-solving schema with question generation of complex short stories. *Reading Research Quarterly, 17,* 166–186.

Smith, N. J. (1977). *The effects of training teachers to teach students different reading ability levels to formulate three types of questions on reading comprehension and question generation ability.* Unpublished doctoral dissertation, University of Georgia.

Wong, B. Y. L., Wong, W., Perry, N., & Sawatsky, D. (1986). The efficacy of a self-questioning summarization strategy for use by underachievers and learning-disabled adolescents. *Learning Disability Focus, 2,* 20–35.

Wong, Y. L., & Jones, W. (1982). Increasing metacomprehension in learning disabled and normally achieving students through self-questioning training. *Learning Disability Quarterly, 5,* 228–239.

Wood, D. J., Bruner, J. S., & Ross, G. (1976). The role of tutoring in problem solving. *Journal of Child Psychology and Psychiatry, 17,* 89–100.

11

ACCOMMODATING STUDENT HETEROGENEITY IN MAINSTREAMED ELEMENTARY CLASSROOMS THROUGH COOPERATIVE LEARNING

Robert J. Stevens
Jill D. Salisbury
Pennsylvania State University

Accommodating student heterogeneity has consistently been a major instructional problem in schools. Regardless of how students are assigned to classes, with a typical elementary or middle-school class of 25 or more students, the teacher must address student heterogeneity in terms of students' prior knowledge, prerequisite skills, motivation, aptitudes, and attitudes toward learning. These cognitive, motivational, and attitudinal differences greatly affect what students learn, how quickly they learn, and how well they learn. As a result, teachers often become concerned about their instructional pace. They fear it may be too slow for the above-average students, causing them to become bored, and too fast for the below-average students, causing them to get lost, overwhelmed, or frustrated. Similarly, teachers are concerned about the difficulty of the tasks they assign during instruction, fearing that the tasks may be too easy and lack challenge for above-average students, while at the same time that they may be too difficult or complex for below-average students to experience success.

Typically, administrators and teachers attempt to accommodate student heterogeneity through structural changes. The most common structural change is grouping students according to their ability either between classes, known as *tracking*, or within a class, known as *ability grouping* (Slavin, 1987). The goal of these structural changes is to make the instructional groups more homogeneous, thereby resolving the instructional pace and task difficulty problems for the teacher. It is also assumed that in ability-grouped and tracked classes teachers will be able to provide more practice and individualized attention based on the needs of the students.

ACCOMMODATING HETEROGENEITY THROUGH GROUPING

Between-Class Ability Groups

Many elementary schools group students into classes based on their general academic ability, a process called tracking (Coldiron, Braddock, & McPartland, 1987). Although this is a fairly common practice, both the logic and research on grouping students for instruction does not support tracking elementary-age students into between-class ability groups. In an exhaustive review of the literature dating back to 1932, Slavin (1987) stated "how unequivocally the research evidence refutes the assertion that ability-grouped class assignment can increase student achievement in elementary school" (p. 307). When students were grouped in relatively homogeneous classes for the entire day there were no consistent positive effects for any students, neither high- nor low-ability.

The logic used to advocate tracking in elementary school is flawed. It assumes that tracking will make instruction easier because teachers can respond better to the individual needs of the students and, theoretically, that teachers can accelerate their instruction for the more advanced students. In reality, with a classroom of 25 or more students it is not that simple. First, it is literally impossible to create a "relatively homogeneous" classroom. Although students' measured ability may be fairly similar, they will still vary greatly on a number of characteristics highly related to learning, including their prior knowledge, motivation, and attitudes. Although it may be possible to create relatively homogeneous classes on one of these important variables (i.e., achievement), it is literally impossible to consider all of them simultaneously when making class assignment decisions.

Research has also shown that the logic in support of tracking is further flawed in that teachers do not adjust to a faster pace for higher ability students in tracked elementary schools (Rowan & Miracle, 1983). Instead, the pace in high-ability classes seems to be similar to that in heterogeneous classes in untracked schools. Meanwhile, the pace in lower ability track classes is much slower than the pace in heterogeneous classes in untracked schools.

The research also indicates that the teachers in the heterogeneous classes allocate more instructional time to the low-ability students within the class. Thus it seems that tracked elementary classes may in fact be significantly *less instructionally responsive* to the needs of low-ability (and possibly to high-ability) students than are heterogeneous classes that use ability grouping within the class for instruction. This research evidence is inconsistent with the logic of the tracking argument that teachers can adjust their pace to be more responsive to both high- and low-ability students when they are in tracked classes.

Another common problem with tracked elementary classes is that the groups are very inflexible. Once a student is assigned to a low- or average-ability class it is highly unlikely that he or she will ever move to a higher ability class (Rosenbaum, 1983). It seems that this kind of grouping assumes a linear growth for students' learning and development. That is, once you determine a student's rate of learning and place them accordingly in a classroom of like-ability students, they will continue to learn at the same rate. However, students' learning and development is not linear. Instead, students learn at varying rates and tend to develop in spurts. The inflexible grouping used in tracked elementary schools is unresponsive to these developmental changes. In contrast, teachers in heterogeneous classes have a structure that could more easily accommodate changes in a student's learning rate. In heterogeneous classes it is possible to accommodate students simply by changing their instructional group or by giving the student other instructional activities, adjustments that are more common and more easily implemented than changing a student's class as would be required in the tracked structure (Dreeben, 1983).

Within-Class Ability Groups

The results of previous research suggest that it is preferable to assign elementary students to heterogeneous classes and if necessary to make ability groups within the class for instruction (Slavin, 1987). For example, this is commonly found in elementary reading instruction. Slavin found that heterogeneous classes with within-class ability groups demonstrated better achievement than did heterogeneous classes without ability groups, with an average effect size of +.34, or a third of a standard deviation. This can be contrasted with tracked classes that showed little or no difference in achievement when compared to heterogeneous classes, with effect sizes clustering from −.15 to +.15 with a median of zero.

However, heterogeneous classes with ability groups have their own problems that may mitigate some of the effects described earlier. During group instruction, one group typically receives instruction from the teacher while the other group(s) works independently on seatwork activities. The advantage of instructing students at the appropriate level and pace offered by ability groups is offset to some degree by the lower on-task rates and potentially less meaningful activities found when students are working independently on seatwork (Anderson, Brubaker, Alleman-Brooks, & Duffy, 1985; Rosenshine & Stevens, 1986). To minimize the negative effects of ability grouping it is important for teachers to (a) keep the instructional groups to a minimum (i.e., only two or three instructional groups); (b) use meaningful seatwork activity that is related to what students do in their instructional groups; and (c) create a physical structure and activity structure within the classroom to help maintain students' on-task behavior (Rosenshine & Stevens, 1986). In a review of ability grouping, Slavin (1987) found that the positive effects for heterogeneous classes with ability groups described earlier were found in classes with only two or three ability groups, and where the ability groups were formed on the basis of specific skills in reading or math and not based on general academic abilities like IQ.

One advantage of heterogeneous classes is that they offer many positive academic models for the average and below-average students. Students learn behaviors and attitudes by observing them in other students. When they see their peers being successful there is the potential that students will learn vicariously from that experience. Teachers in heterogeneous classes can systematically use students to model appropriate cognitive and on-task behaviors to take advantage of the effective models available in a heterogeneous class. Positive academic role models are often not present in homogeneous low-ability classes and student behavior and group norms typically do not support academic behaviors in the classroom (Eder, 1981).

Although both tracking and within-class ability grouping focus on grouping students based on their measured abilities, the message to the students is quite different. In tracked classes it is very common for students in the lower track to recognize their low placement and to think of themselves as "dumb" (Wheelock, 1992). On the other hand, when instructional groups within a heterogeneous class are based on specific skills, they emphasize learning more than general ability. Thus students are less likely to be generically labeled as "smart" or "dumb."

Similarly, an advantage of heterogeneous classes is that it gives students an opportunity to exhibit their strengths among their mixed-ability peers, rather than being globally categorized on limited measures of their abilities. Typically, tracking decisions are based on a few measures of students ability, such as their reading and language arts abilities. However, students seldom have the same ability in all subjects. A student who may be average or below in reading might be average or above in mathematics, social studies, or science. Heterogeneous classes allow students to exhibit their strengths in these other subjects while getting instruction that meets their needs or weaknesses in other areas.

Another strength of heterogeneous classes with ability groups is that teachers tend to have a more rapid pace of instruction for all of the groups than do teachers in tracked classes (Rowan & Miracle, 1983). The more rapid pace of instruction seems to be one appropriate and successful way of accommodating student diversity in heterogeneous classes. In his review, Slavin (1987) found that students at all ability levels benefited from ability grouping within heterogeneous classes. Heterogeneous classes may in fact make teachers more sensitive to student instructional needs without reducing the challenge and pace needed to increase all students' learning.

ACCOMMODATING HETEROGENEITY THROUGH SPECIAL EDUCATION

One method of accommodating students with significantly lower achievement than their agemates is to place them in a special education program. Most special education students spend all or part of their day in separate classes, a form of tracking. Only 35% of students with disabilities are served in their regular classes (Office of Special Education and Rehabilitation Services, 1994). The remainder are segregated either all day in special classes or special schools, or are tracked into resource rooms for instruction for part of the day.

Of those students receiving special education services, over 50% are identified as have learning disabilities (Office of Special Education and Rehabilitation Services, 1994). When students with speech impairments are removed, students with learning disabilities comprise 67% of the special education population. This large population of students has achievement that is significantly lower than others in their grade level, but students with learning disabilities do not seem to be significantly different from other low achievers including those in Title 1 (Chapter 1) programs (Jenkins, Pious, & Peterson, 1988). However, recent data shows that 75% of the students with learning disabilities are segregated from their peers for instruction during part of the day in resource rooms (54%) or for the full day in either separate classes (20%) or separate schools (1%; Office of Special Education and Rehabilitation Services, 1994). This suggests that the majority of schools track students with learning disabilities into relatively homogeneous classes for part or all of the day as a means of accommodating them, rather than keeping them in heterogeneous classes for their instruction.

Beginning in 1975 with the passage of P. L. 94–142, the Education of All Handicapped Children Act, there has been movement toward serving students with special needs in less restrictive and less segregated environments. There has been a significant amount of research and discussion about providing instruction for special education students in mainstreamed regular education classes, particularly for students with learning disabilities. Students with learning disabilities are the most similar in instructional needs and abilities to nonidentified students and they would seem to be the most easily and effectively served in regular classrooms (cf. Gottlieb, Alter, & Gottlieb, 1991; Slavin & Stevens, 1991). In spite of federal mandates and state initiatives to include students with disabilities in regular classrooms, in the past 10 years there has been little change in the percentage of students with learning disabilities who are served in the regular classroom rather than in segregated settings (Office of Special Education and Rehabilitation Services, 1994).

Much of the research on segregated special education programs for students with learning disabilities is similar to the research on tracking. Students who are tracked into segregated special education services, like those in low-ability track classes, tend to have lower achievement, lower self-esteem, and are less socially accepted (cf. Johnston, Allington, & Afflerbach, 1985; Stainback & Stainback, 1984). Many of the advocates of less restrictive and more inclusive school structures and services for special education cite many of the same issues that are used to argue against tracking: the need for social development to prepare for the real world and social justice in a democratic society (Hocutt, Martin, & McKinney, 1991; Reynolds, 1989; Will, 1986). And, as with tracking, the questions about the efficacy and appropriateness of segregated special education programs are not new (Lloyd & Gambatese, 1991).

However, the research on mainstreaming, to date, is less than conclusive and has often raised more questions than answers (Fuchs & Fuchs, 1991; Lloyd, Crowley, Kohler, & Strain, 1988). Research has suggested that simply placing students with learning disabilities in regular education classes is not sufficient to produce significantly better achievement (Marston, 1987). Similarly, regular education teachers often feel unprepared for or incapable of providing adequate instruction for students with learning disabilities who are added to their classes (Gersten, Walker, & Darch, 1988). It seems that effective mainstreaming requires restructuring schools to provide additional support for the instructional needs of learning disabled students in the regular classroom setting (Stainback & Stainback, 1991). Special education needs to be perceived primarily as a service to enhance learning and social development, rather than as a placement. Schools need to develop, implement, or develop *and* implement programmatic changes to support students with special needs in the regular classroom (cf. Gottlieb et al., 1991). Such changes may require restructuring the classrooms and potentially the entire school. They also require training regular education and special education teachers in instructional strategies and classroom processes that will better accommodate the needs of students with learning disabilities as well as all of the students in a heterogeneous class.

USING COOPERATIVE LEARNING TO ACCOMMODATE STUDENT HETEROGENEITY

How can schools accommodate student heterogeneity and, more specifically, students with learning disabilities in a mainstream regular education classroom? One possible alternative is cooperative learning. Cooperative learning has a large body of research documenting its positive impact on students' achievement, attitudes, and social relations (Johnson & Johnson, 1989; Slavin, 1990). Cooperative learning has consistently been effective in improving the social relations between students with and without disabilities in regular education classrooms (see Table 11.1). This is primarily accomplished by integrating students with learning disabilities into the instructional dialogue of the classroom. The interaction and interdependence of cooperative groups encourages more substantial contact among the students, which in turn promotes positive relations among them.

The impact of cooperative learning on the achievement of mainstreamed students with learning disabilities is less straightforward. Previous reviews have suggested that there is a need for more research to substantiate achievement benefits (Lloyd, Crowley, Kohler, & Strain, 1988), and that the existing literature was equivocal regarding impact on achievement (Tateyama-Sniezak, 1990). Recent studies have added substantially to this body of research, but the structure of cooperative learning methods must be considered to disentangle seemingly contradictory results.

For cooperative learning to have a significant positive effect on students' achievement, it must have two essential features: a group goal and individual accountability (Slavin, 1983, 1990). The group goal gives students a reason to cooperate and promotes interdependence among the students. The development of interdependence among the students facilitates improved social relations, but alone is insufficient to lead to a significant impact on students' achievement. Individual accountability gives them a reason to learn, or provides a check of their learning. Cooperative learning that includes both a group goal and individual accountability may be considered well-structured cooperative learning processes. When cooperative learning processes are well structured and include individual accountability along with a group goal, they tend to have consistently positive effect on students' achievement (cf. Slavin, 1990).

Of the 14 studies we located that used cooperative learning programs to mainstream students with academic disabilities, half (7) used programs with a group goal, but without individual accountability (see the top of Table 11.2). The other half of the studies used cooperative learning processes that included both a group goal and individual accountability (the bottom of Table 11.2). Typically, the studies that did not include individual accountability were rather short in duration (2 days to 4 weeks) and had a small number of special education students included in the entire population of the study (6 to 38 students, with 5 having 12 or fewer). None of these studies reported statistical tests on the outcome measures for the students with disabilities in cooperative learning versus students with disabilities in traditional instruction.

Most of the studies cited earlier concluded that students with some form of academic disabilities had higher achievement in cooperative learning than

TABLE 11.1
Cooperative Learning Research: Social Integration and Peer Acceptance of Students With Handicaps

Study	Sample and Duration	Subjects and Grade	Contrasts	Significance	Effect Size
Ballard et al. (1977)	37 classes 37 H 8 weeks	Multimedia project Gr. 3, 4, 5	CL vs. Trad Social accept.	$F = 5.7^*$	+.78
Cooper et al. (1980)	48 NH 12 H 15 days	Englist, science, & geography Gr. 7	Cl vs. Indiv Sociometric	$X^2 = 9.13$ ns	+.85
Armstrong, Johnson, & Balow (1981)	30 NH 10 H 4 weeks	Reading Gr. 5 & 6	Cl vs. Indiv	no test for handicapped only	+
Johnson & Johnson (1981)	32 NH 8 H 16 days	Math Gr. 3	Cl vs. Indiv Sociometric	$t = 1.56^*$	+.49
Johnson & Johnson (1982)	25 NH 6 H 16 days	Math Gr. 11	CL vs. Indiv Sociometric	$t = 2.72^{**}$	+.99
Johnson & Johnson (1982)	41 NH 10 H 15 days	Science Gr. 4	CL vs. Indiv Sociometric	$t = 1.66$ ns	+.46
Johnson & Johnson (1984)	36 NH 12 H 15 days	Social studies Gr. 4	CL vs. Indiv sociometric NH-H interact	$F = 6.4^*$ $F = 3.85$ ns	+.73 +.57
Madden & Slavin (1983)	143 NH 40 H 7 weeks	Math Gr. 3, 4, 6	CL vs. Trad Sociometric	$F = 11.0^{**}$	+.48
Slavin (1984)	418 NH 86 H	Math Gr. 3, 4, 5	CL vs. Trad Sociometric	$F = 3.27^*$	+.39
Stevens & Slavin (1995)	837 NH 76 H	Reading, language arts & math	CL vs. Trad Sociometric # friends picked by NH	$t = 3.42^{**}$ $t = 4.33^{**}$	+.86 +.90

TABLE 11.2
Cooperative Learning Research: Effects on Students' Achievement

Study	Sample and Duration	Subjects and Grade	Contrasts	Significance	Effect Size
Models Without Individual Accountability					
Armstrong, Johnson, & Balow (1981)	30 NH 10 H 4 weeks	Reading Gr. 5 & 6	No individual test	*NA*	NA
Smith, Johnson, & Johnson (1982)	48 NH · 7 H 5 days	Social studies Gr. 6	CL > Indiv retention test		+
Johnson & Johnson (1982)	25 NH 6 H 16 days	Math Gr. 11	Cl vs. Indiv 4 weekly tests		+
Johnson et al. (1983)	39 NH 9 H 10 days	Science Gr. 7	Cl vs. Indic 2 weekly tests	Handicapped only not available	
Johnson & Johnson (1984)	36 NH 12 H 15 days	Social studies Gr. 4	CL vs. Indiv 3 weekly tests		+
Cosden, Pearl, & Bryan (1985)	100 NH 38 H 2 days	Reading Gr. 2-8			+
Johnson et al. (1985)	128 NH 26 H 21 days	Science Gr. 5-6	CL > Indiv		+
Models With Group and Individual Accountability					
Madden & Slavin (1983)	143 NH 40 H 7 weeks	Math Gr. 3, 4, 6	CL vs. Cont math ach.	$F < 1$ ns	+.48
Slavin, Madden, & Leavey (1984a)	387 NH 117 H 10 weeks	Math Gr. 3-5	CL > Cont CL > Indiv math ach.	$F = 1.0$ ns $F = 2.2$ ns	+.16 +.14

TABLE 11.2
(Continued)

Slavin, Madden, & Leavey (1984b)	1258 NH 113 H 10 weeks	Math Gr. 3-5	CL > Cont math comp. math concepts	$F = 6.1^*$ $F = 4.3^*$	+.61 +.46
Stevens et al. (1987) study 2	430 NH 20 H 24 weeks	Reading, Language arts Gr. 3-4	CL > Cont read vocab read comp lang mech Cont > CL lang expr	$F = 4.7^*$ $F = 3.7$ ns $F < 1.0$ ns $F < 1.0$ ns	+.90 +.99 +.10 -.09
Jenkins et al. (1994)	367 NH 30 H 26 weeks	Reading, Language arts	CL > Cont read vocab read comp spelling language	$F = 5.0^*$ $F = 4.1^*$ $F = 1.0$ ns $F = 1.6$ ns	+.72 +.71 +.15 +.62
Stevens & Slavin (1995a)	1162 NH 137 H 2 years	Reading, Language arts Gr. 2-6	CL > Cont read vocab read comp lang mech lang expr	$F = 4.5^*$ $F = 3.9^*$ $F = 1.9$ ns $F = 4.2^*$	+.37 +.32 +.28 +.36
Stevens & Slavin (1995b)	797 NH 76 H 2 years	Reading, Language arts Gr. 2-6	CL > Cont read vocab read comp lang mech lang expr math comp math appl	$F = 13.8^{**}$ $F = 14.4^{**}$ $F < 1.0$ ns $F = 11.4^{**}$ $F = 10.8^{**}$ $F = 3.9^*$	+.76 +.85 +.25 +.74 +.59 +.35

Note. + No statistical test for handicapped students only. Means indicate CL > Individual-istic, but insufficient data to compute an effect size.

in more traditional education. However, these studies presented only the subgroup means and did not provide sufficient information to test whether these differences were statistically significant or to assess the magnitude of the differences relative to the standard deviation of the data (e.g., determine the effect sizes). Therefore, the lack of duration as well as the insufficient data and statistical analyses of these studies offer little if any support for the effectiveness of using cooperative learning to mainstream students with learning disabilities.

The seven studies that used well-structured cooperative learning proc-esses that included both group goals and individual accountability typically were longer in duration (7 weeks to 2 years) and often included a reasonable number of students with academic disabilities in the study (20 to 137 stu-dents) to permit statistical analyses of the results with this subpopulation. All of these studies measured students' achievement on standardized achievement tests and all conducted statistical analyses on the subpopulation of only students identified with academic disabilities (the great majority of them were students with learning disabilities).

Five of the seven studies reported significantly better achievement for students with academic disabilities in cooperative learning than in nonmainstreamed traditional education. (Nonmainstreamed included either part-day pull-out programs and full-day segregated special education programs.) The mean effect size across these seven studies was +.47. Students with academic disabilities who were mainstreamed in well-structured cooperative learning outperformed their peers in traditional special education programs by nearly a half standard deviation on standardized achievement tests.

The fact that these studies tended to be longer in duration helps increase the ecological validity of these results. These were not one-shot, short-term instructional studies potentially fraught with novelty effects. It could be argued that in the schools that used cooperative learning for 2 years (cf. Stevens & Slavin, 1995b), cooperative learning would have been the norm rather than a novelty. On inspecting the bottom of Table 11.2 and the effect sizes presented, it is evident that the four studies which lasted 24 weeks or more also had the largest effects on the achievement of students with disabilities. For example, the effect sizes in reading achievement range from one-third to nearly a full standard deviation. The importance and significance of the magnitude of these effects is enhanced by the fact that they were obtained on standardized achievement tests, rather than on experimenter-designed tests or criterion referenced tests which tend to be more biased to the specific experimental or curriculum treatment (see Rosenshine & Meister, 1994).

IMPLEMENTING COOPERATIVE LEARNING IN A MAINSTREAMED CLASSROOM

Cooperative learning provides a process that can help to accommodate student heterogeneity. It is also important to note, however, that for integrating students with learning disabilities many of the effective studies in Table 11.2 used special education teachers in the regular classroom to team-teach at least a portion of the instruction in reading, language arts, and math (Jenkins et al., 1994; Stevens, Madden, Slavin, & Farnish, 1987; Stevens & Slavin, 1995a, 1995b). Special education teachers provided additional instruction and guided practice to the students who needed it, permitting more flexible use of instructional resources. As suggested by Marston's (1987) research, including students with learning disabilities in regular education classes seems to require additional instructional support from an adult for them to be successful. Although students with disabilities get instructional support from their peers in cooperative learning, the results of these four studies suggest that additional instructional support from a teacher is also needed.

In addition to special education teachers teaching in the regular classroom, in at least two of the studies (Jenkins et al., 1994; Stevens & Slavin, 1995b), the regular and special education teachers also met periodically to determine the instructional needs of the students in the mainstreamed classes. This additional planning time helped the special education teacher work flexibly with the regular education teachers to meet the needs of the special education students along with the demands of regular classroom instruction.

EFFECTS OF COOPERATIVE LEARNING IN HETEROGENEOUS CLASSES

Some argue that cooperative learning is most beneficial to lower ability students who receive the additional instruction and feedback from their higher ability peers. However, this misconception is not supported by research. In well-structured cooperative learning programs there are no differential effects favoring lower ability students over their more able peers (cf. Stevens et al., 1987). One study disaggregated the effects of cooperative learning for gifted, above-average, average, below-average, and special education students, found that gifted students had significantly higher achievement in cooperative learning than in traditional instruction with a gifted pull-out program (Stevens & Slavin, 1995b). In that study, cooperative learning had the largest impact, in terms of the magnitude of the effect sizes, on higher ability students. This provides some evidence that higher ability students do benefit and their achievement certainly is not impeded by cooperative learning.

WHY DOES COOPERATIVE LEARNING WORK IN HETEROGENEOUS CLASSROOMS?

There are a variety of reasons why cooperative learning has significant benefits when used in heterogenous classes, including the motivational and social support that peers give to one another. In terms of the dynamics of learning for all students, perhaps the most significant aspect is the nature of the collaborative dialogue found in cooperative learning. When students work in a setting where they are interdependent—one student's success depends on the success of others—the nature of their academic dialogue is qualitatively different.

Webb and her associates (Webb, 1985; Webb & Kenderski, 1984) found that in cooperative structures students were more likely to ask questions and more likely to receive explanations in response to those questions. Similarly, in cooperative structures students' errors were corrected more frequently and the corrections were more often in the form of explanations of how to arrive at correct answers. As students interact cooperatively on academic tasks they explain strategies to one another in their own words, helping them to further process the complex cognitive activity or content (Brown & Campione, 1986; Wittrock, 1986). Collaborative activity requires students to reflect on their knowledge to make elaborations that they can convey to their peers. Making generalizations and elaborations requires students to understand the cognitive relations of the new knowledge and to relate it to their prior knowledge, which is an effective way to improve their understanding of the information.

Vygotsky (1978) suggested that the importance of collaborative learning and interaction with peers during the learning process may go beyond the effects due to the elaboration process. It seems that collaborative or cooperative learning offers benefits to the students who receive elaborative explanations as well. Observing others and practicing with peer support and dialogue helps learners internalize the cognitive functions that they are attempting to master. When learning complex cognitive tasks, such as reading comprehension or writing, it may be particularly important for students to engage in the collaborative dialogue to improve the efficiency and effectiveness of the learning process.

FUTURE RESEARCH

The research reviewed in this chapter provides the beginning of a picture of the impact that schools can have when students with learning disabilities are included in regular education classes through the use of well-structured cooperative learning processes. Although the findings are consistent, additional replications would help better understand the nature of these findings and their transportability to different settings and schools. The generalizability of these studies is limited because the special education population involved was primarily students with learning disabilities. Future research should investigate whether cooperative learning can be an effective instructional vehicle for including students who have been identified with other disabilites, such as attention deficits, emotional disorders, or behavioral disorders.

Additional research should investigate the academic dialogues in the cooperative teams and whether all of the students adequately participate in them. Recent research in help-seeking behavior suggests that social and academic competence and perceptions of risks in the classroom influence whether students will request help from either their peers or the teacher (Murphy & Pintrich, 1995). This and other related research may have implications for cooperative groups with students with learning disabilities. Research on how students with learning disabilities are participating in the academic discussions would help us gain an understanding of the demands of these situations and the unique needs of students with disabilities in terms of their skills and their perceptions of the classroom.

CONCLUSIONS

Well-structured cooperative learning seems to be an effective way to accommodate student heterogeneity without stigmatizing students based on limited measures of their academic ability. This is particularly true for including students with learning disabilities in regular education classes. Both the research results and the theoretical rationale behind these results suggest that with cooperative learning heterogeneity in classrooms is not necessarily a problem or a weakness; it may instead be a strength. Beyond the obvious social benefits, being able to work with students who differ in their ability and their knowledge may help all students learn more and better understand what they already know.

These results also support Marston's (1987) conclusion that when students with disabilities are included in mainstream classes, it is necessary to provide the teacher with additional support to make inclusion successful. One type of support would be to include the special education teacher in the regular classroom to provide additional instruction to the students with disabilities. Another form of support that is implicit in the studies cited here is training. All of the teachers in the successful studies were trained in instructional methods and curricula that facilitated effective mainstreaming. Effective inclusion of students with disabilities was at least in part due to the instructional training and support the teachers received.

REFERENCES

Anderson, L. M., Brubaker, N., Alleman-Brooks, J., & Duffy, G. (1985). A qualitative study of seatwork in first-grade classrooms. *Elementary School Journal, 86,* 123–140.

Armstrong, B., Johnson, D., & Balow, B. (1981). Effects of cooperative vs. individualistic learning experiences on interpersonal attraction between learning-disabled and normal-progress elementary school students. *Contemporary Educational Psychology, 6,* 102–109.

Ballard, M., Corman, L., Gottlieb, J., & Kauffman, M. (1977). Improving the social status of mainstreamed retarded children. *Journal of Educational Psychology, 69,* 605–611.

Brown, A., & Campione, J. (1986). Psychological theory and the study of learning disabilities. *American Psychologist, 14,* 1059–1068.

Coldiron, J. R., Braddock, J. H., & McPartland, J. M. (1987, April). *A description of school structures and classroom practices in elementary, middle, and secondary schools.* Paper presented at the annual meeting of the American Educational Research Association, Washington, DC.

Cooper, L., Johnson, D., Johnson, R., & Wilderson, F. (1980). Effects of cooperative, competitive, and individualistic experiences on interpersonal attraction among heterogeneous peers. *Journal of Social Psychology, 111,* 243–252.

Cosden, M., Pearl, R., & Bryan, T. (1985). The effects of cooperative and individual goal structures on learning disabled and nondisabled students. *Exceptional Children, 52,* 103–114.

Dreeben, R. (1983). First-grade reading groups: Their formation and change. In P. Peterson, L. Wilkinson, & M. Hallinan (Eds.), *The social context of instruction: Group organization and group processes* (pp. 69–84). New York: Academic Press.

Eder, D. (1981). Ability grouping and self-fulfilling prophecy: A microanalysis of teacher-student interaction. *Sociology of Education, 54,* 151–162.

Fuchs, D., & Fuchs, L. (1991). Framing the REI debate: Abolitionists versus conservationists. In J. W. Lloyd, N. Singh, & A. Repp (Eds.), *The regular education initiative: Alternative perspectives on concepts, issues, and models* (pp. 241–255). Sycamore, IL: Sycamore Publishing.

Gersten, R., Walker, H., & Darch, C. (1988). Relationships between teachers' effectiveness and their tolerance for handicapped students: An exploratory study. *Exceptional Children, 54,* 433–438.

Gottlieb, J., Alter, M., & Gottlieb, B. W. (1991). Mainstreaming academically handicapped children in urban schools. In J. W. Lloyd, N. Singh, & A. Repp (Eds.), *The regular education initiative: Alternative perspectives on concepts, issues, and models* (pp. 95–112). Sycamore, IL: Sycamore Publishing.

Hocutt, A. M., Martin, E. W., & McKinney, J. D. (1991). Historical and legal context of mainstreaming. In J. W. Lloyd, N. Singh, & A. Repp (Eds.), *The regular education initiative: Alternative perspectives on concepts, issues, and models* (pp. 17–28). Sycamore, IL: Sycamore Publishing.

Jenkins, J. R., Pious, C. G., & Peterson, D. L. (1988). Categorical programs for remedial and handicapped students: Issues of validity. *Exceptional Children, 55,* 147–158.

Jenkins, J. R., Jewell, M., Leicester, N., O'Connor, R., Jenkins, L., & Troutner, N. (1994). Accommodations for individual differences without classroom ability groups: An experiment in school restructuring. *Exceptional Children, 60,* 344–358.

Johnson, D., & Johnson, R. (1981). The integration of the handicapped into the regular classroom: Effects of cooperative and individualistic instruction. *Contemporary Educational Psychology, 6,* 344–355.

Johnson, D., & Johnson, R. (1982). The effects of cooperative and individualistic instruction on handicapped and nonhandicapped students. *Journal of Social Psychology, 118,* 257–268.

Johnson, D., & Johnson, R. (1984). Building acceptance of differences between handicapped and nonhandicapped students: The effects of cooperative and individualistic instruction. *Journal of Social Psychology, 122,* 257–267.

Johnson, D., & Johnson, R. (1989). *Cooperation and competition: Theory and research.* Edina, MN: Interaction Books.

Johnson, R., Johnson, D., De Weert, N., Lyons, V., & Zaidman, B. (1983). Integrating severely adaptively handicapped seventh-grade students into constructive relationships with nonhandicapped peers in science classes. *American Journal of Mental Deficiency, 87,* 611–618.

Johnson, R., Johnson, D., Scott, L., & Ramolae, B. (1985). Effects of single-sex and mixed-sex cooperative interaction on science achievement and attitudes and cross-handicap and cross-sex relationships. *Journal of Research in Science Teaching, 22,* 207–220.

Johnston, P., Allington, R., & Afflerbach, P. (1985). The congruence of classroom and remedial reading instruction. *Elementary School Journal, 85,* 465–478.

Lloyd, J. W., Crowley, E. P., Kohler, F. W., & Strain, P. S. (1988). Redefining the applied research agenda: Cooperative learning, prereferral, teacher consultation, and peer-mediated interventions. *Journal of Learning Disabilities, 21*(1), 43–52.

Lloyd, J. W., & Gambatese, C. (1991). Reforming the relationship between regular and special education: Background and issues. In J. W. Lloyd, N. Singh, & A. Repp (Eds.), *The regular education initiative: Alternative perspectives on concepts, issues, and models* (pp. 3–16). Sycamore, IL: Sycamore Publishing.

Madden, N., & Slavin, R. E. (1983). Effects of cooperative learning on the social acceptance of mainstreamed academically handicapped students. *Journal of Special Education, 17,* 171–182.

Marston, D. (1987). The effectiveness of special education. *Journal of Special Education, 21,* 13–27.

Murphy, A., & Pintrich, P. (1995, April). *Should I ask for help?: Adolescent perceptions of costs and benefits of help-seeking in the classroom.* Paper presented at the annual meeting of the American Educational Research Association, San Francisco, CA.

Office of Special Education and Rehabilitation Services (1994). *To assure the free appropriate public education of all children with disabilities: Sixteenth annual report to Congress on the implementation of the Individuals with Disabilities Act* (U.S. Department of Education No. 381-637/10010). Washington, DC: U.S. Government Printing Office.

Reynolds, M. (1989). An historical perspective: The delivery of special education to mildly disabled and at-risk students. *Remedial and Special Education, 10*(6), 7–11.

Rosenbaum, J. (1983). The social organization of instructional grouping. In P. Peterson, L. Wilkinson, & M. Hallinan (Eds.) *The social context of instruction: Group organization and group processes* (pp. 53–68). New York: Academic Press.

Rosenshine, B. V., & Meister, C. E. (1994). Reciprocal teaching: A review of research. *Review of Educational Research, 64,* 479–530.

Rosenshine, B. V., & Stevens, R. J. (1986). Teaching functions. In M. Wittrock (Ed.), *Handbook of research on teaching* (3rd ed., pp. 376–391). New York: Macmillan.

Rowan, B., & Miracle, A. (1983). Systems of ability grouping and the stratification of achievement in elementary schools. *Sociology of Education, 56,* 133–144.

Slavin, R. E. (1983). When does cooperative learning increase student achievement? *Psychological Bulletin, 94,* 429–445.

Slavin, R. E. (1984). Team assisted individualization: Cooperative learning and individualized instruction in the mainstreamed classroom. *Remedial and Special Education, 5*(6), 33–42.

Slavin, R. E. (1987). Ability grouping and student achievement in elementary schools? A best evidence synthesis. *Review of Educational Reseach, 57,* 293–336.

Slavin, R. E. (1990). *Cooperative learning: Theory, research, and practice.* Englewood Cliffs, NJ: Prentice Hall.

Slavin, R. E., Madden, N., & Leavey, M. (1984a). Effects of team assisted individualized instruction on mainstreamed students. *Exceptional Children, 84,* 434–443.

Slavin, R. E., Madden, N., & Leavey, M. (1984b). Effects of team assisted individualization of mathematics achievement of handicapped and nonhandicapped students. *Journal of Educational Psychology, 76,* 813–819.

Slavin, R. E., & Stevens, R. J. (1991). Cooperative learning and mainstreaming. In J. W. Lloyd, N. Singh, & A. Repp (Eds.), *The regular education initiative: Alternative perspectives on concepts, issues, and models* (pp. 177–192). Sycamore, IL: Sycamore Publishing.

Smith, K., Johnson, D., & Johnson, R. (1982). Effects of cooperative and individualistic instruction on the achievement of handicapped, regular, and gifted students. *Journal of Social Psychology, 116,* 277–283.

Stainback, W., & Stainback, S. (1984). A rationale for the merger of special and regular education. *Exceptional Children, 51,* 102–111.

Stainback, W., & Stainback, S. (1991). Rationale for integration and restructuring: A synopsis. In J. W. Lloyd, N. Singh, & A. Repp (Eds.), *The regular education initiative: Alternative perspectives on concepts, issues, and models* (pp. 225–240). Sycamore, IL: Sycamore Publishing.

Stevens, R. J., Madden, N., Slavin, R. E., & Farnish, A. M. (1987). Cooperative Integrated Reading and Composition: Two field experiments. *Reading Research Quarterly, 22*, 433–454.

Stevens, R. J., & Slavin, R. (1991). When cooperative learning improves the achievement of students with mild disabilities: A response to Tateyama-Sniezek. *Exceptional Children, 57*, 276–280.

Stevens, R. J., & Slavin, R. E. (1995a). Effects of a cooperative learning approach in reading and writing on academically handicapped and nonhandicapped students. *Elementary School Journal, 95*, 241–260.

Stevens, R. J., & Slavin, R. E. (1995b). The cooperative elementary school: Effects on achievement, attitudes, and social relations. *American Educational Research Journal, 32*, 321–351.

Tateyama-Sniezek, K. (1990). Cooperative learning: Does it improve the academic achievement of students with handicaps? *Exceptional Children, 56*, 426–437.

Vygotsky, L. (1978). *Mind in society: The development of higher level psychological processes.* Cambridge, MA: Harvard University Press.

Webb, N. (1985). Student interaction and learning in small groups: A research summary. In R. Slavin, S. Sharan, R. Hertz-Lazarowitz, C. Webb, & R. Schmuck (Eds.), *Learning to cooperate: Cooperating to learn* (pp. 211–230). New York: Plenum.

Webb, N., & Kenderski, C. (1984). Student interaction in small-group and whole-class settings. In P. Peterson, L. Wilkinson, & M. Hallinan (Eds.), *The social context of instruction: Group organization and group processes* (pp. 153–170). New York: Academic Press.

Wheelock, A. (1992). *Crossing the tracks.* New York: The New Press.

Will, M. (1986). Educating children with learning problems: A shared responsibility. *Exceptional Children, 52*, 411–416.

Wittrock, M. (1986). Students' thought processes. In M. Wittrock (Ed.), *Handbook of research on teaching* (3rd ed., pp. 297–314). New York: Macmillan.

12

WHOLE LANGUAGE AND PROCESS WRITING: DOES ONE APPROACH FIT ALL?

Steve Graham
Karen R. Harris
University of Maryland

There is a growing concern about the quality of literacy instruction for students with special needs (cf. Allington, 1994; Palinscar & Klenk, 1992). Critics contend there is little special about special education programs for students who have difficulty learning to read and write (Allington, 1994; Allington & McGill-Franzen, 1989; Singer & Butler, 1987). For example, Palinscar and Klenk (1992) found that children in primary-grade special education classrooms spent most of their reading and writing time working alone, completing worksheets, reading directions, and copying board work. They seldom read or wrote for an extended period of time and were "mired in materials that both children and teachers found to be uninteresting and largely irrelevant to their lives" (p. 218).

Critics also claim that literacy instruction for students with special needs focuses too much on the lower level skills of decoding and transcription (cf. McGill-Frazen & Allington, 1991; Palinscar & Klenk, 1992). They indicate that many special education teachers' reading programs primarily concentrate on the teaching of word-attack or word-recognition skills in the context of degraded text or through the use of decontextualized activities such as worksheets. Although such instruction is designed to respond to the difficulties that students with special needs experience with decoding, critics maintain that it limits students' opportunities to learn how to use the "syntactic, semantic, and schematic analysis of text that complement the use of grapho-phonemic analysis" (Palinscar & Klenk, 1992, p. 212). They further indicate that this approach limits students' opportunities for acquiring important background or content knowledge, because an important means for obtaining this information is through extended reading and discussion of text. They contend that these instructional practices may lead students to develop an impoverished understanding of the nature of reading, emphasizing decoding (read fast and correctly) rather than meaning as the purpose for reading. A recent Non Sequitur cartoon offered an especially caustic view on the outcomes of intensive phonics instruction, depicting a panhandler with a cup and the following message on a sign: "Got hooked on phonics—Please help me!"

Similar objections have been voiced about the type of writing instruction provided to students with special needs (cf. Graham & Harris, 1994a). Christenson, Thurlow, Ysseldyke, and McVicar (1989), for instance, looked at the amount of writing done by students receiving special services in 10 urban and suburban elementary schools. On average, slightly more than 20 minutes of the whole school day (across both general and special education classes) were spent writing. This included printing numbers during math, handwriting practice, spelling instruction, filling out worksheets in social studies, and so forth. At least half of the time set aside for writing instruction was allotted to spelling and handwriting, whereas over 60% of students' actual time writing was spent completing paper-and-pencil practice tasks. This approach to writing instruction reminds us of a Peanuts cartoon where Charlie Brown's sister, Sally, is drawing lines on a piece of paper and tells her brother that she is practicing underlining, and that "If I ever write something worth underlining, I'll be ready."

Critics complain that many of the "skills" that students with special needs are taught are only marginally useful when reading or writing (cf. Allington, 1983). For instance, Susan Ohanian (1994), a whole language teacher, questioned the relevance of teaching schwas and the rules for syllabication (two common staples of skill-based literacy programs), as good readers typically do not understand nor use these skills. She further indicated that her experience of filling in for a "direct instruction" teacher convinced her she was tone deaf when it came to hearing the vowel distinctions: "Oh, I could hear the difference between 'O' and 'U' well enough, but I'm talking about the distinction between 'eh' and 'uh.' " She drolly noted that the students were better at making these distinctions than she was—they had been at it for 7 months before she had joined them. Although they were "terrific at circling sounds . . . they hadn't read a book . . . they hadn't even seen a book" (p. 10).

Finally, a fundamental goal for special services during the last 20 years is the acceleration of participants' academic achievement (Allington, 1994). The primary means for achieving this objective has been to employ specially trained teachers to provide students with individually tailored instruction in classrooms containing a relatively small number of students. In some instances, the special teacher was responsible for most, if not all, of a student's literacy instruction. In others, the special education teacher was responsible for only part of the overall program. Communication between special and regular education, however, does not always occur (Graham, Hudson, Burdg, & Carpenter, 1980; Voltz, Elliott, & Cobb, 1994), leading to a fragmented literacy program where services are poorly coordinated (Kulieke & Jones, 1993).

ALTERNATIVES

Is this what literacy instruction for students receiving special services really looks like? Are they provided with reduced or limited opportunities to actually read and write? Are they taught skills that have little value or utility? Do schools fail to provide them with coherent and comprehensive literacy programs?

Although we cannot provide factual answers to these questions (due to a lack of pertinent research), enough dissatisfaction with current practices exists that a number of influential literacy researchers in special education have recommended alternative approaches to literacy instruction for students with special needs (cf. Englert, Raphael, & Marriage, 1994; Gersten & Dimino, 1993; Harris & Graham, 1993; MacArthur, Graham, Schwartz, & Shafer, 1995; Palinscar & Klenk, 1992; Reid, 1993). The common thread underlying most of the recommended alternatives is constructivism.

Although there are many definitions of constructivism, two major principles are included in most constructivism-based approaches to teaching and learning (Harris & Graham, 1994). First, children's active role in the construction of knowledge is emphasized. Constructivists reject the concept of the child as a passive learner, responding to the environment and learning by directly internalizing knowledge given by others. Instead, children are seen as inherently active, self-regulating learners, constructing knowledge in developmentally appropriate ways while interacting with a perceived world. Previous knowledge and experiences are the starting point for new learning, and constructivists believe that real understanding only occurs when children participate fully in their own learning. Full participation is thought to lead to a deeper and richer understanding and use of knowledge, thus promoting access to and application of what has been learned (Pressley, Harris, & Marks, 1992).

Second, constructivists reject the notion of teaching discrete skills in a linear sequence as well as the assumption that demonstrated success on basic skills is a necessary prerequisite to more advanced learning and higher order thinking (Means & Knapp, 1991). Instead, learning is seen as a socially situated activity that is enhanced in functional, meaningful, and authentic contexts (Palincsar & Klenk, 1992; Reid, 1993). The teachers primary role is to assist children in the construction of powerful knowledge, rather than explicitly providing knowledge and information (Tharpe & Gallimore, 1989).

Currently, the most popular constructivitic approaches for teaching reading and writing to children are whole language and the process approach to writing (Graham & Harris, 1994a). In this chapter, we examine the strengths, possible limitations, and issues involved in using these two approaches with students with special needs.

PRINCIPLES UNDERLYING WHOLE LANGUAGE AND PROCESS WRITING

Whole language teachers stress that learning to read and write is as natural as learning to speak and, consequently, is best learned through real use (rather than practice exercises) in meaningful and authentic contexts (Goodman, 1992; Vacca & Rasinski, 1992). They further emphasize that meaning and process, not form, should be the primary focus in reading and writing. Whole language teachers strive to develop a community of learners who share and help each other, make personal choices about what they read and write, take ownership and responsibility for their learning, take risks in their reading and writing, and evaluate their efforts and progress. Literacy learning is also seen as integrative, with learning in any one area of language helping learning in other areas.

The process approach to writing instruction shares many of the same underlying principles as whole language (although the source of their genesis differs), and is often included as part of whole language programs. Process writing teachers provide children with extended opportunities for writing about self-selected topics, emphasizing students' ownership of their writing projects (Atwell, 1987; Graves, 1983). Children write for real purposes and for real audiences. They are perceived as having meaningful things to say, and the teacher's job is to look for ways to help them learn how to say it. The teacher acts as a facilitator, creating an atmosphere (both nonthreatening and supportive) in which students can flourish and take risks. They also use writing conferences, peer collaboration, minilessons, modeling, sharing, and classroom dialogue to deliver personalized and individually tailored assistance and instruction.

SCIENTIFIC EVIDENCE

Whole Language

It is difficult to determine the effects of whole language because there is considerable disagreement as to how to assess it, what to assess, who should assess it, and even if it should be assessed (Edelsky, 1990). This is further complicated because studies of whole language are relatively few in number and often weak in design and analysis (Alamasi, Palmer, Gambrell, & Pressley, 1994). Furthermore, many of the quantitative studies comparing whole language with other approaches to reading instruction (most notably basal readers) have favored the use of conventional reading and writing measures, such as standardized reading tests (Pressley & Rankin, 1994), possibly biasing the evaluation. For example, consider how writing is typically evaluated in studies comparing whole language and skills-oriented instruction. Students are usually asked to write about an imposed topic during a single session. Because whole language teachers advocate student choice in topic selection and writing for extended periods, this set up favors students in skill-oriented classes in which writing for shorter periods of time about assigned topics is more common (Graham & Harris, 1994b).

The most often cited quantitative synthesis on the effects of whole language on children's reading was conducted by Stahl and Miller (1989). Using both meta-analysis and vote-counting procedures, they examined studies conducted prior to 1988 comparing either whole language or language experience programs to basal reading programs. Programs were classified as whole language/language experience approaches if: (a) lessons were child centered, (b) children's own language was used as a medium of instruction, (c) trade books were emphasized, (d) phonics lessons were not directly taught in isolation, or any combination thereof. Overall, they found that whole language/language experience programs and basal reading programs had similar effects on children's reading achievement and attitudes toward reading. One exception to this general finding was that whole language/language experience approaches were more effective than basal programs at the kindergarten level or when compared to a readiness program at the beginning of first grade—this advantage, however, did not extend to formal basal programs in first grade. It was also found that the effects of whole language/language experience approaches were weaker for economically disadvantaged students. This finding runs counter to the claim by some advocates that whole language is especially suitable for these students.

The findings from this synthesis must be interpreted cautiously, not only in terms of the caveats noted earlier, but also because the results are based on an analysis combining both whole language and language experience. Although there are many similarities in the two approaches, there are also a number of important differences, including emphasis on experience charts versus trade books as well as dictated stories versus written stories using invented spelling (Stahl & Miller, 1989). Furthermore, whole language is not easy to define, raising the possibility that the studies selected for review were not representative of whole language/language experience approaches.

Stahl, McKenna, and Pagnucco (1994) conducted a second meta-analysis of studies published since 1988. This review was limited strictly to studies comparing whole language with traditional approaches to reading instruction. Congruent with their earlier findings, they reported that whole language programs were more effective during kindergarten than traditional approaches, but that the two approaches had similar effects across grades on reading attitudes. In contrast to their earlier synthesis, they found that students in whole language classrooms did slightly better on measures of comprehension. There were too few studies, however, to test if this effect was statistically significant. Not surprisingly, students in traditional classrooms did better on measures of decoding, probably because these measures were more closely aligned to the instruction provided in traditional classes.

Thus, synthesis of quantitative evidence on the effects of whole language on reading indicates that whole language is more effective than skills-oriented instruction during kindergarten (when children's concept of the form and function of print are formed) and *may* also provide a slight advantage for older children on measures of reading comprehension. Whole language, however, is not equally effective for all students. As the 1989 synthesis illustrated, economically disadvantaged students tended to fare better in a traditional basal program. Moreover, Nicholson (1989) reported that at least 15% of children in New Zealand, a country heavily committed to the whole language approach, required individual tutelage in reading in their second year of schooling. Qualitative studies of whole language classrooms corroborate these general findings—most students become better readers over the course of the school year, but some show only minimal progress (Allen, Michalove, Shockley, & West, 1991; Dahl & Freppon, 1991).

The research base on the effects of whole language on writing is smaller and more fragmented than the research on reading. In a recent review, we were only able to locate 14 quantitative and qualitative studies examining the effects of whole language on learning to write (Graham & Harris, 1994b). Our analysis of these studies indicated that the writing of students in whole language classes generally improved during kindergarten and the primary grades. As in the area of reading, however, some young children made little progress as writers in whole language classes and some even regressed (cf. Allen, 1988; Dahl & Freppon, 1991), reinforcing the axiom: no one method of instruction is best for all children. Beyond the primary grades, there was simply not enough data available to draw any conclusions about children's progress. The only reliable difference between children in whole language and skills-oriented classrooms involved students' thinking about writing. Students in whole language classes held a meaning-based view of writing, whereas their peers in more conventional classes viewed writing from a skills perspective.

Process Writing

As with whole language, both quantitative and qualitative methods have been used to examine the effectiveness of the process approach to writing. In a meta-analysis of experimental studies in writing, Hillocks (1984) reported that the mean effect size for process writing was positive (.19), but three times smaller than the environmental approach to writing, characterized by structured, problem-solving writing tasks with clear and specific objectives. In examining studies on the National Writing Project (a program aimed at disseminating the process approach to writing), Pritchard (1987) found that students working with teachers trained in the use of process writing were generally better writers than students in traditional composition programs. In addition, teachers who participated in the National Writing Project became more positive about their ability to teach writing. It should be noted that three of the studies in Hillocks' (1984) meta-analysis involved the National Writing Project (one of these was reviewed by Pritchard, 1987). The average effect size (.33) for these three studies was positive, but modest. Thus, studies examining the National Writing Project in both reviews had a similar outcome—training teachers to use a process approach had positive effects on students' writing.

Conclusions regarding quantitative studies on the effectiveness of process writing, however, must be tempered in light of several limitations. First, random assignment of students and teachers to conditions was not possible in many of the studies, allowing competing explanations for obtained differences between treatments. Second, innovative programs typically show superior effects over conventional practice (Pflaum, Walberg, Karegianes, & Rasher, 1980). Receiving "special training" on the process approach to writing, as was done in the National Writing Project studies, may have created a Hawthorne effect, favoring the process writing teachers. Third, most of the available research has been conducted with students in junior high school or above. From a quantitative perspective, we simply know much less about the effects of process writing with young children.

Qualitative researchers, in contrast, have focused considerable attention on the effects of process writing in elementary schools. Graves (1979) and Calkins (1981) have conducted the most influential research in this area. Using a case study approach, they described selected behaviors of a small number of students participating in process writing classrooms. Although this work clearly illustrates how progress can occur in a process writing classroom, Smagorinsky (1987) contended that their work best resembles "journalism about ideas that work well under favorable circumstances, particularly when the instructors have such great enthusiasm for their work that it positively affects students' attitudes" (p. 340). Smagorinsky further argued that the case studies developed by Graves and Calkins are not research, because they did not raise questions about the validity of their evidence nor did they present negative evidence. As other qualitative researchers have demonstrated (cf. Reyes, 1991), process approaches to writing are not uniformly effective with all children.

Students With Special Needs

Although the available evidence suggests that many students fare well in whole language and process writing classes, it is equally apparent that neither of these approaches are a panacea. Some students struggle in these classrooms and, at least in the case of process writing, other instructional approaches may be more effective. Unfortunately, the research base is not sufficiently developed to allow even the most tentative conclusions concerning the effects of whole language or process writing on the literacy development of students with special needs. Only a handful of case studies have examined the effects of whole language and process writing with students with special needs (Cousin, Aragon, & Rojas, 1993; Wansart, 1988; Westby & Costlow, 1991; Zaragoza & Vaughn, 1992; Zucker, 1993). Although the participants in these investigations typically become better readers and writers during the course of the study, too many of these reports resemble the description of journalism offered earlier by Smagorinsky (1987)—whole language or process writing approaches were enthusiastically and uncritically championed.

Because the effectiveness of whole language and process writing with students with special needs is unclear, we next examine possible benefits as well as concerns surrounding these two approaches. This analysis focuses on the basic principles underlying both approaches, paying special attention to issues involving constructivism.

BENEFITS

Respect

Too often teachers set low expectations for students receiving special services and question their abilities to learn (Lilly, 1992). This is reflected in the tendency of schools to track and sort these students and the emphasis on a deficit model, focusing on student weaknesses (Lipsky & Gartner, 1992). A basic tenet of whole language and process writing teachers is that "children should be respected and trusted as competent learners" (Reutzel & Hollingsworth, 1988, p. 407). According to Dudley-Marley (1995), when these teachers see "children who struggle in school, they do not see deficits, deviance, or abnormality" (p. 110). Rather, all students are perceived as capable learners and instruction is based on their capacity and strengths. As one observer noted, students progress at their own rate and are not penalized for being unique (Bock, 1989). Thus, one advantage of whole language and process writing for students with special needs is the respect afforded to each child as a capable learner.

Personalized Assistance

Children receiving special services may not learn as quickly or in the same way as other children. As a result, approaches where instruction is adjusted according to individual needs are particularly important for these students. Several research studies show that whole language and process writing teachers are sensitive to the learning patterns of individual students, especially students likely to struggle with learning to read and write (Allen et al., 1991; Bock, 1989; Dahl & Freppon, 1991). In a study by Dahl and Freppon (1991), for example, kindergarten children who were dependent on the teacher or peers for learning new concepts and reluctant to take risks at the beginning of the school year received considerable scaffolding and extended guidance from their teachers, aimed at helping them extend their writing skills. Similarly, Allen et al. (1991) found that students who were "at risk" in the whole language classrooms they observed received active, intentional support designed to increase their success. As Vacca and Rasinski (1992) noted, providing personalized and individually tailored assistance to students functioning at different levels is one of the key responsibilities of whole language and process writing teachers.

More Time Spent Reading and Writing

Another potential advantage of whole language and process writing is that students will spend more time actually reading, writing, or both. In each approach, there is considerable emphasis on "immersing" students in written language—constantly engaging them in frequent and meaningful reading, writing, or both.

Although there is very little data comparing the amount of time students spend reading or writing in conventional classes versus whole language or process writing classrooms, the differences are quite substantial if studies by Mervar and Hiebert (1989) and Fisher and Hiebert (1990) are representative. The first study found that students in whole language classes read approximately two to three times as much as students in conventional writing classes, whereas the second study found that students in whole language classes spent six times as much time writing. Such differences are noteworthy, as the amount and type of reading and writing students do in school will undoubtedly affect their attitudes toward these processes and the degree to which they make them a useful part of their life.

Ability to Self-Regulate

Students receiving special services often have difficulties with the self-regulation of organized, strategic behavior (Harris, 1982). Self-regulated learning occurs when one uses personal processes (such as goal setting or self-evaluation) to strategically manage the environment or one's behavior (Zimmerman, 1989). In literacy programs with a highly structured curriculum or a restrictive code for classroom conduct (as is the case in some basal programs), opportunities for self-regulated learning and the development of self-regulation skills may be stifled.

Whole language and process writing teachers, in contrast, provide students with plenty of opportunities to learn how to regulate their behavior. Teachers put students "in charge," encouraging them to take responsibility for their own learning and allowing them to make decisions and exercise options about what they read and write (Vacca & Rasinski, 1992). Students are further encouraged to work collaboratively with others, take risks, and evaluate their own efforts. All of these principles are aimed at creating environmental conditions believed to foster self-regulation and self-confidence (Corno, 1992).

Integrative Learning

Whole language teachers emphasize the integrative nature of learning. Reading and writing, for instance, are viewed as equally important, working together to support literacy development (Goodman, 1992). There are numerous examples of how learning in one language area helps learning in others, including acquiring rhetorical knowledge from reading (Bereiter & Scardamalia, 1984), learning the correct spelling of words from reading (Callaway, McDaniel, & Mason, 1972), or using knowledge of word meanings to spell a word (e.g., use a related word to spell a reduced vowel: admire, admiration).

Emphasis on the reciprocal relationship between various language and literacy skills is particularly important for students who struggle with learning to read and write, including those with special needs. This was illustrated in a longitudinal study by Juel (1988), where children who entered first grade with little phonemic awareness became poor readers, and poor readers typically became poor writers and poor spellers. Conventional approaches to literacy, where learning is often compartmentalized, may fail to fully consider or take advantage of the integrative nature of language and learning for these students.

CONCERNS

In a series of letters to the *Washington Post*, published under the title "Can't Read, Can't Write," one parent of three school-aged children referred to whole language as the "Learning to Read By Miracle or By Accident approach." Another parent complained that the problem with whole language for beginning readers and writers could be summed up in a Dennis the Menace cartoon, where a youngster scribbling on a piece of paper says: "I can write, but I am the only one who can read my writing, and I can't read." Still another respondent indicated that she "shuddered to think what is going to happen to this next eager-to-learn group of 6-year-olds" participating in a whole language program.

Are these reactions typical? Are most parents this cynical about the use of whole language and process writing? Although it might be tempting to downplay the comments of the parents quoted here, especially given all of the benefits of whole language and process writing just noted, this would be a mistake, as their viewpoint is not uncommon. In a recent telephone survey of 1,200 Americans conducted by Public Agenda, a New York-based research organization, 60% of those interviewed were highly skeptical of the use of whole language (Willis, 1995). Parents are not alone in their negative reactions to whole language and process writing; educators working with students who are most likely to have difficulty learning to read and write have also expressed concern (cf. Mather, 1992; Pressley & Rankin, 1994; Spiegel, 1992). The two issues that have generated the most "heat" among both parents and professional are considered in the following.

Overcorrection for Meaning and Process

Whole language and process writing teachers place greater emphasis on meaning and process than they do on mechanics and form. This emphasis is, in part, a reaction to conventional literacy instruction where the mechanics of literacy are stressed and children spend only a limited amount of time reading and writing. Some critics maintain, however, that whole language and process writing teachers often go too far—overcorrecting for meaning and process, while underemphasizing the importance of decoding and the mechanics of writing (cf. Spiegel, 1992). Reyes (1991), for instance, expressed concern that teachers may fail to provide the assistance that some students need to be able to master the mechanics of literacy, out of a mistaken desire to remain faithful to the principles underlying whole language and process writing.

We recently observed such a situation in a private elementary school. In response to a request from a number of parents that the school devote more attention to the teaching of "phonics" because their first- or second-grade child could not read, an item in the school newsletter reiterated the school's philosophy that phonics was taught within the context of reading and that it was only one of many processes students used when reading. Although the school was unwilling to place more emphasis on phonics in the classroom, parents whose children were experiencing difficulty were encouraged to hire a tutor who could provide phonics instruction after school. For some of the students experiencing difficulty, this extra help with phonics was all they needed to get them going.

Although we noted earlier that one benefit of whole language and process writing is that teachers are sensitive to the needs of individual students, some critics contend that this responsiveness is constrained by a one-approach-fits-all mentality (cf. Pressley & Rankin, 1994). In the situation described earlier, for instance, some of the parents indicated that they were astonished that the school was bound to this one approach, unwilling to make what they saw as needed modifications, when some children were clearly struggling. Other parents indicated that the teachers in the school were fooling themselves, as they were teaching phonics at home. A similar complaint was posed in the "Can't Read, Can't Write" section of the *Washington Post* cited earlier. The writer complained, "Parents are teaching their children phonics at night while school officials are praising the whole language approach by day."

The need to place greater emphasis on an analytic approach to word recognition in whole language programs may be especially important for students with special needs. A considerable amount of evidence indicates that the primary reading problem for many of these students is a phonological processing difficulty that impedes word learning and word recognition (Stanovich, 1994). Efficient decoding is dependent on discovering and exploiting the principle that spelling matches to sound at the level of letters and phonemes. Critics have charged, however, that whole language teachers do not do enough to ensure that children acquire such pivotal skills as phonemic awareness and the alphabetic principle (Adams, 1990).

We are not implying that whole language teachers should abandon their emphasis on meaning and process. Instead, we are encouraging teachers (who have not already done so) to take an even more responsive approach to individual needs, recognizing that one size does not fit all, and that some children may need and benefit from additional help with phonics. Furthermore, such help does not have to be decontextualized. As Felton (1993) noted, it is quite feasible to teach the alphabetic principle and phonics within the context of a whole language program.

With regard to writing, most students develop enough fluency by the end of the primary grades so that the mechanics of writing do not interfere with the process of getting thoughts onto paper (Scardamalia, Bereiter, & Goleman, 1982). This does not appear to be the case, however, for some children with special needs (Graham, 1990). Although whole language and process writing teachers do address the development of skills such as handwriting and spelling, we are concerned that not enough emphasis is placed on their acquisition (Graham & Harris, 1994a).

In a traditional whole language or process writing class, spelling and handwriting are taught to children within the context of writing, when and if they need it (Manning & Manning, 1995). The accent is on capitalizing on teachable moments, based on needs that have spontaneously arisen during authentic tasks. These needs are then addressed either through conferences, minilessons, or on-the-spot teaching. When teachers observe children working or conference with them individually, however, issues of form and mechanics may not be uppermost in their minds. Fitzgerald and Stamm (1990), for instance, found that teacher–student discussions about writing rarely addressed issues of form. Similarly, DeGroff (1992) reported that process writing teachers' comments on children's first drafts primarily focused on content and process.

Another problem with relying on "teachable moments" to provide minilessons or on-the-spot teaching is that it may lead to haphazard and incomplete instruction (Spiegel, 1992). Teachable moments may not occur for some important literacy skills or may be overlooked in other instances.

It is also important to recognize that capitalizing on teachable moments is basically reactive rather than proactive. In some instances, this can lead to problems that are difficult to correct. In handwriting, for example, on-the-spot teaching and minilessons are usually delivered in response to an established problem or a developing difficulty (Graham, 1992). Once a problem, such as an awkward pencil grip, becomes well established, it is usually difficult to change. Similarly, if developing difficulties, such as inefficient approaches to forming letters, are not identified and addressed promptly, they may well become an established problem. Although systematically teaching young writers how to form letters and hold their writing instrument will not eliminate the need for seizing teachable moments, it should reduce the number of established and developing difficulties the teacher has to address.

Finally, some critics contend that teachers are doing students no favor to suggest, even implicitly, that form is not important in writing. Delpit (1988) contended that, "Students will be judged on their product, regardless of the process they utilize to achieve it" (p. 287). This reminds us of Muggie Maggie, a character in a children's book by Beverly Cleary (1990). Even though she is only in third grade, she forms opinions about her teachers and the school principal based on the neatness of their cursive writing.

As with reading, we recommend a more balanced approach in whole language and process writing in terms of handwriting and spelling. This may be particularly important for students with special needs, who may need and benefit from additional help with these skills.

Overemphasis on Informal Methods of Learning

Whole language and process writing are primarily based on indirect rather than direct methods of instruction. Critics maintain that the methods used by whole language and process writing teachers are not powerful enough to help some students learn the knowledge, skills, or strategies needed to read and write adequately (cf. Mather, 1992; Pressley & Rankin, 1994). A considerable amount of evidence, for example, indicates that many students with special needs do not acquire a variety of cognitive and metacognitive strategies and skills unless detailed and explicit instruction is provided (Brown & Campione, 1990).

As a touchstone for examining this issue more specifically, we return to our earlier discussion on how spelling is typically taught in whole language and process writing classrooms. As noted previously, teachers capitalize on teachable moments ("Do you know how to spell a word that sounds like 'plow'?") and provide minilessons on spelling skills when the child needs them for something the child is working on. Teachers also model correct spelling when writing in class; provide plenty of opportunities for children to share, display, and publish their writing (to increase the likelihood that students will attend to correct spelling in practical and social situations); and encourage students not to worry about misspellings or to invent spellings when working on earlier drafts of a paper, returning to correct their spelling during final editing. More importantly, it is assumed that students' spelling skills will develop "naturally" by providing them plenty of opportunities to read and write for real purposes, much as the ability to speak develops "naturally" (Wilde, 1990).

Are these methods powerful enough for teaching spelling to students with special needs? To answer this question, we begin by examining the belief that students can learn to spell by immersing them in authentic reading and writing; this is the primary mechanism for learning to spell in whole language and process writing. Although research shows that children learn to spell some words as a result of reading and writing, poor readers and spellers are not especially adept at "catching" the spelling of words through incidental methods of learning (Graham & Miller, 1979). Even college students have difficulty learning to spell words as a result of just reading them (Ormrod, 1986). Perhaps just as telling is the observation that many of the words children commonly misspell occur frequently in their reading and writing material (Graham, Harris, & Loynachan, 1993). These findings suggest that advocates for incidental learning in spelling are overly optimistic. It is unlikely that children with special needs (or most other children) will discover all they need to know simply by reading and writing.

What about the other spelling methods used by whole language and process teachers to support the "natural learning" assumption? These techniques provide more direct support to the learner, as some skills are emphasized through minilessons (as the need arises) and others during teachable moments. Although these techniques undoubtedly contribute to learning to spell (just as meaningful reading and writing do), they may not occur with enough frequency to insure that students learn all they need to know (see the discussion in the previous section). They may also not be explicit enough for some students. As Freedman (1993) indicated, when whole language and process writing teachers use direct support, there may be little or no explication. Instead, they may use hints, questions, tactful responding, and so forth to guide students' discovery during conferences, teachable moments, or minilessons.

For example, when a child asks how a word is spelled, instead of providing the answer, the teacher might ask, "How do you think it is spelled?", probing to obtain information about the child's current understanding. This information is then used to generate prompts and hints to encourage the student to rethink the situation (Pressley, in press). To illustrate, the teacher might ask the student, "Do you know how to spell another word that sounds like it?"—inferring that the student did not attempt to use an analogy strategy to spell the word. The teacher might also provide a hint, such as, "This is one where there is not a silent *e* at the end of the word," inferring that the student was overgeneralizing the silent *e* rule.

Although scaffolding provides classroom teachers with an extremely flexible and useful tool, we are concerned that the combination of natural learning techniques and such guided practice (assuming that it occurs with adequate frequency) may still not be powerful enough for many students with special needs. As Pressley (in press) and Harris and Pressley (1991) noted, there are a number of factors that may limit the effectiveness of scaffolding. First, less capable students typically require more scaffolding than more capable ones. In a classroom full of children, teachers will not always have the time nor opportunity to provide the degree of scaffolding needed by each child. Second, despite a teacher's best intentions, students do not always get it. They may not understand what the teacher is "driving at" or their discoveries may be off the mark. Third, some students experience considerable frustration in guided discovery approaches, and their resulting anger may undermine the scaffolding process. Fourth, to scaffold effectively, teachers must know a great deal about both the curriculum and the problems the student is experiencing. Understanding children's difficulties is especially challenging with students with special needs, as they may be less capable of describing the problem precisely.

Similar to our earlier recommendation, we are not suggesting that whole language and process writing teachers abandon their use of informal teaching techniques. Instead, we believe that frequent reading and writing for authentic purposes, scaffolding, and so forth are essential components of the instructional mix. By themselves, they may not be enough, however. For example, in a study by Reyes (1991), students in a bilingual classroom using a process approach to writing did not adopt models of conventional form in their writing even though their teacher modeled correct form, provided minilessons on how to apply correct form, and increased reading and writing activities.

We encourage whole language and process writing teachers (who have not already done so) to take a more balanced approach in the use of indirect and direct methods of instruction, recognizing that some students may need more support—including explicit instruction—to learn all they need to know to be successful and devoted readers and writers. In essence, they need to get enough support—of appropriate quality—to get the job done. Such support should not be limited to just the mechanics of literacy, but should also focus on comprehension and the writing processes of planning and revising. In the area of writing, for example, we have conducted several studies demonstrating that students with special needs in whole language and process writing classes benefit from explicit strategy instruction in planning and revising (cf. Danoff, Harris, & Graham, 1993; MacArthur, Schwartz, & Graham, 1991).

Finally, we would like to point out that explicit and systematic instruction is not synonymous with "mindless" rule following. In spelling, for instance, lessons can be planned to help students discover common orthographic principles. Children's spelling words for a particular week might contain common words for two different spellings of long /o/: h*o*pe and c*o*at. Students could be asked to sort these words into groups with like sounds and spellings to *discover* the underlying features in these words. They could then be encouraged to hunt for words with the same features in their reading and writing material (cf. Graham, Harris, & Loynachan, 1996).

CLOSING COMMENTS

There is much to like about whole language and process writing. Children read and write frequently in a supportive and collaborative environment, where teachers provide personalized and individually tailored assistance. Just as importantly, students are seen as capable learners, who are encouraged to take responsibility for their own efforts. An overreliance on informal methods of learning and overcorrection for meaning and process, however, may weaken the strength of these programs for students with special needs. We do not believe that children who struggle learning to read and write will acquire all they need when given only minimal guidance. Consequently, we encourage a more eclectic approach to reading and writing instruction—one that draws on the best of whole language/process writing and more explicit methods. The key to such instruction, in our opinion, is to keep a balanced perspective, while at the same time remaining responsive to individual needs.

The bridge between whole language/process writing and more explicit methods is not as long as some would suppose. Many teachers already join the two together. Slaughter (1988) reported that most of the whole language teachers she interviewed used both indirect and direct teaching methods. Similarly, Pressley, Rankin, and Yokoi (in press) found that outstanding teachers of reading and writing typically blend together whole language and explicit skills instruction. Examples of using both whole language/process writing and more explicit methods are also becoming more frequent in the research literature (cf. Castle, Riach, & Nicholson, 1994; Englert et al., 1994: MacArthur et al., in press).

Although some whole language advocates would have us believe that you cannot have a little of whole language and a little of something else (cf. Goodman, 1989), many practitioners have already moved beyond these polemics by drawing on different theories and methodologies to meet the needs of individual children. This is especially critical for students with special needs, as one approach does not fit all.

REFERENCES

Adams, M. (1990). *Beginning to read: Thinking and learning about print.* Cambridge, MA: MIT Press.

Alamasi, J., Palmer, B., Gambrell, L., & Pressley, M. (1994). Toward disciplined inquiry: A methodological analysis of whole-language. *Educational Psychologist, 28,* 193–202.

Allen, J. (1988). *Literacy development in whole language kindergartens* (Tech. Rep. No. 436). Urbana: University of Illinois at Urbana–Champaign, Center for the Study of Reading. (ERIC Document Reproduction Service No. ED 300 780)

Allen, J., Michalove, B., Shockley, B., & West, M. (1991). "I'm really worried about Joseph": Reducing the risks of literacy learning. *Reading Teacher, 44,* 458–472.

Allington, R. (1983). The reading instruction provided readers of differing reading ability. *Elementary School Journal, 83,* 548–559.

Allington, R. (1994). What's special about special programs for children who find learning to read difficult. *Journal of Reading Behavior, 26,* 95–115.

Allington, R., & McGill-Franzen, A. (1989). Different programs, indifferent instruction. In D. Lipsky & A. Gartner (Eds.), *Beyond separate education: Quality education for all* (pp. 75–98). Baltimore, MD: Brookes.

Atwell, N. (1987). *In the middle: Reading, writing, and learning from adolescents.* Portsmouth, NH: Heinemann.

Bereiter, C., & Scardamalia, M. (1984). Learning about writing from reading. *Written Communication, 1,* 163–188.

Bock, J. (1989, November). *Portraits of six developing readers in a whole language classroom.* Paper presented at the National Reading Conference, Austin, TX.

Brown, A., & Campione, J. (1990). Interactive learning environments and the teaching of science and mathematics. In M. Gardner, J. Green, F. Reif, A. Schoenfield, A. di Sessa, & E. Stage (Eds.), *Toward a scientific practice of science education* (pp. 112–139). Hillsdale, NJ: Lawrence Erlbaum Associates.

Calkins, L. (1981). Case study of a nine year old writer. In D. Graves (Ed.), *A case study observing the development of primary children's composing, spelling, and motor behavior during the writing process* (pp. 239–262). Durham: University of New Hampshire.

Callaway, B., McDaniel, H., & Mason, G. (1972). Five methods of teaching language arts: A comparison. *Elementary English, 49,* 1240–1245.

Castle, J., Riach, J., & Nicholson, T. (1994). Getting off to a better start in reading and spelling: The effects of phonemic awareness instruction within a whole language program. *Journal of Educational Psychology, 86*, 350–359.

Christenson, S., Thurlow, M., Ysseldyke, J., & McVicar, R. (1989). Written language instruction for students with mild handicaps: Is there enough quantity to ensure quality? *Learning Disability Quarterly, 12*, 219–229.

Cleary, B. (1990). *Muggie Maggie.* New York: Avon Camelot.

Corno, L. (1992). Encouraging students to take responsibility for learning and performance. *Elementary School Journal, 93*, 69–83.

Cousin, P., Aragon, E., & Rojas, R. (1993). Creating new conversations about literacy: Working with special needs students in a middle-school classroom. *Learning Disability Quarterly, 16*, 282–298.

Danoff, B., Harris, K. R., & Graham, S. (1993). Incorporating strategy instruction within the writing process in the regular classroom: Effects on normally achieving and learning disabled students' writing. *Journal of Reading Behavior, 25*, 295–322.

Dahl, K., & Freppon, P. (1991). Literacy learning in whole-language classrooms: An analysis of low socioeconomic urban children learning to read and write in kindergarten. In J. Zutell & S. McCormick (Eds.), *Learner factors/teacher factors: Issues in literacy research and instruction* (pp. 149–158). Chicago: National Reading Conference.

DeGroff, L. (1992). Process-writing teachers' responses to fourth-grade writers' first drafts. *Elementary School Journal, 93*, 131–144.

Delpit, L. (1988). The silenced dialogue: Power and pedagogy in educating other people's children. *Harvard Educational Review, 58*, 280–298.

Dudley-Marley, C. (1995). Whole language: It's a matter of principles. *Reading and Writing Quarterly, 11*, 109–117.

Edelsky, C. (1990). Whose research agenda is this anyway? A response to McKenna, Robinson, and Miller. *Educational Researcher, 19*, 8–11.

Englert, C., Raphael, T., & Marriage, T. (1994). Developing a school-based discourse for literacy learning: A principled search for understanding. *Learning Disability Quarterly, 17*, 2–32.

Felton, R. (1993). Effects of instruction on the decoding skills of children with phonological-processing problems. *Journal of Learning Disabilities, 26*, 583–589.

Fisher, C., & Hiebert, E. (1990). Characteristics of tasks in two approaches to literacy instruction. *Elementary School Journal, 91*, 3–18.

Fitzgerald, J., & Stamm, C. (1990). Effects of group conferences on first graders' revision in writing. *Written Communication, 7*, 96–135.

Freedman, A. (1993). Show and tell? The role of explicit teaching of the learning of new genres. *Research in the Teaching of English, 27*, 22–251.

Gersten, R., & Dimino, J. (1993). Visions and revisions: A special education perspective on the whole language controversy. *Remedial and Special Education, 14*, 5–13.

Goodman, K. (1989). Roots of the whole language movement. *Elementary School Journal, 90*, 113–127.

Goodman, K. (1992). I didn't found whole language. *The Reading Teacher, 46*, 188–199.

Graham, S. (1990). The role of production factors in learning disabled students' compositions. *Journal of Educational Psychology, 82*, 781–791.

Graham, S. (1992). Issues in handwriting instruction. *Focus on Exceptional Children, 25*, 1–14.

Graham, S., & Harris, K. R. (1994a). Implications of constructivism for teaching writing to students with special needs. *Journal of Special Education, 28*, 275–289.

Graham, S., & Harris, K. R. (1994b). The effects of whole language on children's writing: A review of literature. *Educational Psychologist, 29*, 187–192.

Graham, S., Harris, K. R., & Loynachan, C. (1993). The Basic Spelling Vocabulary list. *Journal of Educational Research, 86*, 363–368.

Graham, S., Harris, K. R., & Loynachan, C. (1996). The Directed Spelling Thinking activity: Application with high frequency words. *Learning Disability Research and Practice, 11*, 34–40.

Graham, S., Hudson, F., Burdg, N., & Carpenter, D. (1980). Educational personnel's perceptions of mainstreaming and resource room effectiveness. *Psychology in the Schools, 17*, 128–134.

Graham, S., & Miller, L. (1979). Spelling research and practice: A unified approach. *Focus on Exceptional Children, 12*, 1–16.

Graves, D. (1979). What children show us about revision. *Language Arts, 56*, 312–319.

Graves, D. (1983). *Writing: Teachers and children at work.* Exeter, NH: Heinemann.

Harris, K. R. (1982). Cognitive-behavior modification: Application with exceptional students. *Focus on Exceptional Children, 15*, 1–16.

Harris, K. R., & Graham, S. (1993). Cognitive strategy instruction and whole language: A case study. *Remedial and Special Education, 14*, 30–34.

Harris, K. R., & Graham, S. (1994). Constructivism: Principles, paradigms, and integration. *Journal of Special Education, 28*, 233–247.

Harris, K. R., & Pressley, M. (1991). The nature of cognitive strategy instruction: Interactive strategy instruction. *Exceptional Children, 57*, 392–404.

Hillocks, G. (1984). What works in teaching composition: A meta-analysis of experimental studies. *American Journal of Education, 93*, 133–170.

Juel, C. (1988). Learning to read and write: A longitudinal study of 54 children from first through fourth grade. *Journal of Educational Psychology, 80*, 437–447.

Kulieke, M., & Jones, B. (1993). Cognitive instructional techniques in relation to whole language approaches. *Remedial and Special Education, 14*, 26–29.

Lilly, S. (1992). Labeling: A tired, overworked, yet unresolved issue in special education. In W. Stainback & S. Stainback (Eds.), *Controversial issues confronting special education: Divergent perspectives* (pp. 85–95). Boston: Allyn & Bacon.

Lipsky, D., & Gartner, A. (1992). Achieving full inclusion: Placing the student at the center of educational reform. In W. Stainback & S. Stainback (Eds.), *Controversial issues confronting special education: Divergent perspectives* (pp. 3–12). Boston: Allyn & Bacon.

MacArthur, C., Schwartz, S., & Graham, S. (1991). Effects of a reciprocal peer revision strategy in special education classrooms. *Learning Disabilities Research and Practice, 6*, 201–210.

MacArthur, C., Graham, S., Schwartz, S., & Shafer, W. (1995). Evaluation of a writing instruction model that integrated a process approach, strategy instruction, and word processing. *Learning Disabilities Quarterly, 18*, 278–291.

Manning, M., & Manning, G. (1995). Whole language: They say, you say. *Teaching K–8, 25*, 50–54.

Mather, N. (1992). Whole language reading instruction for students with learning disabilities: Caught in the cross fire. *Learning Disabilities Research and Practice, 7*, 87–95.

Means, B., & Knapp, M. (1991). Cognitive approaches to teaching advanced skills to educationally disadvantaged students. *Phi Delta Kappan, 72*, 282–289.

McGill-Franzen, A., & Allington, R. (1991). The gridlock of low reading achievement: Perspectives on practice and policy. *Remedial and Special Education, 12*, 20–30.

Mervar, K., & Hiebert, E. (1989). Literature selection strategies and amount of reading in two literacy approaches. In S. McCormick & J. Zutell (Eds.), *Cognitive and social perspectives for literacy research and instruction: Thirty-eighth yearbook of the National Reading Conference* (pp. 529–535). Chicago: National Reading Conference.

Nicholson, T. (1989). A comment on reading recovery. *New Zealand Journal of Educational Studies, 24*, 95–97.

Ohanian, S. (1994). "Call me teacher." In C. Smith (Moderator), *Whole language: The debate* (pp. 1–15). Bloomington, IN: ERIC Clearinghouse on Reading, English, and Communication.

Ormrod, J. (1986). Learning to spell while reading: A follow-up study. *Perceptual and Motor Skills, 63*, 652–654.

Palinscar, A., & Klenk, L. (1992). Fostering literacy learning in supportive contexts. *Journal of Learning Disabilities, 25*, 211–225.

Pflaum, S., Walberg, H., Karegianes, M., & Rasher, S. (1980). Reading instruction: A quantitative analysis. *Educational Researcher, 10*, 12–18.

Pressley, M. (in press). The challenges of instructional scaffolding. *Learning Disabilities Research and Practice.*

Pressley, M., Harris, K. R., & Marks, M. (1992). But good strategy instructors are constructivists!! *Educational Psychology Review, 4*, 3–31.

Pressley, M., & Rankin, J. (1994). More about whole language methods of reading instruction for students at risk for early reading failure. *Learning Disabilities Research and Practice, 9*, 157–168.

Pressley, M., Rankin, J., & Yokoi, L. (in press). A survey of instructional practices of primary teachers nominated as effective in promoting literacy. *Elementary School Journal.*

Pritchard, R. (1987). Effects on student writing of teacher training in the National Writing Project Model. *Written Communication, 4*, 51–67.

Reid, D. K. (1993). Another vision of "visions and revisions." *Remedial and Special Education, 14*, 14–16, 25.

Reutzel, D., & Hollingsworth, P. (1988). Whole language and the practitioner. *Academic Therapy, 23*, 405–416.

Reyes, M. (1991). A process approach to literacy using dialogue journals and literature logs with second language learners. *Research in the Teaching of English, 25*, 291–313.

Scardamalia, M., Bereiter, C., & Goelman, H. (1982). The role of production factors in writing ability. In M. Nystrand (Ed.), *What writers know: The language, process, and structure of written discourse* (pp. 173–210). New York: Academic Press.

Singer, J., & Butler, J. (1987). The Education for All Handicapped Children Act: Schools as agents of social reform. *Harvard Educational Review, 57*, 125–152.

Slaughter, H. (1988). Indirect and direct teaching in a whole language program. *The Reading Teacher, 42*, 30–34.

Smagorinsky, P. (1987). Graves revisited. *Written Communication, 4*, 331–342.

Spiegel, D. (1992). Blending whole language and systematic direct instruction. *The Reading Teacher, 46*, 38–44.

Stahl, S., McKenna, M., & Pagnucco, J. (1994). The effects of whole-language instruction: An update and a reappraisal. *Educational Psychologist, 29*, 175–185.

Stahl, S., & Miller, P. (1989). Whole language and language experience approaches for begining reading: A quantitative research synthesis. *Review of Educational Research, 59*, 87–116.

Stanovich, K. (1994). Constructivism in reading education. *Journal of Special Education, 28*, 259–274.

Tharp, R., & Gallimore, R. (1989). *Rousing minds to life: Teaching, learning, and schooling in social contexts.* Cambridge, England: Cambridge University Press.

Vacca, R., & Rasinski, T. (1992). *Case studies in whole language.* Fort Worth, TX: Harcourt Brace Jovanovich.

Voltz, D., Elliott, R., & Cobb, H. (1994). Collaborative teacher roles: Special and general educators. *Journal of Learning Disabilities, 27*, 527–535.

Wansart, W. (1988). The student with learning disabilities in a writing process classroom: A case study. *Reading, Writing, and Learning Disabilities, 4*, 311–319.

Westby, C., & Costlow, L. (1991). Implementing a whole language program in a special education class. *Topics in Language Disorders, 11*, 69–84.

Wilde, S. (1990). Spelling textbooks: A critical review. *Linguistics and Education, 2*, 259–280.

Willis, S. (1995). What the public wants. *Education Update, 37*, 4–5.

Zaragoza, N., & Vaughn, S. (1992). The effects of process writing instruction on three 2nd-grade students with different achievement profiles. *Learning Disabilities Research and Practice, 7*, 184–193.

Zimmerman, B. (1989). A social cognitive view of self-regulated academic learning. *Journal of Educational Psychology, 81*, 329–339.

Zucker, C. (1993). Using whole language with students who have language and learning disabilities. *Reading Teacher, 46*, 660–670.

SPECIAL GROUPS

13

BARRIERS TO THE IMPLEMENTATION OF EFFECTIVE EDUCATIONAL PRACTICES FOR YOUNG CHILDREN WITH DISABILITIES

Judith J. Carta
Charles R. Greenwood
Juniper Gardens Children's Project, University of Kansas

In just 30 years, the state of early intervention/early childhood special education (EI/ECSE) has gone from providing isolated pockets of services offered to families at their own expense, to mandated services for preschoolers with disabilities in all 50 states and the availability of services to infants with disabilities in most states. In this 30-year period, the profession of ECSE has emerged as one of the strongest areas within special education, boasting one of the largest and most active professional organizations, as well as the development of teacher credentialing in most states, the availability of specialized training programs at several institutions of higher education, and an expanding professional literature. These advances have occurred in spite of the fact that prior to 1966, the field had virtually no knowledge on which to base decisions about *what* to teach infants and young children with disabilities or risks, *how* to teach them, *who* should teach these children and what competencies they would need, and *where* educational services should be delivered to these children and their families. Although researchers in ECSE and in related fields of developmental psychology and early childhood education have provided answers to some of these questions, what still awaits is the identification of *effective* educational practices. The larger fields of general and special education have important empirically based knowledge bases identifying effective teaching practices and guiding practice (see Algozzine & Maheady, 1986; Brophy, 1979); however, no similar bodies of information have been generated and diffused to practitioners in

EI/ECSE. This is true in spite of a plethora of empirical studies documenting the effectiveness of individual intervention practices (see Guralnick & Bennett, 1987).

The purpose of this chapter is to examine obstacles to the identification of a set of "effective practices" in ECSE, to explore the difficulties in the systematic diffusion of this information, and to point out the barriers that prevent the high-fidelity implementation and maintenance of these practices. The broader areas of general and special education share many of the same research-to-practice barriers. One challenge that is especially relevant to ECSE, however, has been the difficulty in obtaining consensus on the very definition of effectiveness. The goal of this chapter is to discuss this definitional problem, which lies at the very core of ECSE; examine the barriers that it shares with the other fields of education; and suggest possible solutions to overcome them.

DEFINING EFFECTIVE PRACTICES IN EI/ECSE

Barriers to Identifying Effective Practices

Although barriers exist at each step in the translation of research to effective practices in EI/ECSE, the biggest obstacle for the field lies in the first step of the process: defining effectiveness in a fashion that its multiple constituencies will find acceptable. Many reasons exist for the difficulty in defining effectiveness. First, for many years, instead of identifying effective practices, the field has been sidetracked in a lengthy discussion about whether the field of early intervention itself is effective. Many review articles, syntheses, and meta-analyses have filled journal pages attempting to determine whether providing early intervention is a worthwhile endeavor (Casto & Mastropieri, 1986; Lazar, Darlington, Murray, Royce, & Snipper, 1982; Odom & Fewell, 1983; Shonkoff, Hauser-Cram, Krauss, & Upshur, 1988; Simeonsson, Cooper, & Scheiner, 1982). This discussion, primarily conducted in the years prior to the federal legislative mandate for special education services for preschoolers with disabilities, was a response to policymakers needing a rationale for the provision of services to children younger than school age. Although this dialogue was helpful in creating a body of evidence to support early intervention services to children with disabilities, it postponed a more pragmatic discussion of how those services could most effectively be delivered. In the course of this discussion, many have pointed out that early intervention is not a unitary entity, but rather represents many different interventions, and its effectiveness can only be measured by the quality, intensity, and appropriateness of intervention services actually delivered.

Inconsistencies in Determining Quality Indicators. Throughout its history, the field of EI/ECSE has attempted to define quality practices in various ways. One way has been in the generation of sets of "best practices" or "recommended practices" identified through consensus-based approaches. Although these compilations have been helpful in providing some direction in defining exemplary practices, they have been criticized as a group for their lack of convergence (see Eayres & Jones, 1992). Some agreement exists across the identified sets of practices; however, they have not been identified through a common methodology, nor have they been defined using common criteria. Some authors have developed lists of exemplary practices based on reviews of the professional literature and personal experience (DeStefano, Howe, Horn, & Smith, 1990; Wolery, Strain, & Bailey, 1992). Others have enumerated quality indicators that promote success in mainstream settings (Salisbury, 1991; Vincent et al., 1980). Other authors have subjectively identified best practices based on multiple criteria. For example, according to McDonnell and Hardman (1988), best practices in ECSE should be "integrated, comprehensive, peer- and family-centered, normalized, adaptable, and outcome-based" (p. 332). In some cases, states have developed lists of exemplary practices against which programs in their state can be compared (e.g., Flynn, 1991). Many of these lists of best practices do not explicitly state what the practices are "best" in doing nor what outcomes they are "recommended" for producing.

This lack of definition belies the difficulty in the field of ECSE for identifying a set of common outcomes that form the bedrock for evaluation and the measurement of effectiveness. This difficulty has been exacerbated through the failure of persons in early childhood education (ECE) and ECSE to reach consensus on outcomes for young children in general. In 1987, the primary ECE professional organization, the National Association for the Education of Young Children (NAEYC), published guidelines defining what they termed "developmentally appropriate practice" (DAP) in programs for children from birth through 8 years (Bredekamp, 1987). This effort, motivated by what NAEYC perceived as an increasing emphasis to promote "teacher-directed instruction in narrowly defined academic skills" (p. iv) was organized around a consensus-building approach in which input was obtained from thousands of early childhood practitioners. The result was a comprehensive set of guidelines that identified in behaviorally specific terms a set of practices deemed appropriate and inappropriate for specific age groups of young children. Although this document, described as "perhaps the most influential identification of best practice in early childhood education" (Odom, McLean, Johnson, & LaMontagne, 1995), has served as a mechanism for forging solidarity in the early childhood profession, it has also served as the flashpoint for considerable discussion regarding its applicability in meeting the needs of children with developmental and cultural

differences (Mallory & New, 1994). For example, Williams (1994) has suggested that some of the published guidelines for DAP run counter to traditional values about teaching and learning held by Native Americans. Similarly, others have pointed out that the DAP guidelines do not sufficiently
address important indicators of quality for teaching children with developmental delays (Atwater, Carta, Schwartz, & McConnell, 1994; Carta, Schwartz,
Atwater, & McConnell, 1991; Wolery et al., 1992). Some of these features
include: (a) a consideration in the curriculum for preparing children for their
future environments, (b) the specification of goals and objectives for individual children and continuous monitoring of progress, and finally, (c) an
emphasis on effectiveness and efficiency of program in assisting children in
achieving valued outcomes.

This effort to identify recommended practices in ECE was followed up by
a similar consensus-based approach to identifying recommended practices
for infants and young children with special needs carried out by the Division
of Early Childhood (DEC), a subdivision of the Council for Exceptional Children. This group employed one of the most systematic approaches for
identifying and validating recommended practices to be documented in the
literature in any educational field (Odom et al., 1995). A set of work groups
in 14 areas of early childhood special education (e.g., interventions to promote social skills and emotional development; interventions to promote
motor skills) were established. These work groups including researchers,
practitioners, and parents used a consensus-based approach to identify a
list of recommended practices based on the following six criteria. The practice must be: (a) research based *or* value based; (b) family centered; (c)
multicultural; (d) cross disciplinary; (e) developmentally and chronologi-
cally age appropriate; and (f) normalized. These sets of practices were then
validated by a national sample of 500 people consisting of randomly selected
DEC members, people in high education, and parents. These individuals
rated their level of agreement with each practice and their perception of
the frequency of use of each practice in programs serving young children
with disabilities.

Although the DEC approach to identifying recommended practices in the
field should be lauded as an important first step toward defining the benchmarks of ECSE practice, it should be apparent that a huge gap remains
between defining "recommended" practices and identifying "effective" practices. This concern was articulated recently by Wolery (1995), who asked
what it meant when a given practice is recommended by consensus and
popular vote: "It means simply that a large number of individuals (perhaps
knowledgeable ones) are familiar with the practice and support its use." He
further stated that identification of a recommended practice does not mean
that research exists to document its effectiveness in meeting specific outcomes, nor does it mean that "the practice will benefit the infants, toddlers

or families who experience it or the practitioners who use it" (p. 22). What the DEC process *does* reflect is the social validity of widely recognized practices. The field of early childhood still faces many challenges in documenting a set of effective practices. Foremost among them is lack of agreement in the field regarding the outcomes of early intervention.

Failure to Agree on Outcomes. Fundamental disagreement exists within the ranks of ECSE, and between ECSE and ECE, regarding the goals of educating young children with disabilities. One key disagreement surrounds the basic goal of producing meaningful, measurable changes in children's interactions with their environments. Most people in ECSE recognize that many young children with special needs have delays that keep them from successful independent learning (Wolery et al., 1992). For example, these children's lack of social interaction skills or their inabilities to play with toys may prevent them from opportunities to learn from peers, make friends, or actively explore their environments. Therefore, they require early educational experiences that are carefully designed to promote the learning of needed skills (Bailey & Wolery, 1992).

Although this may appear to be an obvious mission of early intervention, it is not embraced by all. For example, Goodman (1992), in her book *When Slow Is Fast Enough*, argued against the importance of teaching specific skills to young children with disabilities. A vocal proponent of *going slower* in early intervention programs, she contends that fields of EI and ECSE are caught up in changing and speeding up children's development at the expense of children's self-esteem. She rejects the importance of specific behavioral objectives and Individualized Education Plans (IEPs), stating that "rather than dictate behavior, we must find dictates in their behavior. Slowing up will give these children like other children the opportunity for mastery and discovery, for fulfillment of their own drives while they meet expectations set by adults" (p. 254).

This position is based on two myths concerning DAP and its compatibility with effective practices in EI/ECSE. The first is that a program cannot focus on objectives and at the same time be child directed. The second is that a program cannot incorporate direct teaching and at the same time promote active engagement and exploration by young children. Many persons have pointed out that the use of objectives and direct teaching are not incompatible with developmental appropriateness (e.g., Atwater et al., 1994; Carta, 1995; McCollum & Bair, 1994). Objectives themselves do not render a program developmentally inappropriate; rather, it is the content of the objectives and their match to a child's level of functioning. Similarly, direct teaching of children does not negate their active participation in activities; indeed, children with special needs may require direct teaching to facilitate their active involvement in their contexts for learning. Moreover, naturalistic, instructional strategies can also be employed that promote children's learning of specific skills (Cavallaro, Haney, & Cabello, 1993; Wolery & Fleming, 1993). These widely used and naturalistic procedures include: *activity-based instruction*, embedding instructional activities into typical classroom routines and play activities (Bricker & Cripe, 1992); *incidental teaching*, using the child's interests as the basis for an instructional interaction, then providing verbal responses that support more advanced responses by the child (Brown, McEvoy, & Bishop, 1991; Hart, 1985) and *peer-mediated strategies* encouraging the development of children's social interaction skills (Odom & Brown, 1993). These are but a few effective instructional procedures that can be used to teach children specific skills in the context of highly engaging child-directed preschool activities. So although teachers can carry out what looks like a typical early childhood curriculum, what might not be so obvious is the carefully planned opportunities within those activities for specific children to engage in instructional interactions that promote the development of specific skills. Furthermore, what must occur is regular monitoring of those activities to ensure that children are acquiring and applying skills across numerous settings (Wolery et al., 1992).

Disagreement on Effectiveness and Efficiency as Evaluative Criteria.
There is no more basic level of disagreement about evaluating programs and practices for young children than a lack of consensus about their outcomes. However, there is further lack of concordance in EI/ECSE about the yardsticks for evaluating programs. Although effectiveness and efficiency have long been valued as critical indicators of program and practice quality (Carta et al., 1991; Wolery & Bredekamp, 1994), some ECSE authors have suggested that the field of EI/ECSE has placed an overemphasis on these two evaluative criteria. Johnson and Johnson (1994), for example, recently stated that they were dismayed by their "professional colleagues in special education and early intervention constantly harping on effectiveness and efficiency as dimensions for evaluating practice" (p. 345). They suggested that these two factors should not be viewed as ends in themselves but as means to an end. Furthermore, they stated that they feared an emphasis on effectiveness would result in the development of IEP goals that were adult driven and prescriptive, instead of sensitive to the individual child's strengths and needs. They feared an emphasis on efficiency because this criterion focuses on speed of learning instead of "generalizable learning." However, effectiveness/efficiency and generalizability are not mutually exclusive quality indicators; they represent two sides of the same coin. Practices "should result in children learning *and* using the skills listed on the IEPs" (Wolery et al., 1992, p. 103). IEPs should be adult driven and prescriptive and focus on children's strengths, needs, and interests. Therefore, practices should be evaluated on their effectiveness in promoting acquisition of skills as well as promoting their generalization and normalization.

Where does this leave the state of effective practice? In summary, the field of EI/ECSE is without a set of effective practices, unable to agree on outcomes, and unable to determine whether effectiveness is a valued goal. Moreover, as EI/ECSE moves closer to general ECE, the challenges in achieving consensus become even greater regarding how to teach, what to teach, and how we should evaluate programs. Where do we begin in identifying what works in EI/ECSE?

An Action Plan for Identifying Effective Practices

What the field of EI/ECSE needs now is an action plan for the identification of a set of effective procedures to serve as the cornerstone for the development of a science of teaching young children with disabilities. In the following, we describe the important steps the field must take to move in this direction:

First, *we must agree to adopt effectiveness and efficiency as two important criteria for identifying valued practices*. Certainly other criteria such as social validity, developmental and individual appropriateness, ethical groundedness, and cultural appropriateness will round out some of the other dimensions for evaluating programs. However, effectiveness and efficiency are the bottom line against which a program can measure itself relative to each of its stated goals.

Second, *we must come to some agreement on the outcomes that are meaningful goals of EI/ECSE programs*. Although specific goals of programs will of course be individualized to meet the unique needs of individual children, professionals in ECE and EI/ECSE must come to terms about the overriding purposes of their programs. Many persons involved in the education of children with special needs have adopted the following general goals for their programs as identified by Bailey and Wolery (1992):

1. To support families in achieving their own goals.
2. To promote child engagement, independence, and mastery.
3. To promote development in key domains.
4. To build and support children's social competence.
5. To promote the generalized use of skills.
6. To provide and prepare for normalized life experiences.
7. To prevent the emergence of future problems or disabilities. (p. 35)

Third, *we must establish criteria for determining a procedure's effectiveness in reaching one or more of those outcomes*. On what basis do we determine that a procedure "works"? At minimum, an effective procedure should have the following characteristics:

1. Addresses one of the agreed-upon outcomes (e.g., build and support children's social competence).
2. Offers clear and unambiguous evidence in peer-reviewed journal that documents reliable and significant changes in one or more of the agreed-on outcomes.
3. Has sufficient descriptive details that allow for the replication of procedures.
4. Teachers, parents, and other potential consumers have judged both the procedure and the outcomes as acceptable.

Finally, *we must establish a means by which individual practices undergo review based on these or other evaluative criteria* and are thereby deemed "effective." Carnine (1994) has pointed out that other professions must answer to third-party entities which review performance. In education, no such parties exist that review instructional practices and determine whether they are used appropriately. These types of entities need to be developed in early education not only to review practices, but also to support their dissemination to teachers and their integration in personnel preparation programs.

IMPLEMENTING EFFECTIVE PRACTICES IN EI/ECSE

Barriers to the Implementation of Effective Practices

Although no system has been established for reviewing practices and establishing them as effective, the field of EI/ECSE is not without practices that have been shown to change children's behavior in significant and meaningful ways (Guralnick & Bennett, 1987). However, certainly a wide gap exists between the existence of effective practices and their implementation. What do we know about the extent of implementation of these practices?

The Knowledge Gap Between Research and Practice. Not much is known about the implementation of effective practices in EI/ECSE. Little information is available about teachers' knowledge about practices in general (effective or otherwise), which ones they find acceptable, or what practices they are willing to implement. Only a few studies have described the current state of practice in EI/ECSE. Few researchers have gathered information about teachers' opinions about practices or observed actual classroom practice. In their identification and validation of recommended EI/ECSE practices described earlier, Odom et al. (1995) found that most of their survey respondents appeared to be knowledgeable about and in agreement with the 14 sets of DEC recommended practices. Nonetheless, these respondents indicated that although most of the practices were currently being used in intervention programs with which they were familiar, they rated only a small percentage of these practices as being implemented *frequently*. Roberts, Bailey, and Nychka (1991) conducted one of the few observational studies describing the extent of implementation of language interventions in community-based developmental child care settings. They found that, in general, teachers were not using the specific language-intervention strategies demonstrated to be effective in teaching communication skills to children with disabilities.

Obviously, the lack of available information on the implementation of effective practices in EI/ECSE settings suggests limited use of effective practices. Whether teachers are unaware of certain effective practices, know about them but find them unacceptable, or simply lack support for implementing them is still unknown. This lack of information about teachers underscores the gap that exists not only in teachers' implementation of research-based practice, but also in researchers' knowledge about actual classroom practice. Unless researchers interested in having an impact on practice develop a stronger understanding of the factors that influence teachers' implementation decisions, we will not know very much about how practices should be developed and disseminated. What is needed in the early childhood research community is greater knowledge of the diverse cultures of early intervention service delivery and the manner in which factors within those contexts affect practitioners.

The Communication Gap Between Researchers and Practitioners. One reason that research knowledge is used so rarely in early childhood special education practice and in education in general is that researchers and practitioners have limited opportunities to communicate and work together to solve instructional problems (Schwartz, Carta, & Grant, 1996). Instead, these two groups work within separate communities that seldom overlap (Huberman, 1990). Typically, researchers interact with other researchers in determining the instructional problems that need addressing; in identifying and validating teaching strategies that will be judged acceptable to other researchers; in communicating their findings to other researchers in a relatively conservative manner; and then in framing their findings within some broad, difficult-to-apply theoretical principles (Malouf & Schiller, 1995; Shavelson, 1988). Teachers, on the other hand, work in relative isolation, and tend to make intuitive judgments about what works or does not work. They are most likely to get new information "from the teacher down the hall" and to adopt interventions because they are externally imposed (Kaestle, 1993). They have insufficient time, resources, and incentives to learn about research-based practices (Huberman, 1983). What is needed is an avenue for these two communities to work together to improve practice and children's outcomes.

The Reality Gap. Teachers' complaints about the lack of relevance of educational research are legendary. "Educators complain that researchers often ask the wrong questions, produce studies that are of little practical use, and write articles so full of jargon that they are barely comprehensible to non-researchers, in particular to teachers" (Viadero, 1994, p . 24). Teachers often feel that research frequently gives them answers to questions they never asked and solutions to problems they never had (Tinkunoff & Ward, 1983). The instructional procedures generated by researchers in EI/ECSE oftentimes have been developed by individuals removed from actual classroom or early intervention settings (Kohler, 1993). As a result, these procedures may be incompatible with the program's existing needs and constraints (Hall, 1991). Thus, it is understandable that many have questioned the importance of educational research, particularly its contribution to classroom instructional practices (e.g., Greer, 1982; Kaestle, 1993). Researchers attempting to produce solutions to classroom problems in the absence of first-hand knowledge of the classroom often fail to account for contextual factors such as insufficient time and resources, externally imposed curricula, increased student variability, and the "rapid expansion of problems in postmodern society" (Fullan, 1991, p. 1). These are factors that are critical to sustaining an innovation within a classroom setting.

Another barrier to translating educational research into practice has been the lack of concreteness in introducing teaching strategies (Gersten & Woodward, 1992). Too often, educational researchers in general and ECSE researchers in particular have provided only vague and abstract guidelines about the goals or the model underlying an instructional procedure. They fail to provide information about the components of the procedure critical to its effectiveness in a specific context and with a specific group of students (Malouf & Schiller, 1995). However, many studies (McLaughlin, 1990; Sainato, Strain, Lefebvre, & Rapp, 1987) have identified practical and concrete suggestions as basic ingredients in successful efforts in instructional change. When instructional goals are ambiguous, teachers become frustrated, implementation is poor, and impact on children's outcomes is minimal (Stallings, 1975). What is needed is the translation of research principles into carefully defined and manageable teaching strategies so that teachers have a clearer indication of how their teaching must change, and how the classroom setting must be adapted in order to maximize the effectiveness of their instruction.

The Professional Development Gap. Another obstacle separating research and practice has been ineffectual approaches to professional development (Fullan, 1991; Showers, Joyce, & Bennett, 1987; Smylie, 1988). These methods have followed a top-down "transmission model" of telling teachers how to teach (Englert, Tarrant, & Rozendal, 1993). In ECSE and in education in general, training opportunities are typically provided as workshops, special projects, and other abbreviated forms of exposure to new material and ideas. Oftentimes, inservice opportunities provided to ECSE teachers are directed to elementary education teachers and not at all relevant to instructional issues faced by teachers of young children. Moreover, inservice opportunities are seldom selected based on indicators of effective practices (Greenwood & Maheady, in preparation). The greatest indictment of this transmission model for professional development is that it has not produced lasting change (e.g., Firestone & Bader, 1992). Professional communities are needed within schools involving researchers and teachers engaged in authentic activities designed to translate research to practice.

The Support Gap. One final barrier is lack of continuing support for teachers to implement innovative practices, adapt them to their classrooms and their students, and learn from their experimentation. Many teachers have little understanding of how their instructional decisions and behavior affects children's performance in the classroom. Throughout this process, they need a mechanism for getting feedback and collegial support in these endeavors. Few incentives exist for teachers to do a better job (Graham, cited in Kaestle, 1993). Therefore, teachers do not have to seek out information that will help them improve their effectiveness (Kaestle, 1993). Teachers seldom receive backing from administration or peers for trying out new procedures, or producing positive outcomes in children. A teacher who strives to gain instructional skills by learning and implementing new approaches and maintaining effective procedures is typically compensated and recognized in the same measure as a teacher who makes no special effort to improve. What is needed is greater accountability by teachers for the effectiveness of their instruction as well as greater support of teachers to form partnerships with other teachers and with researchers.

Summary. What is evident in this chapter is the compelling evidence contributing to the gap between research and practice. These include: (a) the separateness of the research and practice communities, (b) the limited relevance of educational research to practice, (c) the failure of research to articulate many innovations that are manageable in real classrooms, (d) weak efforts at professional development, and (e) the lack of sustained relationships and common purpose between researchers and teachers to affect learning in early education settings. Arguably, these factors have reduced the probability of research use within classrooms. Work is needed that builds our capacity to channel research findings into the ongoing educational practices in community-based settings.

CONCLUSIONS

As the 1990s draw to a close, the young field of EI/ECSE can be proud of its productive beginnings. It continues to respond to the federal mandate to provide services to children with disabilities at a younger age and in a more comprehensive fashion. The challenge for the next decade will be to provide the most effective interventions possible to young children with special needs. As a field, what must take place is the identification of a set of practices that are most effective based on broadly accepted criteria, the systematic dissemination of those instructional strategies to practitioners, and the infusion of those practices into programs of professional preparation.

REFERENCES

Algozzine, R., & Maheady, L. (Eds.). (1986). In search of excellence: Instruction that works in special education classrooms. *Exceptional Children, 52,* 487–589.

Atwater, J. B., Carta, J. J., Schwartz, I. S., & McConnell, S. R. (1994). Blending developmentally appropriate practice and early childhood special education: Redefining best practice to meet the needs of all children. In B. L. Mallory & R. S. New (Eds.), *Diversity and developmentally appropriate practices: Challenges for early childhood education* (pp. 185–201). New York: Teachers College Press.

Bailey, D. B., & Wolery, M. (1992). *Teaching infants and preschoolers with disabilities* (2nd ed.). Columbus, OH: Merrill.

Bredekamp, S. (Ed.). (1987). *Developmentally appropriate practice in early childhood practice in early childhood programs serving children from birth through age 8.* Washington, DC: National Association for the Education of Young Children.

Bricker, D., & Cripe, J. (1992). *An activity-based approach to early intervention.* Baltimore: Brookes.

Brophy, J. (1979). Teacher behavior and its effects. *Journal of Educational Psychology, 71,* 733–750.

Brown, W. H., McEvoy, M. A., & Bishop, N. (1991). Incidental teaching of social behavior. *Teaching Exceptional Children, 24*(1), 35–38.

Carnine, D. (1994). *Improving educational research.* Unpublished manuscript, University of Oregon, National Center to Improve the Tools of Educators, Eugene, OR.

Carta, J. (1995). Developmentally appropriate practice: A critical analysis as applied to young children with disabilities. *Focus on Exceptional Children, 27*(8), 1–14.

Carta, J. J., Schwartz, I. S., Atwater, J. B., & McConnell, S. R. (1991). Developmentally appropriate practice: Appraising its usefulness for young children with disabilities. *Topics in Early Childhood Special Education, 11,* 1–20.

Casto, G., & Mastropieri, M. (1986). The efficacy of early intervention services: A meta-analysis. *Exceptional Children, 52,* 417–424.

Cavallaro, C. C., Haney, M., & Cabello, B. (1993). Developmentally appropriate strategies for promoting full participation in early childhood settings. *Topics in Early Childhood Special Education, 13*(3), 293–307.

DeStefano, D. M., Howe, A. G., Horn, E. M., & Smith, B. A. (1990). *Best practices: Evaluating early childhood special education programs.* Tucson, AZ: Communication Skill Builders.

Eayres, C. B., & Jones, R. S. P. (1992). Methodological issues and future directions in the evaluation of early intervention programmes. *Child Care, Health, and Development, 18,* 15–28.

Englert, C. S., Tarrant, K. L., & Rozendal, M. S. (1993). Educational innovations: Achieving curricular change through collaboration. *Education and Treatment of Children, 16,* 441–473.

Firestone, W. A., & Bader, B. D. (1992). *Redesigning teaching: Professionalism or bureaucracy?* Albany: State University of New York.

Flynn, L. (1991). *Early childhood special education best practices.* Unpublished manuscript, University Affiliated Program of Vermont, Burlington, VT.

Fullan, M. (1991). *The new meaning of educational change.* New York: Teachers College Press.

Gersten, R. M., & Woodward, J. (1992). The quest to translate research into classroom practice: Strategies for assisting classroom teachers' work with "at-risk" students and students with disabilities. In D. Carnine & E. Kameenui (Eds.), *Higher cognitive functioning for all students* (pp. 201–218). Austin, TX: Pro-Ed.

Goodman, J. F. (1992). *When slow is fast enough: Educating the delayed preschool child.* New York: Guilford.

Greenwood, C. R., & Maheady, L. (in preparation). *Measurable change in student performance: Forgotten standard in teacher preparation?*

Greer, R. D. (1982). Countercontrols for the American Educational Research Association. *The Behavior Analyst, 5,* 65–76.

Guralnick, M. J., & Bennett, F. C. (Eds.). (1987). *The effectiveness of early intervention for at-risk and handicapped children.* Orlando, FL: Academic Press.

Hall, R. V. (1991). Behavior analysis and education: An unfulfilled dream. *Journal of Behavioral Education, 1,* 305–315.

Hart, B. M. (1985). Naturalistic language training techniques. In S. F. Warren & A. K. Rogers-Warren (Eds.), *Teaching functional language* (pp. 63–88). Austin, TX: Pro-Ed.

Huberman, M. (1983). Recipes for busy kitchens: A situational analysis of routine knowledge use in schools. *Knowledge: Creation, Diffusion, Utilization, 4*(4), 478–510.

Huberman, M. (1990). Linkage between researchers and practitioners: A qualitative study. *American Educational Research Journal, 27*(2), 363–391.

Johnson, J. E., & Johnson, K. M. (1994). The applicability of developmentally appropriate practice for children with diverse abilities. *Journal of Early Intervention, 18,* 343–345.

Kaestle, C. F. (1993, January–February). Research news and comment: The awful reputation of education research. *Educational Researcher,* 23–31.

Kohler, F. (1993). Designing a comprehensive and sustainable innovation by blending two different approaches to school reform. *Education and Treatment of Children, 16*(4), 382–400.

Lazar, I., Darlington, R., Murray, H., Royce, J., & Snipper, A. (1982). Lasting effects of early education: A report from the consortium for longitudinal studies. *Monographs of the Society for Research in Child Development, 47*(2–3, Serial No. 195).

Mallory, B. L., & New, R. S. (Eds.). (1994). *Diversity and developmentally appropriate practices: Challenges for early childhood education.* New York: Teachers College Press.

Malouf, D. B., & Schiller, E. P. (1995). Practice and research in special education. *Exceptional Children, 61,* 414–424.

McCollum, J. A., & Bair, H. (1994). Research in parent–child interaction: Guidance do developmentally appropriate practice for young children with disabilities. In B. L. Mallory & R. S. New (Eds.), *Diversity and developmentally appropriate practices: Challenges for early childhood education* (pp. 84–106). New York: Teachers College Press.

McDonnell, A., & Hardman, M. (1988). A synthesis of "best practice" guidelines for early childhood services. *Journal of the Division for Early Childhood, 12,* 328–341.

McLaughlin, M. W. (1990). The RAND change agent study revisited: Macro perspectives and micro realities. *Educational Researcher, 19,* 11–16.

Odom, S. L., & Brown, W. H. (1993). Social interaction skills interventions for young children with disabilities in integrated settings. In C. A. Peck, S. L. Odom, & D. D. Bricker (Eds.), *Integrating young children with disabilities into community programs* (pp. 39–64). Baltimore: Brookes.

Odom, S. L., & Fewell, R. (1983). Program evaluation in early childhood special education: A meta-evaluation. *Educational Evaluation and Policy Analysis, 5,* 445–460.

Odom, S. L., & McLean, M. E., Johnson, L. J., & LaMontagne, M. J. (1995). Recommended practices in early childhood special education: Validation and current use. *Journal of Early Intervention, 19,* 1–17.

Roberts, J. E., Bailey, D. B., & Nychka, H. B. (1991). Teachers' use of strategies to facilitate the communication of preschool children with disabilities. *Journal of Early Intervention, 15,* 358–376.

Sainato, D. M., Strain, P.S., Lefebvre, D., & Rapp, N. (1987). Facilitating transition times with handicapped preschool children: A comparison between peer mediated and antecedent prompt procedures. *Journal of Applied Behavior Analysis, 20,* 285–291.

Salisbury, C. (1991). Mainstreaming during the early childhood years. *Exceptional Children, 58,* 146–155.

Schwartz, I. S., Carta, J. J., & Grant, S. (1996). Examining the use of recommended language intervention practices in early childhood special education classrooms. *Topics in Early Childhood Special Education, 16,* 251–272.

Shavelson, R. J. (1988). Contributions of educational research to policy and practice: Constructing, challenging, changing cognition. *Educational Researcher, 17*(7), 4–11, 22.

Shonkoff, J. P., Hauser-Cram, P., Krauss, M. W., & Upshur, C. C. (1988). Early intervention efficacy research: What have we learned and where do we go from here? *Topics in Early Childhood Special Education, 8,* 81–93.

Showers, B., Joyce, B., & Bennett, B. (1987). Synthesis of research on staff development: A framework for future study and state-of-the-art analysis. *Educational Leadership, 45,* 77–87.

Simeonsson, R. J., Cooper, D. J., & Scheiner, A. D. (1982). A review and analysis of the effectiveness of early intervention programs. *Pediatrics, 69,* 635–641.

Smylie, M. A. (1988). The enhancement function of staff development: Organizational and psychological antecedents to individual teacher change. *American Educational Research Journal, 25,* 1–30.

Stallings, J. (1975). *Follow through program classroom observation evaluation.* Menlo Park, CA: Stanford Research Institute.

Tinkunoff, W. J., & Ward, B. A. (1983). Collaborative research on teaching. *The Elementary School Journal, 83,* 453–468.

Viadero, D. (1994, October). The great divide: The gap between research and practice is wider in education than in other fields, such as medicine and business. *Teacher Magazine,* 22–24.

Vincent, L. J., Salisbury, C., Walter, G., Brown, P., Gruenwald, L. J., & Powers, M. (1980). Program evaluation and curriculum development in early childhood programs for handicapped children: Criteria for the next environment. In W. Sailor, B. Wilcox, & L. Brown (Eds.), *Methods of instruction for severely handicapped students* (pp. 303–328). Baltimore: Brookes.

Williams, L. R. (1994). Developmentally appropriate practice and cultural values: A case in point. In B. L. Mallory & R. S. New (Eds.), *Diversity and developmentally appropriate practices: Challenges for early childhood education* (pp. 155–165). New York: Teachers College Press.

Wolery, M. (1995). Some concerns about process. *Journal of Early Intervention, 19,* 1–17.

Wolery, M., & Bredekamp, S. (1994). Developmentally appropriate practices and young children with disabilities: Contextual issues in the discussion. *Journal of Early Intervention, 18,* 331–341.

Wolery, M., & Fleming, L. A. (1993). Implementing individualized curricula in integrated settings. In C. A. Peck, S. L. Odom, & D. D. Bricker (Eds.), *Integrating young children with disabilities into community programs: Ecological perspectives on research and implementation* (pp. 109–132). Baltimore: Brookes.

Wolery, M. R., Strain, P. S., & Bailey, D. B. (1992). Reaching potentials of children with special needs. In S. Bredekamp & T. Rosegrant (Eds.), *Reaching potentials: Appropriate curriculum and assessment of young children* (pp. 92–111). Washington, DC: National Association for the Education of Young Children.

14

FORGING A RESEARCH PROGRAM ON MULTICULTURAL PRESERVICE TEACHER EDUCATION IN SPECIAL EDUCATION: A PROPOSED ANALYTIC SCHEME

Alfredo J. Artiles
University of California, Los Angeles

Stanley C. Trent
Michigan State University

The increasing cultural diversification of the student population in the United States has recently received more attention in the general and special education fields (Banks & Banks, 1995; Figueroa, Fradd, & Correa, 1989; Obiakor, Patton, & Ford, 1992). As a result, initiatives to develop multicultural education components in teacher education programs have been launched (Gollnick, 1995; Grant & Secada, 1990). Most of these efforts are based on the assumption that teachers will be prepared to work with a diverse student population if they are exposed to information and experiences related to multiculturalism. That is, content and experiences which promote the transformation of schools so that "male and female students, exceptional students, as well as students from diverse cultural, social-class, racial, and ethnic groups will experience an equal opportunity to learn in school" (Banks & Banks, 1989, pp. 19–20).

Teacher educators in general education typically address multiculturalism in foundation courses that provide an overview of issues related to the distinct markers of diversity (e.g., race, gender, language, social class). These sociocultural variables are typically studied in isolation from each other, and the main focus of analysis is on main effects issues (e.g., Does student race affect learning processes?). Thus, it is not surprising that research on the impact of multicultural education on preservice teachers shows mixed results (Grant & Secada, 1990). The truth is, educators do not agree on how to prepare teachers for student diversity. In fact, researchers have concluded that "we know very little about the development of teacher education students' cognitions, beliefs, and skills with respect to the teaching of diverse learners (Grant & Secada, 1990; Sleeter, 1985), including how particular teacher education strategies influence teacher learning" (Zeichner, 1993, p. 21).

This situation might be explained in part by the reported preservice teachers' resistance or opposition to information and experiences that focus on cultural diversity (Ahlquist, 1992; Cross, 1993; Solomon & Levine-Rasky, 1995). The following anonymous letter sent to a minority teacher educator who teaches multicultural education courses illustrates the intensity of preservice teachers' resistance to multicultural education. We are aware that this is an extreme example, but it also shows why—at least in part—multicultural teacher education research has rendered mixed results:

> Professors [in the teacher education program] should reflect the dominant culture and society so that what they teach reflects the views of [the teacher education program] students and society at large. Sociocultural theories are theories invented by communists, atheists, and the lazy or poor who cannot earn a living. Multicultural professors should be reserved for multicultural students, not an elite university like [X].
>
> We came here to learn about methods of teaching; instead, we are subjected to professors who want to change what obviously worked for us. Thank goodness for professors like [XX] and [YY] who agree with us in private that these other professors should be banned. This may sound racist but we'd prefer White professors who have had similar life experiences to ours. Intelligence is not just what's learned from books and research. It's what you've also learned about the dominant culture by living in the dominant culture. So-called minority students need to learn how to live and succeed in this country and yes that means learning to speak English and learning the culture of the dominant society. We do not want to spend the rest of our education focusing on this population. We want to be prepared to teach the dominant student population. We will help others make sure that those who teach multicultural and sociocultural theories go back to where they belong. [Although the letter was not dated, it was left in the professor's mailbox in December of 1994]

Undoubtedly, there are many issues that could be analyzed in this missive. Space constraints, however, prevent us from elaborating on this sad example. The point is that multicultural teacher education in general education is a field plagued with controversial issues that elicit convoluted and complex emotional and cognitive reactions not only from preservice teachers, but also from teacher educators and the general public.

The situation of multicultural teacher education in special education is even more calamitous. In the *Handbook of Research on Teacher Education*

(Houston, 1990), Reynolds (1990) presented little empirical research on the preparation of special educators—due mainly to the absence of such information. In fact, he contended that "very little research has been directed specifically to the preparation of special education teachers" (p. 423), and, we would add, particularly with respect to cultural diversity.

To obtain a general overview of the progress in this field, we conducted a search using broad descriptors (e.g., multicultural education and special education) in the ERIC database for the 1982–1992 period. We located 29 entries on this topic. Sleeter (1995) reported 911 entries during the same period, although she did not distinguish between general and special education. Interestingly, we narrowed our search with the descriptors "multicultural education" and "teacher education" (without distinguishing which education field) and found 151 records. Unfortunately, the number of entries shrank to an alarming 5 when we limited the search to the special education field.

Furthermore, the bulk of the multicultural education literature in special education tends to be comprised of nonempirical manuscripts that call for the inclusion of cultural diversity in numerous areas (e.g., classroom instruction, assessment, curriculum, teacher education; Amos & Landers, 1984; Baca & Amato, 1989; Cloud, 1993; Dean, Salend, & Taylor, 1993; Durán, 1989; Franklin, 1992; García & Malkin, 1993). Although there is nothing wrong with the publication of nonempirical manuscripts (in fact, several of these papers are excellent literature reviews), we argue that we currently possess a basic knowledge base on the interaction between culture and human development to start implementing empirical studies in the area of multicultural teacher education.

We contend that it is dangerous to continue discussing and implementing multicultural education policies in teacher education programs (including special education teacher education) if they are not based on sound empirical evidence. A potential consequence of this practice is that we might conclude in a few years that a focus on diversity has not improved the performance of special educators that work with culturally diverse students. For this reason, we argue that the teacher education field needs to transcend conceptual discussions about how to prepare teachers for diversity. Instead, researchers in this field need to start grappling with the complex area of teacher preparation for cultural diversity. These efforts need to be framed in the context of a systematic program of research. As a first step, we offer an analytic scheme that will allow teacher educators (a) to pose research questions, design and report investigation results, and, ultimately, (b) to summarize and integrate the findings derived from this research program.

For this purpose, we first present a brief discussion on the context of multicultural teacher education research. Next, we present an analytic blueprint to use in a research program on multicultural teacher education. We conclude with a brief discussion of several challenges teacher educators will face when designing and implementing a research program in this field.

THE CONTEXT OF MULTICULTURAL TEACHER EDUCATION RESEARCH

The Nature of Teacher Education Practice and Research

Because there is a dearth of information about multicultural teacher education in special education, we first present a discussion on multicultural teacher education research in general education. Furthermore, we examine the nature of the teacher education field and the issues that confront it before we engage in an analysis of any of its subfields.

Teacher education is defined as "the context and process of educating individuals to become effective teachers or better teachers" (Yarger & Smith, 1990, p. 26). Hence, our discussion of teacher education research does not include the performance or the behavior of teachers within the confines of school classrooms. Rather, it focuses on inquiry on the education of preservice teachers. In turn, a teacher education program is defined as "a set of phenomena *deliberately intended* to help candidates acquire the knowledge, skills, dispositions, and norms of the occupation of teaching" (Katz & Raths, 1990, p. 241; emphasis added). We acknowledge, however, that there are numerous events, incidents, and circumstances in a teacher education program that are not deliberately planned and that have an impact on preservice teachers (e.g., faculty teaching styles that are not consistent with the goals of the teacher preparation program).

The apparent simplicity of these definitions notwithstanding, the field of teacher education has been fraught with myriad problems. For instance, it has been argued that historically, "Teacher education suffered from low prestige and low status, an unclear mission and identity, faculty disquietude, an ill-defined body of study, and program incoherence" (Ladson-Billings, 1995, p. 748). Hence, it is not surprising that teacher educators have traditionally made subjective decisions about the effectiveness of their programs and that the nature of program evaluation in this field is rather rudimentary (e.g., vague outcomes, ill-defined audiences, methodological limitations; Galluzzo & Craig, 1990). Moreover, the lack of consensus and ambivalence about the goals of teacher education impedes progress. To wit:

> Some teacher educators envision the ideal teacher as someone who knows the research findings regarding pedagogy and can apply these principles to each situation encountered; others argue that teaching practices cannot be prescribed and envision, instead, an ideal teacher who can analyze each new

situation, recognizing, for instance, a unique teachable moment when children are suddenly open to an otherwise difficult idea. (Kennedy, 1990, pp. 820–821)

It follows that the "process of teacher education is rarely if ever driven by theory" (Yarger & Smith, 1990, p. 25). Furthermore, because teacher education does not possess a unified theory, the bulk of research tends to be exploratory and descriptive. In addition, the numerous problems and shortcomings of this field presumably explain the lack of substantive advances achieved throughout its history. In this vein, Silberman argued that "teacher education . . . has been the object of recurrent investigation since the end of World War I; indeed, the preparation of teachers has been studied as frequently as the plight of the Black man in America, and with as little effect" (cited in Lanier & Little, 1986, p. 527).

On the other hand, Wideen and Tisher (1990) argued that "as a field of study, teacher education is coming of age" (p. 2). They cited as evidence the creation of specialized research institutions and centers and increasing numbers of conferences and publications devoted to this area of inquiry. Moreover, Wideen and Tisher argued that when assessing the progress achieved in teacher education research, it is important that contextual factors are pondered. They suggested that the nature of teacher education in a particular nation (i.e., how people think of it, the priority given to the field) and the orientation to research prevalent at a given time (e.g., methodological priorities) are critical contextual factors to bear in mind. Each of these factors will determine, to some extent, the nature and quality of research that is conducted in a field. Ultimately, investigators in this area of study ought to define a set of criteria to evaluate teacher education research. Some of the evaluative criteria that have been recommended include (a) usefulness of the generated knowledge to the practice of teacher education, (b) awareness and understanding of phenomena, (c) stimulus for reform, and (d) reflection on systemic situations and actions.

In sum, mixed reviews abound about the nature and efficacy of teacher education programs and teacher education research. Some educators are concerned about the state of teacher education in general whereas others believe that positive changes are on the horizon. Still others are concerned that there is a limited focus on multicultural teacher education research and this neglect will serve to limit the attainment of long range educational goals (e.g., improved academic and social outcomes for all children). We explicate these concerns in the next section.

The Multicultural Teacher Education Research Field

Many educators contend that pervading problems and dilemmas in the teacher education field cannot be dissected from the multicultural teacher education arena. As Ladson-Billings (1995) stated:

Indeed, we must add to these the unique challenges of multicultural education, which include a lack of definitional clarity (Sleeter & Grant, 1987), student resistance to multicultural knowledge and issues (Ahlquist, 1991; King & Ladson-Billings, 1990), and political attacks on and distortion of multicultural education (Bloom, 1987; D'Souza, 1991; Schlesinger, 1992). . . . The responsibility of multicultural teacher education, then, is to ensure that it is placed squarely within the debate about teacher education in general. (p. 749)

Unfortunately, the research on teacher education for diversity in general education is scarce and shows rather inconclusive and mixed results (Grant, 1993; Grant & Secada, 1990; Ladson-Billings, 1995). Grant and Secada's (1990) chapter in the *Handbook of Research on Teacher Education* is one of the very few comprehensive research reviews on this topic. They located 16 studies published on this topic and concluded that this line of research is characterized by geographic, conceptual, and programmatic isolation. Specifically, most studies were conducted in midwestern states, tended to focus on race issues, and were implemented in individual teacher education programs. In addition, Grant and Secada found that most investigators did not define multicultural education, assessed program impact via attitude surveys, and reported mixed results. Although recent reviews have reported more research studies in this domain (e.g., Grant & Tate, 1995, identified 47 studies and Ladson-Billings, 1995, located 43 studies), findings continue to be mixed. In fact, Zeichner (1993) has concluded that "there is still a great deal of uncertainty about both the elements of successful teaching across cultures and about how to prepare teachers for cultural diversity" (p. 22).

Ladson-Billings (1995) found that the dimension that has received the most attention is the integration of multicultural education content into the curricula. She concluded that there is a gap between multicultural teacher education theory and practice. Likewise, Grant and Tate (1995) concluded:

1. There is a movement from research analyzing multicultural workshops to examining courses and field programs on race and gender diversity and social justice.

2. A majority of this research was undertaken by instructors examining their own courses. Further, most of these studies were conducted without external funding.

3. A majority of the courses studied used the Multicultural Education approach or the Human Relations approach.

4. Many of these studies neglected the scholarship and epistemological foundations of previous research on multicultural education.

5. These studies did not provide a critique of their research design and methodology or discuss their limitations.

6. The studies failed to provide a definition of multicultural education and focused mainly on race/ethnicity. (pp. 151–152)

Multicultural Teacher Education in the Special Education Field

Unfortunately, the situation in the special education field is perhaps even worse. Research on multicultural teacher education has received little attention in special education. A review of the scarce literature in this field shows that it is mostly devoted to descriptions of teacher education programs that emphasize cultural diversity (or urban special education, or both) or bilingual special education. Reports seem to focus on inservice teachers. However, participants are sometimes considered preservice teachers even though they had teaching experience in the general education.

This literature includes descriptive accounts of multicultural teacher education models (e.g., Fox, Kuhlman, & Sales, 1988; Fradd, Weismantal, Correa, & Algozzine, 1988), but others also include data on program impact—most of which are based on quasi-experimental designs, qualitative models, or both (Burstein & Cabello, 1989; Burstein, Cabello, & Hamann, 1993; Ellsworth, 1993; Harry, Torguson, Katkavich, & Guerrero, 1993; Kozleski, Sands, & French, 1993). Several of these reports are formative evaluations of ongoing projects and it seems that results tend to be positive. Other topics of interest in this field include the integration of culturally diverse families in the work of teachers (Harry et al., 1993) and recruitment and retention models to attract minority teachers to the special education field (Franklin & James, 1990).

Again, it is unfortunate that comprehensive reviews of the special education literature in this domain are not available. We speculate that the lack of attention to this area in special education is explained by at least three factors. First, special educators tend to work in isolation from their colleagues in general education. Thus, the knowledge base on teacher education for cultural diversity that is emerging in general education (Banks & Banks, 1995; Grant, 1992; Zeichner, 1993) rarely informs the efforts of teacher educators in special education.

Second, the area of multicultural teacher education research has received alarmingly low levels of financial and professional support. For instance, moneys to conduct research in this area—particularly in special education—are virtually nonexistent. The federal funds allocated for "personnel preparation" projects are typically used to fund the recruitment and training of special education teachers. Although projects have been funded to recruit and retain minority teachers, teacher educators concentrate their efforts in the successful achievement of program objectives, and generally project directors are not concerned with internal validity issues to document the impact of programs with a multicultural focus.

Third, policymakers and administrators send mixed messages to the teacher education field. For example, national and state reform initiatives have not always monitored the implementation and have not documented the impact of efforts in this arena. In her review of the literature, Gollnick (1995) found that although the National Council for Accreditation of Teacher Education (NCATE) has included multicultural education requirements in teacher education programs since the late 1970s, "not all institutions had yet incorporated multicultural education and cultural diversity into their programs." She concluded that "curriculum content was the only area in which improvement was recorded" (p. 58). It appears, then, that the teacher education community observes on one hand that attention to cultural diversity is "mandated," but on the other hand, they learn quickly that such reforms are not monitored or evaluated in a substantive manner.

Hence, from our review of the literature on multicultural teacher education research in both general and special education, we conclude that in order to strengthen this area, we must develop a sound conceptual framework to guide future inquiry. More specifically, we contend that multicultural teacher education research must become broader in scope (i.e., include, but not be confined to, race), must be generated using both quantitative and qualitative methodologies, must be conducted not only in the college classroom, but also within the context of field placements, and must be conducted longitudinally (e.g., data must be collected on students at the preservice level through their beginning years of teaching). We now provide a blueprint for multicultural teacher education research which incorporates these components.

A BLUEPRINT FOR A RESEARCH PROGRAM ON MULTICULTURAL PRESERVICE TEACHER EDUCATION

The blueprint we outline in this chapter could be used in at least two fashions. First, researchers can use it as a rubric to design studies and to report their findings. This will contribute to promote consistency in this field to both study important dimensions and to use similar report formats. Second, researchers can use it as a framework to guide literature reviews and research syntheses. In turn, this will help to appraise and guide systemic progress. We are aware that this blueprint cannot encompass all aspects of multicultural teacher education research in special education. Nevertheless, our ultimate goal is to promote discussions and applications of this model so that it can be transformed and refined as the field moves forward.

The analytic scheme we propose is multifaceted and comprised of at least three main dimensions, namely (a) the foci of teacher education research, (b) the approach to multicultural education embedded in research studies,

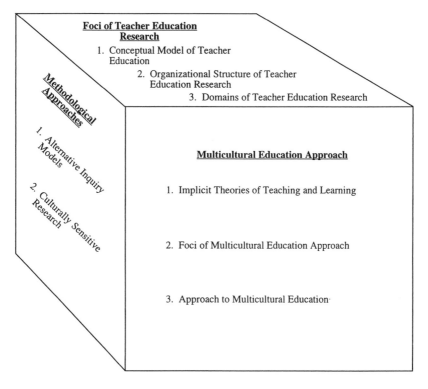

FIG. 14.1. An analytic scheme to conduct multicultural teacher education research.

and (c) the methodological approaches utilized in inquiries (see Fig. 14.1). Because the multicultural teacher education literature is alarmingly scarce in the special education field, most of the literature used to craft our model focuses on general education teacher education.

Facet 1: Foci of Teacher Education Research

There are three interrelated issues relevant to a discussion on the foci of teacher education research: (a) the conceptual model of teacher education underlying a program, (b) the organizational structure of teacher education research, and (c) the domains of study in teacher education research (see Sikula, Buttery, & Guyton, 1996, for a comprehensive review of research on teacher education).

Conceptual Models of Teacher Education. All teacher education programs are based on a particular conceptual model. Zeichner contended that this century's four traditions of practice in the U.S. teacher education field are:

(a) an academic tradition that emphasizes teachers' knowledge of subject matter and their ability to transform that subject matter to promote student understanding; (b), a social efficiency tradition that emphasizes teachers' abilities to thoughtfully apply "a knowledge base" about teaching that has been generated through research on teaching; (c) a developmentalist tradition that stresses teachers' abilities to base their instruction on their direct knowledge of their students—their current understandings of the content under study and their developmental readiness for particular activities; and (d) a social reconstructionist tradition that emphasizes teachers' abilities to see the social and political implication of their actions and to assess their actions and the social contexts in which they are carried out, for their contribution to greater equality, justice, and humane conditions in schooling and society. (as cited in Ladson-Billings, 1995, p. 749)

These conceptual models have implications for the implementation of multicultural education components in teacher education programs. For instance, the academic tradition would concentrate on the content that will be taught and on issues of teacher knowledge of cultural diversity; the social efficiency model could focus on what is considered effective pedagogy for culturally diverse learners; the developmentalist tradition would focus on the best time to address issues of ethnic identity or prejudice with pupils; and, finally, the social reconstructionist approach would focus on the study of curricula, strategies, and procedures that lead to values clarification, decision making, and actions on the part of teachers and students.

Traditionally, however, teacher education programs in special education do not acknowledge explicitly their underlying conceptual models. Reynolds (1990), for instance, categorized the different models of teacher education in special education in terms of issues or alternatives debated/used in this field. Specifically, he listed alternative models that include (a) undergraduate versus graduate preparation; (b) single versus dual preparation (i.e., certifications in general and special education); (c) categorical versus noncategorical preparation; (d) K–12 versus separate-level preparation (i.e., preschool, elementary, secondary); and (e) direct versus indirect services (e.g., via consultation). Nonetheless, it is difficult to infer from this list the conceptual models that inform each of these alternatives because they seem to focus on distinct dimensions or aspects of the teacher education enterprise. Obviously, conceptual models are critical elements of teacher education programs because they contain basic assumptions and definitions of fundamental constructs (e.g., functions and goals of education, definitions of teaching and learning) that guide the work of teacher educators and shape the emphases, formats, and procedures adopted in a teacher education program.

Similarly, conceptual models inform the conceptualization of multicultural education components in teacher education programs. In other words, "how we understand the philosophy and purposes of a multicultural teacher education program requires the understanding of teacher education in general at specific institutions" (Ladson-Billings, 1995, p. 749). As we discuss in a subsequent section, the conceptual model of teacher education adopted in a particular program will have consequences for the approach used to incorporate multicultural education.

The Organizational Structure of Teacher Education Research. It follows that teacher education research must be conducted in the context of the conceptual model that underlies a given program. However, it may prove useful to have an analytic framework that is generic enough to assist researchers in the design, evaluation, or both of teacher education research. For this purpose, we adopted Yarger and Smith's (1990) basic organizational framework of teacher education research. They purported that this research focuses on one or more of the following aspects and their linkages: antecedent, process, and outcomes of teacher education. Antecedents are "conditions and variables that affect teacher education without being directly related to process, but rather influence and guide that process" (p. 27). Examples of antecedent variables include faculty, student, and institutional characteristics, physical conditions of the program, the structure of the university setting within which the teacher education program is located, and the legislative and policy contexts (e.g., state/federal mandates, accreditation requirements and concerns).

In turn, process variables include "any factor associated with the intervention of a teacher education program" (Yarger & Smith, 1990, p. 28) (e.g., the structure of the program, the components of the structure, the implementation procedures and the extent of implementation). Finally, outcome variables are the "learned or provoked behaviors exhibited by the recipients of teacher education that occur as a direct result of an intervention." Teacher and student behaviors are included in this category. These outcome variables, however, are relevant to this discussion only as they relate to antecedents and processes.

Note that studies which focus on isolated components of this model are rare. Research linking these components, however, is more common. The three components can be linked in at least four different ways, namely antecedent–process, antecedent–outcomes, process–outcomes, and antecedent–process–outcomes. In the antecedent–process studies, researchers are interested in looking at how antecedent variables (as defined earlier) influence the process of teacher education and vice versa. Yarger and Smith (1990) also argued that research could focus on both types of effects simultaneously, such as how "the availability of funds for paying cooperating teachers influences the extent to which these teachers are involved in the teacher education process" (p. 28).

Antecedent–outcomes studies are concerned with the link between antecedent and outcome variables (e.g., teacher behaviors or cognitions). Obviously, the role of process variables is disregarded in this type of inquiry.
The third type of linkage is process–outcomes studies. As its name indicates,
investigators look at how the teacher education intervention impacts
teacher behaviors/cognitions, student behaviors/cognitions, or both. Of all
types of research, this kind of study is the most common approach. "However, studies in this domain are broader than simple process–product research but also include evaluation studies (the applied aspect), which allows
one to examine the effects of outcomes on subsequent process" (Yarger &
Smith, 1990, p. 28).

Finally, studies that aim to examine simultaneously antecedent–process–
outcome variables are rather scarce. In part this is explained by the fact that
this type of research is not affordable to individual researchers. Most likely,
studies of this kind are represented by national or regional large-scale studies.

The Domains of Study in Teacher Education Research. So far, we have
proposed that the foci of teacher education research should take into consideration the underlying conceptual models that inform these programs
and that this inquiry is scrutinized or pursued through an organizational
lens. The next issue relates to the *content* of this research (i.e., *what* will be
studied?). We purposely avoided the development of a list of topics to be
investigated in this field because "the [research] agenda is specific to the
individual author; there is no consensus on what research is most important
in teacher education or where to begin" (Yarger & Smith, 1990, p. 26). Instead,
we provide a few examples of alternative ways in which research topics
have been organized in this realm.

Katz and Raths (1990) identified several parameters that can be used as
a framework to guide teacher education research. In their own words, "The
varied phenomena constituting a teacher education program are characterized, defined, influenced and circumscribed by broad classes of variables
we refer to as 'parameters.' The term 'parameter' is used here to indicate
a category of variables that applies to every teacher education program"
(pp. 241–242). The parameters include (a) goals; (b) characteristics of the
candidates; (c) characteristics of the staff; (d) content (e.g., knowledge base,
skills, techniques, competencies, philosophical basis, texts, curricula, topics); (e) methods (e.g., fieldwork, observation in schools, student teaching);
(f) time/timing (i.e., duration, timing, and sequencing); (g) ethos (i.e., affective quality prevalent in the program); (h) regulations (e.g., graduation
requirements, certification requirements); (i) resources (fiscal, material, and
human); (j) evaluation practices; and (k) impacts of the program. Katz and
Raths proposed to use a matrix in which the 11 parameters are depicted in
both rows and columns. Thus, each cell of the matrix can be used to

summarize or design research on the two parameters represented in a given cell.

Likewise, Lanier and Little (1986) organized their review of the teacher education research literature around broad themes that include (a) teacher educators, (b) preservice teachers, (c) the curriculum, and (d) the milieu. Grant and Tate (1995), on the other hand, identified research on preservice multicultural teacher education that dealt with seven topics, namely, studies that examine the influence of university workshops, university courses, university programs, university field experiences, field immersion plus course sequence, placement in culturally diverse classrooms and communities, and cooperating teachers and supervisors. Similarly, Zimpher and Howey (1990) summarized the research on teacher education in the United States and developed the following list of six research themes:

1. Learning to teach.
2. The purposes, structure, and character of teacher education programs.
3. Specific contexts and modalities for learning to teach.
4. Education faculty and students.
5. Clinical teacher education.
6. The induction and socialization of beginning teachers.

Moreover, Reynolds (1990) reported three broad topics "believed to be essential for special education teachers" (p. 427). The topics include (a) legal and ethical principles, (b) curriculum, and (c) educational models and approaches (e.g., direct instruction, behavioral principles, classroom management, teaching basic literacy skills, teaching self-regulation and strategic behavior, interactive teaching for cognitive change, social skills, working with parents, communication and consultation).

Based on this review, it appears that, independent of the theme or topic we choose to investigate, we must be aware of the conceptual assumptions and premises on which a teacher education program is founded. In turn, these conceptual foundations determine the way teacher education programs are organized and managed. It is in the context of these theoretical and organizational structures that a program's approach to multicultural education is nested. We now turn to the issue of approaches to multicultural education.

Facet 2: Approaches to Multicultural Education

Three main issues are relevant to this discussion. First, researchers must specify the underlying theories of learning and teaching that support their view of multicultural teacher education. Second, it is important that the foci of the multicultural education approach be explicitly stated. Third, the approach to multicultural education has to be described.

Theories of Teaching and Learning. We should keep in mind that all approaches to multicultural education contain implicit models of teaching and learning. Nowadays, a cognitive view of learning and instruction is favored in education. In this view, students use what they have learned to make sense and construct knowledge from their experiences. Other sociolinguistic (e.g., classroom participation structures), cognitive (e.g., self-regulatory processes), cultural (e.g., values, culturally valued practices) and affective (e.g., identity, self-esteem) variables are relevant to understand student learning. More importantly, it is critical that multicultural teacher education research be grounded in a theory of teachers as learners. Hence, teachers should also be seen as learners that learn through similar processes (Kennedy, 1991).

Thus, multicultural teacher education programs need to state explicitly an underlying philosophy of student and teacher learning. This is critical because foundations and methods courses will be based on these paradigms. Similarly, the ways in which the intersection between culture and student learning are described will depend on these theories. In fact, these theories also inform the definition of a teacher's task—a pivotal construct implicitly embedded in preservice foundations and methods courses.

Foci of Multicultural Education. Depending on the conceptual orientations and interests of teacher educators, specific variables are emphasized in multicultural teacher education programs. For example, a common focus of these programs is issues of race and ethnicity. Other areas include gender, social class, language, religion, and sexual orientation. Because some teacher educators see these variables as being dynamic and interactive, other programs focus on a combination of these factors (Artiles, Chow, & McClafferty, 1995; Trent, Pernell, & Stephens, 1995). Generally, the focus on a particular variable is related to the implementors' beliefs about teaching and learning. Thus, implications for teaching are also presented to preservice teachers. It is imperative, then, that teacher educators make a conscious decision about the foci of their multicultural education program. Moreover, their decision should be grounded in a model of multicultural education that is congruent with identified theories of teaching and learning.

Approaches to Multicultural Education. There are several typologies to classify multicultural education approaches. These typologies classify approaches to multicultural education according to the philosophy, main goals, and focus of the model as well as the strategies used to implement the approach. Banks (1993), for instance, proposed that there are five dimensions represented in the multicultural education field, namely, content integration, knowledge construction, prejudice reduction, equity pedagogy, and empowering school culture. Sleeter and Grant (1994), on the other hand, identified five approaches to multicultural education. These include teaching the culturally different or exceptional children, human relations, single-group studies, multicultural approaches, and education that is multicultural and social reconstructionist (see the cited references for detailed discussions of these typologies).

It is obvious that each model within these typologies differs from each other in terms of the foci, goals, and depth with which multicultural education issues are treated. For instance, some are more superficial than others and some are more theoretically grounded than others. We argue that teacher educators need to analyze carefully each of these models so that they choose the options that represent the most equitable education model for culturally diverse exceptional learners (e.g., multicultural approaches, education that is multicultural and social reconstructionist, equity pedagogy, empowering school culture). Unfortunately, the literature shows that most U.S. prospective teachers are not exposed to a social reconstructionist model (Grant & Tate, 1995; Ladson-Billings, 1995). Even when preservice teachers are exposed to critical models of multicultural education, they tend to disregard equity issues and the political dimension of education (Artiles & McClafferty, in press).

Within the context of approaches to multicultural education, we must also consider the service delivery model adopted by program implementors. Often, teacher education programs offer isolated courses on cultural diversity. By using this approach, "the students and the institution are tacitly, but not so subtly, saying that multicultural concerns are not real concerns of teaching and learning" (Ladson-Billings, 1995, p. 749). That is why it is critical that teacher educators are aware of the need to make an informed selection of a multicultural education approach and develop ways to incorporate and infuse content throughout the span of the program. If teacher educators understand the theoretical roots of these approaches and envision the enormous implications of multicultural education, they will be able to avoid what typically happens in this field. To wit:

> Too many teacher educators (and teachers) believe that they can implement an effective multicultural education program without effecting fundamental change in the classrooms and schools in which they teach. This belief contributes to the superficial and trivial treatment of issues of race, class, and gender in elementary and secondary school classrooms. (p. 755)

In sum, as we develop schemes to conduct multicultural teacher education research in special education, we must be able to explicate contextual information such as theories of teaching and learning, foci of multicultural education, and the program's approach to multicultural education. Identifying these contextual aspects is extremely important so that we can begin to "generalize about the impact of various case contexts—particularly their normative and political dimensions" (Wells, Hirshberg, Lipton, & Oakes, 1995, p. 19). Furthermore, attention paid to context—as we develop an abundance of case studies on multicultural teacher education in special education—might help us to identify characteristics and attributes that are more likely to influence the beliefs, decisions, and actions of preservice teachers. As we identify the contextual variables associated with multicultural education approaches and with the foci of teacher education research, we must begin to develop methodological approaches that help us to assess the efficacy of our practice. We discuss this critical issue in the next section.

Facet 3: Methodological Approaches

Although we have argued earlier that most teacher education research tends to be exploratory and descriptive, it is also necessary that research questions that stipulate the directionality of relationships between variables or that aim to manipulate variables are posed in the near future. It is possible that the lack of support given to teacher education inquiry explains the descriptive focus of this research. Most likely, teacher educators tend to conduct research on their own initiative and they are probably motivated by the unique needs of their programs. However, the descriptive nature of teacher education research raises questions about the generalizability of findings in this area of study, particularly because of the unique configuration of factors that characterize programs and samples selected by convenience of access. One potential way to address this issue is to present detailed descriptions of the operationalization of the independent and dependent measures as well as contextual factors (Yarger & Smith, 1990). This will contribute to the replicability of findings.

Independent of the type of research question that guides a study, it is necessary that researchers attempt to use varied methodological approaches. We now possess numerous quantitative and qualitative approaches that can enrich findings in this area of study. In addition, it is critical that research on multicultural teacher education is planned and conducted following specific guidelines for a culturally sensitive research program. We discuss briefly these two interrelated aspects.

Alternative Inquiry Models. Currently, advances in both quantitative and qualitative analysis procedures can be used in an integrated manner to study multicultural teacher education in special education. In this vein, quantitative methods such as hierarchical linear models, and qualitative methods such as action research and case studies of a longitudinal nature might be used to explore issues related to course or program development, student change or growth, and students' thinking and behavior during internship and novice teaching experiences. To illustrate, faculty desiring to document the development and implementation of a new course focused on multicultural education—after identifying conceptual and organizational aspects of their program and defining components of the multicultural education approach to be used—might design a study that uses multiple measures and methodologies to generate data. An action research project designed to "improve the quality of an organization and its performance (Calhoun, 1993, p. 62) might be used to assess course effectiveness and incite editing, modifications, and revisions on an ongoing basis. To accomplish this goal, faculty might tape, transcribe, and analyze discourse from preliminary planning meetings, actual lectures and presentations, and evaluative sessions.

This ongoing analysis and evaluation of content, activities, assignments, and presentations could be complemented by data collection related to (a) preservice teacher satisfaction, (b) perceived change and growth, and (c) preservice teacher knowledge/skill transfer to the classroom level. Preservice teacher satisfaction might be determined based on attendance, feedback sheets, and course evaluation data. Perceived change and growth could be determined through analysis of interview data, dialogue journals, and pre- and postconcept maps (Morine-Dershimer, 1993; Trent et al., 1995). For example, Morine-Dershimer used concept maps to trace conceptual change in preservice teachers about teacher planning. To identify differences between pre- and postconcept maps she conducted a discriminant function analysis and found that "elementary and secondary majors differed significantly in their patterns of reference to the three major categories on their pre maps" (p. 19).

Trent et al. (1995) replicated Morine-Dershimer's study and used pre- and postconcept maps to trace conceptual change in preservice teachers enrolled in a special education/multicultural education introductory course. The course—the first in a sequence of courses of a restructured program—introduced a broad definition for diversity and multicultural education that was infused and further developed throughout the remaining teacher education coursework. Student characteristics were studied in the context of culturally mediated and socially constructed identities (Cushner, McClelland, & Safford, 1992). In addition, the professors focused on the development of beliefs and practices consistent with the social action approach outlined by Banks and Banks (1989).

Informants were asked to construct pre and post maps depicting their conceptions about teaching children from culturally diverse backgrounds. In addition to the quantitative analysis, the constant comparative method

(Glaser & Strauss, 1967) was used to generate multiple-level categories that characterized participants' changes from the beginning to the end of the course. In turn, the instructors triangulated these data with interview and dialogue journal data to determine the extent to which their goals and objectives were accomplished. In addition, results were used to make course modifications and revisions where deemed appropriate.

To examine the link between teacher thinking and behaviors, researchers could collect observational data during preservice teachers' practica and internship experiences. In addition, data from follow-up interviews and observations could be compared to data generated during student matriculation (e.g., concept maps and dialogue journals) to determine the extent to which teachers appropriated course/program information into their instructional practices (e.g., Artiles & Barreto, in preparation; Artiles et al., 1995).

To conclude, we want to stress that teacher educators and educational researchers have a wealth of methodological approaches at their disposal. Indeed, a research program on multicultural preservice teacher education should benefit from the use of multiple methodological means. This will not only enrich the nature of findings derived from this program, but will also strengthen the eclectic nature of this knowledge base. However, it is critical that we keep in mind a rule of thumb for sound inquiry: "The research question and the theoretical perspective embedded in the question should permeate the selection of methodological approaches." Thus, research in this area needs to be theory driven. The formulation of questions that are based on particular conceptualizations of teacher education and of multicultural education will determine the methodological strategies utilized in inquiries. At the same time, independent of the theory or method selected for a study, this research ought to make a deliberate effort to be culturally sensitive.

Considerations to Conduct Culturally Sensitive Research. Researchers are only starting to recognize the need for a culturally sensitive research agenda. Let us take, for example, the case of research with ethnic groups. The assumption that color blind (or should we say "objective") research is the most sound inquiry has been recently challenged in the educational research community (Cochran-Smith, 1995; Stanfield & Dennis, 1993). Although referring to the mental health field, Rogler's definition of culturally sensitive research is germane to the discussion of teacher education research with ethnic groups:

> Research is made culturally sensitive through a continuing and open-ended series of substantive and methodological insertions and adaptations designed to mesh the process of inquiry with the cultural characteristics of the group being studied. . . . The insertions and adaptations span the entire research

process, from the pretesting and planning of the study, to the collection of data and translation of instruments, to the instrumentation of measures, and to the analysis and interpretation of the data, Research, therefore, is made culturally sensitive through an incessant, basic, and active preoccupation with the culture of the group being studied throughout the process of research. (cited in Padilla & Lindholm, 1995, p. 99)

In this vein, Padilla and Lindholm posed that investigators must be aware of at least four pivotal issues when conducting research with ethnic groups. First, samples need to be properly identified, selected, and described. Unfortunately, very few studies are conducted in special education and psychology with ethnic minority informants (Artiles, Trent, & Kuan, in press; Graham, 1992). When ethnic minorities are included in studies, researchers tend to use them as a comparison group against the "standard" performance of White populations. Further, many of these studies typically focus on documenting minorities' difficulties in distinct developmental spheres (Padilla & Lindholm, 1995).

Padilla and Lindholm (1995) recommended that researchers be concerned with several issues that relate to sampling ethnic minority subjects. Recommendations include to understand the demographic characteristics of the population, particularly to get a sense of the within-group variance. This will also help researchers to determine if a random and representative sample can be drawn and how. Furthermore, they recommend to be attentive to the presence of confounding variables. To wit:

In order that culture, ethnicity, and social class not be confounded, it is important to understand the unique cultural features of the group. For example, issues of generation of residence, language usage, and acculturation are salient for Hispanic, African American (particularly immigrant), and Asian American families. (p. 102)

Another critical aspect is the recognition of the heterogeneity within ethnic groups. Despite increasing evidence on the contrary, researchers tend to make the fallacious assumption of homogenous intragroup variance and of monolithic identity when working with ethnic minorities (Stanfield, 1993). Similarly, cultural and language barriers (e.g., suspicion of government involvement in research projects, dialect differences in the use of terms or concepts) can complicate a researcher's task when working with ethnic minority groups. Finally, concerns about instrumentation and measurement should be central to investigators doing research with ethnic groups (e.g., appropriateness of instruments, need to develop special instruments to measure ethnic characteristics, response patterns of ethnic respondents; Padilla & Lindholm, 1995).

Moreover, researchers should avoid making the fallacious assumption that isolated demographic variables can be used as proxies of culture. The notion of culture is extremely complex and dynamic. Often, researchers use variables such as race or ethnicity to draw inferences about people's functioning in other life spheres. For instance, referring to ethnic minority research in psychology, Betancourt and López (1993) contended:

> Direct measures of cultural elements are frequently not included, yet cultural factors are assumed to underlie ethnic group differences. Furthermore, ethnic minority research often lacks sufficient attention to psychological theory. It appears that investigators of ethnicity are more inclined toward description than testing theoretically derived hypotheses. (p. 634)

They recommended that culturally sensitive research should include theory and conceptualize and measure group-specific sociocultural variables (e.g., beliefs, values) so that "we can advance the understanding of the role of culture as well as contribute to theory development and applications" (p. 636).

In summary, researchers who now focus on multicultural teacher education in special education can benefit from the wealth of information we currently posses on alternative methodological approaches. However, the design and implementation of this research must be theory driven and culturally sensitive. The guidelines for culturally sensitive research outlined earlier imply that traditional approaches to multicultural education (e.g., tourist and culture-fair approaches) be avoided. This is supported by quantitative and qualitative research on ethnic groups that have documented the rich diversity within and between ethnic groups. The within-group diversity of ethnic populations is becoming more apparent in these postmodern times of rapid sociocultural transformation and mobility. This research has also shown that the study of cultural diversity must transcend the scrutiny of individual variables as the source of cultural variance. This demands us to rethink our notions of multicultural teacher education practice and research. Heath's (1995) discussion on the future of ethnographic research in ethnic minorities' communities aptly summarizes our point:

> Many of today's young do not see their community or their identity as that of a single ethnic group, place, or family; instead they pick and choose, change and reshape their affiliations of primary socialization. Multicultural education will be hopelessly caught in cultural lag if it tries to plead for the dignity of cultural differences and respect merely through repeated portrayals of individuals of color who have conquered their oppressive backgrounds to contribute to mainstream society, or in capsule histories of the immigration patterns of certain nationalities. Discussions of African American, Hispanic, Latino, Asian American, or Pacific cultures that present all members of each of these

groups as homogeneous and securely locked within the membranes of their ethnic membership and identity as "a community" also reflect an inability to stay in touch with the out-of-school socialization networks of today's youth. Multicultural education must go considerably further than the introduction of new content into literature, social studies, and art and music classes. (p. 126)

In sum, as we develop a scheme for investigating the implementation and efficacy of multicultural teacher education in special education, we must begin to use integrated research designs that are grounded in theory and that combine quantitative approaches with ethnographic, phenomenological approaches. In addition, these approaches must honor the dynamic aspects of culture and the variability that exists within cultural groups.

CHALLENGES TO MULTICULTURAL TEACHER EDUCATION RESEARCH

The implementation of a research program in this field is not an easy task. The field is plagued with myriad problems that range from conceptual vagueness to the nature of the special education field. A brief discussion on several of these challenges follows.

Conceptual Clarity: Goals and Scope of Multicultural Education

Researchers need to be aware of the need to define clearly the concept of multicultural education used in their investigations. Researchers have documented that this is a term which is not always clearly defined (Grant, 1993; Sleeter & Grant, 1987). In fact, it has been reported that most research studies do not define multicultural education (Grant & Secada, 1990) and that there is disagreement on how to define it.

On the other hand, despite the controversy and heated discussions about the definition, aims, need, and impact of multicultural education in the United States (see Sleeter, 1995, for a review of critiques in this field), there is a "high level of consensus about [the] aims and scope in the literature written by multicultural education theorists" (Banks, 1993, p. 3). In turn, Sleeter and Grant (1994) purported:

Multicultural education has emerged as an umbrella concept that deals with race, culture, language, social class, gender, and disability. Although many educators still apply it only to race, it is the term most frequently extended to include additional forms of diversity. (p. 33)

Interestingly, the multicultural education literature rarely makes distinctions between the general and special education fields. This complicates the use of multicultural education in special education. For instance, special educators might ask: Should we adapt the multicultural education knowledge base to use in the special education field? Are there systemic or disciplinary considerations that special educators should be aware of when using the multicultural education knowledge base? We attempt to provide brief answers to these questions in the next section.

Disciplinary and Systemic Considerations

There are several considerations related to the nature of multicultural education and of special education that we must be aware of when trying to integrate these two areas of work.

First, a distinctive feature of multicultural education is its interdisciplinary nature. To illustrate, anthropologists and educators have shed light on the influence of culture on ethnic groups' construction of values and world views that shape their performance in social institutions such as schools (Delgado-Gaitán, 1994; Delgado-Gaitán & Trueba, 1991; Weisner, Gallimore, & Jordan, 1988). Developmental psychologists, sociologists, and anthropologists have offered evidence on the ways in which certain sociocultural variables interact with distinct contexts to produce unique developmental pathways (Greenfield & Cocking, 1994; Rogoff, 1990; Spencer & McLoyd, 1990; Stigler, Shweder, & Herdt, 1990; Tharp, 1989). Sociolinguists have produced evidence of the value and meaning of dialects among different racial groups (Labov, 1972). Ethnic-studies specialists, educators, and psychologists have shown how ethnic identity influences self-perception and intergroup relations (Bernal & Knight, 1993; Heath & McLaughlin, 1993). Indeed, multicultural education is an interdisciplinary field of study. As a result of efforts in these domains of study, educators possess an interdisciplinary body of knowledge on the ways student learning is mediated by culture.[1]

Nonetheless, the interdisciplinary nature of this field of study has advantages and disadvantages. On one hand, the field benefits from a truly expanded view of human development in which alternative world views, theoretical assumptions, and inquiry traditions mingle to provide an eclectic

---

[1]Although we realize this knowledge base is only starting to emerge, we think this baseline information could be used to begin conducting research in the teacher education field. It is beyond the scope of this chapter, however, to summarize this basic knowledge base. We must assume that readers are familiar (a) with the research on the role of sociocultural variables in learning and instructional processes (e.g., see Banks & Banks, 1995; Cloud, 1993; Figueroa et al., 1989; García, 1993; Obiakor et al., 1992; Rogoff & Morelli, 1989; Tharp, 1989; Trent & Artiles, 1995) and (b) with reviews of this literature (see, e.g., Irvine & York, 1995; Ladson-Billings, 1995; Zeichner, 1993).

account of culture and human growth. On the other hand, conceptual barriers (e.g., use of terminology), difficulties in synthesizing and interpreting research findings from different theoretical and methodological traditions, and, perhaps more importantly, the difficulties inherent to the translation of this knowledge base to the language of practitioners are only a few examples. However, as discussed earlier, educators have developed several approaches to multicultural education that range from rather superficial ways to deal with diversity (e.g., the "tourist" approach to cultural diversity; content infusion in the curriculum about minority groups) to more radical analyses of the struggle of minority groups to promote equity and their empowerment (see Banks, 1993, and Sleeter & Grant, 1994, for a review of alternative approaches and dimensions of multicultural education).

Professionals in the general education system have developed guidelines and ideas to implement multicultural education for isolated "markers of difference" (e.g., race, gender, language, or disability). Interestingly, although "multicultural education theorists are increasingly interested in how the interaction of race, class, and gender influences education" (Banks, 1993, p. 4), there is a paucity of information on how educators in the general education system can address the interactions of such variables in their classrooms. That is, the bulk of the teacher education literature focuses on the "main effects" of sociocultural variables (e.g., How does gender influence student learning?).

This is an interesting issue because in reality most sociocultural variables included in the multicultural education discourse interact in people's lives. Unfortunately, many teacher educators use the "main effects" view when interpreting the notion of multicultural education. Thus, they merely infuse in the curriculum information on other racial groups' history, customs, and traditions. The relevance of such information to pupils' lives is not always addressed. Moreover, the fact that the influence of race, gender, language, and social class is embedded in everybody's identities and daily routines is typically not acknowledged.

Notably, the embeddedness of sociocultural variables is even more apparent in the special education system. Special educators, for instance, typically have a hard time trying to identify the proportion of the variance in a student's educational performance that is accounted for by a disability and by other sociocultural variables (e.g., limited English proficiency).[2] Consequently, special educators should avoid constraining themselves by posing the main effects question that pervades in the general education system

---

[2]We recognize this argument is based on the assumptions that disability is a clearly defined construct or that disabilities are discrete conditions. For heuristic purposes, we chose to use this argument because the view of disability as a discrete variable still pervades in the special education field. We are aware, however, of the debates on the noncategorical view of mild disabilities and on the socially constructed nature of disability. Unfortunately, we cannot address these issues due to space constraints.

(e.g., What is the impact of language on student learning?). Instead, they are compelled to pose at least two other types of questions. First, they need to pose interaction effects questions in which disability is always part of the matrix of analysis (e.g., How does disability interact with distinct sociocultural variables in the learning process of students?). Second, they need to pose phenomenological questions that move beyond linear, cause–effect hypotheses and lead to the examination of context and sociocultural variables that influence students' learning processes (e.g., What is the contribution of personal, interpersonal, and community forces in the development of children's understanding of literacy tasks? What is the role of cultural values in shaping children's problem solving skills?). Obviously, this situation complicates the work of special educators with culturally diverse learners and it entangles the translation and application of the multicultural education literature to the work of teacher educators in special education. Further research in this area will help elucidate this issue.

Other Challenges

There are many other challenges that teacher educators will confront when conducting research in this field. Because of space constraints, however, we only mention briefly two other challenges, namely the teacher education faculty and academic ethnocentrism and elitism.

Teacher educators need to be familiar and accept the philosophy and practice of multicultural education if a research program is to be launched in this domain. However, an examination of the demographic composition of teacher educators suggests that this may not be the case. Grant (1993) reported that 93% of professors of education are White and 70% of this group are male. The mean age for a full professor is 53, for an associate professor is 47, and for an assistant professor is 42. Similarly, Zabel and White (1988) reported data on special education teacher educators. They found that the average age for assistant professors is 41, for associate professors is 45, and for full professors is 52. Data were not reported by race. In contrast to the male-dominated situation in the general education field, the proportion of women in their sample comprised 60% of respondents.

In light of these data, it can be assumed that the majority of faculty in general and special education "has had little formal instruction in multicultural education during their formative years of professional development" (Grant, 1993, pp. 50–51; see also García, 1990, for a discussion on bilingual education faculty). Reasons supporting this assumption include that it was not until recently that multicultural education information started to be systematically infused in courses and textbooks (Foster & Iannaccone, 1994; Grant, 1993). In addition, professional development courses and training for faculty in teacher education programs are rare, particularly in the area of multiculturalism.

Another challenge to researchers is academic ethnocentrism and elitism. It is important that research on multicultural education is accepted and valued in institutions of higher education. In this way, researchers can pursue programs of research in this area without fearing sanctions or penalties from academic personnel committees. Grant (1993) contended that "there has been and continues to be academic ethnocentrism and elitism directed toward scholars who wish to study multicultural issues and issues related to race, class, and gender" (p. 52). In the same vein, Padilla (1994) argued that ethnic minority scholars experience even more obstacles in this area "at all levels of professional development" (p. 25). He asserted further that as doctoral students and junior faculty, many ethnic minority scholars experience difficulty finding mentors who wish to conduct "ethnic related research" or who are willing to provide them with intense research apprenticeships that will equip them with the skills needed to be successful in major research institutions. Padilla also discussed the failure of mainstream educational journals to publish studies that focus on ethnic-related research and encourages ethnic minority scholars to publish in ethnic journals such as the "*Journal of Black Psychology, Journal of Negro Education*, and the *Hispanic Journal of Behavioral Sciences*" (p. 25). Although we agree with Padilla's recommendation, we also assert that if major institutions of higher learning espouse to honor and value diversity, they must begin to consider and publish research that focuses on ethnic-related and other multicultural issues.

CONCLUSIONS

We began this chapter by identifying the current dilemmas that exist in the area of multicultural teacher education research in both general and special education fields. More specifically, although a considerable amount of writing has focused on multicultural teacher education, most of it has been conceptual in nature. Unfortunately, this situation has created an ever-widening gap between theory and practice and created at least three problems that threaten the development and sustainment of multicultural education as a vital component of teacher education programs. First, it appears that we are changing significantly the organization of programs and courses without knowledge about the components and approaches that yield the most positive results. Second, as we have determined in our review of the literature, little multicultural education research has focused either directly or indirectly on student outcomes, or the many mediating variables or interactive effects that might affect student outcomes. Third, it appears that many programs and courses view multicultural education from a very narrow standpoint and studies have determined that the content and foci of courses often perpetuate stereotypes and overgeneralizations about certain minority groups.

It is imperative, therefore, that we develop a research framework that focuses on two major contextual components. These components include (a) the foci of teacher education research and (b) the approaches used to teach multicultural education. In addition, we must begin to develop research designs that integrate both quantitative and qualitative approaches and employ multiple measures. These practices will allow us to document the development and evolution of the models, characteristics, and components of programs that affect the thinking and actions of teachers in positive ways. Finally, we need to determine if and how these refined programs affect social and academic outcomes for students.

In sum, the time has come for us to move beyond advocacy discussions about multicultural education and begin to focus on empirical work designed to strengthen the field and affect positively the performance of teachers who will instruct increasing numbers of students from diverse cultural, linguistic, and other nonmainstream backgrounds. Research in this area should be based on a theory of teachers as learners and it should take into account the conceptualizations of teacher education and multicultural education that underlie preservice programs. Similarly, the use of multiple methodological strategies and culturally sensitive designs will enrich the depth and sophistication of a knowledge base on multicultural preservice teacher education.

In addition, our work must begin to frame policies in this area so that decisions about restructuring programs will be based on analysis of longitudinal and generalizable data. We believe that the field of multicultural preservice teacher education represents a promising area that might influence positively the education of neophyte teachers and their subsequent practice. However, failure to move the field beyond its present position will not result in the widespread implementation of equitable educational practices for all children.

ACKNOWLEDGMENTS

The authors wish to thank Diane Haager, Festus Obiakor, and the volume editors for their review of previous drafts of this chapter. The chapter authors (listed alphabetically) contributed equally to the preparation of this manuscript.

REFERENCES

Ahlquist, R. (1992). Manifestations of inequality: Overcoming resistance in a multicultural foundations course. In C. A. Grant (Ed.), *Research and multicultural education: From the margins to the mainstream* (pp. 89–105). London: The Falmer Press.

Amos, O. E., & Landers, M. F. (1984). Special education and multicultural education: A compatible marriage. *Theory Into Practice, 23,* 144–150.

Artiles, A. J., Chow, V., & McClafferty, K. (1995, April). *Learning to teach in multicultural contexts: Exploring preservice teachers' knowledge change.* Paper presented at the annual meeting of the Council for Exceptional Children, Indianapolis, IN.

Artiles, A. J., & McClafferty, K. (in press). Learning to teach culturally diverse learners: Charting change in preservice teacher thinking about effective teaching. *Elementary School Journal.*

Artiles, A. J., & Barreto, R. (in preparation). *Tracing the evolution of teacher thinking about multicultural teaching: Two case studies of novice teachers.* Los Angeles: University of California.

Artiles, A. J., Trent, S. C., & Kuan, L. A. (in press). Learning disabilities empirical research on ethnic minority students: An analysis of 22 years of studies published in selected refereed journals. *Learning Disabilities Research and Practice.*

Baca, L., & Amato, C. (1989). Bilingual special education: Training issues. *Exceptional Children, 56,* 168–173.

Banks, J. A. (1993). Multicultural education: Historical development, dimensions, and practice. *Review of Research in Education, 19,* 3–49.

Banks, J. A., & Banks, C. M. (Eds.). (1989). *Multicultural education: Issues and perspectives.* Boston: Allyn & Bacon.

Banks, J. A., & Banks, C. M. (Eds.). (1995). *Handbook of research on multicultural education.* New York: Macmillan.

Bernal, M. E., & Knight, G. P. (Eds.). (1993). *Ethnic identity.* New York: State University of New York Press.

Betancourt, H., & López, S. R. (1993). The study of culture, ethnicity, and race in American psychology. *American Psychologist, 48,* 629–637.

Burstein, N. D., & Cabello, B. (1989). Preparing teachers to work with culturally diverse students: A teacher education model. *Journal of Teacher Education, 40,* 9–16.

Burstein, N., Cabello, B., & Hamann, J. (1993). Teacher preparation for culturally diverse urban students: Infusing competencies across the curriculum. *Teacher Education and Special Education, 16,* 1–13.

Calhoun, A. J. (1993). Action research: Three approaches. *Educational Leadership, 51,* 62–65.

Cloud, N. (1993). Language, culture and disability: Implications for instruction and teacher preparation. *Teacher Education and Special Education, 16,* 60–72.

Cochran-Smith, M. (1995). Color blindness and basket making are not the answers: Confronting the dilemmas of race, culture, and language diversity in teacher education. *American Educational Research Journal, 32,* 493–522.

Cross, B. E. (1993). How do we prepare teachers to improve race relations? *Educational Leadership, 50,* 64–65.

Cushner, K., McClelland, A., & Safford, P. (1992). *Human diversity in education: An integrative approach.* New York: McGraw-Hill.

Dean, A. V., Salend, S. J., & Taylor, L. (1993). Multicultural education: A challenge for special educators. *Teaching Exceptional Children, 26*(1), 40–43.

Delgado-Gaitán, C. (1994). Socializing young children in Mexican-American families: An intergenerational perspective. In P. M. Greenfield & R. R. Cocking (Eds.), *Cross-cultural roots of minority child development* (pp. 55–86). Hillsdale, NJ: Lawrence Erlbaum Associates.

Delgado-Gaitán, C., & Trueba, H. (1991). *Crossing cultural borders: The education of immigrant families in America.* London: The Falmer Press.

Durán, R. P. (1989). Assessment and instruction of at-risk Hispanic students. *Exceptional Children, 56,* 154–158.

Ellsworth, N. J. (1993). Trainees' perceptions of types of instructional practices modeled in an urban teacher education program. *Teacher Education and Special Education, 16,* 34–41.

Figueroa, R. A., Fradd, S. H., & Correa, V. I. (Eds.). (1989). Meeting the multicultural needs of the Hispanic students in special education. *Exceptional Children, 56,* 102–178.

Foster, H. L., & Iannaccone, C. J. (1994). Multicultural content in special education introductory textbooks. *The Journal of Special Education, 28*, 77–92.

Fox, C. L., Kuhlman, N. A., & Sales, T. B. (1988). Cross-cultural concerns: What's missing from special education training programs. *Teacher Education and Special Education, 11*, 155–161.

Fradd, S. H., Weismantal, M. J., Correa, V. I., & Algozzine, B. (1988). Developing a personnel training model for meeting the needs of handicapped and at-risk language-minority students. *Teacher Education and Special Education, 11*, 30–38.

Franklin, M. E. (1992). Culturally sensitive instructional practices for African-American learners with disabilities. *Exceptional Children, 59*, 115–122.

Franklin, M. E., & James, J. R. (1990). Nontraditional approaches to recruiting and retraining minority future special educators: Two comprehensive models. *Teacher Education and Special Education, 13*, 50–53.

Galluzzo, G. R., & Craig, J. R. (1990). Evaluation of preservice teacher education programs. In W. R. Houston (Ed.), *Handbook of research on teacher education* (pp. 599–616). New York: Macmillan.

García, E. E. (1990). Educating teachers for language minority students. In W. R. Houston (Ed.), *Handbook of research on teacher education* (pp. 717–729). New York: Macmillan.

García, E. E. (1993). Language, culture, and education. *Review of Research in Education, 19*, 51–98.

García, S. B., & Malkin, D. H. (1993). Toward defining programs and services for culturally and linguistically diverse learners in special education. *Teaching Exceptional Children, 26*(1), 52–58.

Glaser, B. G., & Strauss, A. L. (1967). *The discovery of grounded theory*. Chicago: Aldine.

Gollnick, D. M. (1995). National and state initiatives for multicultural education. In J. A. Banks & C. M. Banks (Eds.), *Handbook of research on multicultural education* (pp. 44–64). New York: Macmillan.

Graham, S. (1992). Most of the subjects were White and middle class: Trends in published research on African Americans in selected APA journals, 1970–1989. *American Psychologist, 47*, 629–639.

Grant, C. A., (Ed.). (1992). *Research and multicultural education: From the margins to the mainstream*. London: The Falmer Press.

Grant, C. A. (1993). The multicultural preparation of U.S. teachers: Some hard truths. In G. K. Verma (Ed.), *Equality and teacher education: An international perspective* (pp. 41–57). London: The Falmer Press.

Grant, C. A., & Secada, W. (1990). Preparing teachers for diversity. In W. R. Houston (Ed.), *Handbook of research on teacher education* (pp. 403–422). New York: Macmillan.

Grant, C. A., & Tate, W. F. (1995). Multicultural education through the lens of the multicultural education research literature. In J. A. Banks & C. M. Banks (Eds.), *Handbook of research on multicultural education* (pp. 145–166). New York: Macmillan.

Greenfield, P. M., & Cocking, R. R. (Eds.). (1994). *Cross-cultural roots of minority child development*. Hillsdale, NJ: Lawrence Erlbaum Associates.

Harry, B., Torguson, C., Katkavich, J., & Guerrero, M. (1993). Crossing social class and cultural barriers in working with families. *Teaching Exceptional Children, 26*(1), 48–51.

Heath, S. B. (1995). Ethnography in communities: Learning the everyday life of America's subordinated youth. In J. A. Banks & C. M. Banks (Eds.), *Handbook of research on multicultural education* (pp. 114–128). New York: Macmillan.

Heath, S. B., & McLaughlin, M. W. (Eds.). (1993). *Identity and inner-city youth: Beyond ethnicity and gender*. New York: Teachers College Press.

Houston, W. R. (Ed.). (1990). *Handbook of research on teacher education*. New York: Macmillan.

Irvine, J. J., & York, D. E. (1995). Learning styles and culturally diverse students: A literature review. In J. A. Banks & C. M. Banks (Eds.), *Handbook of research on multicultural education* (pp. 484–497). New York: Macmillan.

Katz, L. G., & Raths, J. D. (1990). A framework for research on teacher education programs. In R. P. Tisher & M. F. Wideen (Eds.), *Research in teacher education: International perspectives* (pp. 241–254). London: The Falmer Press.

Kennedy, M. M. (1990). Choosing a goal for professional education. In W. R. Houston (Ed.), *Handbook of research on teacher education* (pp. 813–825). New York: Macmillan.

Kennedy, M. M. (1991, Spring). An agenda for research on teacher learning (NCRTL Special Rep.). East Lansing: National Center for Research on Teacher Learning, Michigan State University.

Kozleski, E. B., Sands, D. J., & French, N. (1993). Preparing special education teachers for urban settings. *Teacher Education and Special Education, 16,* 14–22.

Labov, W. (1972). *Language in the inner city: Studies in the Black English vernacular.* Philadelphia: University of Pennsylvania Press.

Ladson-Billings, G. (1995). Multicultural teacher education: Research, practice, and policy. In J. A. Banks & C. M. Banks (Eds.), *Handbook of research on multicultural education* (pp. 747–759). New York: Macmillan.

Lanier, J. E., & Little, J. W. (1986). Research on teacher education. In M. C. Wittrock (Ed.), *Handbook of research on teaching* (pp. 527–569). New York: Macmillan.

Morine-Dershimer, G. (1993). Tracing conceptual change in preservice teachers. *Teaching and Teacher Education, 9,* 15–26.

Obiakor, F., Patton, J., & Ford, B. (1992). Special issue: Issues in the education of African-American youth in special education settings. *Exceptional Children, 59,* 104–171.

Padilla, A. M. (1994). Ethnic minority scholars, research, and mentoring: Current and future issues. *Educational Researcher, 23*(4), 24–27.

Padilla, A. M., & Lindholm, K. J. (1995). Quantitative educational research with ethnic minorities. In J. A. Banks & C. M. Banks (Eds.), *Handbook of research on multicultural education* (pp. 97–113). New York: Macmillan.

Reynolds, M. C. (1990). Educating teachers for special education students. In W. R. Houston (Ed.), *Handbook of research on teacher education* (pp. 423–436). New York: Macmillan.

Rogoff, B. (1990). *Apprenticeship in thinking: Cognitive development in social contexts.* New York: Oxford University Press.

Rogoff, B., & Morelli, G. (1989). Perspectives on children's development from cultural psychology. *American Psychologist, 44,* 343–348.

Sikula, J., Buttery, T. J., & Guyton, E. (Eds.). (1996). *Handbook of research on teacher education* (2nd ed.). New York: Macmillan.

Sleeter, C. E. (1995). An analysis of the critiques of multicultural education. In J. A. Banks & C. M. Banks (Eds.), *Handbook of research on multicultural education* (pp. 81–94). New York: Macmillan.

Sleeter, C. E., & Grant, C. A. (1987). An analysis of multicultural education in the U.S. *Harvard Educational Review, 57,* 421–444.

Sleeter, C. E., & Grant, C. A. (1994). *Making choices for multicultural education: Five approaches to race, class, and gender* (2nd ed.). Columbus, OH: Merrill.

Solomon, P., & Levine-Rasky, C. (1995, March). *Tensions and contradictions in teachers' responses to antiracist education.* Paper presented at the annual meeting of the American Educational Research Association, San Francisco, CA.

Spencer, M. B., & McLoyd, V. C. (Eds.). (1990). [Special issue on minority children]. *Child Development, 61,* 263–589.

Stanfield, J. H. (1993). Epistemological considerations. In J. H. Stanfield & R. M. Dennis (Eds.), *Race and ethnicity in research methods* (pp. 16–36). Newbury Park, CA: Sage.

Stanfield, J. H., & Dennis, R. M. (Eds.). (1993). *Race and ethnicity in research methods.* Newbury Park, CA: Sage.

Stigler, J. W., Shweder, R. A., & Herdt, G. (Eds.). (1990). *Cultural psychology: Essays on comparative human development.* Cambridge, England: Cambridge University Press.

Tharp, R. G. (1989). Psychocultural variables and constants. *American Psychologist, 44,* 349–359.

Trent, S. C., & Artiles, A. J. (1995). Serving culturally diverse students with behavior disorders: Broadening current perspectives. In J. M. Kauffman, J. W. Lloyd, T. A, Astuto, & D. P. Hallahan (Eds.), *Issues in the educational placement of pupils with emotional or behavioral disorders* (pp. 215–249). Hillsdale, NJ: Lawrence Erlbaum Associates.

Trent, S. C., Pernell, E., & Stephens, K. (1995, April). *Preservice teachers' beliefs about teaching culturally and linguistically diverse exceptional learners.* Paper presented at the annual meeting of the Council for Exceptional Children, Indianapolis, IN.

Weisner, T. S., Gallimore, R., & Jordan, C. (1988). Unpackaging cultural effects on classroom learning: Native Hawaiian peer assistance and child-generated activity. *Anthropology & Education Quarterly, 19,* 327–351.

Wells, A. S., Hirshberg, D., Lipton, M., & Oakes, J. (1995). Bounding the case within its context: A constructivist approach to studying detracking reform. *Educational Researcher, 24*(5), 18–24.

Wideen, M. F., & Tisher, R. P. (1990). The role played by research in teacher education. In R. P. Tisher & M. F. Wideen (Eds.), *Research in teacher education: International perspectives* (pp. 1–10). London: The Falmer Press.

Yarger, S. J., & Smith, P. L. (1990). Issues in research on teacher education. In W. R. Houston (Ed.), *Handbook of research on teacher education* (pp. 25–41). New York: Macmillan.

Zabel, R. H., & White, W. J. (1988). Demographic characteristics of special education teacher educators. *Teacher Education and Special Education, 11,* 111–122.

Zeichner, K. M. (1993, February). *Educating teachers for cultural diversity* (NCRTL Special Rep.). East Lansing: National Center for Research on Teacher Learning, Michigan State University.

Zimpher, N. L., & Howey, K. R. (1990). Scholarly inquiry into teacher education in the United States. In R. P. Tisher & M. F. Wideen (Eds.), *Research in teacher education: International perspectives* (pp. 163–190). London: The Falmer Press.

15

ANTISOCIAL GIRLS AND THE DEVELOPMENT OF DISRUPTIVE BEHAVIOR DISORDERS

Elizabeth Talbott
University of Illinois at Chicago

Kevin Callahan
University of North Texas

Boys dominate classes for students with emotional and behavioral disorders (Callahan, 1994), referrals for mental health services (Achenbach & Edelbrock, 1981), and arrests for violent crime (Chesney-Lind & Shelden, 1992). However, girls' disruptive behavior disorders are as disturbing to parents as the disorders of boys (Moore & Mukai, 1983), and their disorders are more likely than boys' to co-occur with depression, anxiety, and delinquency during adolescence (Loeber & Keenan, 1994). Furthermore, girls with a history of disruptive behavior disorders during childhood are more likely than girls without such a history to experience early sexuality and pregnancy, school dropout, and substance use during adolescence (Cairns & Cairns, 1994; Serbin, Peters, McAffer, & Schwartzman, 1991). Disruptive behavior disorders (i.e., conduct disorder and oppositional defiant disorder, according to the *DSM–IV*), are the second most common of the psychiatric disorders that girls experience (American Psychiatric Association, 1994; Zoccolillo, 1993). To prevent disruptive behavior disorders and their comorbid problems from continuing through adolescence, it is best to identify and treat them early in the course of their development. However, girls' disruptive behavior disorders may not be easily identified in childhood and they do not proceed as clearly as the behavior disorders of boys. In this chapter, we address critical issues in the study of girls' disruptive behavior disorders across and within developmental periods. These issues include measurement, prediction, and comorbidity.

CRITICAL ISSUES IN THE DEVELOPMENTAL STUDY OF ANTISOCIAL GIRLS

In order to understand the nature of disruptive behavior disorders among girls in the population, researchers must measure the characteristics of girls as accurately and reliably as possible (Buka & Lipsitt, 1994). Applying accurate measurement tools, researchers can establish continuity in behavior disorders across developmental periods (childhood, early adolescence, and adolescence). Researchers have studied community and clinical samples to understand the behavior disorders of girls and have employed developmental (i.e., longitudinal follow-up and cross-sectional cohort designs) and nondevelopmental designs to establish continuity. It is from a large and diverse body of literature that we draw conclusions and hypotheses about the progression of disruptive behavior disorders in girls.

Studies of representative community samples provide estimates of the prevalence and course of disruptive behavior disorders within the general population, facilitate generalizability of findings, and lead researchers to identify antecendents of disorders so as to prevent them (Buka & Lipsitt, 1994; Verhulst & Koot, 1991). Studies of clinical samples yield a rich understanding of girls' behavior disorders, and drive researchers to develop hypotheses that can be tested in large community samples. It is from studies of these two types of samples that we identify the critical issues facing researchers who study girls' disruptive behavior disorders: measurement, prediction, and comorbidity.

Measurement issues pervade the study of disruptive behavior disorders, particularly in the study of girls. Valid, reliable, and diverse measurement techniques are critical to describing and predicting behavior disorders across developmental periods. Measurement and prediction are intricately related. In order to predict which members of the population are at risk for developing a disorder, one must be able to accurately measure the disorder (Buka & Lipsitt, 1994). The use of multiple methods is required to measure and predict the disruptive behavior disorders of girls. Measurement and prediction are complicated by the fact that comorbid problems (e.g., depression, anxiety, and delinquency) often occur with disruptive behavior disorders in girls.

Measurement of Disruptive Behavior Disorders

Measurement is a central and pervasive issue in the study of any disorder, and in the study of the disruptive behavior disorders of girls, researchers have not agreed about what they are attempting to measure. Zoccolillo (1993) claimed that researchers should measure aggression in females that is comparable to aggression in males. However, Zahn-Waxler (1993) objected to this view of girls as "miniature males" and argued that conduct problems for girls are qualitatively different from those for boys. Cairns and Cairns (1994) argued that aggression in girls both resembles and differs from that in boys.

The longitudinal work of Cairns and Cairns (1994) shows that, for a subset of girls, disruptive behavior disorders are not significantly different from those of boys. Girls and boys whom they identified in elementary school as aggressive did not differ from each other in terms of frequency or severity of hostile exchanges. However, by seventh grade the nature of aggressive acts between girls had changed, from the physical and verbal acts of childhood to nonphysical acts of social ostracism that characterized adolescence. The nature of aggressive acts between boys at seventh grade persisted in the same style as fourth grade. Although aggression between young adolescent girls differed from that between young adolescent boys, it was no less hurtful or hostile. It appears that the aggressive and disruptive behavior of girls is both similar and different from that of boys, depending on the developmental period during which it is measured.

The study of girls' disruptive behavior has included three types of assessment: observations of girls at school and at home prior to adolescence; observations of structured family interactions during adolescence; and the ratings of parents, teachers, peers, and girls themselves across development. Observations conducted in natural settings or during structured family activities provide a description of girls' problems in the context of family relationships and are particularly enlightening when paired with raters' views. Although raters are not likely to agree about the characteristics of children's problems, different raters provide a view of girls' functioning in different contexts (Achenbach, McConaughy, & Howell, 1987). Additional records must be collected to aid in the description and prediction of girls' disruptive behavior disorders across developmental periods. These include records of girls' contact with schools and courts and histories of the relationships (e.g., with family and friends) that they develop over time (Cairns & Cairns, 1994). The collection of such diverse records can help to depict change and continuity in aggression and disruptive behavior over time (Buka & Lipsitt, 1994).

Prediction of Disruptive Behavior Disorders

To develop an understanding of girls' disruptive behavior disorders, one must be able to describe and predict their problems across development. Researchers can predict delinquency in adolescence for highly aggressive boys as early as age 8 (Walker, Colvin, & Ramsey, 1995), but they cannot do the same for highly aggressive girls. The aggressive and disruptive behavior of boys during childhood (e.g., fighting, vandalism) occurs at relatively high rates and resembles their delinquent activities in adolescence (e.g., vandalism, theft, violent crime; Chesney-Lind & Shelden, 1992). In contrast, the aggressive and disruptive behavior of girls during childhood and early adolescence (e.g., verbal, physical, and social aggression) does not resemble their delinquent activities during adolescence (e.g., drug and alcohol use, running away, and early sexual activity). Tremblay et al. (1992) found that girls who were considered by their female peers to be disruptive during first grade were not necessarily the same girls who reported delinquent behavior at age 14 (whereas such had been the case for boys); Stattin and Magnusson (1989) found that girls who were considered by their teachers to be aggressive at age 10 were not necessarily more likely than girls who were not aggressive at 10 to commit crimes during adulthood (but such had been the case for boys). Girls' aggressive activities are difficult to describe and detect across the course of development.

Likewise, in the study of boys' disruptive behavior the reports of single raters (either teachers or parents) have been adequate predictors of delinquency, aggression, and mental health problems (i.e., Stattin & Magnusson, 1989; Tremblay et al., 1992; Verhulst, Koot, & Van der Ende, 1994); however, the same has not been true for girls. More than one rater is required to predict the adolescent experiences of antisocial girls. Parent and teacher reports together improved the prediction of mental health referrals, academic and behavior problems at school, police contact and suicide attempts for girls by 42% over parent reports alone and 37% over teacher reports alone. In contrast, prediction for boys improved 11% over parent reports alone and 9% over teacher reports alone (Verhulst et al., 1994).

Comorbidity With Other Disorders

To further complicate measurement and prediction, girls who engage in disruptive behavior may be more likely than boys to have comorbid problems (Loeber & Keenan, 1994). "Once girls qualify for a disruptive behavior disorder they have a higher probability of incurring other disorders than do disruptive boys . . . the risk for developing comorbid conditions is higher in girls than in boys" (p. 500). Loeber and Keenan grounded this assumption in the theory of gender paradox, wherein fewer females are identified with disruptive behavior disorders, but their disorders are more severe than males (Eme, 1992). Although this theory does not yet have substantial empirical support, there is empirical support for comorbidity of disruptive behavior disorders with anxiety, depression, and delinquency. Comorbidity of these disorders can begin during childhood, with conduct disorders and depression in a community sample of fourth graders co-occurring twice as often as expected (Cole & Carpentieri, 1990). During adolescence, disruptive behavior disorders of girls co-occur with anxiety disorders, depression, and delinquency (Bowen, Offord, & Boyle, 1990), making girls' adjustment to an independent and autonomous adulthood a difficult one (Joffe, Offord, & Boyle, 1988).

Measurement issues pervade the study of comorbid problems, making use of multiple raters and methods critical throughout development. When researchers use a single method to assess two or more disorders, the comorbidity of symptoms is due in part to the use of only one method (Cole & Carpentieri, 1990). The use of multiple methods is critical to untangling the contributions of multiple problems to outcomes for girls.

DISRUPTIVE BEHAVIOR DISORDERS
ACROSS DEVELOPMENTAL PERIODS

Longitudinal, prospective research has identified two types of disruptive behavior disorders: those that persist across developmental periods and those that are limited to adolescence (Moffitt, 1993). For girls who experience the effects of disruptive behavior disorders throughout development, childhood consists of physical and verbal aggression that rivals that of boys; adolescence yields delinquent activities and comorbid problems; and adulthood consists of unsuccessful marriages, failed employment, and poor parenting skills. For the life-course persistent antisocial group of girls, it is plausible to map the course of their disorders so as to predict and prevent the effects of disruptive behavior disorders.

The second type of disruptive behavior disorders is present only during adolescence. During this period, girls engage in delinquent activities without having had a prior history and without maintaining a pattern of antisocial behavior. Those for whom antisocial behavior is limited to adolescence are vulnerable because their delinquent activities put them at risk for disease, death, or arrests (e.g., early sexual activity results in sexually transmitted diseases or pregnancy; driving while intoxicated results in accidents or death; and stealing or taking drugs results in arrests). Nearly all adolescents engage in some form of delinquent activities (Moffitt, 1993); therefore, the adolescence-limited group of antisocial girls is more diverse than those who persist in antisocial acts throughout the life course.

The studies that we review in the subsequent sections have generated findings about the characteristics of girls' disruptive behavior disorders across and within developmental periods. They yield a rich description of girls who have been identified with these disorders and girls who have not been identified. From these studies of clinical and community samples, we generate hypotheses about the characteristics of girls with disruptive behavior disorders that persist throughout life and the characteristics of those disorders that are limited to adolescence. We begin by reviewing studies of these disorders within the developmental periods of childhood, transition between childhood and adolescence, and adolescence.

Childhood

During childhood, the characteristics of girls with disruptive behavior disorders do not differ significantly from the characteristics of boys. Epstein and colleagues found that special education teachers rated 6–11-year-old girls with behavior disorders as being equally aggressive and disruptive as young boys (Epstein, Kauffman, & Cullinan, 1985). Likewise, 7–10-year-old girls with behavior disorders in special education classes have received their highest scores from teachers who taught students with conduct problems. Fights, disruptions, temper tantrums, disobedience, and arguments were more common among the girls in this sample than were personality problems, immaturity, or delinquency (Cullinan, Epstein, Cole, & Dembinski, 1985). These studies explored the views of teachers about girls from clinical samples; others have explored the characteristics of young girls with conduct disorders in the context of family relationships.

O'Leary and colleagues (Emery & O'Leary, 1982; Johnson & O'Leary, 1987) used multiple methods to describe the characteristics and family relationships of 10-year-old girls in a clinical sample. Parents' ratings of girls' conduct problems were significantly correlated with girls' feelings of nonacceptance by their parents (Emery & O'Leary, 1982); mothers of girls with conduct disorders were significantly more hostile to their spouses than were mothers of girls without conduct disorders (Johnson & O'Leary, 1987). Although parents of girls with conduct disorders rated their daughters as more aggressive than did parents of girls without conduct disorders, parents of girls in both groups rated their daughters as equally skilled in social competence. Children with disruptive behavior disorders evoked negative responses from members of their families (Caspi, Elder, & Bem, 1987), but parents in these studies of preadolescents continued to see their daughters possessing social competence skills.

Moore and Mukai (1983) observed the aggressive behavior of first-grade girls and boys who were referred to clinics by their parents for aggression and disobedience. The children were observed at home; Moore and Mukai recorded the behavior of the aggressive child and the person to whom that behavior was directed. They found that girls and boys did not differ in rates of verbal aggression, passive dependent, or disobedient behavior in the home. Instead, they found that girls referred for clinical services by their parents used verbal aggression, passive dependent, and disobedient behavior at home in nearly the same fashion and at the same rate as boys. Each of these studies (Cullinan et al., 1985; Emery & O'Leary, 1982; Epstein et al., 1985; Johnson & O'Leary, 1987; Moore & Mukai, 1983) has revealed continuity between the disruptive behavior of girls and boys from clinical samples in early childhood, although they did not address comorbidity. Researchers (Lyons, Serbin, & Marchessault, 1988; Mattison, Morales, & Bauer, 1991) have addressed comorbid problems of girls in elementary school by using multiple methods.

Mattison and colleagues obtained information from diverse sources about a sample of elementary school-aged girls who were receiving special education for behavior disorders. They examined girls' educational and family backgrounds, obtained psychiatric interviews with girls and their parents, and obtained teachers' responses to checklists. Mattison and colleagues reported significantly more comorbid problems among girls with behavior disorders in elementary school than among their peers, but did not find the same for girls in secondary school. More than one third of girls in elementary school with behavior disorders had repeated a grade in the past and were receiving additional educational services (i.e., for learning disabilities); 81% of these girls had a history of psychiatric disorder in the family. Depression was the most common disorder among their mothers; substance abuse and antisocial behavior were most common among their fathers (Mattison et al., 1991).

Sixty-three percent of girls in Mattison's elementary sample had more than one psychiatric diagnosis and externalizing disorders were the most common single diagnosis. Teacher ratings also indicated multiple problems, with the average rating for young girls with behavior disorders being two standard deviations above the mean for hyperactivity, conduct disorders, emotional problems, and withdrawal. In this clinical sample, the young girls experienced multiple problems, including diagnosed disorders, disorders among their parents, teacher ratings of significant problems, and the absence of treatment (besides educational treatment) for their problems (Mattison et al., 1991).

Lyons et al. (1988) also examined comorbid problems in a community sample of young girls and boys who had been identified by their same-gender peers as either aggressive, withdrawn, or aggressive and withdrawn. Lyons and colleagues found that girls and boys in the aggressive group were active and involved in social interaction, physical contact, and physical activity on the playground. Aggressive girls initiated nonaggressive touching and aggressive acts toward peers at high rates and were more likely than girls in any other group to retaliate when their peers initiated aggressive acts. Girls in the aggressive group were the targets of about half as many aggressive acts as they initiated toward others; girls in the aggressive and withdrawn group appeared to be their victims. In fact, aggressive and withdrawn girls received almost twice as many aggressive acts as they initiated. Girls in the control group were ignored when they aggressed against peers, whereas girls who were considered deviant by their peers (aggressive or withdrawn or both) were as likely as deviant boys to be involved in aggressive acts, either as victims or as perpetrators.

From the research we have reviewed here, we can hypothesize about the continuity between girls' and boys' disruptive behavior disorders in early childhood. Girls and boys from clinical samples are equally likely to exhibit disruptive behavior, and if they have comorbid problems, are frequently the recipients of aggressive acts. However, the disruptive behavior disorders of girls in early childhood also differ from those of boys, as Cairns and Cairns (1984) demonstrated with data obtained (individual interviews, teacher ratings, and peer nominations) for students from a community sample of fourth and fifth graders and for a subgroup of highly aggressive students within that sample.

Cairns and Cairns obtained perfect prediction of teacher and peer ratings for the subgroup of highly aggressive girls from fourth to fifth grade. This group of aggressive girls was distinctly different from unselected girls; their behavior was stable over time and, unlike aggressive boys, they did not lose their aggressive status over time. Two groups of girls were present in this community sample. One was highly aggressive, with characteristics that were disturbing to teachers and principals who nominated them. The remaining unselected girls engaged in social and verbal aggression that they themselves considered more disturbing than did their teachers (Cairns & Cairns, 1984). Girls reported that they ignored the provocations of other girls, only to retaliate later using means that were not physical. The aggression of girls in late childhood appeared to be subtle, social, and verbal.

Transition Between Childhood and Adolescence

During the transition between childhood and adolescence, more and more youth from nonclinical samples engage in predelinquent and delinquent activities. For girls from community samples, there are distinct changes in types of conflict that occur during this period of development (i.e., from fourth to seventh grade). Gradually, conflicts become less overt and more covert: aggression between girls changes from physical to verbal and includes active rejection from a group, slander and defamation of others' reputation by gossip, and alienation of affection (Cairns, Cairns, Neckerman, Ferguson, & Gariepy, 1989). Measurement issues are paramount during this period of development, as observations in natural settings become difficult to employ and interviews with girls, parents, and teachers become particularly useful. In this section, we examine issues that affect girls' disruptive behavior disorders at the transition between childhood and adolescence.

Cairns et al. (1989) followed girls and boys whom they had tested in fourth grade in a previous study (Cairns & Cairns, 1984). They conducted interviews with teachers and students and obtained peer and school nominations for aggression. From the interviews, researchers obtained information about aggressive interactions between girls, identifying peers with whom they had experienced conflict, and naming troublemakers. Cairns and colleagues found from their interviews that girls from the community sample showed a developmental decrease in statements about physical aggression. In fourth grade, 10% of girls reported themes of social alienation and ostracism; by seventh grade over one third of the conflicts among girls involved manipulation of group acceptance through alienation, ostracism, or character defamation. This type of aggression was rarely mentioned by boys (Cairns et al., 1989).

Cairns and colleagues found that the proportion of girls rated with extreme aggression scores was the same as the proportion of boys with extreme scores. Over time, however, the proportion of boys—not girls—with extreme scores diminished. They also found that for boys there was a single aggressive factor that remained stable across the developmental transition. For girls, the factor structure changed from fourth to seventh grade, from a single aggressive factor similar to boys' in fourth grade, to two factors in seventh grade. The second factor included self-reports of social alienation in conflicts with other girls. Social alienation (i.e., active rejection of persons from a clique, slander and defamation of reputation by gossip, and alienation of affection) emerged as a distinct theme.

Clearly, a proportion of girls experience social aggression during the transition from childhood to adolescence. Certain girls are more vulnerable to aggressive social attacks than others. The data reported by Lyons and colleagues indicate that girls with comorbid problems (i.e., aggression and withdrawal) are especially vulnerable. French's (1990) data indicate that withdrawn girls may be most vulnerable. Aggressive girls and girls with comorbid problems are vulnerable to peer rejection, a characteristic that is central to the lives of antisocial boys (Walker et al., 1995). The transition between childhood and adolescence appears to be an important developmental period for prediction and prevention of disorders. For the life-course persistent antisocial girls, this transition may mark the time that their problems become worse, and for the adolescence-limited antisocial girls, this transition may mark the time that their problems emerge.

Gillmore et al. (1991) found that a three-factor model (school troubles, delinquency, and substance use) best fit the data for preadolescent girls from a community sample. School troubles were measured by teacher reports of aggression and acting out and self-reports of getting in trouble at school. Delinquency was measured by self-report and was categorized in three types: (a) breaking and entering, fights, and assault; (b) throwing objects and shoplifting; and (c) stealing and vandalism. In validation of girls' reports, teacher ratings of aggression and acting out were significantly correlated with girls' reports of two of three types of delinquency (breaking and entering, assaults, and fights; throwing objects and shoplifting) and smoking. Continuity between behavior of girls from community and clinical samples occurs during the transition to adolescence, with Cullinan and colleagues finding no significant differences between preadolescent girls with and without behavior disorders on teacher measures of delinquency (Cullinan et al., 1985).

Adolescence

Adolescence is the period during which delinquent activities peak because of the behavior of two groups of teens: one that has engaged in antisocial acts throughout life, and another that engages in antisocial acts just during adolescence (Moffitt, 1993). Conflict and alienation are part of the interactions that occur in families of adolescents (Steinberg, 1981); the role of family members in their interactions with troubled girls has been explored by Kavanaugh and Hops (1994) and by Henggeler and colleagues (Henggeler, Edwards, & Borduin, 1987). Other researchers have explored the prevalence of social impairments and comorbid problems in community samples of adolescent girls (i.e., Offord, Boyle, & Racine, 1991; Sanford, Offord, Boyle, Peace, & Racine, 1992). In this section we examine the results of those studies and their contributions to the understanding of disruptive behavior disorders during adolescence.

Kavanaugh and Hops (1994) observed the family interactions of adolescent girls from a clinical sample during a structured problem-solving activity. They obtained scores for negative engagement (negative verbal behavior, verbal attack, coercion, negative physical acts, statements with negative affect) and positive engagement (positive verbal behavior, statements of endearment, requests, positive touch, statements with positive affect) from these interactions, as well as parent, teacher, and youth reports of problem behavior. Teachers identified girls from this sample as high on the measure of delinquency. Girls' and teachers' reports of problems were significantly and negatively correlated with girls' positive interactions with their parents, meaning that the absence of positive engagement in family interactions was more of a problem for girls and their teachers than the presence of negative engagement.

The presence of conflict was a distinct problem for families with delinquent daughters in a study conducted by Henggeler and colleagues. In observations of structured family problem-solving activities, they found that mother–daughter dyads in families with delinquent girls had higher rates of conflict than mother–son dyads, and that parents of female delinquents had higher rates of conflict among themselves than did parents of male delinquents (Henggeler et al., 1987). Henggeler's conclusion was that family relations were highly disturbed to support the presence of delinquency in daughters. Perhaps families were reacting to the severity of disorders in daughters.

Studies of preadolescent girls with conduct disorders have supported high levels of conflict in their families (Emery & O'Leary, 1982; Johnson & O'Leary, 1987), and for preadolescent girls who attained low status among their peers, severity of family disturbance was the best single predictor of delinquency (Roff & Wirt, 1984). In one community sample (Ontario Child Health Study), adolescent girls reported higher rates of impairment in social relationships (frequent or constant problems in getting along) than in academic functioning (Sanford et al., 1992). In a separate community sample, marital discord, recent separation, and living in a single-parent home amplified female delinquency (Dornfeld & Kruttschnitt, 1992). It could be that deterioration in family relations are distinct signs of vulnerability for adolescent girls, and that families suffer from the absence of positive, facilitative interactions with their daughters. Certainly children's behavior disorders evoke aversive responses from family members (Caspi et al., 1987). If girls experience comorbid problems at the same time that their facilitative and positive interactions in the family decline, the frequency of negative family interactions can only increase.

Anxiety, depression, and delinquency have been found to occur with disruptive behavior disorders for girls during adolescence. In the Ontario Child Health Study, the highest rate of comorbidity for individuals with conduct disorders was for adolescent girls, who had comorbid emotional disorders (Offord et al., 1991). Anxiety disorders have been diagnosed more frequently in females than in males from clinical and community samples (American Psychiatric Association, 1994). In a clinical school sample, Epstein et al. (1985) found that teacher ratings of aggression and disruption had a strong anxiety component (including tension, nervousness, and crying over minor annoyances); Zoccolillo and Rogers (1991) found that anxiety and phobias occured in more than half of their sample of adolescent girls with conduct disorders; and Myers, Burket, Lyles, Stone, and Kemph (1990) found that nearly half of the adolescents from a clinical sample of delinquent girls met the criteria for anxiety disorder. In a community sample, Anderson, Williams, and Silva (1987) found that conduct disorders and anxiety co-occurred at greater-than-chance levels for adolescent girls, and researchers with the Ontario Child Health Study found that nearly half of adolescent girls with conduct disorder also met criteria for anxiety disorders (Bowen et al., 1990). Because adolescent girls are at higher risk for anxiety disorders than are adolescent boys, they are at higher risk for comorbid anxiety disorders (Loeber & Keenan, 1994).

Such could also be the case for depression. During adolescence, girls are more likely to be depressed than boys (Rutter, 1988). In clinical samples of adolesent girls with conduct disorders, major depression affected one third of the sample in one study (Zoccolillo & Rogers, 1991) and half of a clinical sample of adolescent girls with behavior disorders in a school setting in another study (Mattison et al., 1991). In the community sample assessed by researchers in the Ontario Child Health Study, one third of preadolescent girls with conduct disorders had comorbid emotional disorders, and nearly half of adolescent girls with conduct disorders had emotional disorders (Offord, Alder, & Boyle, 1986). Girls with conduct disorders may be particularly vulnerable to experiencing suicidal ideation and attempting suicide. Joffe et al. (1988) reported that girls with conduct disorders were significantly more likely than boys with conduct disorders to consider and attempt suicide. Kashani, Goddard, and Reid (1989) reported higher rates of distress in families with suicidal girls than in families with suicidal boys; antisocial acts were displayed by 14% of girls who had committed suicidal acts.

Delinquency occurs for girls from clinical samples in the context of ongoing disruptive behavior disorders; for girls from community samples, delinquency emerges without the context of previous disruptive behavior disorders (Loeber & Keenan, 1994). Zoccolillo and Rogers (1991) found that half of adolescent girls with conduct disorders had been arrested within 2–4 years after their psychiatric hospitalization and nearly half had run away from home. Girls in the Zoccolillo and Rogers study had demonstrated high frequencies of disruptive behavior and delinquency, including chronic lying, violations of rules, fighting, drunkenness or substance abuse, running away, prostitution, truancy, and vandalism. Adolescent girls from community samples report engaging in delinquent activities and substance use with greater frequency than their parents report (Chesney-Lind & Shelden, 1992). For example, girls in community samples report using alcohol, drugs, and tobacco during early adolescence (Gillmore et al., 1991). For a sample of girls in special education classes with behavior disorders, teachers reported no significant difference between adolescents with behavior disorders and their peers with regard to delinquent activities (Cullinan et al., 1985).

Although the delinquent activities reported by adolescent girls from clinical and community samples are similar, girls with a history of disruptive behavior disorders are significantly more likely than girls without such a history to associate with delinquent peers and engage in delinquent acts by age 13 (Caspi, Lynam, Moffitt, & Silva, 1993). Thus, girls from clinical samples may be vulnerable at young ages to engage in risky delinquent activities with older and experienced peers. Young girls may not be emotionally or psychologically prepared to engage in the common delinquent acts of adolescence. For example, young adolescents are less likely than older adolescents to use birth control when they have sex, and more likely than older adolescents to use alcohol or drugs when doing so (Zabin & Hayward, 1993). For the life-course persistent antisocial girls, it will be critical to identify their problems early to prevent their engagement in delinquent acts with older peers.

SUMMARY OF THE CRITICAL ISSUES

Measurement, prediction, and comorbidity are the critical issues that we have identified in the study of the disruptive behavior disorders of girls. Measurement is central among these issues and pervades prediction and comorbidity. Valid, reliable, and diverse measurement techniques are critical to predicting behavior disorders across developmental periods and teasing out the influence of other disorders. The difficulty in capturing girls' disruptive behavior disorders appears to occur during the transition between childhood and adolescence, when the nature of aggression between girls changes. At that point in development, teacher and parent ratings and observational data may no longer be as sensitive at capturing aggressive exchanges as they were during childhood. Researchers may continue to collect data from teachers and parents and by observation, but they must add interviews with adolescents themselves to capture the content of their aggressive exchanges (i.e., Cairns & Cairns, 1994). Each of these kinds of data must be collected prospectively from representative samples of girls, so that researchers can ascertain the course of disruptive behavior disorders across developmental periods (Buka & Lipsitt, 1994). Furthermore, antisocial activities must be assessed repeatedly from childhood through adolescence to capture stability and change over time (Moffitt, 1993). Only by using such rigorous longitudinal and prospective research designs can researchers establish a model for the development of antisocial behavior in girls.

Although the prediction of disruptive behavior disorders across development is most enhanced by the study of representative samples of girls, studies of girls from clinical samples are required to understand the nature of disorders among members of the population who already experience them, and to develop hypotheses about these disorders as they occur in the general population. Members of the clinical population may represent the life-course persistent antisocial girls. The study of clinical samples is relevant to understanding antisocial acts and their persistence among members of a most troubled group.

Researchers have begun to establish continuity across developmental periods in the disruptive behavior of girls from clinical samples. Morris, Escoll, and Wexler (1956) correctly predicted that girls who had experienced aggressive behavior disorders during childhood (i.e., truancy, stealing, lying, cruelty, disobedience, restlessness, destruction, and tantrums) would later experience adjustment problems as adults, and Robins (1966) identified theft and sexual problems as effective predictors of poor adult adjustment for girls from a psychiatric sample. Cairns and Cairns (1994) identified highly aggressive girls as having been rejected by their non-aggressive peers, experiencing lower academic competence, and developing friendships with other aggressive peers during childhood. As adolescents and adults, these highly aggressive girls dropped out of school, became teenage mothers, abused substances, and had encounters with the criminal justice system (Cairns & Cairns, 1994). The clinical population of girls is likely to experience multiple problems in adulthood and is worthy of study in its own right.

Comorbid psychological problems are more common for life-course persistent antisocial girls than for adolescence-limited antisocial girls (Moffitt, 1993). The assessment of comorbid problems must be advanced and applied across developmental periods. Weiss and Catron (1994) have found support for comorbid relationships between the broad-band externalizing and internalizing disorders rather than between the narrow-band disorders (i.e., aggression and depression). If such is the case, then prediction of comorbid problems at the broad-band level should be more successful than prediction of narrow-band problems across development. As accurate and reliable measurement of disruptive behavior disorders improves, so should the measurement and prediction of comorbid problems. Each of the critical issues—measurement, prediction, and comorbidity—must be addressed as part of the establishment of a theoretical model to explain the developmental course of girls' disruptive behavior disorders.

DISCUSSION

There are not yet theoretical models to describe the developmental course of disruptive behavior disorders and delinquency for the two groups of girls. The continuity of disruptive behavior disorders as they are observed in diverse antisocial acts across developmental periods needs to be established for girls. Models for the life-course persistent and adolescence-limited antisocial girls can be developed independently and integrated later. One model would describe the development of girls for whom aggressive behavior is consistent, severe, and stable (Cairns & Cairns, 1994; Cairns et al., 1989). A second model would describe the development of girls who become delinquent during adolescence without a previous or subsequent history of disruptive behavior disorders (Moffitt, 1993). After the independent models are developed, the two models can be integrated.

Social aggression as defined by Cairns and colleagues (i.e., manipulation of group acceptance through alienation, ostracism, or character defamation) is one of the variables that may link the two models. Researchers can develop hypotheses from interviews with girls about how social aggression operates and address the following research questions. Do the same groups of adolescent girls persist in this type of aggression throughout development? Are girls with certain characteristics (i.e., comorbid problems) singled out for alienation? Who are the aggressors (i.e., girls with disruptive behavior disorders?), and what are the long-term effects for them and for their victims? Are the victims of social aggression likely to develop comorbid problems with anxiety and depression during adolescence? These are the types of questions that need to be addressed about social aggression in ongoing longitudinal research.

Delinquency is another variable that links the two groups of girls. How are individuals initiated in delinquent acts and what are the characteristics of girls that place them at risk for engaging in early delinquent acts? The work of Caspi and colleagues indicates that a history of externalizing behavior disorders and an association with older peers places some girls at risk (Caspi et al., 1993); the work of Stattin and Magnusson (1990) indicates that girls from community samples who develop early and associate with delinquent peers may also be at risk. Clearly, the assessment of social aggression and early delinquency will require the development of new measures, drawn from interviews with girls regarding social networks, characteristics of conflict, delinquent activities, and timing of pubertal development. Once researchers develop independent models of disruptive behavior and delinquency for the two groups of girls, a single model can be tested with a large and diverse community sample, collecting data over the life course. Researchers must also assess multiple components of an antisocial lifestyle during adulthood, including characteristics of family violence (are antisocial girls the victims of spousal abuse?) and child maltreatment (are antisocial mothers the aggressors?).

Much has been written about the deleterious effects of antisocial boys' behavior over the long term, but few researchers have discussed the long-term effects of the behavior of antisocial girls. However, Serbin and colleagues found that girls who had been aggressive during childhood were more likely than girls who had not been aggressive to experience gynecological problems, sexually transmitted diseases, and pregnancy during adolescence (Serbin et al., 1991). Having had a history of childhood aggression was a predictor of unresponsive parenting on the part of adolescent mothers. That unresponsive parenting contributed to developmental delays for offspring. Furthermore, the behavior problems of children have been positively correlated with their mothers' nondrug offenses, such as assault, shoplifting, fraud, theft, and vandalism (Martin & Burchinal, 1992). Girls with a history of aggression are more likely than their nonaggressive peers to have children when they are young, to persist in antisocial acts, and to demonstrate poor parenting skills. The most deleterious long-term effects of antisocial girls' disruptive behavior is in their parenting. Antisocial girls who become adolescent mothers contribute to the development of antisocial behavior in their offspring.

Researchers can begin to identify the markers of girls at risk only if they describe and measure antisocial behavior in its diverse forms across the life span and identify change and continuity in antisocial acts. The results of these efforts can contribute to the establishment of effective interventions for girls. The development of treatment for antisocial children in the context of their families, schools, and neighborhoods should also be an integral part of establishing a theoretical model to explain the developmental course of disruptive behavior disorders in girls.

REFERENCES

Achenbach, T. M., & Edelbrock, C. S. (1981). Behavioral problems and competencies reported by parents of normal and disturbed children aged four to sixteen. *Monographs of the Society for Research in Child Development, 46* (1, Serial No. 188).

Achenbach, T. M., McConaughy, S. H., & Howell, C. T. (1987). Child/adolescent behavioral and emotional problems: Implications of cross-informant correlations for situational specificity. *Psychological Bulletin, 101*, 213–232.

American Psychiatric Association (1994). *Diagnostic and statistical manual of mental disorders* (4th ed.). Washington, DC: Author.

Anderson, J. C., Williams, S., & Silva, P. A. (1987). *DSM–III* disorders in preadolescent children. *Archives of General Psychiatry, 44*, 69–76.

Bowen, R. C., Offord, D. R., & Boyle, M. H. (1990). The prevalence of overanxious disorder and separation anxiety disorder—results from the Ontario Child Health Study. *Journal of the American Academy of Child and Adolescent Psychiatry, 29*, 753–758.

Buka, S. L., & Lipsitt, L. P. (1994). Toward a developmental epidemiology. In S. L. Friedman & H. C. Haywood (Eds.), *Developmental follow-up: Concepts, domains, and methods* (pp. 331–350). San Diego: Academic Press.

Cairns, R. B., & Cairns, B. D. (1984). Predicting aggressive patterns in girls and boys: A developmental study. *Aggressive Behavior, 10*, 227–242.

Cairns, R. B., & Cairns, B. D. (1994). *Lifelines and risks: Pathways of youth in our time.* New York: Cambridge University Press.

Cairns, R. B., Cairns, B. D., Neckerman, H. J., Ferguson, L. L., & Gariepy, J. L. (1989). Growth and aggression: I. Childhood to early adolescence. *Developmental Psychology, 25*, 320–330.

Callahan, K. (1994). Wherefore art thou, Juliet? Causes and implications of the male-dominated sex ratio in programs for students with emotional and behavioral disorders. *Education and Treatment of Children, 17*, 228–243.

Caspi, A., Elder, G. H., & Bem, D. J. (1987). Moving against the world: Life-course patterns of explosive children. *Developmental Psychology, 23*, 308–313.

Caspi, A., Lynam, D., Moffitt, T. E., & Silva, P. A. (1993). Unraveling girls' delinquency: Biological, dispositional, and contextual contributions to adolescent misbehavior. *Developmental Psychology, 29*, 19–30.

Chesney-Lind, M., & Shelden, R. G. (1992). *Girls, delinquency, and juvenile justice.* Monterey, CA: Brooks/Cole.

Cole, D. A., & Carpentieri, S. (1990). Social status and the comorbidity of child depression and conduct disorder. *Journal of Consulting and Clinical Psychology, 58*, 748–757.

Cullinan, D., Epstein, M. H., Cole, K., & Dembinski, R. (1985). School behavior problems of behaviorally disordered and nonhandicapped girls. *Journal of Clinical Child Psychology, 14*, 162–164.

Dornfeld, M., & Kruttschnitt, C. (1992). Do the stereotypes fit? Mapping gender-specific outcomes and risk factors. *Criminology, 30*, 397–418.

Eme, R. F. (1992). Selective female affliction in the developmental disorders of childhood: A literature review. *Journal of Clinical Child Psychology, 21,* 354–364.

Emery, R. E., & O'Leary, K. D. (1982). Children's perceptions of marital discord and behavior problems of girls and boys. *Journal of Abnormal Child Psychology, 10,* 11–24.

Epstein, M. H., Kauffman, J. M., & Cullinan, D. (1985). Patterns of maladjustment among the behaviorally disordered. II: Boys aged 6–11, boys aged 12–18, girls aged 6–11, and girls aged 12–18. *Behavioral Disorders, 10,* 125–135.

French, D. C. (1990). Heterogeneity of peer-rejected girls. *Child Development, 61,* 2028–2031.

Gillmore, M. R., Hawkins, J. D., Catalano, R. F., Day, L. E., Moore, M., & Abbott, R. (1991). Structure of problem behaviors in preadolescence. *Journal of Consulting and Clinical Psychology, 59,* 499–506.

Henggeler, S. W., Edwards, J., & Borduin, C. M. (1987). The family relations of female juvenile delinquents. *Journal of Abnormal Child Psychology, 15,* 199–209.

Joffe, R. T., Offord, D. R., & Boyle, M. H. (1988). Ontario child health study: Suicidal behavior in youth age 12–16 years. *American Journal of Psychiatry, 145,* 1420–1423.

Johnson, P. L., & O'Leary, K. D. (1987). Parental behavior patterns and conduct disorders in girls. *Journal of Abnormal Child Psychology, 15,* 573–581.

Kashani, J. H., Goddard, P., & Reid, J. C. (1989). Correlates of suicidal ideation in a community sample of children and adolescents. *Journal of the American Academy of Child and Adolescent Psychiatry, 28,* 912–917.

Kavanaugh, K., & Hops, H. (1994). Good girls? Bad boys? Gender and development as contexts for diagnosis and treatment. In T. H. Ollendick & R. J. Prinz (Eds.), *Advances in clinical child psychology* (Vol. 16, pp. 45–79). New York: Plenum.

Loeber, R., & Keenan, K. (1994). Interaction between conduct disorder and its comorbid conditions: Effects of age and gender. *Clinical Psychology Review, 14,* 497–523.

Lyons, J., Serbin, L. A., & Marchessault, K. (1988). The social behavior of peer-identified aggressive, withdrawn, and aggressive/withdrawn children. *Journal of Abnormal Child Psychology, 16,* 539–552.

Martin, S. L., & Burchinal, M. R. (1992). Young women's antisocial behavior and the later emotional and behavioral health of their children. *American Journal of Public Health, 82,* 1007–1010.

Mattison, R. E., Morales, J., & Bauer, M. A. (1991). Elementary and secondary socially and/or emotionally disturbed girls: Characteristics and identification. *Journal of School Psychology, 29,* 121–134.

Moffitt, T. E. (1993). Adolescence-limited and life-course persistent antisocial behavior: A developmental taxonomy. *Psychological Review, 100,* 674–701.

Moore, D. R., & Mukai, L. H. (1983). Aggressive behavior in the home as a function of the age and sex of control-problem and normal children. *Journal of Abnormal Child Psychology, 11,* 257–272.

Morris, H. H., Escol, P. J., & Wexler, R. (1956). Aggressive behavior disorders of childhood: A follow-up study. *American Journal of Psychiatry, 112,* 991–997.

Myers, W. C., Burket, R. C., Lyles, B., Stone, L., & Kemph, J. P. (1990). *DSM–III* diagnosis and offenses in committed female delinquents. *Bulletin of the American Academy of Psychiatry Law, 18,* 47–54.

Offord, D. R., Alder, R. J., & Boyle M. H. (1986). Prevalence and sociodemographic correlates of conduct disorder. *American Journal of Social Psychiatry, 4,* 272–278.

Offord, D. R., Boyle, M. H., & Racine, Y. A. (1991). The epidemiology of antisocial behavior in childhood and adolescence. In D. J. Pepler & K. H. Rubin (Eds.), *The development and treatment of childhood aggression* (pp. 31–54). Hillsdale, NJ: Lawrence Erlbaum Associates.

Robins, L. N. (1966). *Deviant children grown up: A sociological and psychiatric study of sociopathic personality.* Baltimore: Williams & Wilkins.

Roff, J. D., & Wirt, D. (1984). Childhood aggression and social adjustment as antecedents of delinquency. *Journal of Abnormal Child Psychology, 12,* 111–126.

Rutter, M. (1988). Epidemiological approaches to developmental psychopathology. *Archives of General Psychiatry, 45*, 486–495.

Sanford, M. N., Offord, D. R., Boyle, M. H., Peace, A., & Racine, Y. A. (1992). Ontario Child Health Study: Social and school impairments in children aged 6 to 16 years. *Journal of the American Academy of Child and Adolescent Psychiatry, 31*, 60–66.

Serbin, L. A., Peters, P. L., McAffer, V. J., & Schwartzman, A. E. (1991). Childhood aggression and withdrawal as predictors of adolescent pregnancy, early parenthood, and environmental risk for the next generation. *Canadian Journal of Behavioural Science, 23*, 318–331.

Stattin, H., & Magnusson, D. (1989). The role of early aggressive behavior in the frequency, seriousness, and types of later crime. *Journal of Consulting and Clinical Psychology, 57*, 710–718.

Stattin, H., & Magnusson, D. (1990). *Pubertal maturation in female development.* Hillsdale, NJ: Lawrence Erlbaum Associates.

Steinberg, L. (1981). Transformations in family relations at puberty. *Developmental Psychology, 17*, 833–840.

Tremblay, R. E., Masse, B., Perron, D., Leblanc, M., Schwartzman, A. E., & Ledingham, J. E. (1992). Early disruptive behavior, poor school achievement, delinquent behavior, and delinquent personality: Longitudinal analyses. *Journal of Consulting and Clinical Psychology, 60*, 64–72.

Verhulst, F. C., & Koot, H. M. (1991). Longitudinal research in child and adolescent psychiatry. *Journal of the American Academy of Child and Adolescent Psychiatry, 30*, 361–368.

Verhulst, F. C., Koot, H. M., & Van der Ende, J. (1994). Differential predictive value of parents' and teachers' reports of children's problem behaviors: A longitudinal study. *Journal of Abnormal Child Psychology, 22*, 531–546.

Walker, H. M., Colvin, G., & Ramsey, E. (1995). *Antisocial behavior in school: Strategies and best practices.* Monterey, CA: Brooks/Cole.

Weiss, B., & Catron, T. (1994). Specificity of the comorbidity of aggression and depression in children. *Journal of Abnormal Child Psychology, 22*, 389–401.

Zahn-Waxler, C. (1993). Warriors and worriers: Gender and psychopathology. *Development and Psychopathology, 5*, 79–89.

Zoccolillo, M. (1993). Gender and the development of conduct disorder. *Development and Psychopathology, 5*, 65–78.

Zoccolillo, M., & Rogers, K. (1991). Characteristics and outcome of hospitalized adolescent girls with conduct disorder. *Journal of the American Academy of Child and Adolescent Psychiatry, 30*, 973–981.

Zabin, L. S., & Hayward, S. C. (1993). *Adolescent sexual behavior and childbearing.* Newbury Park, CA: Sage.

LEGISLATION AND POLICY

A DIVERSITY OF RESTRICTIVE ENVIRONMENTS: PLACEMENT AS A PROBLEM OF SOCIAL ECOLOGY*

James M. Kauffman
Daniel P. Hallahan
University of Virginia

The overriding policy issue in special education in the 1990s has been the assignment of students to a place of schooling. Many special education reformers have centered attention on the least restrictive environment (LRE) provisions of the Individuals with Disabilities Education Act (IDEA), suggesting that the inclusion of all students with disabilities in general education classes in their neighborhood schools—and only such inclusion—will fulfill the letter and spirit of the law (e.g., Gartner & Lipsky, 1989; Laski, 1991; Lipsky & Gartner, 1991; Stainback & Stainback, 1991). Policymakers' enthusiasm for inclusion rhetoric and the assumption that the general education classroom in the neighborhood school is, in fact, least restrictive for all students has resulted in rapid erosion of placement options for students with disabilities, especially those identified in the categories of learning disabilities, emotional and behavioral disorders, and mild mental retardation. Many communities have seen the not-so-gradual disappearance of special self-contained classes, and in some schools pull-out programs of any kind have virtually disappeared.

The rapid policy shift from commitment to a full continuum of placement options, which in fact is mandated by IDEA, toward a severe limitation of options has occurred in the absence of adequate consideration of the logical or empirical bases for grouping students for schooling. Our purpose is to

---

*Portions of this chapter were published in: Kauffman, J. M. (1995). Why we must celebrate a diversity of restrictive environments. *Learning Disabilities Research and Practice, 10*, 225–232.

extend the discussion we have begun elsewhere (e.g., Hallahan & Kauffman, 1994; Kauffman, 1988, 1989, 1991, 1993, 1994; Kauffman & Hallahan, 1993; Kauffman & Lloyd, 1995) by considering the meaning of LRE in ecological perspective.

As we have pointed out elsewhere, *place*—that is, physical location, not to mention rank or status—is a highly emotionally charged issue (Kauffman & Lloyd, 1995). In fact, place is so highly emotionally charged that it tends to breed fanatics—zealots willing to sacrifice everything else for the sake of a place. Fanatics of nearly every stripe elevate some aspect of place to the supreme value, which they then use to justify illogical and morally indefensible behavior. The tribal, ethnic, religious, and national warfare of the 20th century demonstrates how reverence for holy places can produce rage and violence. Temples and other holy places, motherlands, fatherlands, and promised lands have been the excuses for the coercive tactics of terror, torture, degradation, slaughter, and vandalism used by religious, nationalistic, and political zealots. These observations led Kauffman (1992) to articulate the hope that in the 21st century "we will understand that special education has no holy place and no promised land" (p. 344).

Our concern is that the inclusion movement is leading to designation of the general education classroom in the neighborhood school as the "promised land" or a "holy place" for students with disabilities. The implication is that special education is in danger of being radicalized into a group who will justify whatever tactics are necessary to claim that promised land for students with disabilities. The claim that all students should be promised placement in general education classes is based on the assumption that the general education classroom is least restrictive for all, which is a serious misunderstanding of LRE.

MISUNDERSTANDING OF LRE AND THE MEANING OF ENVIRONMENT

A basic assumption of proponents of full inclusion is, apparently, that any placement other than the general education classroom is inherently more restrictive and, therefore, less desirable. This assumption reflects a common misunderstanding about environments in general and the general education classroom environment in particular—that an environment can be either least restrictive for all or totally nonrestrictive.

Every environment is inherently restrictive. "Nonrestrictive environment" is an oxymoron, like "universal excellence" or "an elite education for everyone." The concept of environment implies surroundings—both physical and social—that impinge on our behavior. Surroundings by definition constrain what we can and may do. That is, physical and social contexts alter the probability that we can and may do certain things. The significance of an environment is not that it is restrictive in a general sense but that it is restrictive of specific things. As Cruickshank (1977) suggested, a given environment can be less restrictive of social interaction but more restrictive of learning than another; talk of environmental restrictiveness is therefore essentially meaningless unless we ask, "Restrictive of what?"

To make an environment least restrictive of some things—academic learning or socialization, for example—other things may need to be made more restrictive, such as the tasks presented, the responses demanded, the consequences provided, and so on. In fact, the restrictions placed on antecedents, behaviors, and consequences are the very stuff of education. What IDEA envisions is the least restriction of the educational environment *that will produce the desired educational outcomes for individual students.* Restrictions are necessary to produce outcomes, and the same restrictions will not produce the same outcomes for all students. Furthermore, *a single environment cannot contain all manner of restriction, for no environment is infinitely flexible.*

A common assumption of the proponents of full inclusion is that the LRE concept embodied in Public Law 94–142 (now called IDEA) requires that students be placed in the schools and classes they would attend if they were not identified as having disabilities. This assumption probably is the basis for the argument by some that the LRE for all students is, in fact, the general education classroom in the neighborhood school. However, the assumption that there exists a universally least restrictive place is at odds with both the law and with the best available scientific evidence (see Bateman, 1994; Bateman & Chard, 1995; Huefner, 1994, for commentary on legal issues).

The framers of IDEA made no assumption that the general education classroom in the neighborhood school would be least restrictive for all students. Clearly, they thought that a cascade of placement options ranging from general education classrooms and resource rooms through special self-contained classes to residential or hospital care would be necessary to achieve the appropriate education of all children and that each of these placements would be least restrictive for some but not for others (Hocutt, Martin, & McKinney, 1991). The law is consistent with the principles of ecological psychology that had emerged a decade before Public Law 94–142 was enacted in 1975.

IMPLICATIONS OF ECOLOGICAL CONCEPTS FOR SPECIAL EDUCATION PLACEMENT

The restrictiveness of environments requires consideration of human ecologies. Ecological principles have important implications for human services, including special education. They are especially critical in constructing the social ecologies in which particular academic and social goals for individual students can be reached. Human and nonhuman social ecologies are in many ways governed by the same principles, but it is important to note some differences between them.

In natural biological ecologies, things are in balance. Various species, varieties, groups, and individuals may support each other's survival, often by one species, group, or individual preying on another to sustain itself and keep another in check. We accept the natural order as good, although it may involve the violent aggression of one species, variety, group, or individual against another. We do not try to turn raptors into eaters of cereal or even carrion. Only a real kook, like the demented Dr. John Harvey Kellogg of Boyle's (1993) novel *The Road to Wellville*, would claim to have trained—or even try to train—a wolf to be vegetarian.

In subhuman social ecologies, the concept of a "natural" order also applies. Dominance, pecking order, flocking, schooling, and congregation into a closed group or segregation of individuals from the group are typically merely observed by scientists, not manipulated. Scientists often worry that the manipulation of subhuman social ecologies might upset the ecological balance. Another important aspect of subhuman ecologies is that the individual is not typically essential to ecological balance or to what is considered acceptable. There are sacrificial lambs. We do not want to prevent the fox from eating the mouse or those species that do so from eating their young, nor do we intervene to prevent the harsh domination of one primate by another in its natural environment. The individual's life is expendable, and the individual's social standing in the group is accepted, whether the individual is a despot or an outcast. The group, the species, is the center of concern.

In contrast, in human social ecologies the concept of "natural" is ambiguous. We do not admire the feral child. We describe uncontrolled human social ecologies as having devolved to the law of the jungle, to predatory behavior. We see the manipulation of individuals and groups as not only acceptable but desirable or essential. Acceptable human social ecologies are constructed deliberately, and we are constantly seeking to refine them, to make them more caring, more supportive of prosocial behavior. In human social ecologies, especially in Western cultures, the focus of concern is at least as much on the individual as on the group; the individual is seldom deemed to be expendable.

Perhaps Mark Twain was right in his assessment that we humans are morally inferior to the so-called "lower" animals. He observed that, "To create man was a quaint and original idea, but to add the sheep was tautology" (Library of America, 1976, p. 946). Mark Twain's unsettling wit notwithstanding, we must proceed as if we are superior to subhumans in intelligence and in our ability to construct deliberately a social habitat that supports the kind of behavior we want to flourish and to suppress the kind of behavior we consider destructive. However, we ignore the basic principles that govern all species only at our own risk. We are part of a social ecosystem as surely as the sheep or the baboon. The behavior of individual human beings is interconnected, and the basic principles of ecological systems apply in large measure to human social intercourse and the structure of human social groups.

Since the early work of ecological psychologists (e.g., Barker, 1968; Hobbs, 1966), we have understood that the behavior of individuals shapes and is shaped by the environment—by those physical and social restrictions that are the stuff of an environment. More recently, Gallagher (1993) has said:

> The same environmental unit provides different inputs to different persons, and different inputs to the same person if his behavior changes . . . the whole program of the environment's inputs changes if its own ecological properties change; if it becomes more or less populous, for example. (p. 205)

Taking an ecological perspective, whether in biology or psychology or special education, requires consideration of the totality or pattern of relationships between individuals and their environments. Educators and social scientists with an ecological bent are interested in the development and structure of human communities and the ways in which the presence of individuals with certain behavioral characteristics alters the pattern, rhythm, or course of social interactions or relationships.

Interest in applying ecological concepts to the study of special education dates back at least to the 1960s (e.g., Hobbs, 1966; Rhodes, 1967). Contemporary psychological and behavioral research includes relatively sophisticated ecobehavioral analyses of the problems of maintaining and teaching individuals with disabilities in specific social environments (e.g., Kamps, Leonard, Dugan, Boland, & Greenwood, 1991; McWilliam & Bailey, 1995). The work of Farmer and his colleagues applies developmental and ecological concepts to the study of social networks in general education and special classes (e.g., Farmer, 1994; Farmer & Farmer, 1996; Farmer & Hollowell, 1994; Farmer, Pearl, & Van Acker, 1995; Farmer, Stuart, Lorch, & Fields, 1993).

Two terms important for understanding sociobehavioral ecologies are *niche* and *ecodeme*. Niche refers to a site or habitat supplying the support necessary for an individual or group to survive. It also refers to the role of an individual or group in an interdependent community, especially its way of life in a community and the effects of its behavior on the environment. Thus, an ecological niche involves both location and interaction. An ecodeme is a population occupying a particular ecological niche. In sociobehavioral ecology, the ecodeme is comprised of the group occupying the location and forming the community and structure into which an individual might be introduced or from which an individual might be ejected.

The concept of ecological niche has very important implications for special education placements. It is important to remember, for example, that certain ecological niches are notoriously hospitable to some species, varieties, and individuals and equally notoriously inhospitable to others. An ecosystem may be thrown out of balance or destroyed by the introduction of certain individuals or groups, and individuals or groups that find a particularly hospitable niche may, if uncontrolled by others, destroy the very ecosystem that initially sustained them. Our own uncontrolled behavior as a species, for example, threatens to destroy our entire ecosphere. All experienced teachers understand how a given individual can undermine and quickly destroy the social structure of a class.

Natural scientists who are concerned with ecologies study the limits of the adaptability of various species, varieties, and individuals to various habitats and the effects of niches on survival. However, social and behavioral scientists, including educators, are interested in more than survival; they study also how the quality of human life of an individual or group is altered by someone's occupying a given niche and how humans create and maintain ecodemes and niches for themselves and others.

CREATION OF EDUCATIONAL ECOLOGIES

Social ecologies are constructed and maintained in large measure through two processes: by the congregation and segregation of individuals. Congregation and segregation are not peculiar to humans; they are pervasive biological processes. Subhuman species congregate into groups, separate individuals from groups, and segregate themselves from other groups in the interests of survival. These processes of congregation and segregation are part of the natural order. However, human beings have the capacity and the moral duty to construct a social order that does more than protect the species. We must construct a social order that also serves humanely the interests of the individual. Nevertheless, we cannot avoid congregation and segregation, because these are basic processes in any social ecology. The conceptual bases and strategies for clustering individuals in certain locations—the rationales for and the construction of ecodemes and niches through congregation and segregation—are the turning points for controversies about placement.

For example, it is important to recognize that on the one hand the legal racial segregation of American society has been rightly condemned as a great evil and that de facto segregation resulting in lowered opportunities is often and rightly decried. On the other hand, the segregation of dangerous criminals from the general society for most or all of their lives and the segregation of people with specific medical needs in hospitals are practices that most would agree are not only just but necessary to the preservation of a humane social fabric.

Likewise, congregation, depending on the purposes and circumstances, may be judged either an evil or a good. On the one hand, we condemn the congregation of people for evil purposes, such as lynching or performing violent acts in a gang. On the other hand, we condone or extol the virtues of congregating people in many other ways for mutual support, comfort, and special purpose. We approve of families, family reunions, and social, civic, recreational, and political clubs of great variety—some even though they are congregations determined primarily by race or ethnicity or gender. The congregation of African Americans in churches, colleges, and other social or political organizations is often defended as not only legal but ethical, advantageous, and worthy of preservation. Our point is that we must understand the words *congregation* and *segregation* in their broader meanings as we examine placement issues and not make the assumption that segregation and congregation for educational purposes are equivalent (Hallahan & Kauffman, 1994; Kauffman & Hallahan, 1993; Kauffman & Lloyd, 1995; Semmel, Gerber, & MacMillan, 1994).

The ideals of a democratic society include the freedoms of movement and association. Consequently, we view the assignment of someone to a special ecodeme or niche with great caution, if not suspicion, fearing that the assignment may be coerced or result in restricted opportunities. The contemporary ideals of American society also include tolerance if not deliberate maintenance of a rich social and behavioral diversity. Consequently, we view the removal of an individual from an established ecodeme or niche with great wariness, if not misgiving, fearing that removal may limit awareness and tolerance of those who are different. The primary focus of intervention in some human social ecologies, such as schools and classrooms, is therefore on altering the behavior of individuals within a given location— that is, the focus is on refurbishing the existing social habitat in some way to modify the individual's niche. We are hesitant to move a child to a new location, place him or her with a different ecodeme, and require the child to find a new niche in that group.

A common suggestion, for example, is that special services be brought to students in the habitat of their general education classroom and school; that is, that students should not be brought to services offered at another place. Another is that we should try to develop friendships in an existing group rather than move a child to a new group where other friendships might be developed. The inclusionary bias is to foster academic learning and desirable social networks for children with disabilities among an ecodeme comprised of nondisabled peers in a general education class of the neighborhood school rather than to offer academic instruction and introduce children with disabilities to social networks in special classes or special schools in which their peers have similar disabilities.

An inclusionary bias may be proper and ethical, as long as it does not lead to ignoring important realities. Unfortunately, the ideology of full inclusion ignores or distorts the literature on social ecologies, and in so doing ignores or distorts the realities our students and teachers must face daily. It ignores or distorts the responsibilities we have to construct the most habilitatively restrictive environments we can for our students. The study of human social ecologies, including the social ecologies of schools and classrooms, may lead to the recognition of several realities that will temper but not lead to the abandonment of a bias toward refurbishing the ecodemes and niches of students with disabilities and highlight the value of moving *some* students to different ones. An ecological approach to placement issues requires the recognition of the complexity, variety, and purposes of social systems.

Complexity

Full inclusion ideology seems to imply that the congregation of students in neighborhood schools for general education purposes is sacrosanct, that this congregation has superior moral status for all students, and that this ecodeme is the one to which all students should belong regardless of their characteristics or preferences. The assumption is that being educated alongside their general education classroom peers is the only acceptable solution to the challenge of meeting the special needs of students for academic instruction and socialization, that constant proximity to normal peers in regular classrooms is necessary to foster learning and appropriate social relationships. However, this simplistic view is inconsistent with the science of social systems. It denies the complexity of social relationships. Consider, for example, Dunbar's (1988) comments on the social systems of primates. Dunbar pointed out that a problem with the traditional conception of societies is that sociality or social interaction has been seen as synonymous with living in a group:

> But this is a very simplistic conception of what is involved in a social existence, at least in mammals as advanced as primates. In these species, groups exist through time not because animals are arbitrarily forced to associate, as, for example, dungflies do on a cow dropping, but because of the relationships that they have with each other. Those relationships exist independently of whether or not the animals actually live in physical proximity in the same group. Just because animals live semi-solitary lives, it does not follow that their relationships with each other are not as complex as those in species that live in formal groups. (p. 11)

Full inclusionists make much of the notion of the neighborhood school. They insist, for example, that students with disabilities be educated in the same schools as those of their peers, and in making this argument they frequently refer to these schools as "neighborhood schools." We have to wonder if they are not holding to a rather outdated notion of neighborhood schools. Forty or 50 years ago, schools tended to be either rural or urban, and the latter often were, indeed, neighborhood schools in the sense that virtually everyone knew everyone else and every child lived within walking distance of the school. The suburbanization of the United States, however, has resulted in a large percentage of the school-age population living relatively great distances from each other and from the schools they attend. The idea of a neighborhood school, in the traditional sense, has disappeared for many students. With this disappearance, the supposed advantages of having students with disabilities attend the same schools as students from their neighborhoods has greatly diminished.

The point here is not that grouping students is unimportant, but that physical proximity is neither necessary nor sufficient to ensure social relationships, either in subhumans or in human beings. Socialization is far more complex a phenomenon than much of the rhetoric about full inclusion suggests (see Schroeder, 1990). For example, recent work with young children with and without disabilities in various social groupings (McWilliam & Bailey, 1995) "challenges us to understand the complexity of various environmental influences—particularly, the social dimensions of environments" (Wolery, 1995, pp. vii–viii). Research by Schroeder et al. (1982) showed that the presence or absence of a single newcomer or disruptive individual dramatically changed the rates of many behaviors, both adaptive and maladaptive, of other individuals in group settings. Commenting on these findings, Mulick and Meinhold (1994) noted:

> It was as if the entire habitual set of social and individual interactions in the setting had been thrown out of balance by such intrusions. This is what we mean by a social ecology. Literally, changes in one part of such complex social environments produce dramatic changes in other parts of the social environments. The reality of these potential effects is the context in which teaching and treatment procedures, as well as new social relationships, are imposed on people with handicaps by planners and programmers. (p. 119)

The suggestion that environments judged "normal" will facilitate the emergence of "normal" behavior of all individuals is contradicted by the fact that aberrant behavior often develops and is sustained in normal environments. Furthermore, we know that nonnormal environments are sometimes required to produce normal behavior. Contrary to ideological reasoning about normalization, normal environments are not equally habilitative for everyone, and a single environment cannot be engineered to include all of the features necessary to produce desirable outcomes for every individual. Every environment imposes limitations on what is possible and what is feasible. Mulick and Meinhold (1994) concluded that:

Normal-appearing environments by themselves, even environments characterized by social advantage, do not assure normal behavioral outcomes. Handicaps sometimes require extraordinary environmental modifications, including modifications of quite normal rules for social conduct. We do not suggest that segregation and devaluation of people with handicaps is indicated by a scientific analysis, just that rules derived from an abstract and idealized sociopolitical analysis may not be useful in developing effective individualized treatment approaches. . . . Normal environments make some things easier and some things remarkably harder. (p. 121)

The way children learn through observation and social interaction is often grossly oversimplified. A very common part of the rationale for full inclusion is that placement of students with disabilities in the general education classroom in their neighborhood schools is important because that is where they will see appropriate peer models. This rationale is suspect to those who work in the area of emotional and behavioral disorders, not only because it is simplistic but, in the words of John Irving's character Owen Meany, "MADE FOR TELEVISION" in its obfuscation of reality. As Rhode, Jenson, and Reavis (1992) have stated about the students they call "Tough Kids":

By definition, Tough Kids exhibit significant social skills deficiencies when they are compared with their successful peers. There are those who propose that students with severe behavior problems need only spend time with their normal peers to learn the desired skills. However, Tough Kids are poorly accepted by their "normal" peers, resulting in minimal interaction between them even when they do spend time together. When interaction does occur, it is often negative. It becomes clear that if all that was needed was to expose Tough Kids to their normal peers in order for them to acquire appropriate social skills, they would have acquired acceptable social skills already. (p. 95)

The simplistic notion that appropriate peer models is the key to behavioral improvement is suspect for several reasons. First, if children tend always to imitate appropriate peer models, then one might expect the behavior of children in general education classes—where, presumably, the appropriate peer models exist—to become progressively more tractable. If appropriate peer models are indeed a more powerful influence than are the contingencies arranged by teachers, then a much higher proportion of students in general education classes than now do should be expected to imitate the appropriate behavior of their peers and thus avoid ever being identified as having emotional or behavioral disorders. Furthermore, those students who exhibit disruptive behavior might be just as likely, or perhaps even more so, to imitate other disruptive students in regular classrooms (Patterson, Reid, & Dishion, 1992). Finally, it may be possible for students to find appropriate and effective peer models in special classes (Farmer et al., 1993).

The truth is that socialization through modeling and imitation is far more complex than the proponents of full inclusion have let on (Gresham, 1982). As Hallenbeck and Kauffman (1995) pointed out in a review of research on observational learning, if regular classroom teachers are to make effective use of appropriate peer models, then they have a very substantial job cut out for them. They must find ways to (a) provide explicit models, including explicit instructions to imitate certain behaviors, plus guided practice in exhibiting those behaviors; (b) monitor the extent to which desirable imitation occurs; (c) provide direct and frequent reinforcement for imitation of desired behaviors; (d) make the models salient to the observers by increasing the observers' perceptions of similarity to the models; (e) decrease the likelihood that students with emotional or behavioral disorders will respond to seeing others obtain reinforcement as if they (observers) were being punished; and (f) create regular class conditions in which students with emotional or behavioral disorders do not experience frequent academic or social frustration.

Variety

Animal societies, including human societies, include many different groupings constructed for different purposes at different times. Dunbar (1988) described how a population of primates might group itself into coalitions, units, teams, bands, and communities. All levels of grouping serve specific functions in the community, and individuals may sort themselves or be sorted by the social system into different groups at different times (see also Chance & Jolly, 1970). In primate societies, for example, groups may be formed to protect against predators, to defend resources, to increase efficiency in foraging, or to improve caregiving. Humans form groups for the purposes of teaching and learning new skills, transporting or marketing goods and services, observing religious rites, engaging in athletics, celebrating kinship, providing the national defense, providing health care, creating the legal rules for the society, advocating legal rights, and so on. In fact, our daily lives can be characterized by movement from one social group to another for varying periods of time and for various purposes. We are constantly being pulled out of, being pushed into, and selecting ourselves in or out of groups—and most of these groups are not formed on the basis of prior physical proximity.

One line of argument is that students should not be pulled out of general education classrooms because it does not prepare them for life after school. As we have heard suggested more than once, "We don't live in a pull-out world." Nevertheless, the everyday social world of most adults includes a lot of pull-out groups, most of which are considered functional, ethical, and self-enhancing or self-protective. People are pulled out of a group and put in another or they move themselves out of one group and into another for training, work, moral support, recreation, and self-protection, and most individuals do not define themselves or their existence simply by reference to a single group with which they affiliate. One could make the case that preparing students to live in the adult world requires that they be taught to adopt a variety of group affiliations and be prepared to move and be moved from one to another.

Purpose

Analysis of placement decisions demands that we ask why we form groups for purposes of education: Just what are we trying to accomplish? How do we define place for educational purposes? What constraints or restrictions does the place of instruction put on how we accomplish our goals? Ultimately, we must ask what kind of social ecology is best for accomplishing each of our purposes.

Special education should be designed to accomplish two things, both of which are necessary and neither of which is alone sufficient to claim success: first, to offer effective instruction in the academic and social skills students should acquire; second, to foster social networks that induce and sustain desirable social behavior and that lead to satisfying relationships. Educational placement is defined by more than the physical space students occupy. It also involves the methods, materials, and equipment used in instruction, the particular students being taught, the teacher or teachers who provide instruction, and the tasks students are asked to perform. Clearly, the number and characteristics of the students present, the training and expertise of the teacher, and the instructional methods are constraints on the effects any placement might have. These dimensions of an educational environment are restrictive. The difficult task is designing an environment that is restrictive in the most helpful way for individual students.

Students with disabilities present an extremely varied set of instructional problems. The question for advocates of full inclusion is: Are these needs met most effectively for all students in the context of a general education classroom? We think it strains credulity to believe so. More important, the best available evidence to date suggests that a substantial proportion of students with disabilities are very poorly served in general education classrooms, even when strenuous and sustained efforts are made to accommodate their special needs (e.g., Zigmond et al., 1995). Moreover, the best available research belies the claim that the most effective instruction is provided in heterogeneous groups (Grossen, 1993). Students sometimes make greater academic progress in pull-out settings than in regular classes (e.g., Marston, 1987–88). The fact that they *sometimes* make greater gains in separate settings is an important qualifier. As we have argued elsewhere (Hallahan & Kauffman, 1994), in comparing students' progress under fully inclusive versus separate settings, if researchers were to find significant differences favoring the former, this should not be used to justify the elimination of separate settings unless *all* students progressed better under the inclusive setting. When comparing two groups of students, those in inclusive settings and those in separate settings:

> There is almost always some overlap of the distributions. . . . Because of the mandate to provide the most appropriate education to *each* student with a disability, it would be unethical to eliminate special classes unless research consistently demonstrated that general education classes were superior to special classes and there was virtually no overlap between the distributions on the dependent variables. (p. 502)

Some might object that using such a stringent criterion in deciding what placement options to make available loads the deck in favor of having a wide assortment of placements available. To this, we readily admit and point out that this is precisely why the framers of IDEA were so wise in insisting on a variety of placement alternatives. Furthermore, special classes and special schools are places in which students with serious behavior problems can be taught self-evaluation, self-control, and other important social skills (e.g., Cosden, Gannon, & Haring, 1995; Kern et al., 1995). In short, the best evidence we have indicates that differently restrictive instructional environments are necessary to provide the best learning outcomes for all students.

The constraints of placement on socialization need to be examined more closely. We want students to learn important social skills and to develop social networks that enhance and sustain their social behavior. The outcomes we want depend on instruction in social skills, opportunities to practice under controlled conditions and obtain feedback on their performance, and the presence of a peer group containing members with whom they are likely to develop a desirable social network. For many students, placement in the general education classroom does or can provide the ecology we want, at least with careful management by the teacher. For some students, however, it is highly questionable whether the general education classroom can meet the requirements of desirable ecodeme and niche. As Farmer and his colleagues have found, students tend to form social networks based on homophily—on the basis of similarity of salient characteristics (Farmer & Farmer, 1996). For example, students gravitate socially to others who share their shyness, their prosocial behavior, or their antisocial behavior.

The niche a student fills in a classroom depends in large measure on the peer group available and the social networks already formed in the class.

More important, habilitative social networks may be found in special classes or residential schools, and undesirable social networks can be developed in general education classes. We need much more knowledge of how students who exhibit problem behavior negotiate social ecologies of various types, and we need to know more about how to help students construct social networks that are most supportive of prosocial behavior. In all likelihood, increasing support will be found for well-implemented special classes and schools as ecologies that are most beneficial for some students during some phases of their development.

The preponderance of the evidence supports the conclusion that human responses to any given environment are extremely varied. People are diverse in their perceptions of how hospitable an environment is, in their ability to learn specific skills under specific environmental conditions, and in the friendship networks that support prosocial behavior in a given environment. True, we may be able to write a general prescription for the environment in which many or even most individuals will find a niche that we consider desirable. However, if we wish to construct a general social system that is hospitable to all, it must include a variety of places—a variety of environments with restrictions calculated to address the varied characteristics of individuals in the population.

Finally, we note the potential value of recognizing the culture of disability. Some groups of persons who receive special education services view themselves as cultural groups. Those who are blind and especially those who are deaf make it a point to emphasize the cultural aspects of their conditions. Many people who are deaf, for example, have their own set of cultural norms and behaviors (Padden & Humphries, 1988). Rather than seeing separate settings as evil, those who are blind or deaf often advocate for separate settings. They see congregating with other deaf or blind people as important for maintaining their culture. They emphasize their differences from the larger, nondisabled society and seek to maintain their identities as blind or deaf. A large part of their reasoning is that, by congregating, younger deaf or blind children can learn the ways of the culture from their elders and each other.

Elsewhere, we have speculated that there might be value in other populations of people with disabilities, such as those with learning disabilities, considering themselves as part of a culture (Hallahan & Kauffman, 1994). For example, adults with learning disabilities who are not hesitant to refer to themselves as learning disabled, who see their learning disability as a part of their identity, are more likely to be successful than those who tend to deny their disability (Gerber, Ginsberg, & Rieff, 1992; Spekman, Goldberg, & Herman, 1992).

Full inclusionists have argued that separate settings are detrimental to students with disabilities because they learn inappropriate behaviors from others who have the same disabilities. Ironically, it may be that students with disabilities may actually have the potential to be positive role models for other students with the same or similar disabilities:

> Perhaps association with others who have similar problems could be used to transmit the culture of what it is like to be learning disabled, mentally retarded, and so forth. This would require a shift, however, in how disability and disability labeling is viewed. In our view, we should weigh the possibility and probability of reducing stigma and increasing learning by banning labeling and grouping by disability against the feasibility and likelihood of reducing stigma and increasing learning by developing esprit de corps among congregations of people with disabilities. (Hallahan & Kauffman, 1994, p. 505)

For decades, we special educators have found coherence, unity, and mutual support in the notion that we should celebrate the diversity of the characteristics of children and youth. We have been, to be sure, congregated and united by our dedication to the task of changing for the better the characteristics of our students who have disabilities. However, we are in no way disparaging of the students whose characteristics we hope to change. We value these young people in all their diversity for who they are and hope that our profession will soon stop disparaging special placements and see renewed value in retaining a diversity of alternatives.

For a variety of reasons, our profession has been seriously divided, and therefore weakened, by the ideology of full inclusion. The doctrine of full inclusion defines diversity of placement as morally suspect, if not the Great Satan of special education. It seeks the elimination of placement options under the assumption that only one environment can be least restrictive, that the general education classroom is the promised land of all children. Special educators should reject the notion of a special education promised land and become united around another celebration—the celebration of the diversity of restrictive environments that are necessary to meet the needs of students with a wide variety of exceptionalities.

At present, we special educators are having trouble knowing just where we fit in the scheme of public education. Perhaps we will be more willing to celebrate a diversity of restrictive environments when we feel that our own niche in public education is secure.

REFERENCES

Barker, R. G. (1968). *Ecological psychology*. Stanford, CA: Stanford University Press.

Bateman, B. D. (1994). Who, how, and where: Special education's issues in perpetuity. *The Journal of Special Education, 27*, 509–520.

Bateman, B. D., & Chard, D. J. (1995). Legal demands and constraints on placement decisions. In J. M. Kauffman, J. W. Lloyd, D. P. Hallahan, & T. A. Astuto (Eds.), *Issues in educational placement: Students with emotional and behavioral disorders* (pp. 285–316). Hillsdale, NJ: Lawrence Erlbaum Associates.

Boyle, T. C. (1993). *The road to Wellville*. New York: Penguin.

Chance, M. R. A., & Jolly, C. (1970). *Social groups of monkeys, apes and men*. London: Jonathan Cape.

Cosden, M., Gannon, C., & Haring, T. G. (1995). Teacher-control versus student-control over choice of task and reinforcement for students with severe behavior problems. *Behavioral Education, 5*, 11–27.

Cruickshank, W. M. (1977). Guest editorial. *Journal of Learning Disabilities, 10*, 193–194.

Dunbar, R. I. M. (1988). *Primate social systems*. Ithaca, NY: Cornell University Press.

Farmer, T. W. (1994). Social networks and the social behavior of youth with emotional and behavioral disorders: Implications for intervention. *B.C. Journal of Special Education, 18*, 223–234.

Farmer, T. W., & Farmer, E. M. Z. (1996). The social relationships of students with exceptionalities in mainstream classrooms: Social networks and homophily. *Exceptional Children, 62*, 431–450.

Farmer, T. W., & Hollowell, J. H. (1994). Social networks in mainstream classrooms: Social affiliations and behavioral characteristics of students with emotional and behavioral disorders. *Journal of Emotional and Behavioral Disorders, 2*, 143–155, 163.

Farmer, T. W., Pearl, R., & Van Acker, R. (1995). *Expanding the social skills deficit framework: A developmental perspective, classroom social networks, and implications for the social growth of students with disabilities*. Unpublished manuscript, University of North Carolina, Chapel Hill, NC.

Farmer, T. W., Stuart, C. B., Lorch, N. H., & Fields, E. (1993). The social behavior and peer relations of children with emotional and behavioral disorders in residential treatment: A pilot study. *Journal of Emotional and Behavioral Disorders, 1*, 223–234.

Gallagher, W. (1993). *The power of place: How our surroundings shape our thoughts, emotions, and actions*. New York: Poseidon.

Gartner, A., & Lipsky, D. K. (1989). *The yoke of special education: How to break it*. Rochester, NY: National Center on Education and the Economy.

Gerber, P. J., Ginsberg, R., & Rieff, H. B. (1992). Identifying alterable patterns in employment success for highly successful adults with learning disabilities. *Journal of Learning Disabilities, 25*, 475–487.

Gresham, F. R. (1982). Misguided mainstreaming: The case for social skills training with handicapped children. *Exceptional Children, 48*, 422–433.

Grossen, B. (1993). Focus: Heterogeneous grouping and curriculum design. *Effective School Practices, 12*(1), 5–8.

Hallahan, D. P., & Kauffman, J. M. (1994). Toward a culture of disability in the aftermath of Deno and Dunn. *Journal of Special Education, 27*, 496–508.

Hallenbeck, B. A., & Kauffman, J. M. (1995). How does observational learning affect the behavior of students with emotional or behavioral disorders? A review of research. *Journal of Special Education, 29*, 45–71.

Hobbs, N. (1966). Helping the disturbed child: Psychological and ecological strategies. *American Psychologist, 21*, 1105–1115.

Hocutt, A. M., Martin, E. W., & McKinney, J. D. (1991). Historical and legal context of mainstreaming. In J. W. Lloyd, N. N. Singh, & A. C. Repp (Eds.), *The regular education initiative: Alternative perspectives on concepts, issues, and models* (pp. 17–28). Sycamore, IL: Sycamore Press.

Huefner, D. S. (1994). The mainstreaming cases: Tensions and trends for school administrators. *Educational Administration Quarterly, 30*, 27–55.

Kamps, D. M., Leonard, B. R., Dugan, E. P., Boland, B., & Greenwood, C. R. (1991). The use of ecobehavioral assessment to identify naturally occurring effective procedures in classrooms serving students with autism and other developmental disabilities. *Journal of Behavioral Education, 1*, 367–397.

Kauffman, J. M. (1988). A revolution can also mean returning to the starting point: Will school psychology help special education complete the circuit? *School Psychology Review, 17*, 490–494.

Kauffman, J. M. (1989). The regular education initiative as Reagan–Bush education policy: A trickle-down theory of education of the hard-to-teach. *Journal of Special Education, 23*, 256–278.

Kauffman, J. M. (1991). Restructuring in sociopolitical context: Reservations about the effects of current reform proposals on students with disabilities. In J. W. Lloyd, A. C. Repp, & N. N. Singh (Eds.), *The regular education initiative: Alternative perspectives on concepts, issues, and methods* (pp. 57–66). Sycamore, IL: Sycamore Press.

Kauffman, J. M. (1992). Special education into the 21st century: An educational perspective. In *Challenge for change: Reform in the 1990s. Conference proceedings, 16th national conference of the Australian Association of Special Education* (pp. 343–344). Perth, Western Australia: Australian Association of Special Education.

Kauffman, J. M. (1993). How we might achieve the radical reform of special education. *Exceptional Children, 60*, 6–16.

Kauffman, J. M. (1994). Places of change: Special education's power and identity in an era of educational reform. *Journal of Learning Disabilities, 27*, 610–618.

Kauffman, J. M., & Hallahan, D. P. (1993). Toward a comprehensive delivery system for special education. In J. I. Goodlad & T. C. Lovitt (Eds.), *Integrating general and special education* (pp. 73–102). Columbus, OH: Merrill.

Kauffman, J. M., & Lloyd, J. W. (1995). A sense of place: The importance of placement issues in contemporary special education. In J. M. Kauffman, J. W. Lloyd, D. P. Hallahan, & T. A. Astuto (Eds.), *Issues in educational placement: Students with emotional and behavioral disorders* (pp. 3–19). Hillsdale, NJ: Lawrence Erlbaum Associates.

Kern, L., Wacker, D. P., Mace, F. C., Falk, G. D., Dunlap, G., & Kromrey, J. D. (1995). Improving the peer interactions of students with emotional and behavioral disorders through self-evaluation procedures: A component analysis and group application. *Journal of Applied Behavior Analysis, 28*, 47–59.

Laski, F. J. (1991). Achieving integration during the second revolution. In L. H. Meyer, C. A. Peck, & L. Brown (Eds.), *Critical issues in the lives of people with severe disabilities* (pp. 409–421). Baltimore: Brookes.

Library of America. (1976). *Mark Twain: Collected tales, sketches, speeches, & essays 1891–1910.* New York: Author.

Lipsky, D. K., & Gartner, A. (1991). Restructuring for quality. In J. W. Lloyd, N. N. Singh, & A. C. Repp (Eds.), *The regular education initiative: Alternative perspectives on concepts, issues, and models* (pp. 43–57). Sycamore, IL: Sycamore Press.

Marston, D. (1987–88). The effectiveness of special education: A time series analysis of reading performance in regular and special education settings. *Journal of Special Education, 21*(4), 13–26.

McWilliam, R. A., & Bailey, D. B. (1995). Effects of classroom social structure and disability on engagement. *Topics in Early Childhood Special Education, 15*, 123–147.

Mulick, J. A., & Meinhold, P. M. (1994). Developmental disorders and broad effects of the environment on learning and treatment effectiveness. In E. Schopler & G. B. Mesibov (Eds.), *Behavioral issues in autism* (pp. 99–128). New York: Plenum.

Padden, C., & Humphries, T. (1988). *Deaf in America: Voices from a culture.* Cambridge, MA: Harvard University Press.

Patterson, G. R., Reid, J. B., & Dishion, T. J. (1992). *Antisocial boys.* Eugene, OR: Castalia.

Rhode, G., Jenson, W. R., & Reavis, H. K. (1992). *The tough kid book: Practical classroom management strategies.* Longmont, CO: Sopris West.

Rhodes, W. C. (1967). The disturbing child: A problem of ecological management. *Exceptional Children, 33*, 449–455.

Schroeder, S. R. (Ed.). (1990). *Ecobehavioral analysis and developmental disabilities: The twenty-first century.* New York: Springer.

Schroeder, S. R., Kanoy, J. R., Mulick, J. A., Rojahn, J., Thios, S. J., Stephens, M., & Hawk, B. (1982). Environmental antecedents which affect management and maintenance of programs for self-injurious behavior. In J. C. Hollis & C. E. Myers (Eds.), *Life-threatening behavior* (Monograph No. 5). Washington, DC: American Association on Mental Deficiency.

Semmel, M. I., Gerber, M. M., & MacMillan, D. L. (1994). Twenty-five years after Dunn's article: A legacy of policy analysis research in special education. *The Journal of Special Education, 27*, 481–495.

Spekman, N. J., Goldberg, R. J., & Herman, K. L. (1992). Learning disabled children grow up: A search for factors related to success in the young adult years. *Learning Disabilities Research and Practice, 7*, 161–170.

Stainback, W., & Stainback, S. (1991). A rationale for integration and restructuring: A synopsis. In J. W. Lloyd, N. N. Singh, & A. C. Repp (Eds.), *The regular education initiative: Alternative perspectives on concepts, issues, and models* (pp. 226–239). Sycamore, IL: Sycamore Press.

Wolery, M. (1995). Foreword. *Topics in Early Childhood Special Education, 15*, vii–viii.

Zigmond, N., Jenkins, J., Fuchs, L. S., Deno, S., Fuchs, D., Baker, J. N., Jenkins, L., & Couthino, M. (1995). Special education in restructured schools: Findings from three multi-year studies. *Phi Delta Kappan, 76*, 531–540.

17

THE LEGALIZATION
AND FEDERALIZATION
OF SPECIAL EDUCATION

Dixie Snow Huefner
University of Utah

It has been 20 years since the passage of Public Law 94–142, the Education for All Handicapped Children Act. The 20th anniversary is a good time to pause and evaluate the act and what its implementation over two decades has wrought. It is also a good time to ponder the future and what the next 20 years may bring.

At the time of the original passage of P.L. 94–142 in 1975, special education advocates had worked patiently for a decade to extend the federal role in the education of children with disabilities. Following the model of Title I of the Elementary and Secondary Education Act, they sought federal grants-in-aid to underwrite more services for these students than states could provide on their own. They also successfully advocated for individual identification of each student with a disability, and funding to each state based on the number of children so identified. For the special education community, the victory was hard fought, the mood expansive, the time full of hope for state and federal cooperation to serve all children with disabilities, including the most severe, who typically had been excluded from public schools across the nation.

In the intervening years, P.L. 94–142, which is a permanently authorized funding statute, has been amended a number of times and is currently Part B of the Individuals with Disabilities Education Act (hereinafter, IDEA or the Act).[1] The Supreme Court has ruled seven times on different aspects of the

---

[1]20 U.S.C. § 1400 et seq.

Act. Pressures on the federal government to deregulate threatened the Part B regulations in the early 1980s. Currently, some of the basic premises of the Act itself are receiving scrutiny.

This chapter examines the accomplishments of Part B of IDEA, as well as its limitations. First, it reviews the statute itself and its key amendments over time. Second, it assesses major judicial interpretations of the statute. Finally, the author reflects on what the legalization and federalization of special education have produced and where we should go from here.

THE LEGISLATION

Part B of IDEA provides both substantive and procedural rights to students with disabilities in states accepting funds under the statute, which is now all of them. Those rights include, first and foremost, the right to a free appropriate public education (FAPE),[2] that is, publicly funded and specially designed instruction to meet a special education student's individual needs. Second, that education is to be provided, to the maximum extent appropriate, in a setting with nondisabled students[3]; this concept is captured in the IDEA regulations under the heading of "least restrictive environment."[4] Third, both the student's program and placement must be governed by a written individualized education program (IEP) in which the student's goals, needed services, and the extent of interaction with nondisabled students are projected on an annual basis.[5] The IEP also includes measurable short-term objectives.

Prior to receipt of special education services under IDEA, a student must be evaluated as fitting within one of the eligible categories of disability and needing special education as a result of the disability.[6] The evaluation must be performed by more than one person, that is, by a "multidisciplinary team," and must consist of multiple measures; in particular, an IQ test alone cannot be the basis for a disability label.[7] Additionally, various protections must be honored to avoid misclassification based on racial, ethnic, and cultural (language) difference.

Procedurally, the parents of eligible students with disabilities can exercise extensive rights on behalf of their children.[8] Among them are the following:

---

[2]*Id.* at §§ 1401(18), 1412(2)(B).

[3]*Id.* at § 1412(5)(B).

[4]See 34 C.F.R. § 300.550.

[5]20 U.S.C. §§ 1401(20), 1414(a)(5); 34 C.F.R. § 300.346.

[6]20 U.S.C. § 1401(a)(1)(A). Students aged 3–5 inclusive need only be identified as developmentally delayed and in need of special education and related services. *Id.* at § 1401(a)(1)(B).

[7]See 34 C.F.R. 530–532.

[8]See generally 20 U.S.C. § 1415.

- The right to receive notice of actions proposed or rejected by the education agency.[9]
- The right to withhold consent to initial evaluation for eligibility and initial placement in a special education program.[10]
- The right to an Independent Educational Evaluation, often at public expense.[11]
- The right to participate in the development of their child's IEP.[12]
- The right to access their child's records[13] and to prevent unauthorized access by others.[14]
- The right to an administrative decision by an impartial hearing officer if a conflict arises with respect to the student's identification, evaluation, program, or placement as a special education student.[15] Ultimately, the parent has the right to go to court to uphold the provisions of the statute.[16]

Subsequent to the initial passage of P.L. 94–142 in 1975 and the corresponding regulations promulgated in 1977, the following major statutory or regulatory changes have occurred:

1. The Act now extends to 3–5 year olds, with added flexibility in identifying, evaluating, and placing eligible preschoolers.[17] The per-student funding base for this age group is more generous than the per-student funding amount for school-age children.

2. The Education Department issued an "Interpretation of the IEP" that constitutes an Appendix to the IDEA regulations and that provides important regulatory guidance to states and local education agencies.[18]

3. The Act now includes transition requirements to ensure that education agencies, along with other community agencies, as appropriate, plan for the transition of students with disabilities from public school to postschool environments.[19]

---

[9]34 C.F.R. § 300.504(a).
[10]*Id.* at § 300.504(b).
[11]*Id.* at § 300.503.
[12]*Id.* at § 300.344-345.
[13]*Id.* at § 300.502.
[14]See the Family Educational Rights and Privacy Act, 20 U.S.C. § 1232(g) and 34 C.F.R. § 99.30.

[15]34 C.F.R. §§ 300.506-507.
[16]*Id.* at § 300.511.
[17]20 U.S.C. § 1401(a)(1)(B); see also note following 34 C.F.R. § 300.552.
[18]34 C.F.R. Part 300, Appendix C.
[19]20 U.S.C. § 1401(a)(19)-(20).

4. Autism and Traumatic Brain Injury are now discrete, separate categories of disability under IDEA.[20]

5. Assistive technology devices and services have been added to the Act and can be considered either special education, related services, or supplementary aids and services, as the case may be.[21]

6. Rehabilitation counseling and therapeutic recreation have been added to the list of examples of potential related services.[22]

7. An early intervention program (Part H of IDEA) offers federal subsidies to states that establish programs for children from birth to age 3 who are developmentally delayed or at risk of developmental delay.[23]

8. Mediation is encouraged in the regulations as a precursor to the due process hearing; states are not yet required to offer such a procedure, however.[24]

9. State compliance review procedures have been tightened by requiring written findings within 60 days of the filing of a complaint.[25]

10. The Education Department's Office of Special Education Programs (OSEP) has shifted its federal audits from every year to every 3 years to provide some relief to state agencies and to recognize the reality of staff constraints within OSEP.

11. The Act includes a provision for reimbursement of attorney's fees to prevailing parents.[26] The amendment, entitled the Handicapped Children's Protection Act, also includes a clarification that Section 504 of the Rehabilitation Act and Section 1983 (a civil rights statute) are available as remedies in suitable cases, provided that administrative remedies are exhausted first in applicable situations.[27]

Alongside these important changes, it is equally important to declare what has not been changed, sometimes in spite of attempts to do so:

1. The definition of serious emotional disturbance (SED) has not been rewritten, despite earnest attempts to broaden the category to include students with character and conduct disorders. Children with these disorders cause many problems in the schools and arguably cannot be well differentiated from many of those characterized as SED. Nonetheless, politics thus

---

[20]*Id.* at § 1401(a)(1).

[21]*Id.* at § 1401(a)(25)-(26); 34 C.F.R. § 300.308.

[22]20 U.S.C. § 1401(a)(17).

[23]*Id.* at § 1471 et seq.

[24]Note accompanying 34 C.F.R. § 300.506.

[25]34 C.F.R. § 300.661.

[26]20 U.S.C. § 1415(e)(4)(B).

[27]*Id.* at § 1415(f).

far has dictated against broadening the pool of eligible students, although the issue is not dead.

2. Attention Deficit Disorder/Attention Deficit Hyperactivity Disorder has not been added to the list of disabilities. Again, politics and funding constraints have thus far dictated against broadening the pool of eligible students. Many of these students, however, are being served under other special education labels, such as learning disabilities, SED, and other health impaired.

3. Funding has not kept pace with original congressional intent, but remains at about 8% of the national average per pupil expenditure (APPE) or approximately $415 per student. Initially, Congress had hoped to be able to contribute 40% of APPE to the excess costs of educating children with disabilities but reached a high of 12% in the early 1980s and then dropped back to approximately 8%, a percent that has remained stable over the past decade.

4. Crucially, the basic propositions of FAPE in the LRE with an IEP, accompanied by extensive procedural safeguards remain intact. The definition of FAPE in the statute has not changed, nor has the mandate to educate students with disabilities with nondisabled students "to the maximum extent appropriate." The IEP and due process safeguards have not diminished, and in fact each has been embellished by the addition of transition-programming requirements and reimbursable attorney's fees for prevailing parents, respectively.

JUDICIAL RULINGS

Supreme Court Rulings

The first and still most important of the U.S. Supreme Court's seven rulings under IDEA is its interpretation in *Hendrick Hudson District Board of Education v. Rowley*[28] of the statutory meaning of FAPE. The *Rowley* case confirmed that FAPE was a right not just a statutory preference and that FAPE required more than mere access to public school. The Supreme Court's interpretation established a modest but nonetheless meaningful FAPE standard: Schools must provide an individualized educational program tailored to the student's specific needs and the IEP must be designed to provide some educational benefit to the student. In other words, access must go beyond baby sitting or day care for the disabled. The Court also affirmed the importance of the Act's procedural safeguards, and reminded the lower courts that matters of educational methodology were to be left to the states and local education agencies.

---

[28]458 U.S. 176 (1982).

In the aftermath of *Rowley*, many circuits of the U.S. Court of Appeals have required some sort of meaningful progress as the measure of whether the benefit required under the Act is sufficient to provide FAPE.[29] If an IEP has been implemented, then measures of progress are available; if the IEP has not been implemented, then the measure of FAPE is whether the IEP is "reasonably calculated" to produce meaningful benefit (see Huefner, 1991). Courts generally have missed the boat, however, in terms of recognizing the value of IEP goals and objectives as a means to measure progress. Instead, they have too often focused narrowly on specific student characteristics, needed services, and on whether the student generally was making educational progress. The *Rowley* decision is a case in point.

The second Supreme Court decision, which dealt with related services, is arguably the second most important. *Irving Independent School District v. Tatro*[30] affirmed that school health services such as catheterization are distinguishable from medical services and can constitute a related service under the Act when needed to enable the student to benefit from special education. The distinction between a health service and a medical service is at times a fine one, and lower courts have struggled to define the boundary, as more and more medically fragile children with life-threatening conditions have entered the public school system. When the care approaches private duty nursing, the courts have judged the care to be essentially medical in nature even though not provided by a licensed physician.[31] Nonetheless, the overall impact of *Tatro* has been to affirm the need for education agencies to shoulder financial burdens that go well beyond the provision of educational services.

Two private school decisions by the Court have also confirmed the financial burdens that education agencies must bear under IDEA. *Burlington School Committee v. Massachusetts Department of Education*[32] and *Florence County School District v. Carter*[33] together stand for the proposition that if an education agency fails to provide FAPE and a parent places a child unilaterally in a private school, the education agency will be liable for the reasonable costs of the private schooling, so long as the private placement was proper and regardless of whether the private school was on a state-approved list.

Collectively, these four Supreme Court cases have the effect of balancing the extent of the financial obligation of education agencies by establishing

---

[29]See, e.g., Burke County Bd. of Educ. v. Denton, 895 F.2d 973 (4th Cir. 1990); Doe v. Smith, 879 F.2d 1340 (6th Cir. 1989), *cert. denied*, 112 S.Ct. 730 (1990); Central Susquehanna Intermediate Unit 16, 853 F.2d 171 (3d Cir. 1988), *cert. denied*, 488 U.S. 1030 (1989); Evans v. District No. 17, 841 F.2d 824 (8th Cir. 1988); Abrahamson v. Hershman, 701 F.2d (1st Cir. 1983).

[30]484 U.S. 883 (1984).

[31]See, e.g., Neely v. Rutherford County Sch., 68 F.3d 965 (6th Cir. 1995); Detsel v. Board of Educ. of Auburn, 820 F.2d 587 (2d Cir. 1987), *cert. denied*, 108 S.Ct. 495 (1987); Granite Sch. Dist. v. Shannon M., 787 F. Supp. 1020 (D. Ut. 1992); Bevin H. v. Wright, 666 F. Supp. 71 (W.D. Pa. 1987).

[32]471 U.S. 359 (1985).

[33]114 S.Ct. 361 (1993).

a modest FAPE standard in *Rowley* while affirming the potential breadth and reach of the financial obligation under *Tatro, Burlington*, and *Florence County*.

The Supreme Court has ruled on one discipline case, *Honig v. Doe*,[34] and supported the proposition, first stated in *Mills v. District of Columbia Board of Education*,[35] that students should not be excluded unilaterally from public education for misbehavior that relates to their disability. *Honig* held that a suspension or expulsion for longer than 10 days is a change of placement under IDEA and therefore invokes the procedural protections of IDEA, such as convening a multidisciplinary placement team to validate any proposed change of placement. The parties in *Honig* stipulated that the misbehavior in question was related to the disability, and the Court's decision did not address what disciplinary actions are legal if the misbehavior is not related to the disability. As a result, the holding has created considerable confusion.

In the last few years, public reaction to the increasing student use of firearms at school has propelled the Congress to enact legislation to the effect that states wishing to receive federal funds under the Elementary and Secondary Education Act (now entitled the Improving America's Schools Act) must pass a law requiring education agencies to expel any student from their current placement for at least a year if that student brings a firearm to school.[36] Some modification in the policy was adopted to conform to IDEA requirements, but it still allows students with disabilities who bring firearms to school to be expelled from the current placement for up to 45 days.[37] In other words, even for these students some kind of long-term suspension or expulsion is available as a disciplinary option. As a result, a 45-day interim placement (e.g., home or an alternative school) is now the placement of choice for students with disabilities who bring a firearm to school. Procedural protections must still be invoked during this period to reevaluate the appropriateness of the IEP and the placement in which the misbehavior occurred, but the interim placement may precede the procedures. In addition, if the parents file for a hearing to challenge the school's actions or recommendations, the interim placement becomes the "stay-put" placement while the proceedings are pending. Furthermore, if a knowledgeable team determines that the misbehavior is not caused by the disability, expulsion for up to a year may take place, although not all educational services to the student may cease.

In response to growing belief that dangerous students with disabilities should be subject to the same ultimate disciplinary sanctions as other

---

[34] 484 U.S. 305 (1988).

[35] 348 F. Supp. 866 (D.D.C. 1972).

[36] See the Gun-Free Schools Act of 1994, Sections 14601–14602 of Improving America's Schools Act (IASA), Pub. L. 103-382, 108 Stat. 3907 (to be codified at 20 U.S.C. § 8921). See also the Jeffords Amendment to IDEA at Title III, Part A of the IASA, 108 Stat. 3931 (to be codified at 20). U.S.C. § 1415(e)(3)(B).

[37] 20 U.S.C. § 1415(e)(3)(B).

students, legislation has been introduced in the 104th Congress that would allow total expulsion for firearms violations if the misconduct is unrelated to the disability. (H. R. 3268, 1996; S. 1578, 1996). In addition, the proposed legislation would require expulsion for possession of other dangerous weapons and illegal drugs. Disability advocates have been extremely concerned that the proposed legislation would deny the hard-fought right to FAPE to affected students. As of this writing, the outcome of the proposed legislation had not been determined.

The Supreme Court's other two rulings under IDEA have both been rendered ineffective by subsequent congressional amendments to IDEA. The Court in *Smith v. Robinson*[38] interpreted IDEA to preclude payment of attorney's fees to prevailing parents. In response, Congress amended IDEA[39] to clarify its intent to allow reimbursement for attorney's fees in proper cases. Congress also opened the possibility of damage awards under Section 504 and Section 1983.[40]

Under the attorney's fee provision, a majority of the lower court decisions have allowed reimbursement for attorneys' fees at the hearing and even some prehearing stages,[41] generating a huge surge of attorney's fee cases in federal court. One can question whether it is a wise use of judicial resources to hear cases where the only issue is the availability of attorney's fees for work done at a prelitigation stage.

Finally, in *Dellmuth v. Muth*[42] the Supreme Court ruled that IDEA did not abrogate a state's sovereign immunity from suit in federal court under the Eleventh Amendment because the Act did not explicitly declare such an intent. In response, Congress amended IDEA to establish explicitly that states could be sued in federal court for alleged violations of IDEA.[43] Thus, two of the Court's interpretations of the Act were rejected by Congress and no longer are good law.

Additional Key Issues in the Lower Courts

A number of significant issues not heard by the Supreme Court have been effectively resolved by decisions in various circuits of the U.S. Court of Appeals. *Timothy W. v. Rochester, New Hampshire, School District*[44] established

---

[38]468 U.S. 992 (1984).

[39]20 U.S.C. § 1415(e)(4)(B–F).

[40]*Id.* at § 1415(f).

[41]See, e.g., Moore v. District of Columbia, 907 F.2d 165 (D.C. Cir. 1990), *cert. denied,* 111 S.Ct. 556 (1991); McSomebodies v. Burlingame Elem. Sch. Dist. 886 F.2d 1558 (9th Cir. 1989), *as supplemented,* 897 F.2d 974 (1990); Mitten v. Muscogee County Sch. Dist., 877 F.2d 932 (11th Cir. 1989); Duane M. v. Orleans Parish Sch. Bd., 861 F.2d 115 (5th Cir. 1988); Eggers v. Bullitt County Sch. Dist., 854 F.2d 892 (6th Cir. 1988).

[42]491 U.S. 223 (1989).

[43]20 U.S.C. § 1403.

[44]875 F.2d 954 (1st Cir. 1989), *cert. denied,* 110 S.Ct. (1990).

that a student with multiple, profound disabilities was eligible for services under IDEA even in the absence of demonstrable ability to benefit from those services. Although the *Rowley* FAPE standard requires the IEP team to produce an IEP reasonably calculated to produce benefit, the court in *Timothy W.* concluded that the ability to benefit cannot be a precondition for eligibility to receive an IEP. The effect of this decision has been for schools to accept all children with disabilities and presume capability to benefit from some form of special education. Some schools have even accepted comatose children, although this is an overreading of the decision itself.

Larry P. v. Riles[45] and *PASE v. Hannon*[46] established that multidisciplinary assessment using multiple measures was an important means of reducing racial discrimination in evaluation procedures. We have yet to see, however, an equivalently strong ruling dramatizing the need to avoid misclassifying as disabled those students who are instead limited English proficient (LEP). The existing criteria should be sufficient to allow accurate classification of LEP students, but the criteria are often honored more in the breach than in the observance, so some new judicial statement of their importance in the LEP context would be helpful.

The right to an extended school year (ESY) as an extension of the right to FAPE has been established in enough circuits of the U.S. Court of Appeals to be uniformly accepted as the law.[47] If as a result of failure to provide services over holiday breaks, especially the summer break, a student's right to FAPE is effectively denied or significantly jeopardized, then services must be provided in spite of any limitations under state law to the contrary.

The right to compensatory education, after a slower start, is now widely accepted as an appropriate extension of the Supreme Court's private school decision in *Burlington*.[48] The logic of providing compensatory education past the age at which a student would have lost eligibility is that it provides a remedy to parents whose child was denied FAPE, yet who could not afford to remove that child from public school and then seek private school tuition reimbursement.

Although consensus has emerged with respect to the aforementioned issues, mainstreaming/inclusion issues remain the largest and toughest set

---

[45]793 F.2d 969 (9th Cir. 1984).

[46]506 F. Supp. 831 (N.D. Ill. 1980).

[47]See, e.g., Johnson v. Indep. Sch. Dist. No. 4 of Bixby, 921 F.2d 1022 (10th Cir. 1990), *cert. denied*, 111 S.Ct. 1685 (1991); Cordrey v. Euckert, 917 F.2d 1460 (6th Cir. 1990), *cert. denied*, 111 S.Ct. 1391 (1991); Alamo Heights Indep. Sch. Dist. v. State Bd. of Educ., 790 F.2d 1153 (5th Cir. 1986); Battle v. Pennsylvania, 629 F.2d 269 (3d Cir. 1980), *cert. denied*, 449 U.S. 1109 (1981).

[48]See, e.g., Pihl v. Massachusetts Dep't of Educ., 9 F.3d 184 (1st Cir. 1993); Lester H. v. Gilhool, 916 F.2d 865 (3d Cir. 1990), *cert. denied sub nom. Chester-Upland Sch. Dist. v. Lester H.*, 449 U.S. 923 (1991); Burr v. Sobol, 888 F.2d 258 (2d Cir. 1989), *cert. denied*, 494 U.S. 1005 (1990); Jefferson County Bd. of Educ. v. Breen, 853 F.2d 853 (11th Cir. 1988); Miener *ex rel* Miener v. Missouri, 800 F.2d 749 (8th Cir. 1986).

of issues to elude clear consensus. Under IDEA, decisions must be individualized, emerging from rather than preceding the IEP.[49] The statutory right to placement in settings with nondisabled students "to the maximum extent appropriate" reflects the balance between the preference for mainstreaming and the need for FAPE. Honoring the potential tension between mainstreaming and FAPE, the federal regulations require school districts to make available a continuum of placement options[50] so that each student may be placed in the "least restrictive environment," that is, the placement closest to the mainstream in which FAPE can be delivered. Blanket policies determining placement on the basis of categories such as disability label or degree of severity violate the IDEA.

Different tests have evolved in different federal circuits to determine when a student can be placed appropriately in the regular classroom. The two-part test established by the 5th Circuit in *Daniel R.R. v. Texas State Board of Education*[51] is the dominant standard and has been adopted by the 3rd and 11th Circuits.[52] Essentially, the standard requires, first, that an education agency make sufficient efforts to accommodate an instructionally mainstreamed student and consider both academic and nonacademic goals in determining whether a child can benefit from education in a regular classroom with supplementary aids and services. Second, it requires that other kinds of opportunities for interaction with nondisabled students be considered if instructional mainstreaming in the regular classroom is not appropriate. In the view of this author, the 9th Circuit's test, articulated in *Sacramento City Unified School District v. Rachel H.*,[53] is less carefully constructed than *Daniel R.R.* because, among other things, it lacks the second part of the *Daniel R.R.* standard.

The feasibility test adopted by the 6th Circuit in *Roncker v. Walter*[54] remains the dominant standard for determining when services should be provided in a regular education setting such as a neighborhood school, that is, the school the student would attend if not disabled. It has been adopted by the 4th and 8th Circuits.[55] It considers cost as well as benefit in assessing the feasibility of transporting allegedly superior services in a separate facility to a neighborhood school. *Roncker* and its progeny recognize the poten-

---

[49]34 C.F.R. § 300.342.

[50]34 C.F.R. § 300.551.

[51]874 F.2d 1036 (5th Cir. 1989).

[52]See Oberti v. Clementon Sch. Bd., 995 F.2d 1204 (3d Cir. 1993); Greer v. Rome City Sch. Dist., 950 F.2d 688 (11th Cir. 1991), *op. withdrawn*, 956 F.2d 1025 (1992), *reinstated*, 967 F.2d 470 (1992).

[53]14 F.3d 1398 (9th Cir.), *cert. denied*, 114 S.Ct. 2679 (1994).

[54]700 F.2d 1058 (6th Cir.), *cert. denied sub nom. Cincinnati City Sch. Dist. v. Roncker*, 464 U.S. 864 (1983).

[55]See Schuldt v. Mankato Indep. Sch. Dist., 937 F.2d 1357 (8th Cir. 1991), *cert. denied*, 112 S.Ct. 937 (1992); Barnett v. Fairfax County Sch. Bd., 927 F.2d 146 (4th Cir.), *cert. denied*, 112 S.Ct. 175 (1991).

tial value of centralized services and the need to allocate resources equitably within the disability population.

Virtually all cases looking at the neighborhood school issue have concluded that the Act does not compel placement in the neighborhood school so long as students are educated with their nondisabled peers to the maximum extent appropriate and so long as placements are determined on an individual basis. In other words, the nondisabled peers with whom a disabled student should have the opportunity to interact need not be the child's neighborhood friends. The feasibility cases reach this result, as do recent neighborhood school cases such as *Murray v. Montrose County School District*[56] and *Urban v. Jefferson County School District R–1*.[57]

In addition to not having decided either an inclusion or a neighborhood school case, the Supreme Court has not yet ruled on whether IDEA requires certain kinds of on-site special education services for disabled children placed in parochial school by their parents for reasons other than denial of FAPE at the public school. Although the Supreme Court's decision in *Zobrest v. Catalina Foothills School District*[58] concluded that the Establishment Clause of the First Amendment to the U.S. Constitution was no bar to the services of a sign language interpreter on parochial school premises, the question remains whether IDEA itself requires such necessarily on-site special education and related services if a FAPE remains available in the public setting. At least five district court decisions in 1995 and 1996 have now concluded that certain kinds of services must be provided on site under IDEA. One was upheld on appeal, one was reversed, and at least two others are awaiting appellate decisions.[59] At some point one of these cases would seem destined for Supreme Court review, especially because OSEP's interpretation of the IDEA/EDGAR requirements differs in some respects from these judicial interpretations.

THE RESULTS

Achievements and Challenges

Looking back over the past two decades, one can begin to assess what the legalization and federalization of special education law has produced. First

---

[56]51 F.3d 921 (10th Cir. 1995).

[57]89 F.3d 720 (10th Cir. 1996).

[58]113 S.Ct. 2462 (1993).

[59]See Russman v. Sobol, 85 F.3d 1050 (2d Cir. 1996) (affirming district court decision in Russman v. Board of Educ. v. Watervliet, No. 93-CV-905 (N.D. N.Y. 1995)); K.R. v. Anderson Community Sch. Corp., 81 F.3d 673 (7th Cir. 1996) (reversing 887 F. Supp. 1217 (S.D. Ind. 1995)). See also Fowler by Fowler v. Unified Sch. Dist. No. 259, 900 F. Supp. 1540 (D. Kan. 1995) (on appeal to the 10th Circuit); Cefalu by Cefalu v. East Baton Rouge Parish Sch. Bd., 907 F. Supp. 966 (M.D. La. 1995) (on appeal to the 5th Circuit); Natchez-Adams Sch. Dist. v. Searing, 918 F. Supp. 1028 (S.D. Miss. 1996).

and foremost, it has provided public school access to virtually all children with disabilities, and especially to children with severe and profound disabilities—many of whom have been deinstitutionalized as a result of IDEA. Schools understand quite clearly their obligation to educate all children who are age eligible, regardless of the extent of their disability. State funding for special education has increased as a result of the federal law; more special educators have been trained and hired, more students with disabilities have been completing high school, and their employment rate has been increasing (see U.S. Dep't of Education, 1995a). The challenge is to continue to upgrade and extend the training and retention of skilled educators, to sustain the funding, and to improve the outcomes for more students with disabilities.

A related achievement has been the funding for early intervention and preschool programming, both intended to reduce or even in some cases prevent the need for extensive school-age special education services. The increased attention to transition planning is also targeted at long-term outcomes, that is, the need to reduce or even prevent the need for extensive adult services and to increase the opportunities for independent living and employment. Both the early intervention and the transition service requirements increase the need for services from agencies other than the education agencies. Sometimes turf battles are the result, but in any event difficult cost-sharing burdens arise. Interagency collaboration is in its infancy, and whether the schools can become a center for coordinated education, health, mental health, social services, and correctional services, when the need arises, remains to be seen. Ironically, because of the need for all kinds of related services, the effect of IDEA probably has to been to burden states financially more than it has helped them.

Also an achievement and continuing challenge is the introduction of procedural protections for parents of special education students and the invitation to parents to become involved in their child's education in unprecedented ways. Extending numerous due-process safeguards to parents reflects recognition of the need to protect children with disabilities from decisions driven by administrative convenience rather than the needs of the student and to avoid the harm that comes from misclassification and misplacement.

Has this experiment in creative home–school cooperation worked? Only partly, although the assessments vary. Although school districts have provided parents with written explanations of their rights, those statements are frequently lengthy and written in legalese, obscuring the import of the basic rights. Although school districts now engage parents in development of annual IEPs, those IEPS are typically routinized and sometimes computerized, and have generated complaints from school personnel about the paperwork. In addition, some parents have misunderstood the extent of their IEP role and have demanded certain methods or materials that properly remain within the domain of professional educators; others have never caught the vision and have remained passive and uninvolved—an equally undesirable result. Finally, although the involvement of parents has restrained school districts from acting in a way that compromises the needs of students with disabilities, that very involvement has also generated more litigation than one would have hoped, with federal and state court cases now numbering over a thousand (see Maloney & Shenker, 1995).

Providing an administrative hearing mechanism for the resolution of disputes was intended to allow for impartial third party decision making while keeping most disputes out of the courts. The use of attorneys at the hearings, however, was a primary contributor to the adversariness that has developed. Once one party started bringing an attorney to the table, the other side felt compelled to do likewise. With the arrival of reimbursable attorney's fees, the number of suits in federal court raising just the issue of fees has grown exponentially. One way to reduce the filings would be to allow the due-process hearing officer to award reasonable attorney's fees. Another would be to eliminate the availability of fees for work done at the prehearing stage that resulted in a settlement. A third would be to eliminate the fee provision entirely, something that has occasioned sporadic interest among individual members of Congress, but which could deny some parents access to court.

An intermediate step already being taken to reduce the extent of adversarial proceedings is encouragement of the use of mediation prior to the administrative hearing. Many states already use mediation, and the pressure to require all states to do so has been growing in Congress. Even if not optional to the states, however, it should remain optional to the parties and, under current law, cannot be used to prevent a parent from exercising the right to an administrative hearing.

An additional step is being advanced in schools that are training their educators in Fisher and Ury's (1991) strategies of "Principled Negotiation." These techniques, used already in international diplomacy and in commercial disputes, are in their infancy in the schools. Their primary application would be at negotiation stages, such as, IEP meetings, evaluation requests, and all the routine points of contact between home and school (see Goldberg & Huefner, 1995). Hopefully this technique, which explores common interests rather than bottom-line positions, could reduce the number of disputes that should never have reached the hearing stage.

A fourth result of the federal special education law has been the extended interaction between the Department of Education (OSEP in particular) and state educational agencies. Leadership on special education matters has shifted to Washington in large part, and states have bought the federal standards in order to get the funds. Lobbying that used to occur primarily at the state level has shifted to the federal level. Of course, Section 504 of the Rehabilitation Act of 1973 and the Americans with Disabilities Act have also brought visibility nationally to disability issues. The interaction of these statutes with IDEA has strengthened the federal role in special education and created new litigation thrusts as well. As more rights are extended, the challenge remains to educate persons with disabilities as well as their non-disabled counterparts to understand their responsibilities to one another.

Current Federal Initiatives

In an attempt to benefit from the experience of the last 20 years, the Clinton Administration and Congress are proposing significant amendments to Part B of IDEA as part of the current reauthorization cycle for the discretionary grant titles of the Act (Parts C–G). Some of the changes fall under the category of fine tuning; others implicate the basic premises underlying the original P.L. 94–142. The Administration circulated its own drafts of proposed amendments (OSEP, 1994; U.S. Dep't of Education, 1995a), and the House of Representatives and the Senate each introduced its own separate bill. All three versions are similar in many respects but also differ in significant respects. The House passed its version (H.R. 3268) on June 10, 1996. The Senate adjourned for the August 1996 recess without having acted on its bill (S. 1578, 1996). Only a few of the important issues are identified here—to illustrate what the author considers the difference between fine tuning and major reform thrusts. As this chapter goes to press, the situation is fluid and the actual congressional outcome uncertain, but the issues identified will remain regardless of the amendments that are eventually enacted.

An example of fine tuning is OSEP's proposed consolidation of annual IEP goals and measurable short-term objectives into measurable annual objectives in an attempt to simplify the IEP process (OSEP, 1994). The proposed change is based on the widespread view that IEPs have not worked well because their basic purpose has been misinterpreted. To minimize the paperwork burden, educators too often have developed standardized objectives and prepared the IEP prior to meeting with parents in the hopes of expediting the meeting and quickly obtaining parental consent for proposed services.[60] Such IEPs miss the essential nature of the IEP meeting as a collaborative opportunity to explore with parents what the school should be addressing and to plan together how to implement needed changes and track progress. Eliminating short-term objectives is intended to refocus the efforts properly.

Other OSEP refinements to IDEA would require more specific and frequent progress reports to parents, as well as the inclusion of parents on

---

[60]For a highly intelligent and useful discussion of good and bad IEP development, see Bateman (1992).

the placement team, just as they are now included on the IEP team. These too can be seen as fine tuning because they do not require extensive training and do not suggest underlying shifts in philosophy. They simply attempt to increase the involvement of parents at meaningful points. Interestingly, in spite of language in House bill 3268 requiring frequent progress reports to parents, elimination of short-term objectives was resisted by those who feared loss of intermediate evaluation measures, and the House reinstated the requirement of short-term objectives.

In contrast to the efforts at fine tuning, the proposal to require the participation of a regular educator on the IEP team represents a major shift. Although IEPs address only special education services, they simultaneously specify the amount of time the student is to spend in regular education settings. However, a regular educator may well be uninformed about the student's special education goals and therefore unable to coordinate regular classroom activities and services with those being implemented by the special educator. The proposed involvement of a regular educator makes eminent sense, yet the legal mandate alone will be insufficient if regular and special educators do not grasp the opportunity to truly collaborate. This, of course, takes time away from other pursuits, and whether regular educators will find IEP participation helpful or burdensome remains to be seen. In any event, the training implications are significant.

The proposed inclusion of children with disabilities in district and state-wide assessments also represents a significant change—one that regular education has not fully endorsed as yet. Like the efforts to improve progress reports, it too reflects a greater interest in results or outcomes—a widespread trend appearing also in regular education, higher education, and health care debates.

Among other major reform thrusts are two that also implicate regular educators in a significant way. OSEP is deeply interested in the participation of all special education students in the general curriculum, believing that separate special education programs often have not demanded enough of special education students. OSEP's conceptualization of special education as a service rather than a place or program and OSEP's desire to decategorize special education students and use the Section 504 functional definition of disability both represent an underlying view that regular and special education should be meshed in important ways. Although OSEP couches these proposals in the rhetoric of preserving the original intent of the law, the proposals are directed at an integration of regular and special education that was not contemplated by P.L. 94–142. Such an integration is well motivated and defensible, but it also has the possibility of producing a serious decline in the level of services available to special education students. Many in the special education community are concerned that this current OSEP direction may not reflect the needs or desires of a majority of that community.[61] Although many advocates for persons with mental retardation and severe developmental disabilities see decategorization and participation in regular education classrooms as an important way to reduce discrimination, others view these directions as potentially harmful. For instance, many advocates for students with learning disabilities, hearing impairments, visual impairments, communication disorders, and behavioral disabilities still prefer a degree of separation in order to receive more specialized training than is typically available in a busy and diverse regular education classroom.[62] They are not unlike proponents of gifted students in this regard.

Although OSEP's proposed amendments to IDEA continue to pay lip service to individualized placement decisions and the need for a continuum of placement options, new language emphasizing access to the "general curriculum" can be easily read as eroding the ability of a school to separate a student from the regular classroom environment. In fact, many inclusionists are reading it this way in spite of the fact that access to the general curriculum is not the same thing as access to the general education classroom. The IEP definition in House bill 3268 not only echoes but actually extends the OSEP proposals by requiring that the education agency write "measurable annual goals, including benchmarks or short-term objectives, related to (i) meeting the child's needs that result from the child's disability to enable the child to be involved in and progress in the general curriculum" (H.R. 3268, 1966, § 602(11)). It also requires the agency to specify "any program modifications or support necessary for the child (i) to progress toward the attainment of the annual goals . . . and (ii) to be involved and progress in the general curriculum . . . and to participate in extracurricular and other nonacademic activities." Finally, it would also require the agency to provide "justification of the extent, if any, to which the child will not be educated with nondisabled children." This last sentence would seem to move the current preference for mainstreaming into a presumption that a regular education classroom is the appropriate one for each student unless proven otherwise.

One danger with creating a presumption that inclusion in the regular classroom is appropriate for all students is that it is too easy for educational administrators with fiscal problems to return special education students to general education classes without providing the requisite support services and funding. OSEP's proposed funding changes that would allow special educators to simultaneously serve disabled and nondisabled students with-

---

[61]For an earlier critique of related reform thrusts, see Fuchs and Fuchs (1994).

[62]Among the statements in the author's possession that express concerns about full inclusion are those from the Learning Disability Association of America (LDA), The Council of Administrators of Special Education (CASE), Children with Attention Deficit Disorder (CHADD), the National Federation of the Blind, and the Deaf Education Initiative of the National Association of State Directors of Special Education.

out incurring federal financial penalties may help sustain special services in regular classes, but this OSEP proposal nonetheless carries the risk of dilution of funding to special education students themselves. In the past, allowing special education its own identify increased the funding available to it, so the potential decrease in identity is not without risks (see Martin, 1995).

Another risk of the current emphasis on the integration of regular and special education is that of backlash from the general education community, which did not initiate the move to integrate the two disciplines and which looks askance at the possibility of having students with serious behavior problems, in particular, "dumped" back into the regular classroom. That same community of educators and parents is concerned about the possible "dumbing down" of the curriculum and about the burdens of having to provide a parallel curriculum to students who are mainstreamed in regular classrooms but who cannot handle the regular curriculum. A number of regular education groups have opposed the concept of full inclusion out of just such fears.[63] Encouraging educators to hold high academic expectations for students with disabilities is laudable, as is the desire to encourage the participation of these students in the general curriculum to the extent appropriate. In fact, the vast majority of students with disabilities have mild enough cognitive, physical, and behavioral disabilities to already allow their participation in the general curriculum. What is more worrisome, however, is to what extent these goals will be undermined by educators who have not participated in developing them and who misunderstand them. There are risks inherent in requiring that annual objectives for students with disabilities enable participation in the general curriculum: the risk that special educators will be asked to perform as general classroom aides and that undertrained tutors will do too much of the work for the student. We lose sight at our peril of the fact that separate and specialized curricular methods and materials, functional curricula, and parallel curricula as well were introduced for an educational not a discriminatory purpose. In short, the danger of a pendulum swing that produces an overemphasis on the general curriculum at the expense of a developmentally appropriate curriculum carries the risk of throwing the baby out with the bath water.

Accompanying the OSEP desire to serve more special education students in regular education settings is its proposal, now modified in response to adverse reaction, to decategorize special education students by adopting the Section 504 definition of disability. OSEP argues that the evaluation process currently specified in the law produces an overemphasis on classification for eligibility and an underemphasis on evaluation for programming

---

[63]Among statements in the author's possession that express concerns by regular education or private groups about full inclusion are those from the National Education Association (NEA), The American Federation of Teachers (AFT), and the Committee for Economic Development.

purposes. A move toward decategorization, it argues, will force more emphasis on individual programming needs. This may be true, but both emphases are desirable and serve important functions. The real question may be how to support the legitimacy of both rather than one to the exclusion of the other. To lose the label is sometimes to lose the justification for certain individualized services. Although disability labels carry the risk of stigmatization, they are also the vehicle for certain kinds of services unavailable under a generic label of disability. Parent groups who fought for recognition of their children's particular disability, such as learning disability, autism, and traumatic brain injury, are convinced that correct diagnosis helps to target effective programming alternatives.

An alternative approach to the problem of inadequate evaluation for programming purposes might be to ask the multidisciplinary evaluation team to generate programming implications when it determines eligibility for special education services. Another might be to require that the current levels of performance on the IEP reflect both informal and formal assessment data and that the annual objectives be directly linked to academic and behavioral performance levels. The proposed amendment to increase the attention to programming at the 3-year reevaluation also is a reasonable approach to the problem.

How Much Can the Law Do for Us?

Law has been characterized by anthropologist Paul Bohannan (1968) as in many ways the "reinstitutionalization" of custom. The civil law achieves it purposes with minimal tension when it reflects cultural norms. Arguably it works even better when it shapes customs in new directions that widen our appreciation for humanity and our ability to live together peacefully and constructively, but it can only lead well if it leads the public in the direction it is prepared to go, thereby catalyzing acceptable change. It works less well when it attempts to impose values for which society is not prepared or which are not embedded, at least in nascent form, in the cultural fabric of that society. Federal special education law has been generally successful because it is in harmony with the basic and fundamental value of equal opportunity, and most citizens philosophically agree that all students should be provided with an opportunity to learn. The challenge of the future is to know how far the federal government should push the civil rights agenda and in what direction. IDEA must protect access to appropriate learning opportunities while acknowledging the schools' need to balance the legitimate interests of all students and to provide orderly and good learning environments for everyone.

The rights established by legislation and judicial enforcement have not been enough to produce widespread acceptance of all students with disabilities in regular schools and regular classrooms; new sources of money and new training of educators and parents have also been required. When and where sufficient training and funds have been made available, the education community generally has seen the benefit. When training and resources have been lacking, old fears arise. Rights that push the society to adapt its customs and overcome its prejudices must be accompanied by the ability to actualize those rights through the expenditure of time, energy, skills, and money.

Underlying the Clinton Administration's approach to IDEA reauthorization is a view of placement in separate classes as a major civil rights issue and categorization as a tool to perpetuate discrimination. Even if this view is correct, and it may be, it is a shift from the original premises of P.L. 94–142. Lacking consensus within the education community and the society itself, it may invite backlash that P.L. 94–142 itself did not generate.

Part of what underlies this disagreement on placement and labels is the question of to what extent federal law (or any law) can mandate acceptance of all students with disabilities by their peers and the education community and still preserve the notion of special rights and entitlements. Minow's (1990) *Making All the Difference* poses the dilemma nicely: Can those with disabilities preserve the legitimacy of their different needs for the purpose of receiving specialized, individualized, and generally more expensive services and yet simultaneously argue that they deserve to be accepted and treated as equals by their nondisabled peers?[64]

This chapter concludes on a cautionary note. It is tempting to impose one's values on the society regardless of whether the research base and practical experience document their effectiveness and regardless of whether those values are in harmony with the beliefs of the society. Whether special education and regular education can successfully merge and generate the resources to support individualized services for students at risk, including special education students, is problematic. A generation of successful experimentation would be helpful. With the current weakening of support for the Goals 2000 legislation and the movement to return control to the states, it would seem far wiser to allow educational experiments to proceed in communities that support them than to impose them on a recalcitrant public.

Perhaps more than other groups, we as educators tend to look for panaceas. Because we have not solved many of the educational needs of students with disabilities, we look for new avenues, including legal ones. Special education is engaged in a grand experiment to see if we can truly individualize educational opportunities based on particularized needs. In contrast, some of the current reform thrusts seem to presume that one place and a generic

---

[64]Minow offered a few tentative solutions to the dilemma she posed, but the solutions seem to this author to be far ahead of where the public currently is.

disability label is best for all students. May not such a presumption devalue the complexity of individual needs and actually undermine those needs?

At this point in time, special educators have taken a number of initiatives that go beyond the current federal legal framework. The Regular Education Initiative (a misnomer because it was initiated by special educators) is an example. So is the inclusion movement; so is the interest in outcomes, authentic assessment, and decategorization. At what point should these initiatives be adopted as legal mandates? What if they have not yet been institutionalized as customs; can they successfully be reinstitutionalized as law? It may well be that IDEA's future will be better assured if we try to consolidate what we have, allow experimentation to continue without legalizing it, and work to change the system from within rather than prematurely imposing major new legal mandates from without.

REFERENCES

Bateman, B. (1996). *Better IEPs* (2nd ed.). Longmont, CO: Sopris West.

Bohannan, P. (1968). Law and legal institutions. *International Encyclopedia of the Social Sciences, 9,* 75. New York: Macmillan.

Fisher, R., & Ury, W. (1991). *Getting to yes* (2nd ed.). Boston: Houghton Mifflin.

Fuchs, D., & Fuchs, L. (1994). Inclusive schools movement and the radicalization of special education reform. *Exceptional Children, 60,* 294–309.

Goldberg, S. S., & Huefner, D. S. (1995). Dispute resolution in special education. *West's Education Law Reporter, 99,* 703–711.

H.R. 3268, 104th Cong., 2d Sess. (1996).

Huefner, D. S. (1991). Judicial review of the special educational program requirements under the Education for All Handicapped Children Act: Where have we been and where are we going? *Harvard Journal of Law & Public Policy, 14,* 492–516.

Maloney, M., & Shenker, B. (1995). *The continuing evolution of special education law 1978 to 1995.* (Individuals with Disabilities Education Law Report, Special Rep. No. 12). Horsham, PA: LRP Publications.

Martin, E. W. (1995, December). Funding dedicated to serving special education students essential. *CEC Today, 2,* 14.

Minow, M. (1990). *Making all the difference.* Ithaca, NY: Cornell University Press.

Office of Special Education Programs, *Improving the Individuals with Disabilities Education Act* (Draft Memorandum, Dec. 14, 1994), Washington, DC: Author.

S. 1578, 104th Cong., 2d Sess. (1996).

U.S. Department of Education. (1995a). *17th annual report to Congress on the implementation of the Individuals with Disabilities Education Act.* Washington, DC: Author.

U.S. Department of Education. (1995b). *Making a good law better: The Individuals with Disabilities Education Act Amendments of 1995.* Washington, DC: Author.

18

BRIDGING THE RESEARCH-TO-PRACTICE GAP

Douglas W. Carnine
National Center to Improve the Tools of Educators

A key goal of research in the social and behavioral sciences is the improvement of practice. Basic research is designed to add to an extant knowledge base by formulating, expanding, or evaluating a theory, and is valued because it is concerned with the development of knowledge, which in turn can have implications for altering practice. Applied research is designed to find a solution to an immediate problem, and is valued because it is concerned with the solution of everyday problems that have implications for altering practice. Recently, the extent to which educational research has influenced educational practice has been the focus of professional discussions.

Some researchers argue that a "research-to-practice" gap exists because their research is not designed to make a practical difference (i.e., it is basic research with implications, not direct applications, for practice). They also argue that the problem is that practitioners do not see the implications of their research and therefore contribute to the gap. Practitioners argue that too much research addresses esoteric topics with limited anchoring in the real world. They also argue that researchers create the research-to-practice gap by not involving them in the decision making. With continued arguing, the chasm widens, and an "us-and-them" mentality develops to make making a difference with research even more difficult.

Educational research could and should be a vital resource to teachers, particularly when they work with diverse learners—students with disabilities, children of poverty, limited English speaking students. It is not. This chapter suggests that teachers and others have legitimate concerns about the quality of educational research findings in terms of trustworthiness, useability, and accessibility. On the other hand, researchers can justly claim that even "quality" findings are routinely ignored. The focus here is how to move beyond continuing this stalemate. Issues and concerns about what researchers can do are acknowledged and remedies offered. Similarly, the issues and concerns about what other groups can do are acknowledged and remedies offered. The problems associated with the shortcomings of research and its underutilization must be addressed comprehensively and concurrently if improvements in practice are to be realized.

ISSUES AND CONCERNS

Quality of research can be evaluated in terms of trustworthiness, useability, and accessibility. Trustworthiness reflects the confidence generated by research findings by people who use them. Useability refers to the practicality of the research-based practices for those who attempt to put them into practice. Accessibility provides a measure of the extent to which the findings are available to those who want to use them. The terms and their implications for improving educational practice are related, and each bears strong witness in analyses of issues and concerns faced in bridging the research-to-practice gap.

Trustworthiness

Trustworthiness, which is defined by technical considerations of methodology and analysis, determines the confidence with which a given set of findings can be acted on by practitioners, policymakers, publishers, and other knowledge consumers (Carnine, 1995a). The prestigious National Research Council of the National Academy of Sciences issued a scathing report on the trustworthiness of educational research because of "methodologically weak research, trivial studies, an infatuation with jargon, and a tendency toward fads with a consequent fragmentation of effort" (Atkinson & Jackson, 1992, p. 20). They warned that without high-quality and credible evaluations, school districts will never be able to choose wisely among available innovations. Special education researchers share some of those problems. A review of about 200 studies of students with learning disabilities found that 39% involved the experimental evaluation of some educational practice, a substantial drop from 61% found in a 1980 review (Durrant, 1994). Out of the approximately 80 studies that experimentally investigated an educational practice, Durrant reported that most (93%) resulted in a significant effect; however, because the majority (71%) did not include control groups, the findings of the studies must be interpreted with caution.

Useability

Useability refers to the likelihood that the research will be used by those who have the responsibility for making decisions that impact students and by those who actually teach or provide services to them. To be useable, research findings must be clearly written and deal with topics of importance to practitioners. The special education research community can be proud of the useability of its research relative to other areas of education. The Division of Innovation and Development (DID):

> Was singled out by the National Academy of Education in its report *Research and the Renewal of Education*. The Academy recognized the DID program as "an example of the type of consensus building and priority setting" that would benefit the research goals of all education programs. (McKenna, 1992, p. 27)

In general, however, educational research is often seen as not being as useable as it needs to be. The National Academy of Science carried out a study of federally funded educational research:

> The question of use and usefulness was repeatedly raised by the key staffers we spoke to in the U.S. Senate and House as we began the study. Several said bluntly that all other questions about the enterprise [of research] are of little interest to Congress until these two are answered in a satisfactory manner. (Bick & Jackson, 1992, p. 8)

An interdisciplinary National Academy of Science committee "was struck by how much of education research was 'small science' with little hope of big discoveries, much of which 'has been dysfunctional and will need to change'" (Sroufe et al., 1995, p. 26).

Accessibility

Accessibility has to do with the ease and quickness with which practitioners can obtain research findings and extract the necessary information related to a certain goal. If it is difficult and time-consuming for knowledge consumers to locate and interpret research, they are not likely to make the effort. An informal survey study of a small number of teachers in Washington and California illustrates the difficulty and time involved in trying to find research (Carnine, 1995b). The subject of the teachers' search was beginning reading, a topic that probably has more research, in terms of quality and quantity, than any other topic in education. The question the teachers asked was this: "What information do you have about research-based practices for teaching beginning reading?" The federally funded ERIC system produced 222 references on beginning reading of which 47 of these were research syntheses that did not deal extensively with practical implications. Obtaining these lists would take about 3 hours for an experienced ERIC user. It is safe to estimate that less than one half of one percent of teachers are experienced ERIC users.

Other organizations also were of little help. Calls to the International Reading Association produced six references, none directly related to teaching beginning reading; the National Education Association referred the question to the National Center for Educational Statistics. The American Federation of Teachers had a well-put-together research synthesis, but specific, practical implications were limited. State departments and local districts were of even less help. In short, it was time-consuming and difficult both to obtain the findings and to extract the necessary information.

Implications of Lack of Quality

Problems with research not being trustworthy, useable, and accessible undermine the demand for research findings. These shortcomings pose two challenges for educational researchers: (a) to commit to the concept of continuous improvement of the trustworthiness, useability, and accessibility of research findings while increasing the visibility and credibility of research's accomplishments; and (b) to nurture a market demand for research findings. The possible radical changes in the political landscape—funding based on results rather than funding based on need—and a corresponding move to shift authority and funding from the federal government to the states makes it prudent for the education research community to take a proactive stance in helping practitioners and families produce results with students within a context of accountability.

IMPROVING TRUSTWORTHINESS, USEABILITY, AND ACCESSIBILITY OF RESEARCH

Trustworthy findings result from replicated, well-designed, and executed studies. Research findings must be sufficiently trustworthy to justify dissemination through personnel preparation, regional resource centers, and technical resource centers. Suggestions for improving the trustworthiness of educational research by improving the process and creating a critical mass of knowledge appear in Table 18.1. The research process can be improved by making research questions more relevant to improved practices, describing participants and interventions more clearly to facilitate replication and generalizability, aligning dependent measures more closely to objectives to maintain internal consistency in investigations, and providing evidence that interventions actually took place. Providing contingencies

TABLE 18.1
Suggestions for Improving Trustworthiness of Research

Action	Guidelines
Improve research process	• Address shortcomings of research.
	- Improve significance of research questions.
	- Describe subjects more carefully.
	- Specify interventions clearly.
	- Align measures and objectives.
	- Ensure treatment fidelity.
	• Develop a process for translating practice into research that targets replicated, highly effective practices.
	• Provide incentives for support.
	- Adjust funding criteria.
	- Adjust tenure and promotion criteria.
	- Adjust publication criteria.
Create critical mass	• Employ systematic, broad-based process to synthesize practical value of research.
	• Distribute research syntheses.

and showcasing studies with practical value at federal, state, and local levels will speed the process.

Research directed to decision makers has to consider whether the demands for implementation and use are reasonable. The demands have to be reasonable in terms of available time and expertise *and* in terms of support that can be provided to increase the available time and expertise of practitioners. Research knowledge about effective practices and successful use should align with teacher needs and should be "teacher friendly." Suggestions for improving the useability of research appear in Table 18.2. Addressing questions grounded in practice, involving practitioners, focusing on interventions that are efficient and easy to implement, collaborating with practitioners to establish feasibility, broadening the context for successful research demonstrations, and increasing interest in doing school-based research provide an excellent basis for efforts to improve the perceived and actual useability of research.

Information based on research findings that are trustworthy and useable needs to be readily available to educators during both preservice and inservice. For example, the core of preservice programs should be based on useable, trustworthy information. Similarly, practicing teachers should have ready access to trustworthy, useable information through ERIC and professional development experiences. Suggestions for improving accessibility include deciding what types of information should be more widely distributed, developing a variety of alternatives for dissemination reports (e.g., regional presentations, brochures, workshops, presentations at professional

TABLE 18.2
Suggestions for Improving Usability of Research

Action	*Guidelines*
Increase relevance	• Address practitioner and family questions.
	• Involve practitioners in research.
Increase practicality	• Focus on interventions that can be used.
	• Collaborate with practitioners.
Increase transportability	• Extend implementation settings.
	• Highlight high-performing schools.
	• Describe context more completely.
Increase interest	• Provide incentives for change.
	- Adjust funding criteria.
	- Adjust tenure and promotion criteria.
	- Adjust publication criteria.

meetings, "sales" presentations), altering current methods of dissemination (e.g., ERIC and Regional Resource Centers), and providing incentives (e.g., "bonus points" for personnel preparation grants that build on useable, trustworthy information) for implementation by university preparation programs.

Accessibility has to do with more than just the avenues of distribution. It is also very important that when the information is disseminated it is comprehensible and addresses the important questions educators might have. Questions to use in organizing and evaluating trustworthy and useable information for dissemination are provided in Table 18.3.

NURTURING DEMAND FOR RESEARCH FINDINGS

The current lack of marketplace demand for research findings is due in part to flaws and omissions that render results inconclusive or difficult to act on. The audience for educational research is frequently assumed to be other researchers and theoreticians, rather than practitioners and families. Many

TABLE 18.3
Organizing Research Findings for Consumers

- Does the information provide evidence that an approach is effective?
- Does the information clearly describe the approach and its outcomes?
- Does the information describe an accountability system in the approach?
- Does the information describe a management plan for teachers and administrators?
- Does the information describe effects for different populations?
- Does the information describe and reflect reasonable costs?

reports are too difficult to comprehend. Researchers can remedy these shortcomings.

Although researchers have almost sole responsibility for the trustworthiness of research, they are not solely responsible for making research accessible and useable. These research-into-practice challenges are the joint responsibility of researchers and other groups that take a leadership role in trying to improve American education.

Similarly, changing the marketplace demand for research findings is not solely or even primarily the role of researchers. At this time, major educational decisions are influenced by the actions of four broadly defined groups: influence producers, regulation producers, knowledge producers, and knowledge consumers (Carnine, 1995c). Members of each group, as well as their interrelationships, are summarized in Fig. 18.1.

Influence producers are the trendsetters in education. Educational organizations in this category usually create and sanction popular education in-

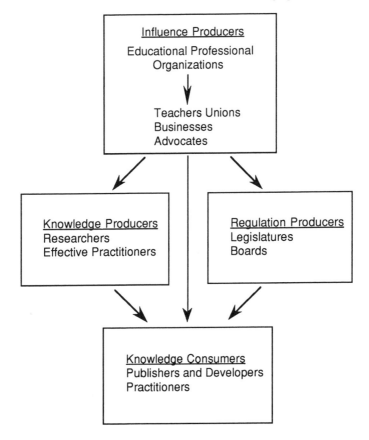

FIG. 18.1. Interrelationships between producers and consumers.

novations. Influence producers in education tend to promote innovations before they have been tested to determine whether they are effective (Worrall & Carnine, 1994). Education curriculum experts have been the most influential. Education curriculum experts are district and state curriculum specialists, college of education faculty in curriculum areas, leaders in national curriculum organizations, and curriculum experts in the educational publishing industry.

Knowledge producers are researchers and successful practitioners. Researchers have not been influential in part because of the shortcomings of their research and in part because of the lack of market demand for research findings. The lack of market demand stems from researchers not finding enough answers to important problems and practitioners not looking to researchers for answers. Knowledge producers have been and are less important than influence producers.

Knowledge consumers are publishers and practitioners who receive most of their information about innovations and effective practices, either directly or indirectly, from educational organizations and their leaders. Because influence producers dominate education, they hold sway over knowledge consumers. Knowledge consumers take their lead from the presentations, writings, and actions of influence producers.

Regulation producers are governmental agencies that dictate what teachers must do to become certified to work in schools (and to maintain that certification), what constitutes an acceptable course of study in college for prospective teachers, what makes for acceptable educational tools, what factors determine whether schools or school districts are performing at acceptable levels, which topics should be researched, and so forth. Regulation producers turn to influence producers for guidance, just as knowledge consumers do. Regulation producers are likely to produce legislation and regulations based on the advice of influence producers.

New Ways of Operating

Increased market demand for trustworthy, useable, and accessible information will change the way in which these four broad groups operate. Influence producers and knowledge producers will become a single group with much closer ties. The traditional influence producers will become more demanding of knowledge producers, insisting that research findings be sufficiently trustworthy and useable to evaluate innovations and provide information on how to reliably disseminate effective practices.

Merging influence producers and knowledge producers will be of great benefit to knowledge consumers, and practitioners will have more efficacious tools. Publishers and developers will turn more to knowledge producers to gain information about innovations and effective practices so that effective practices can be incorporated in the educational tools they publish. In addition, practitioners implementing effective practices will receive more trustworthy and useable support. Finally, regulation producers will make knowledge about innovations and effective practices and how effective practices can be disseminated a cornerstone for teacher certification, school accreditation, and other professional development requirements.

What could cause the groups to operate in these new ways? A number of incentives would influence knowledge producers. For example, the University of Nebraska is piloting a new promotion and tenure policy based on a scholar–practitioner role that will give greater weight to professional work in schools. In addition, publication requirements and journal missions could be redirected toward more practitioner-oriented research (e.g., identifying and studying high-performing schools and special education programs). Similarly, useable knowledge could be made a priority for research funding decisions. A few knowledge producers are beginning to explore these types of changes on their own.

Because the workings of influence producers, regulation producers, and knowledge consumers are so interdependent, they will need to work in consort to create incentives to change how they operate. One powerful way in which these broad groups could increase the marketplace demand for trustworthy, useable, and accessible knowledge would be for them to come to a consensus about standards for educational reform.

Building such a consensus will require an extensive and ongoing educational effort concerning standards for reform and the need for such standards. The force and clarity of these public messages about the importance of such standards will be essential to inform and convince decision makers, who must understand and believe that poorly conceived and executed innovations will do little to improve American education, particularly for students with disabilities. As both the general public and decision makers in the four groups accept the importance of standards for reform, specific incentives will be put into place to ensure that the standards are heeded.

The first step is to agree on standards for reform and how to communicate those standards. The standards might address assessment, identification and implementation of effective practices, restructuring, and systemic reform. A sample of what might be included in such a set of standards appears in Table 18.4.

CONCLUSION

Research is not just science, but craft and art as well. Nevertheless, bolstering the scientific contribution of research to education is critical. Clearly, research must become more trustworthy, useable, and accessible if confi-

TABLE 18.4
Goals and Standards for Responsible Educational Reform

Goals for Organizations

- Provide information on instructional and assessment practices that have been proven effective, or shown promise for further investigation.
- Work to improve research support for dissemination of information about validated educational practices and high-performing schools.
- Avoid supporting popular beliefs that have not improved student achievement in the past.

Standards for Organizations

- Support and encourage community review of any learning and instructional standards under consideration.
- Review education practices and tools to determine whether they are unproved innovations to be evaluated, or effective practices to be emulated.
- Identify and promote the development and use of valid and reliable assessment tools for "high stakes" and other important evaluations.
- Support identification and replication of validated tools and practices used in high-performing schools.
- Restructure or remove any barriers to the development of effective schools.
- Promote systemic reform by identifying and promoting "best practices" and implementing them.
- Hold itself accountable by maintaining a clear focus on achievement

---

dence in it is to increase. On the other hand, confidence must begin to grow to motivate researchers and policymakers to expend the effort needed to address the shortcomings of research. In short, researchers and other groups must begin work concurrently to deal with shortcomings that undermine the value of research. Solutions to these problems will bring enormous benefits to teachers and students as well as society as a whole. Many more diverse learners, particularly students with disabilities, will thus meet higher social and academic performance standards.

ACKNOWLEDGMENT

This research was supported in part by Grant No. H180M10006–94, from the Office of Special Education Programs. The views expressed within this chapter are not necessarily those of the U.S. Department of Education.

REFERENCES

Atkinson, R. C., & Jackson, G. B. (Eds.). (1992). *Research and education reform: Roles for the Office of Educational Research and Improvement.* Washington, DC: National Academy of Sciences.

Bick, K., & Jackson, G. B. (1992). *Research and education reform: Highlights and implications of a recent United States study.* Paper prepared for the OECD/OERI International Seminar on Educational Research and Development.

Carnine, D. (1995a). Becoming a better consumer of research. *The School Administrator, 6*(62), 10–16.

Carnine, D. (1995b). Trustworthiness, useability, and accessibility of educational research. *Journal of Behavioral Education, 5*(3), 251–258.

Carnine, D. (1995c). Rational schools: The key to innovation, reform, restructuring, and choice. *Behavior and Social Issues, 5*(2), 5–19.

Durrant, J. E. (1994). A decade of research on learning disabilities: A report card on the state of the literature. *Journal of Learning Disabilities, 27*, 25–33.

McKenna, B. (1992). Special education research priorities focus on action. *Educational Researcher, 21*, 27–29.

Sroufe, G., Goertz, M., Herman, J., Yarger, S., Jackson, G. B., & Robinson, S. P. (1995). The federal education research agency: New opportunities and new challenges for researchers. *Educational Researcher, 24*(4), 24–30.

Worrall, R. S., & Carnine, D. (1994). *Lack of professional support undermines teachers and reform—a contrasting perspective from health and engineering.* Eugene: University of Oregon, National Center to Improve the Tools of Educators.

INTEGRATION

19

EDUCATING STUDENTS WITH DISABILITIES: THE FUTURE OF SPECIAL EDUCATION

Naomi Zigmond
University of Pittsburgh

This volume has addressed many issues of great importance to the education of students with disabilities, namely: Who has a disability? What do we need to know to plan and monitor instruction for students with disabilities? What assessments do we need to do to find that out? What are appropriate instructional models for students with disabilities? What special attention should be provided to particular groups of students with disabilities? Where do we go from here, in legislation, in policy, in research, and in practice?

In this text, chapters by Kavale, Forness, Lerner, and Speece and Harry have tackled problems relating to the definition of disability: Who is learning disabled? Who is to be classified as emotionally disturbed or behavior disordered? Who has attention deficit disorder? How can classification schemes utilized in the schools serve, rather than stigmatize, both children and their families? Chapters by Howell and Davidson, Deno, and Haager and Vaughn have addressed the what and how of assessment; the chapter by Tankersley and Landrum described the problems in assessment when issues of comorbidity are considered. Englemann as well as Stevens and Salisbury discussed approaches to schooling that improve the overall quality of mainstream instruction and address the heterogeneity currently existing in classrooms whether students with disabilities are included or not. The chapter by Rosenshine summarized advances in instructional research that can and should be used to guide teaching and learning in the general education classrooms. In the chapter by Graham and Harris, the authors searched for and found sensible, common ground in the sometimes contentious debate between cognitive–behavioral and constructivist perspectives in writing instruction. Authors Carta and Greenwood, Talbott and Callahan, and Artiles and Trent each addressed the unique needs of special populations of students with disabilities. Finally, chapters by Huefner, Kauffman and Hallahan, and Carnine dealt with issues related to legislation and public policy: Huefner's chapter is a fine review of current thinking as IDEA moves through reauthorization; Kauffman and Hallahan's chapter explores broadly the meaning of "place" in the education of students with disabilities; and Carnine's chapter tackles the research-to-practice gap.

The authors of this book admit that issues related to educating students with disabilities will not easily be resolved, yet their chapters give testament to continuing and creative efforts to make progress toward some resolution. In doing so, the authors of this book honor Barbara Bateman, a pioneer and leader who personifies our field's willingness to be reflective, to look inward, to be self-critical, and to grow.

WHAT IS *SPECIAL EDUCATION*?

In this concluding comment to the book, I want to raise an additional issue of importance to the education of children with disabilities. It is an issue that has been dealt with only tangentially in the preceding chapters. It concerns the meaning and practice of *special education*, now and in the future.

Historically, educating students with disabilities meant providing special education. The presence of a disability made these children a burden to the general class teacher and vulnerable to failure in schoolwork and ridicule from classmates. Special education programs were developed to protect and nurture children with disabilities. The predominant educational strategy was to organize programs that were segregated by handicapping condition and isolated from the mainstream.

By the mid-1960s, however, the emphasis in special education shifted from nurturance to instruction, not only for researchers and practitioners concerned about students diagnosed as learning disabled, emotionally disturbed, or behavior disordered, but also for those concerned about children with severe and profound disabilities. Now, special education was what was "done to youngsters [with disabilities] *educationally*" (Smith & Neisworth, 1975, p. 13, emphasis added). It was the "*instructional* activity [for children with disabilities] carried on outside the regular classroom by an expert" (Reynolds & Birch, 1992, p. 13, emphasis added). It referred to "those aspects of education that are unique and/or in addition to the instructional program for all children" (Kirk & Gallagher, 1962, p. 13). It was "the application of procedures" (Reynolds & Birch, 1992, p. 14) that were aimed at "the prevention, reduction, or elimination of those conditions that produce significant defects in the academic, communicative, locomotive, or adjustive functioning of children" (Smith & Neisworth, 1975, p. 398).

Certainly, those of us grounded in traditions within LD or BD remember how optimistic we were about the outcomes for students who received properly implemented special education. It "fixed" them. It taught them things they had not learned before, despite opportunities to learn in the mainstream or in the community. Special education taught what could not be learned anywhere else.

In addition, the special education teacher was uniquely prepared for the task. She or he had learned how to figure out what each individual student assigned to her needed to know and how to teach it. Sometimes she just asked; sometimes she observed; sometimes she tested. Then she designed instructional activities, made materials, and taught. The special educator was detective and diagnostician. She was clever and creative. She knew a lot about children and about instruction, and she knew that students were depending on her to help them achieve. Above all else, however, she was relentless. She did not give up until she and her students had been successful.

These were principles I had been taught. These were the reasons that the field of learning disabilities attracted me. What we, as special education teachers, were charged to do was important, and urgent. It took planning at the individual student level, with careful selection and prioritizing of the many things that needed to be learned. It took persistence, searching this way and that for a way into each child's thinking, teaching the same thing over and over again, but differently each time. Some called what we did "clinical teaching" (Johnson & Myklebust, 1967; Lerner, 1971), or "diagnostic teaching" (Myers & Hammill, 1969), or "response contingent instruction" (Zigmond, Vallecorsa, & Silverman, 1983). It was teaching as problem solving. It was very special teaching, indeed.

The teachers who left teacher preparation programs in those early years had a mission: They knew they were responsible for finding out what was wrong; for choosing carefully what to teach from among all the things a child could not do; for finding out how each individual child processed information in order to learn; for devising a strategy for teaching each student what he or she needed to know; for changing to another strategy if they did not get through; and for not giving up until they found a strategy that worked. They were prepared to teach intensively, preferably one-to-one.

"SNAPSHOTS" OF PULL-OUT SPECIAL EDUCATION SERVICES

However, what these teachers encountered in the real world were large class lists, tight schedules, and multiple demands. There were too many students to teach them one at a time. There was too much to teach to focus on basic skills. There was too much to "help with" to focus on instruction.

These days, as I travel to schools, I barely recognize the special education my former students are implementing.

Picture This Self-Contained, Special Education Class in an Elementary Building

There are 18 students, grades 1–6, assigned to this room, each for varying amounts of time, each with different subjects on the IEP. As many as 16 of the 18 students might be present for instruction at any one time; however, students are always coming and going, because they attend some content subjects and "specials" (art, music, or physical education) with age-appropriate mainstream peers.

There are 14 students in the room when this "snapshot" is taken. Twelve are at their desks completing individual seatwork assignments: 2 of the students are in a reading lesson with the teacher at a table in the corner of the room. The teacher is the only adult in the room, and her schedule says that the next 2 hours will be devoted to reading. Her plan is to provide 20-minute, one-to-one or small-group lessons to students divided by grade level. Until she is ready for them, the rest of the students will complete the worksheets she has prepared. Some of her students will work independently for the next 100 minutes until it is their turn for 20-minutes of teacher-directed instruction.

Or, Picture This High School Resource Room

There are eight students who come to this room during third period—two are freshmen, assigned there for English/Reading instruction; four are sophomores assigned for math; and two are seniors who are there to fulfill a science requirement in biology. The teacher distributes a sheaf of worksheets to each student, and spends her time roaming around the room giving students encouragement as they work through their assignments.

Or Picture This

A school district in Pennsylvania has adopted the Madeline Hunter model of instruction; there has been district-wide inservice training, and now all teachers, including those of children with disabilities, are to be observed by their principals teaching whole-class groups, beginning each lesson with a statement of the objective, encouraging discussion and higher level thinking. The intermediate grades special education teacher has changed her math program from individualized to whole-class instruction to accommodate the model.

Or This

The special education teacher has planned a very specific, teacher-directed reading activity for Linda during her next period in the resource room, but Linda arrives with materials sent by the fifth-grade teacher of work Linda did not finish in her mainstream class. A note from the mainstream teacher asks that the work be completed in the resource room.

Or This

The students in Mrs. Kelly's resource room, fourth period, are feeling very pressured about the science test coming up on Friday. They do not want to spend the period working on test-taking strategies; they want to be coached on the contents of the science textbook.

Or This

The fourth-grade teacher has sent a note with Ramone asking his special education teacher to read the social studies chapter to him so that he will be better able to follow tomorrow's lesson on mountains.

Are these pictures of *special education*? Is this "specially designed instruction which meets the unique needs of an exceptional child [including] special materials, teaching techniques, equipment or facilities [as] may be required" (Hallahan & Kauffman, 1978, p. 4)? Is this what Kirk and Gallagher (1962) meant by "practices that are unique, uncommon, of unusual quality" (p. 12). Reading instruction is certainly appropriate for elementary students with LD assigned to a self-contained special education classroom, but the number and diversity of students present in the special education class at the same time has forced this teacher into a structural arrangement that has students spending most of their time teaching themselves; that hardly constitutes providing a special education. Even if it were sensible for a high school resource room teacher to teach English, math, and biology to students with learning disabilities, it is certainly not sensible for her to do all three in one 40-minute period; and completion of worksheets, however well they are prepared and however much that completion is supervised, is hardly special education. Designing a math lesson to accommodate a principal's need to see whole-class instruction rather than to accommodate the individual learning needs of the special education students is not what is meant by a special education. Helping a child with learning disabilities complete their mainstream work, study for a mainstream test, or preview a social studies lesson that will be taught in the mainstream are all nice and helpful things for a special education teacher to do, but do they constitute providing a special education?

I am not questioning the value of these services provided in the name of special education. I acknowledge the evidence that pull-out placements can be advantageous in terms of academic skill development for students diagnosed as LD or BD (Carlberg & Kavale, 1980; Madden & Slavin, 1983; O'Connor, Stuck, & Wyne, 1983), and that special education may even enhance teacher and student perceptions of academic progress and personal social adjustment for this population of students with disabilities. What I am questioning is whether the services that I have been describing are *special education*.

"SNAPSHOTS" OF IN-CLASS SPECIAL EDUCATION SERVICES

In the last decade, for understandable reasons, pull-out special education settings have come under severe attack. Alternative, more inclusive models of special education services have been proposed. The impetus for placing students with disabilities (particularly those with LD) into general education classrooms *in lieu of* providing them with pull-out special education services derived in large part from the call by Will (1986) for a greater sharing of responsibility for students with learning problems between general education and special education. The movement, dubbed the Regular Education Initiative (REI), received additional impetus from advocacy groups that considered access to the general education class setting a right of *all* students, even those in need of a *special* education (Gartner & Lipsky, 1987; Snell, 1991; Stainback & Stainback, 1989). REI was also spurred by the growing national criticism of another large pull-out program, Chapter 1 (see Allington & McGill-Franzen, 1988; Allington, Steutzel, Shake, & Lamarche, 1986).

Advocates of inclusive models reminded us that "special education procedures, materials, and equipment are readily adaptable for use by *all* teachers" (Reynolds & Birch, 1992, p. 14, emphasis added). The place in which special education was delivered began to shift from the pull-out setting to the mainstream classroom. There were many variations on the theme (see Jenkins, Jewell, Leicester, Jenkins, & Troutner, 1990; Reynaud, Pfannenstiel, & Hudson, 1987; Stevens, Madden, Slavin, & Farnish, 1987; Wang, 1987; Zigmond & Baker, 1990), but in each of them, students who would otherwise have attended special education classrooms full or part time were returned full time to general education classes. Was *special education* delivered in these inclusive classrooms? Again, some snapshots might be instructive.

First, Picture a Third-Grade Classroom in an Elementary School in Kansas

Eight students with learning disabilities are integrated with 16 general education students. Two teachers are in the room, one is the general education teacher and the other is a special education teacher who used to teach in a self-contained classroom. The two of them will be teaching together for a full 3 hours this morning, as they do every morning. It is time for reading.

One teacher stands on each side of the room and together they teach the lesson. They finish each other's sentences, elaborate on each other's explanations. Even a sophisticated observer would not be able to tell them apart. They both discipline and praise everyone. When the students are assigned a follow-up writing task to write a story, the students are paired up so that an able child is working with a child with disabilities. The "study buddies" coach the students with LD through the assignment while the two teachers circulate throughout the room.

Or This. It Is a Fifth-Grade Classroom in Virginia

Seven students with LD are integrated into a class of 16 general education students. There are two teachers in the room during this 90-minute reading and language arts block. The block begins with the special education teacher leading the whole class in a lesson on a writing strategy. Then she takes half the class to a table at the back of the room to continue work on writing, while the general education teacher takes half the class to work on a reading story. Twenty minutes later, the two teachers change groups and they repeat their lessons. Everyone gets everything.

Or This Fourth-Grade Classroom in Kansas

Students are in cooperative learning groups completing a science activity; only the general education teacher is in the room. There are 4 students with LD integrated into this class of 22 students. The special education teacher enters and stands at the back of the room for a few minutes "to get a lay of the land." Then she approaches one of the groups that seems to be having trouble; it is not one of the four cooperative learning groups that has a student with LD in it. She listens, then asks some questions, and tries to coach them through their task. After a few minutes, she leaves the room to check in next door.

Or This Second-Grade Classroom in Pennsylvania

A nonreader, diagnosed as LD, is integrated into this class of 25 children. During the first half of the reading lesson, this little guy sits quietly and listens to the teacher talk about this week's book, *Blueberries for Sal*. He seems to follow along, but he does not raise his hand and he does not answer any questions.

About 30 minutes into the lesson, a special education teacher arrives, and quickly the class forms two groups. The smaller group of about 8 students goes with the special education teacher to a table on the side of the classroom; our nonreader is part of that group, as are 2 other higher functioning students also diagnosed as LD. The 17 students form a second reading group at their seats with the general teacher. Both groups continue the reading lesson related to *Blueberries for Sal*. The special education teacher is using flashcards to preview the vocabulary in the story. Students in her group take turns reading the flashcards and creating a deck of such cards for themselves. The nonreader repeats the word after it is given to him by the teacher, and spends most of his time copying the letters of the words from the teacher's sample to his cards. Then this small group spends time drawing an illustration of the word on the back of each flashcard. After 30 minutes, the special education teacher quietly packs her things away and leaves. The eight students in her group return to their seats.

Or Picture This

In an empty classroom in one of these buildings (the room used to be a resource room), a meeting is taking place: Present are two second-grade teachers meeting with the Chapter 1 teacher, the special education teacher, and the teacher of the gifted. All three "special teachers" are scheduled to coteach in the second-grade classrooms; the special education teacher will spend 30 minutes there, 4 days per week. The purpose of the meeting is to plan next week's coteaching periods. The special education teacher is offering suggestions on alternative ways to accomplish the objectives the second-grade teachers have laid out. The suggestions all involve classwide adaptations, and are all based on "stereotypic" interpretations of the needs of children with learning disabilities.

Are these pictures of special education? Is having two teachers in the classroom the same as providing a special education? Is being helped through a writing assignment by a competent second-grade peer (study buddy) the same as getting a special education? Is any instruction delivered by a person certified in special education what is meant by receiving a special education? Is learning what everyone else learns, and doing what everyone else does the same as receiving a special education? Is planning instruction and modifying instruction based on stereotypic generalizations rather than individual assessment data what we mean by special education?

Would integration into the direct instruction classrooms in the schools described by Englemann (Chapter 9, this volume) constitute providing special education? Do the cooperative learning strategies described by Stevens and Salisbury (Chapter 11, this volume) constitute special education? Are the practices described by Rosenshine (Chapter 10, this volume) special education? I think not.

REINVENTING SPECIAL EDUCATION

As others have said before me (see Fuchs & Fuchs, 1995; Scruggs & Mastropieri, 1995), special education is, first and foremost, instruction focused on individual need. It is carefully planned. It is intensive, urgent, relentless, and goal directed. It is empirically supported practice, drawn from research. To provide special education means to set priorities and select carefully what needs to be taught. It means teaching something special and teaching it in a special way. To provide special education means using the techniques and procedures described by Howell and Davidson (Chapter 6, this volume) for defining the special education curriculum appropriate for each student that will be designated on the annual IEP. To provide special education means monitoring each student's progress in the manner described by Deno (Chapter 5, this volume), and taking responsibility for changing instruction when the monitoring data indicate that sufficient progress is not being made. None of this was visible in the classrooms that I have been describing.

How to restore special education services to those who need them? It will take several decisive initiatives:

1. *Redefine the responsibilities of general and special education.* Although a trend in the field in the 1990s has been to blur the lines between general and special education in both school programs and teacher preparation, to restore needed special education services to students with disabilities will require, instead, more explicit definition of the fiscal and educational responsibilities of general education. We have always known that not every student who has a disability is in need of a special education. Both EHA and IDEA are clear on that point. There are children with disabilities for whom reasonable accommodations made by the general education teachers are sufficient to guarantee a satisfactory education. Little has been said in the literature to date about a district's obligations under Section 504 of the Rehabilitation Act of 1973, or under the Americans with Disabilities Act of 1990. Attention has been drawn to these provisions in the course of current debates over adding ADD/ADHD to the categories of disability listed in IDEA. Failing to achieve that objective, and denied eligibility for special education services through IDEA entitlements, parents and advocates for children with hyperactivity and attention deficit disorders have demanded reasonable accommodations for their children by virtue of Section 504, or through state provisions for "otherwise handicapped students" (i.e., meaning students who have a disability but are not in need of a special education, or students who have a disability but not one "authorized" in IDEA; see, for example, Pennsylvania State Code, Chapter 15).

Children with ADHD are not the only children with disabilities to whom these provisions would apply. Take the case of the child with spina bifida who is functioning well in his second-grade classroom; or the hearing-impaired child who is getting Bs and Cs in all of her middle school subjects; or the anorexic or severely depressed, perhaps even suicidal, teenager who, when not hospitalized, achieves passing grades in high school. All of these are students with disabilities. However, if they are functioning *adequately* in a regular education classroom, they are not in need of a *special* education (i.e., a special curriculum and specially designed instruction). Similarly, students with attention problems, or poor handwriting, or atrocious spelling, or inadequate social or organizational skills, may be diagnosed as having a severe discrepancy, a learning disability, but if they are performing *adequately* in the ordinary school program, they are not in need of a *special* education. Recent experiments in full inclusion of students with learning disabilities, the largest group of students currently served in special education (see Zigmond et al., 1995), have demonstrated that half of the students with LD in six elementary schools implementing full-inclusion models made satisfactory progress academically and socially when reasonable accommodations were made. These accommodations required the deployment of additional personnel into general education classes, and adaptation of instruction, curriculum, materials, tests, and grading procedures. They required use of cooperative learning strategies and peer tutoring, but they did not involve delivering special education (see Baker, 1995a, 1995b, 1995c; Zigmond, 1995a, 1995b).

These students with disabilities, and the resources with which to provide reasonable accommodations, are the responsibility of general education; achieving these reasonable accommodations in the mainstream should not use up federal, state, or local *special education* resources, as it does now (see Baker & Zigmond, 1995). Redefining fiscal and education responsibility will not only reduce the rosters of special education programs, but also free up entitlement resources with which to provide more appropriate and needed services.

2. *Reinvent special education.* For the "other half" of the students with LD and for all other students with disabilities who are in need of a special education (i.e., a *special* curriculum—not available to other students—taught in a *special* way, using different texts, different ways of presenting the information, different pacing of instruction, different amounts of guided practice, different examinations, different grading standards) we must provide a truly *special education.* I do not mean a return to "business as usual," but I do mean a return to special education as it was conceived in the 1960s and 1970s. I mean special education provided by a highly trained professional capable of assessing the child, of planning a teaching program based on this assessment, and of implementing the teaching plan (Lerner, 1971). I mean special education that is temporary, intensive, and delivered in a pull-out setting. Temporary, to "help children organize themselves for increased independent learning so that they will be able to eventually return to normal classes" (p. 258); the goal would be to have students acquire a significant number of skills and strategies in a relatively short period of time. Intensive, because "intensity of instruction" is what would distinguish the special education students were to receive from the general education they were al-

ready getting (Meyen & Lehr, 1980). And delivered in a pull-out setting, because the general education classroom learning environment is not conducive to intensive instruction. Such a setting would provide opportunities for sustained and consistent time on task, immediate and appropriate feedback, regular and frequent communication of expectations for achievement, and progress monitoring—the building blocks of special education. However, students would be pulled out *only* for the period of time they received direct, one-to-one instruction from a special education teacher, and *only* until they could be responsibly reintegrated (Fuchs, 1992) into the ongoing instruction and curriculum. Worksheets and workbook pages would be completed in the general education class while they wait their turn.

3. *Preserve a unique preparation for special educators*. Preservice and inservice preparation for general education teachers must continue to emphasize the ways in which the general education teacher can accommodate the needs of diverse learners, students with disabilities among them. General education teachers must also be prepared for collaborative, not isolated, teaching roles, for participation in problem-solving building-level teams, and for working more effectively with parents.

To deliver to students with disabilities the special education that I am proposing, however, there will continue to be a need for special educators with unique and specialized skills. Regardless of how well-prepared a general educator is, the focus of general education practice is on the group: managing instruction for a large group of students, managing behavior within a large group of students, designing assessments suitable for a large group, and so forth. The special educator's focus has always been, and would continue to be, on the individual, providing unique and response-contingent instruction, teaching socially appropriate behavior, designing tailored assessments that are both diagnostic and summative, and so on. This focus includes a "dedication . . . to success measured one student at a time" (Murphy, 1995, p. 210), a commitment to setting individual goals, to monitoring individual progress, and adapting pacing, intensity, structure, and materials to the unique needs of each individual child. These are strategies that all teachers *could* learn, if there were unlimited time in a teacher preparation program. However, they are also strategies that get honed with practice—practice that consists of intensive one-to-one or very small group instruction, not classroom teaching.

THE FUTURE OF SPECIAL EDUCATION

The title of this volume is *Issues in Educating Children With Disabilities*. It is about education, and it is about entitlement. The issue of who has a disability has always been critical to these educational discussions because only children with disabilities are entitled to special consideration from the school system. Ordinary children get standard treatment—the same educational opportunities, the same curricula, the same teachers, the same tests as other children in the school system. Ordinary children get the same individual attention or lack thereof given to everyone else in the school system. Ordinary children get special consideration if a kind, considerate, compassionate adult believes it is necessary. However, ordinary children are not *entitled* to treatment that is beyond the ordinary.

People with disabilities are entitled to treatment out of the ordinary! Through Section 504 of the Rehabilitation Act of 1973, children with disabilities are entitled to reasonable accommodations. Through IDEA, those who have a disability and are in need of a special education are entitled to one. These entitlements are a burden to a school system. They compel a school district to recognize the special needs of some of their students, and to take action to meet those special needs. They require a school district to expend additional resources in the provision of reasonable accommodations, and even more resources in the provision of a special education, although some of these latter resources are supplied by federal and state funds specifically set aside for that purpose. These entitlements impose paperwork requirements that document actions taken and provisions implemented. They also "tie the hands" of a school district in dealing with troubled and troublesome pupils.

It is not surprising that defining who exactly is entitled is a persistent issue in educating children with disabilities. In the real world of schools, debates about diagnostic criteria, about who is and who is not disabled, are not exercises in rhetoric, or logic, or science. They are pragmatic debates: Definitions of disability delimit entitlement. They establish, for a school district, whose problems can be dismissed, whose must be "reasonably" accommodated, and whose deserve special education. It is certainly understandable why administrators, school directors, and others would seek narrower definitions, limiting the numbers who might be diagnosed, and therefore limiting the extent of resources that must be expended. It is also understandable that parents and advocates would press for broader definitions, if such definitions entitle their children to special considerations (unless, of course, they perceive a stigma attached to those special considerations; see Speece & Harry, Chapter 4, this volume).

At the heart of the entitlement is special education. Even strong advocates of inclusive educational practices have seen *special education* as something unique and separate from general education. How else to understand the conclusion of Reynolds and Birch (1992) that "an exceptional child's individualized education program is usually *a combination of regular and special education*" (p. 14, emphasis added). Those who see little value in special education will make strong arguments for the resources attached to this entitlement to be invested toward the general good. It will be difficult to counter those arguments if the pot at the end of the rainbow contains nothing but "fool's gold."

Special education was once worth receiving; it could be again. In many schools, it is not now. Here is where practitioners, policymakers, advocates, and researchers in special education need to focus—on defining the nature of special education and the competencies of the teachers who will deliver it. Here is where the research-to-practice gulf must be bridged. Here is the issue we must resolve, or the hard-fought promise of IDEA will be empty, indeed.

REFERENCES

Allington, R., & McGill-Franzen, A. (1988). *Coherence or chaos? Qualitative dimensions of the literacy instruction provided low-achievement children.* Albany: State University of New York. (ERIC Document Reproduction Services No. ED 292 060)

Allington, R., Steutzel, H., Shake, M., & Lamarche, S. (1986). What is remedial reading? A descriptive study. *Reading Research and Instruction, 26*, 15–30.

Baker, J. M. (1995a). Inclusion in Minnesota: Educational experiences of students with learning disabilities in two elementary schools. *The Journal of Special Education, 29*(2), 133–143.

Baker, J. M. (1995b). Inclusion in Virginia: Educational experiences of students with learning disabilities in one elementary school. *The Journal of Special Education, 29*(2), 116–123.

Baker, J. M. (1995c). Inclusion in Washington: Educational experiences of students with learning disabilities in one elementary school. *The Journal of Special Education, 29*(2), 155–162.

Baker, J. M., & Zigmond, N. (1995). An exploration of the meaning and practice of inclusion for students with learning disabilities. Themes and implications from the five cases. *The Journal of Special Education, 29*(2), 163–180.

Carlberg, C., & Kavale, K. (1980). The efficacy of special versus regular class placement for exceptional children: A meta-analysis. *The Journal of Special Education, 14*, 295–309.

Fuchs, D. (1992). Case-by-case reintegration of students with learning disabilities: Special issue: Integrating learners with disabilities in regular education programs. *Elementary School Journal, 92* 261–281.

Fuchs, D., & Fuchs, L. S. (1995). What's 'special' about special education? *KAPPAN, 76*, 522–530.

Gartner, A., & Lipsky, D. K. (1987). Beyond special education: Toward a quality system for all students. *Harvard Educational Review, 57*, 367–395.

Hallahan, D. P., & Kauffman, J. M. (1978). *Exceptional children: Introduction to special education.* Englewood Cliffs, NJ: Prentice-Hall.

Jenkins, J. R., Jewell, M., Leicester, N., Jenkins, L., & Troutner, N. (1990, April). *Development of a school building model for educating handicapped and at-risk students in general education classrooms.* Paper presented at the annual meeting of the American Educational Research Association, Boston, MA.

Johnson, D., & Myklebust, H. (1967). *Learning disabilities.* New York: Grune & Stratton.

Kirk, S. A., & Gallagher, J. J. (1962). *Educating exceptional children* (3rd ed.). Boston: Houghton Mifflin.

Lerner, J. W. (1971). *Children with learning disabilities: Theories, diagnosis, and teaching strategies.* Boston: Houghton Mifflin.

Madden, N. A., & Slavin, R. E. (1983). Mainstreaming students with mild handicaps: Academic and social outcomes. *Review of Educational Research, 53*, 519–569.

Meyen, E. L., & Lehr, D. H. (1980). Evolving practices in assessment and intervention for mildly handicapped adolescents: The case for intensive instruction. *Exceptional Education Quarterly, 1*(2), 19–26.

Murphy, J. (1995). Insights on "the context of full inclusion" from a nonspecial educator. *The Journal of Special Education, 29*(2), 209–211.

Myers, P., & Hammill, D. D. (1969). *Methods for learning disorders.* New York: Wiley.

O'Connor, P. D., Stuck, G. B., & Wyne, M. D. (1983). Effects of a short-term interaction resource room program on task orientation and achievement. *Journal of Special Education, 13*, 375–385.

Reynaud, G., Pfannenstiel, T., & Hudson, F. (1987). *Park Hill secondary learning disability program: An alternative service delivery model. Implementation Manual.* (ERIC Document Reproduction Services No. ED 28931)

Reynolds, M. C., & Birch, J. W. (1992). *Teaching exceptional children in all America's schools.* Reston, VA: The Council for Exceptional Children.

Scruggs, T. E., & Mastropieri, M. A. (1995). What makes special education special: Evaluating inclusion programs with the PASS variables. *The Journal of Special Education, 29*(2), 224–233.

Smith, R. M., & Neisworth, J. T. (1975). *The exceptional child: A functional approach.* New York: McGraw-Hill.

Snell, M. E. (1991). Schools are for all kids: The importance of integration for students with severe disabilities and their peers. In J. W. Lloyd, N. N. Singh, & A. C. Repp (Eds.), *The regular education initiative: Alternative perspectives in concepts, issues, and models* (pp. 133–148). Sycamore, IL: Sycamore Press.

Stainback, W., & Stainback, S. (1989). Practical organizational strategies. In S. Stainback, W. Stainback, & M. Forest (Eds.), *Educating all students in the mainstream of education* (pp. 71–87). Baltimore: Brookes.

Stevens, R., Madden, N., Slavin, R., & Farnish, A. (1987). Cooperative integrated reading and composition: Two field experiments. *Reading Research Quarterly, 22*, 433–454.

Wang, M. (1987). Toward achieving educational excellence for all students: Program design and student outcomes. *Remedial and Special Education, 8*(3), 25–34.

Will, M. C. (1986). Educating children with learning problems: A shared responsibility. *Exceptional Children, 52*, 411–415.

Zigmond, N. (1995a). Inclusion in Kansas: Educational experiences of students with learning disabilities in one elementary school. *The Journal of Special Education, 29*(2), 144–154.

Zigmond, N. (1995b). Inclusion in Pennsylvania: Educational experiences of students with learning disabilities in one elementary school. *The Journal of Special Education, 29*(2), 124–132.

Zigmond, N., & Baker, J. M. (1990). Project MELD: A preliminary report. *Exceptional Children, 57*, 176–185.

Zigmond, N., Jenkins, J., Fuchs, L., Deno, S., Fuchs, D., Baker, J. N., Jenkins, L., & Couthino, M. (1995). Special education in restructured schools: Findings from three multi-year students. *KAPPAN, 76*, 531–540.

Zigmond, N., Vallecorsa, A., & Silverman, R. (1983). *Assessment for instructional planning in special education.* Englewood Cliffs, NJ: Prentice-Hall.

Author Index

A

Abbott, R., 313, 316, 321
Abrams, J. C., 11, 22
Achenbach, T. M., 136, 137, 148, 305, 307, 320
Ackerman, P., 31, 41, 42
Adams, M., 250, 255
Afflerbach, P., 226, 235
Ahlquist, R., 276, 280, 300
Alamai, J., 243, 255
Alder, R. J., 316, 321
Alexander, P. A., 117, 123, 125
Alexson, J., 57, 61
Algozzine, B. J., 105, 112, 128, 281, 302
Algozzine, R., 261, 272
Alleman-Brooks, J., 223, 234
Allen, J., 244, 247, 255
Allen, N., 65, 72
Allington, R., 226, 235, 239, 240, 255, 257, 382, 389
Alper, A., 56, 60
Alter, M., 225, 226, 235
Alton-Lee, A., 116, 127
Alvermann, D. E., 207, 209, 217
Amato, C., 301, 277
Amos, O. E., 277, 301
Anderman, E. M., 113, 123, 125
Anderson, J. C., 315, 320
Anderson, L. M., 223, 234
Anderson, T. H., 210, 211, 213, 218
Anderson, V., 211, 218
Andre, M. D. A., 210, 211, 213, 218
Appelbaum, M. I., 68, 72
Applegate, B., 33, 42

Aragon, E., 246, 256
Archer, A. L., 40, 42, 117, 126
Aristotle, 16, 22
Armstrong, B., 228, 234, 229
Arter, J. A., 107, 115, 126
Artiles, A. J., 275, 288, 289, 292, 293, 296, 301, 304
Asher, S. R., 138, 140, 143, 148, 151
Atkinson, R. C., 364, 372
Atwater, J. B., 264, 265, 272
Atwell, N., 242, 255

B

Babigian, H., 138, 149
Baca, L., 277, 301
Bader, B. D., 271, 273
Bailey, D. B., 135, 148, 263, 264, 265, 266, 267, 269, 272, 274, 329, 333, 341
Bailey, K. D., 67, 71
Bair, H., 265, 273
Baker, J., 104, 127
Baker, J. M., 382, 386, 389
Baker, J. N., 96, 101, 104, 113, 128, 342, 386, 390
Baker, S., 96, 98
Ballard, M., 228, 234
Balow, B., 228, 229, 234
Bangert-Drowns, R. L., 110, 127
Banks, C. M., 275, 281, 301, 396
Banks, J. A., 275, 281, 288, 295, 296, 297, 301
Barbetta, P. M., 38, 42
Barker, R. G., 329, 339
Barkley, R. A., 27, 28, 29, 33, 42

SUBJECT INDEX

A

Accelerated Student Achievement Project (ASAP), 188
Accommodations in general education classrooms, 35, 37, 56
ADHD, *see* attention deficit disorders
Aggression Replacement Training (ART), 40
American Psychiatric Association, 27, 29, 31, 32, 41, 46, 53, 59
Americans with Disabilities Act, 356
Antisocial girls, 305-320
Applied behavior analysis, 91
Arithmetic, 129-147
Art, 40
Assessment, 77-147, 153
  academic performance, 79-97
  antisocial behavior, 306
  attention deficit disorder, 34
  comorbidity and, 163-164
  disruptive behavior, 306
  instructional placement, 101-125
  progress monitoring, 77-97
  social competence, 129-147
  student mastery, 216
Attention deficit disorders, 27-41
  coexisting disabilities and, 29
  emotional and behavioral disorders and, 29, 53
  historical definitions, 30-33
  Individuals with Disabilities Education Act and, 33, 347
  learning disabilities and, 14, 29

Association for Children with Learning Disabilities, 12, 22
Attention
  increasing, 36

B

Behavior disorders
  see emotional or behavioral disorders, 4, 21
Boats, 101, 108, 111, 114, 118

C

Cascade of services
  see continuum of alternative placements
Central nervous system dysfunction, 8-9, 11-13, 15, 19-21
Change in placement, 349-350
Children and Adults with Attention Deficit Disorder, 33, 35, 42
Classification, 63-70, 153
  comrbidity and, 164-165
Classwide Peer Tutoring (CWPT), 38
Coexisting disabilities
  see comorbidity
Cognitive processing
  instruction and, 197
Cognitive strategies
  teaching, 205-217
Comorbidity, 29, 153-173
  assessment and, 163-164
  behavior disorders of girls, 308
  classification and, 164-165

405

NATIONAL UNIVERSITY
LIBRARY SAN DIEGO